Ben-Gurion

Ben-Gurion

His Later Years in the Political Wilderness

Avi Shilon

Translated by Naama Zohar

ROWMAN & LITTLEFIELD
Lanham • Boulder • New York • London

Published by Rowman & Littlefield
A wholly owned subsidary of The Rowman & Littlefield Publishing Group, Inc.
4501 Forbes Boulevard, Suite 200, Lanham, Maryland 20706
www.rowman.com

Unit A, Whitacre Mews, 26-34 Stannary Street, London SE11 4AB

British Library Cataloguing in Publication Information Available

Library of Congress Cataloging-in-Publication Data
Names: Shilon, Avi, author.
Title: Ben-Gurion : his later years in the political wilderness / by Avi Shilon.
Description: Lanham, Maryland : Rowman & Littlefield, [2015] | ?2015 |
    Includes bibliographical references and index.
Identifiers: LCCN 2015041632 | ISBN 9781442249462 (cloth : alk. paper) |
    ISBN 9781442249479 (electronic)
Subjects: LCSH: Ben-Gurion, David, 1886-1973. | Prime ministers—Israel—Biography.
Classification: LCC DS125.3.B37 S5375 2015 | DDC 956.9405/2092—dc23
LC record available at http://lccn.loc.gov/2015041632

♾ ™ The paper used in this publication meets the minimum requirements of American National Standard for Information Sciences—Permanence of Paper for Printed Library Materials, ANSI/NISO Z39.48-1992.

Printed in the United States of America

Contents

Foreword

1

In the years after David Ben-Gurion declared the establishment of the state of Israel, there were three separate instances in which he surprisingly announced his resignation. The first time was when he left the post of prime minister in 1953 and settled in Kibbutz Sde Boker in the Negev. He wanted then to recharge his mental resources and to present himself as a personal model for the reclamation of the desert. He also wanted to develop new ways of bestowing the pioneer spirit to the young generation. But concerns over defense matters made him resume the premiership after two years.

In June 1963, at the age of seventy-seven, he retired once more from the premiership. By now he was thoroughly exhausted after decades of public activities, and preferred to leave the management of current affairs to his successor Levi Eshkol. But he thought that the goals of Zionism had not been completely fulfilled by establishing the state of Israel and that the struggle to buttress the nation must go on, and therefore he wanted to educate the leadership and the people in maintaining the ideals of pioneering and *Mamlachtiut* (statism: the principle marking the shift from sectorial, partisan, and religious interests to general interests and from an era of semi-voluntarism to a binding obligation to the state). However, he soon became engulfed in political and personal struggles with *Mapai* leadership and by 1965 he found himself an Opposition Member of Knesset.

In May 1970, a few months after establishing a new party, the National List, he resigned from the Knesset. He felt the waning of his power and wished to forego "any national role." But his sense of duty had not left him. It was important for him to bequeath to the public and to the leadership the understanding that the revolutionary period was not over yet and that a further effort was required. He decided to emphasize this in the memoirs he intended to write.

Ben-Gurion left his last term as member of Knesset disappointed and angry. In April 1970, one month before his resignation, he gave a long speech, replete with bitterness and frustration, in which he mocked the issue that had split the political system since 1967 War. The debate over the future of the Occupied Territories, he claimed, should not divide the Zionist parties. He had demanded a Greater Israel up to the Peel Commission in 1937, but later, especially after the Biltmore Conference in 1942, he supported the partition of the land. Now, in a similar vein, he asked the state's leadership to consider its policy according to the realistic options it faced.

Partition and a move toward a peace accord were necessary in his eyes, but as long as no proposal for a "true peace" was forthcoming, he saw the debate over the future of the territories as a delaying factor. Instead, he urged the political system to concentrate on encouraging Jewish immigration to Israel, populating the Negev, and realizing the aspiration to be the Chosen People, that is, to create an ethical and intellectual society that would be a moral model to the nations of the world. His speech in Sde Boker drew upon the principles of "utopian realism" that guided him as a leader: striving to achieve the maximum alongside the ability to make do with the optimum. The ability to maneuver between the possible and the impossible was in his view the key to breaking out of the paralysis induced by a leadership that would only pursue the achievable, while avoiding the failure that would be brought about by a leadership that would pursue the unachievable.

Few listened to him in those days. For seven years he had accused the state's leaders of "sins against statism," and now many regarded him as a grumpy old man criticizing his successors over his frustration due to the loss of his influence. Words he said and wrote in that period had little resonance.

In writing this book I wished to encapsulate a fascinating period in the history of the people of Israel: the years in which Ben-Gurion observed from the outside what was happening with the country. I wanted to know what were the things he had wanted to correct; what did he regret; what was he proud of; how did he see the future of the state; did he fully embrace the "melting pot" policy; what was his attitude toward Jewish religion, socialism, relations with the United States, and many other subjects.

When I studied in the Department of Philosophy and History of the Jewish people in Tel Aviv University in the early 2000s, the major tendency while researching Ben-Gurion was to confront his Zionist way, to study his mistakes. Certainly he made mistakes, but I think that from the distance of years, it is more interesting today to try to understand him.

My curiosity was also aroused toward Ben-Gurion the person. How did this person, endowed with a Promethean desire for eternal change, deal with the neutralizing of his power in his later years? What did he think of life? What was its purpose in his eyes? Who remained loyal to him? Who abandoned him? Who did he miss?

I traced him mainly through his archive. I relied on his diary, which he continued to write until the last year of his life; on the hundreds of letters, which he considered highly important, he wrote to citizens of the country and of the world; on his articles; on minutes of meetings he held; on interviews he granted; and on research papers and personal memoirs containing various details on him. I also based my research on interviews not yet publicized from the Ben-Gurion Archives and on interviews I made with persons from his inner circle, from his security guard, and his doctor to decision-makers and politicians.[1]

The more I delved into the material, the more I became exposed to an untilled field of historical research and to the fascinating world of Ben-Gurion in the last years of his life.

Even though the book deals mainly with his later years, it is clearly impossible to study Ben-Gurion and his cogitation without referring to the story of his life and to his early positions. Therefore, I endeavored to incorporate the story of his waning years into the general context of his accomplishments, and along the way to try to discover changes or consistencies in his world view.

I think that due to the irregular feature inherent in this monograph—telling Ben-Gurion's story from its end—this foreword is highly important.

2

Ben-Gurion's life until his retirement from the Knesset was rich with deeds and vicissitudes. His leadership extended over almost fifty years, during which he stood at the head of the *Yishuv* (the pre-state Jewish population in Palestine) and later the state. Ben-Gurion was a practical leader, a founder, a creator. This was, perhaps, the most significant aspect of his leadership. His basic purpose was to unite the Jewish people and to forge it from a collection of groups interconnected by a religious bond into one people living in its land and establishing its state according to both the values of the Bible and Western progress. He did not wish to found Israel as one state among others and to be satisfied with finding a place under the sun for the Jews. He wished to form society in the spirit of the prophets' vision as an *Am Segula* that will be a "light unto the nations."

For this purpose he both strengthened and unraveled the bond between the people and its ancient culture. The stories of the Bible indeed stood at the center of the myth in whose light he wanted to form the spirit of the people, but this was to be accomplished while secularizing their holiness in order to incorporate the social-moral-national values he found in them. In this sense his view was anchored in a kind of secular messianism, and Israel was formed in the spirit of his political theology. The process of creating the renewed nation included actions at many stages of history, each of which setting in motion the one following it.

Ben-Gurion was born in Plonsk in 1886. As a youth he was one of the founders of the Ezra movement, which strove to encourage immigration to Palestine and to teach Hebrew. He dedicated himself to leadership since he was fourteen years old, as we know from the diary he began writing then. At the age of twenty he immigrated to Palestine and joined the Zionist-Socialist Poaley Zion Party. In 1918, he served in the Jewish Battalion of the British Army. Together with Berl Katznelson he established the *Ahdut Ha-Avoda* party, based on a union between Poaley Zion and nonpartisan activists. A year later he began to set up the *Yishuv*'s institutions and was one of the founders of the *Histadrut* (the general labor union). In 1930, he pushed for a union between *Ahdut Ha-Avoda* and Hapoel Hatzair, leading to the establishment of *Mapai*, a workers' party that gradually became a popular party supported by all levels of society.

From 1935 onward Ben-Gurion headed the Jewish Agency, which together with the National Council functioned as what could be termed "the provisionary Government." By virtue of this, he also led the *Yishuv*'s most important defense institution, the Hagana.

Ben-Gurion's policy changed according to the way he viewed historical developments. Until World War I he viewed Turkey as supportive of the Zionist aspirations. After the war he worked to gain Britain's support. And after the St. James Conference in 1939 he changed the Zionist Movement's orientation and turned to the United States for help.

Until the late 1930s he demanded recognition of Greater Israel as the Jewish national home. But in the 1942 Biltmore Conference he demanded that a sovereign Jewish state be created, even if it meant partitioning the land, and called for opening the country's gates to immigration. In 1947, he led the Zionist Movement to adopt the partition plan. After the declaration of the establishment of the state of Israel he led the people in the War of Independence.

He based the Israel Defense Forces (IDF), the Israeli Army, whose organization was completed in practice during the fighting, on the Hagana. Views differ on his capabilities as a military leader, but there is no doubt that the IDF was better prepared for war, among other things because Ben-Gurion was already in 1946 one of the first to regard the Arab states—not the British or the Palestinians, as others thought—as the main enemy in the expected war.

The focus of his fears was the need to instill in the Jews what he termed a "sense of civics." He feared that people, not accustomed to a proper political life in the Diaspora, would find it hard to function as one body having awareness of accepting rulings by majority and of acceding to governmental authority. Ben-Gurion fought, against the background of the establishment of the state, with internal forces which in his opinion were liable to threaten order and the democratic rules of the game.

Two well-known decisions stand out in this context. In June 1948 he ordered the IDF to open fire on the *IZL* ship *Altalena* because its people refused to hand over the arms they brought from the United States even after the organization had agreed to disarm and to merge into the IDF. Similarly, if less violently, he insisted in November 1948 on disbanding the *Palmah* Brigade over his fears that its troops would constitute a military body not obligated to commands of the government but to the authority of the *Yishuv*'s Leftist faction.

Ben-Gurion knew how to seek a compromise, but risked unraveling the delicate thread that bonded the newly crystallized society and also endangered his leadership because he thought that in order to unify the nation under one law, firm decisions must be made in an unambiguous way, unlike interpretations of the Talmud in the time of the Diaspora. In order to form the first coalition he made a pact with the religious parties and not with the second-largest party *Mapam*, which was to his left. After clashing both with the Revisionist and Leftist camps, his willingness to compromise with the Rabbinic establishment could be seen as fulfilling the dialectic process of formulating society on the basis of a broad consensus. Eventually, he also abolished the existing education structure, in which the different ideological streams maintained independent education systems, in favor of a national system of education.

At the time of the establishment of the state the Jewish population numbered 600,000 inhabitants. Between 1949 and 1951 Ben-Gurion headed the huge immigration enterprise that doubled the population. This too was not a simple decision. Despite the harsh economic conditions that necessitated imposing an austerity program, he led a process of mass absorption contrary to the demands for selective and cautious immigration (although in certain stages he too tended to discriminate the immigrants according to their quality).

He wished to assimilate the immigrants into the *Yishuv*'s veteran population in a fast, painful, but necessary process. The "melting pot" program was intended to define a new and unified Israeli identity: the pioneering Sabra living in the Middle East but functioning in the spirit of Western European values. For this purpose Ben-Gurion required the immigrants to relinquish the old traditions and cultures they brought with them from their countries of origin in favor of an Israeli culture. But alongside the advantages of the "melting pot," he caused the destruction of thousand-year-old family structures and disrupted grand traditions.

He held a mixed attitude toward the "Arab Question." His long-term belief was that Israel would sign a Jewish-Arab treaty that would renew the area's ancient Golden Age. But after concluding in the 1930s that the Palestinians would not be reconciled with the Zionist initiative, not even in exchange for promises of aiding their economic development, he concentrated his efforts on buttressing a Jewish defense force. After the establishment of the state, he worked toward setting up armament industries, making agreements of purchase of military equipment, and basing the IDF on a concept of defensive activism. He fervently believed, more than in any other defense enterprise, in the necessity of the nuclear initiative at Dimona, in which he saw the real answer to preventing a reoccurrence of the Holocaust. At the same time he pushed for quick reconciliation with West Germany in return for the Reparations Agreement and military support.

In 1953, he retired from all his duties and moved to live in Kibbutz Sde Boker in the Negev. Foreign Minister Moshe Sharett took over as premier, and Pinhas Lavon was appointed minister of defense.

Upon his return to his post late in the winter of 1955, he conceived the Sinai Campaign, which had colonialist characteristics, together with the leaders of Britain and France. In a swift operation Israel conquered from Egypt the Gaza Strip and the Sinai Peninsula, displaying a surprising military might, although quite shortly withdrew under international pressure. Simultaneously, he formulated the strategy of the "Peripheral Treaty"—fostering relations with Iran, Turkey, Sudan, the Kurds, and Ethiopia—intended to bypass the belt of hostile states along Israel's border.

Ben-Gurion stood at the head of the state until June 1963, when he suddenly resigned. He announced that he intended to write his memoirs. But his main purpose was to exchange his leader's mantle for the cloak of the prophet, the guide. He was troubled that the weary Israeli society, having absorbed the large waves of immigration, was straying from its proper path of realizing its ideals, and so he wished to continue guiding the people and its leadership to further efforts—but from outside of the government.

These are, it seems, the most general outlines of his history as a leader.

3

Ben-Gurion did not even have a matriculation diploma. He was forced to forge one so that he could enroll in law school in Constantinople, but he widened his education independently and was not only a constructive leader but on a wide range of subjects. He immersed himself in matters of political philosophy, texts from Ancient Greece, Spinoza, Cervantes, and the prophets of Israel. To use Shlomo Aharonson's definition, he led as a "renaissance man." Until the day he died he wrote dozens of books and hundreds of articles and speeches on various subjects.

As a young man he researched the history of Palestine and the origins of its inhabitants and determined that the Arab fellaheen were descendants of the Jews of the Second Temple. He offered independent interpretations of biblical issues, most of which were intended to prove that Jewish nationalism predated acceptance of the Torah and that the ties between the people and its land were never disrupted. He also wished to decide the question of Jewish identity that he wanted to base on a national-secular culture, and never ceased from seeking answers about God's existence and his essence.

His horizons reached beyond Judaism and political science: he was interested in Buddhism as a relief of spiritual pains, believed in a connection of body and soul reminiscent of present-day New Age ideas, wished to understand the secrets of mind and brain, and very many other subjects.

But he was also a centralist and obstinate leader; the only truth he accepted was his. He excluded central groups in Israeli society, among them the revisionist camp and the communist fringe. He imposed military rule on the Israeli Arabs and strove to bend society in its whole to *mamlachtiut*—that is, preferring the state institutions over all other organizations. Ben-Gurion was optimistic as to man's ability to change reality, but his views on the nature of the spirit of humankind were skeptical and not heartening. He would not have otherwise wished to establish the state by means of a strict national mechanism he positioned at its center—the army—which by its very nature forcefully enforced its authority.

Nonetheless, he carried out his decisions in a democratic manner, while engaging in complex political struggles. This is no small achievement considering that Ben-Gurion operated in a fragmented society including immigrants from all corners of the earth, only very few of whom brought with them a system of democratic values from their countries of origin.

Even his critics, to say nothing of his admirers, will easily contend that Israel had no other leader so active in the two fields of execution and ideology. It is doubtful if such a leader will arise in the near future. It is doubtful if the spirit of the period enables such a leader to rise.

4

Ben-Gurion's variegated activities serve as a fertile background for research. A considerable number of biographies, monographs, and good and fascinating studies have been written about him and his worldview.[2] In addition, there are books written by those who surrounded him, personal memoirs casting light on his character and enlightening articles about him. His actions and opinions still engender both admiration and criticism. It is no wild conjecture to assume that many more books and research papers will be written about him. But despite the abundance of material written on the subject of Ben-Gurion, only scant research exists on his later years, save for a fascinating article written by Prof. Zeev Tzachor, who was also his secretary.[3]

Ben-Gurion's later years to which I refer is a six-year period from January 1968—after the members of *Rafi*, the party he established in 1965, abandoned him and merged with *Mapai*—up to his death on December 1, 1973. This period is mentioned briefly in a small number of biographies and in a few articles. This is not accidental. These are the years of the winter of Ben-Gurion's life, after he lost his influence. Therefore, I naturally feel the need to apologize, to explain what motivated me to deal with this period specifically out of the myriad subjects concerning him. Is there anything from these years to research and to write about? Isn't the very choice of this time frame an injustice to the man?

A sudden thought regarding the symbolic closeness of dates between the Yom Kippur War and his death piqued my curiosity. The fact that Israel's founding father passed away over the background of its society's national fault line was in my eyes more than a tragic coincidence. It was, as it were, a message that a reassessment of his waning years was required.

While browsing his archive I found the minutes of a long conversation he held with one of *Mapam*'s leaders four years before the sirens' wail that shocked the state's citizens, in which he said:

> The IDF won the three wars, among other things because it grew out of the ground of a country based on truth, justice, and honesty. If the state of Israel does not shake free from a leadership based on non-truth and immorality, it behooves that the IDF will be the same. And such an army cannot fight and win, and the state will have no friends in the international arena. Therefore I will not desist from shouting, from telling the truth.[4]

It was as if the things he said in this conversation were written by future historians who examined the war and retroactively revealed the leadership's shame. His warning had fallen on unheeding ears. The post-June 1967 Israelis wanted to savor the fruits of victory, to relax in their armchairs, to let go. Ben-Gurion pointed them at the sublime, but in the same way that in certain circumstances the sublime tends to be regarded as pathetic, his calls to extend the pioneering era were seen anachronistic.

So my answer to the question why I chose to deal with this period is simple: a curiosity about his voice in the years when his words and deeds no longer had any audience, when nobody tried to understand him anymore.

I endorse Prof. Tuvia Friling's statement that all his life Ben-Gurion was a man full of fear: fear about the possibility of establishing the state, and after that—fear for its continuing existence. Therefore, even after the dissolution of *Rafi*, he did not intend to relax. The establishment of Israel was in his eyes merely one step on the way to achieving the national goals. The fact that the majority of the people did not yet reside in its land; the lack of a statist tradition following the Diaspora years; and the divisions characterizing the people even when it became sovereign, all these encouraged him to demand from the Israelis and their leadership to continue the joint effort.

As for the moral point of view, he continued to bear the banner of the insistence to overcome the Diaspora mentality which in his eyes manifested itself in many ways, especially in a hysterical leadership, unable to function in the spirit of *realpolitik*, and a fragmented society turning its back on its national duties.

In practice, Ben-Gurion worked to thwart the *Mapai* regime: surprisingly, he stated that his natural place was in *Mapam*; he tried to enlist Menachem Begin in his struggle against the government; and after his failure, established another party, the National List. In the political arena, due to his assessment that an agreement with Egypt was a possible and even expected goal, he tried to influence Golda Meir to adopt the Rogers Plan.

In the spirit of the classic Zionist narrative he saw the Palestinian national movement as a late reaction to the national Jewish enterprise. Ben-Gurion publicly announced that the Palestinian people were a historical invention. But I was surprised to discover the extent of his efforts to find a solution to the Palestinian problem. A meeting documented in his diary under the code name "Musa" hid an initiative for a renewed historic meeting with the leader of the Palestinian national movement during the days of the *Yishuv*, Musa Alami. The draft discussed in the meeting, which was held in 1969 and was reported to the foreign ministry under a Top Secret classification, included a proposal for direct negotiations between Israel and a Palestinian delegation chosen from the territories and the Palestinian Diaspora, with an intention to seek autonomy or a confederation with Jordan.

I will not go into the details of the meeting and its contents in this foreword; its very existence is enough to reveal a previously untold side of Ben-Gurion—his recognition de facto of the existence of Palestinian people. This attests once more to the fascinating duality between the practical and the declarative dimensions of his policy. This example is enough to answer affirmatively the question: is there any interesting material previously untold about his later years?

As for the third question: precisely in his weakness, removed from the aura of his power, Ben-Gurion tended to disclose a more "humane" dimension, open to reevaluation, true to the confessions he abstained from during his days of glory. I have found that Ben-Gurion, in the eclipse of his life, is no less fascinating than in his golden age.

5

The core of the story—his life following his resignation from the Knesset—cannot be understood separately from the events that took place in the previous seven years. A considerable part of his activities and positions in his later years ensued from his failure to realize his will of influencing the regime's patterns of operation and the spirit of the people. Therefore, I divided the book into two parts. The first is a long exposition reviewing the years 1963–1970 and the background story of his political decline.

The research of the first five years listed in the exposition did not begin from thin air. It is another step based on those made previously. Good researchers have already mapped out these years and I tried to add and to contribute details and insights of my own. The years 1968–1970 are missing from works written about Ben-Gurion. Their description is based here on my primary sources and interviews kept in his archive as well as interviews I held with persons involved with his affairs.

The first part begins with an attempt to understand the reasons for his surprising retirement from the premiership. This decision had various reasons but one thing is perfectly clear: Ben-Gurion did not retire from his mission. On the contrary, when he could act without a need to consider political constraints, he wished as aforementioned to warn about a relaxing from the common efforts, as he demanded during the days of the *Yishuv* and the early years of the state.

A series of decisions and moves made by his successor Levi Eshkol convinced Ben-Gurion that the state was deviating from the path he had assigned. For instance, Eshkol in fact gave up on the demand to change the electoral system to a regional one. Ben-Gurion saw this as a threat to Israeli society, having diagnosed its tendency to split into groups fighting irresponsibly with each other. Even Eshkol's agreement to authorize the reinterring of Zeev Jabotinsky's bones was dangerous in his opinion, not only because he saw it as giving legitimacy to the views of Menachem Begin, leader of *Herut*, but also because Eshkol's move was intended to ease up on the people, to lead them "normally" after the conclusion of the pioneering enterprises; and in Ben-Gurion's eyes the time had not yet come to relax the effort. He demanded from the citizens to continue fulfilling their obligations to the mission of rebirth, as he saw them.

Other decisions and psychological reasons deepened the rift between Eshkol and Ben-Gurion and inflamed the latter's rage. But their major confrontation erupted over the background of the Lavon Affair, which was disclosed in 1954 following the exposure of an Israeli spy ring in Egypt. An investigation into the affair unearthed failures, falsifications, and faults in the defense establishment. On the surface, the inquiry dealt with identifying those responsible for falsifying documents and with finding out "who gave the order" to send the group to Egypt to sabotage American institutions. In fact, from the 1960s onward the vestiges of the affair constituted the background for a struggle between two conflicting worldviews regarding the formulating character of Israel.

It is no coincidence that only from 1960 onward did Ben-Gurion involve himself with all his might in pushing for the establishment of a judicial commission of inquiry to investigate the affair and the meetings of the ministerial committee that exonerated then Defense Minister Pinhas Lavon from responsibility for running the Israeli intelligence cell in Egypt.

What troubled Ben-Gurion was not the need to convict Lavon, but the patterns of Lavon's struggle and his readiness to threaten the defense establishment with exposure and leaks in order to clear his name. Ben-Gurion saw this as the beginning of an era of "careerism," a renouncing of the commitment to the collective and damage to the "rules of the game" he wished to instill. At the same time he saw the willingness of Prime Minister Eshkol and the *Mapai* heads to be satisfied with the conclusions of the ministerial committee in order to maintain "industrial peace" and avoid damage to the party's image as patterns of exile leadership, whose only goal was survival.

Ben-Gurion wanted Lavon to be a model pioneer citizen. Such a citizen, even if personally wronged, must clarify the accusations against him by the duly established state institutions and not by the media or other kinds of trickery. And he expected the leadership to ensure that the judicial branch would investigate the executive branch and prevent an investigation of the defense establishment by the ministers. Ben-Gurion's vision of a Utopian leadership and of pioneer citizens committed to the state institutions was seen by leading intellectuals of the time—historian Yaakov Talmon, philosopher Martin Buber, and others—as yet another step in the suppression of personal rights in order to protect the state institutions.

The grounds for the accusations against him cannot be ignored, but on his part, sacrifice of the self for the sake of the collective did not cause damage to the individual. On the contrary, as a proponent of the Platonic school he believed that a proper state is what enables the individual to attain mental wholeness. Moreover, in regard to the crystallization of Israeliness, he feared that society would crumble if it were not bonded together by mutual commitment to its basic values. His struggle over the Lavon Affair was yet another part of a series of struggles he fomented in order to pass on his heritage to the future generation.

Was he right? In principle it is enough to consider two affairs exposed in Israel in the following decades after the Lavon Affair—the Bus 300 affair of 1984, and even the affair of the Harpaz Document from 2010—to understand that he identified in advance the dangers inherent in infringing the "rules of the game" between the institutions of the state and the persons staffing them.[5]

However, these affairs precisely might attest that failures of human nature will always overcome any institution, proper as it may be. Thus, one can understand Eshkol, who with his special sense of human nature, rightly saw the Lavon Affair as the fruit of human weakness and preferred to let it go after justice was done with the guilty and innocent.

Perhaps Ben-Gurion demanded from Israeli society and from the damaged Pinhas Lavon a correction beyond human capability. But this was how he interpreted the term "the Chosen People"—over-obligations, not over-rights.

I want to broaden the discussion of the affair because the values Ben-Gurion tried to express in its duration, which were perceived as a political and personal struggle, remained in the center of his worldview to the end of his days.

6

Politically and personally Ben-Gurion failed in his fight over the affair. His demand to establish a judicial commission of inquiry was rejected. He soon found himself outside *Mapai*. In his rage he initiated in 1965 the establishment of *Rafi*, the first centrist party, intended to bring about a deep change in the political establishment, but also expressed a blatant and deep personal frustration over losing the power of his influence.

In the 1965 elections *Rafi* gained only ten seats. The sixth Knesset's voting public found it hard to understand why the person who set up the establishment suddenly demanded to foment a revolution against it. Israeli society was tired of Ben-Gurion's rallying projects, and in the days of mediocrity of the 1960s the political system wanted some respite from his demands. For the first time in the history of the state he was pushed to the opposition. In a sense, he was a victim of his Nietzscheian view: his belief in the "superman" ideal and in the power of the will to overcome difficulties of reality and to propose a further revolution.[6]

The tense days of waiting before 1967 War offered him a rare opportunity to return to central stage. The panic about the imminent war that grasped the public and the political system renewed the longing for him. Even his rival Menachem Begin joined Shimon Peres in returning him to the National Unity government that was established at the time. At the end of the political maneuvering Eshkol remained prime minister while *Rafi* joined the coalition and sent Moshe Dayan to the government as minister of defense.

Ben-Gurion grudgingly acceded to this move only because he thought that he could influence Dayan and thus save Israel from annihilation. He opposed the war and cautioned that the government was needlessly escalating the situation. But his own protégé thought that he was "living in the past," relying on France and ignorant of the IDF's might, and so ignored his advice.

It is historically ironic that the war that ended in Israel's most resounding victory signified the end of the era of the person who declared the state. After Ben-Gurion's gloomy predictions were proven false, he was considered superfluous. Although he well identified the blight of victory—and called on the government to return most of the territories—his words after the war had little resonance. His stature's decline was rapidly translated into political results: in January 1968 even his most stalwart adherents, who left *Mapai* with him and joined *Rafi*, abandoned him and returned to the Labor Party.

Historical research about him also stopped after the dissolution of *Rafi*. Thus, the period 1968–1970, two fascinating years of his history as a member of Knesset, "disappeared." These were the years in which he struggled single-handedly against *Mapai*'s rule, sought ways of solving the Israeli-Arab conflict, made predictions about the future of the world, coped with his loneliness, established another party, and more. We will go into all this in detail further in the book.

7

The story of Ben-Gurion in his later years since relinquishing his Knesset seat is described in the second part of the book. During this fascinating time he searched his soul: having created Israel's establishment and then disconnected himself from it, he was able to analyze it from without and within.

His fear of the exile mentality, which was "imprinted in the Jewish Genome," continued to guide him; it is woven like a silken thread in most of his views. This mentality was used by him to explain many weaknesses in society and leadership: a tendency to split, to act selfishly, to be blind, to reject mutual responsibility, to oscillate between mania and depression. Therefore, even when many began to accept the damages of the "melting pot," Ben-Gurion to his last day did not reject its necessity. He saw the process of creating the "new Jew" as the major element of the Zionist enterprise. Even the ethnic discrimination was in his view an outcome of the days of exile that created hierarchies among the Jews, and so he opposed affirmative action toward minority groups, which in the 1970s was already considered a way of correcting past mistakes.

His remarks on lack of political talent among the leaders of the Jewish people seem to have been written today. He wrote a fiery article about the people of Israel being able to produce esteemed figures in various fields, but that ever since Biblical times its leaders were unworthy. The global political system, he reminded again and again, is based on changing interests, while Israelis tended to scrutinize the nations of the world from a misplaced Jewish perspective: "are you for us or for our enemies?"

This is one of the reasons that especially during the Cold War he used to emphasize the support given by the Russians in the days of the creation of the state. About Israeli-American relations he warned of over-reliance on another nation, however strong and friendly.

In his years at Sde Boker, in contrast to those as prime minister, he tried to speed the efforts to recognize the country's Arab population and to check with it the possibilities of peace. His efforts ensued from his doubts about the state's chances of surviving another era of war. It is not by chance that precisely at the end of his 1972 tour of the Military Industries he admitted for the first time that the myth of the "Few against the Many" in the War of Independence was not accurate and that from the purely military point of view the Jewish power was preponderant. He hinted that Israel should not rely only on its sword although he believed it should keep it sharp.

As for his views on the post-1967-War Greater Israel, it is difficult to place him on the left or Right in the present-day context. He was convinced that the Golan Heights, due to their strategic value, and Hebron and Jerusalem, due to their historic importance, should remain under Israeli sovereignty in any case. He wanted to give back the rest of the territories in return for peace. The Left could take up his cry to return the territories, while the Right would identify in his demand for a "real peace" (a term encompassing establishment of cultural, social, and economic relations), the setting of a political threshold proving that the time for peace had not yet come. About the settlement enterprise, which began in the beginning of the 1970s, his position was complex. He acceded to building them, while assessing that in the future they could remain under foreign rule. His pragmatism is too complex to be subjected to any particular school of thought.

He was not a historian, although like many of Zionism's founders he strove for a revolution in the Jews' attitude toward to the people's collective memory. This was his path of reconciling the distant past with the statism of the present. In his later years he consistently strove to establish a common Jewish myth, not based only on the orthodox religious tradition. To this end he refined his interpretations of the biblical stories, whose purpose was to prove that Jewish nationalism preceded religion. Thus, for example, he praised Moses not only as the one who sealed the covenant between the people and their God, but as a national leader who led his people to revolt against the rule of their masters.

Along with this, the last chapter of Ben-Gurion's life holds a surprise concerning the softening of his attitude toward the significance of Jewish religion in the time of the Diaspora. It seems that after more than twenty years of the state's existence, he came to realize that the danger to the future of Zionism lay not in the return to religious tradition but in the abandonment of national values. He did not become closer to religion in his later years, as some say, but occupied himself intensively with his attitude toward God and despite adhering for most of his life to the view of Spinoza, who equated God with nature, he wrote that he was unable to determine if the god in which he believed was outside nature or part of it.

He did not regret his decision to mix religion and state in Israel. The reason was practical. He assessed that despite mutual complains, secular and religious Jews in Israel live their lives undisturbed, and time had not ripened for this separation. But he also expressed his sorrow that he did not strive to allow civil marriage, among other things as a personal lesson from the fact that in his waning year his granddaughter was disallowed from being married by the Rabbinate. Another interesting idea he wished to promote in regard to religion and state lies in the term "Jewifying" that was intended to replace conversion. According to the principle of Jewification, joining the Jewish people in Israel would be done according to national criteria: settling in the country, knowledge of the biblical stories, and realization of citizenship.

Immediately after the establishment of the state Ben-Gurion claimed that this step negated the term Zionist for whoever does not realize his obligation to settle in the country. Even at the age of eighty-six he stated in a provocative speech, in front of the members of the Zionist Congress in particular, that the Jews of the Diaspora who maintain an affinity with the state are "supporters of Israel" and not Zionists. But in his waning days he accepted that his hope to nullify the model created in the days of the Second Temple in regards to Center and exile would not come to fruition. He identified the major danger of assimilation of the diaspora Jews and called upon world Jewry to expand Hebrew education, to invest in Israel, and to visit it.

In regards to the internal Zionist narrative, he never ceased from confronting the historiography of the secessionist underground movements *IZL* and *Lehi*, especially in regard to the damage they caused to the Zionist enterprise in his opinion by defying the National Institutions' authority. He never regretted his part in the *Altalena* affair.

Nevertheless, when he deduced that the threat from Left and Right to the authority of the government had dissipated, and accepted that Menachem Begin, *Herut*'s leader, had become an inseparable part of the establishment, he was ready to define the *Altalena* affair "stupidity" and not a "threat to the government." Accordingly, although in the time of the *Yishuv* he called the actions of *IZL* and *Lehi* "terror acts," in his later years he even defended them. He firmly rejected any comparison between their patterns of operation and those of the Arab organizations for the liberation of Palestine. He reasoned that the buds of the post-Zionist view had precisely begun to flower and that his reservations about the "dissidents" would support the defamation of Zionism as a whole.

Also interesting is his assuming responsibility for the failure of the agreement he formulated with Zeev Jabotinsky in 1934, in an attempt to relieve the tensions between the labor movement and the Revisionists after the murder of one of the labor movement's leaders, Haim Arlosoroff. Ben-Gurion strictly opposed Jabotinsky and his worldview. But in 1934 he came to the realization that the status of the Revisionist Movement's leader within his party had weakened and that over the background of the tension prevailing in the *Yishuv* following Arlosoroff's murder, a chance had arisen to sign an agreement that would help to bend Jabotinsky to his will. Subsequently Ben-Gurion agreed to meet him for a series of fascinating meetings, in the end of which the two agreed to sign the London Accords between *Ha-Tzohar* (the Revisionist Party) and the workers' movement.[7] But when the *Histadrut* members rejected the accord, Ben-Gurion forgot the compliments he heaped on Jabotinsky and went back to regard him as a symbol of Zionist fascism.[8]

In the 1930s, the attacks on Jabotinsky were also necessary to achieve hegemony in the *Yishuv*,[9] but in his waning years Ben-Gurion regretted that the agreement they signed had not materialized. He attributed the failure to unpropitious timing. He admitted that he was mistaken when he asked the *Histadrut* members to ratify the agreement too near to the murder of Arlosoroff, while they were still agitated: "after a year or a year and a half they would have ratified it. There was nothing against the *Histadrut* in the agreement, but it was conceived while the things that were done to the workers' camp were fresh, and the hatred then towards the revisionists was very deep."[10] He did not elaborate on his part in instigating the hatred, but thirty-nine years after blaming Jabotinsky that his grief over the murder of Arlosoroff was characterized by "crocodile tears [...] cheap hypocrisy,"[11] he emphasized: "Jabotinsky himself certainly had no hand in the deed."[12]

From the other side, his attitude toward socialism as a method overwent a gradual process of distancing, which became apparent in his waning years. In fact, from the beginning of his Zionist way he subjugated the socialist dimension to the national one. During the 1970s his reservations became more acute; he explained that the socialism in which he believed meant supporting "cooperation," not "equality." He insistently emphasized that he did not settle in Sde Boker because it was a kibbutz but because it was situated in the Negev, which was to be made to bloom, and in any case he "hated living in the big city." He even proposed to prohibit strikes in the fields of education and health.

It is interesting to try to understand Ben-Gurion also against the background of issues he addressed only infrequently, among them the Holocaust. His talks, speeches, and writings in his later years hardly touched on it. He was undoubtedly influenced by the Holocaust; his efforts to set up the nuclear enterprise in Dimona were fueled by his fears of its recurrence. So the question arises if his silence on this subject was due to his discomfort over the paucity of the Zionist establishment's attempts to save the Jews in Europe.

He left this question unanswered. I tend to assume that he believed that in any case he could not have done more to save them, and he was also disgusted by the internal political usage of the memory of the Holocaust in Israel. He used the Holocaust as a political argument about the need to establish the state; but as a proponent of constructive Zionism, once it was created he was occupied with building up the nation and not with woe over past catastrophes. This was also his attitude to Masada. Regardless of his attempts to instill a myth of national heroic deeds, he was against suicide; there was nothing to be learned from it, in his view.

These are but a few of the positions Ben-Gurion held in his waning years. He also gave much thought to the occupation's negative influence on realizing the idea of "Hebrew Labor," to the future of the world, to globalization, to the decline of the United States, to the rise of China's power, and to many other subjects widely reviewed in this book.

8

In one of his speeches in a *Mapai* Congress he wished to clarify the term "Pioneerism" (*Halutziyut*) and linked it among other things with the constant need of "non-acceptance of reality."[13] This same nonacceptance guided him in his private life as well. Ben-Gurion is commonly portrayed as a strict, adamant, humorless, and "no-nonsense" person, as Shimon Peres described him. His later years open a window on the life of Ben-Gurion the man, finding himself in an unaccustomed situation necessitating him to deal with his approaching final stop in the circle of life. These years witnessed his frustrating tension between the essence of his existence—striving for a further effort—and his few real remaining options. For a man who saw action as the key to eternal redemption, this period was also fraught with a deep melancholy. One of the touching disclosures in this regard is his doctor's secret mission in 1972 to seek the secret of longevity in an antiaging clinic in Switzerland.

As weird as it sounds, only a mere few years after Ben-Gurion ruled the *Yishuv* and the state with a firm hand, he was forgotten and neglected. His archive holds an apologetic testimony by Ezer Weizmann that he preferred telling Ben-Gurion that he was busy over having to have lunch with him. Indeed, in his waning years he lived in a not-so-splendid solitude. There were instances when unbeknownst to him his security detail invited visitors to his cabin so he could unlimber his thoughts to them.

It is no coincidence that the first things he wrote in his diary after retiring from the Knesset concerned his memories of Nechemiah Argov, his personal assistant during the 1950s, who took his own life, and his wife Paula. In his loneliness he longed for those whose loyalty to him was absolute. Nevertheless, his spirit remained strong as before. Even though he longed for the love of his youth, Rachel Nelkin, he rejected her offers to renew their acquaintance because he understood it was too late.

His personal life encompassing his loves, hates, familial relations; his frustration over his failure to write the autobiography; and his moments of content are widely described in the second part of the book, owing to the natural curiosity about Ben-Gurion the person and also because the attempt to understand the man helps us to understand his positions and actions.

It is an open secret that with the passing of time his memory became flawed. Ben-Gurion was troubled about this and, as was his wont, tried to find his own solution. He tried to improve his memory and to crack the secret of the human genome. From time to time his memory lapses caused him a bad moment. Minutes of his talks and memories of those surrounding him attest to this. But to his dying day the Ben-Gurionist lightning and thunder never left him. I do not ignore his weakness, but I have placed his good moments in the center of my description of his last years. There is no beauty in a person's dissolution, even if it is a chapter in the epic story of the greatest leader the state of Israel ever had.

Ben-Gurion passed away unrequited. He knew the value of his Zionist enterprise and of his success, but like Moses he felt that he did not live to enter the promised land of his dreams. In my opinion his acceptance of his fate is one of the reasons he chose to be buried in a plot overlooking Wadi Zin, described in the Bible as the stream the people of Israel crossed on their way to their land.

9

An interesting question is what he would have thought had he been able to see the present-day state. The forty years since his death attest that in many senses his fears were well-based. Israeli society is fragmented into tribes;

the Bible on which he tried to base the binding mythos was pushed aside in favor of the ascending power of religion as it developed in the Diaspora; the IDF, intended to be the principal body linking pioneerism to statism, is no longer exactly the "army of the people"; the issue of the territories still divides the people and hinders society from concentrating its efforts on striving to be a "light to the nations"; the governmental system has not yet been changed; the issue of conversion continues to bar between Israeli Jews and many Israelis who are not Jews according to the Halacha; and it is difficult to ignore that the Diaspora spirit still permeates the leadership and society itself in innumerable contexts.

However, Israel is a substantial, flourishing, and technologically advanced country having a powerful military. The pioneering spirit is manifested, among other things, in the myriad original initiatives in the fields of hi-tech and scientific developments; whereas the statist element has strengthened after even groups that were considered to be outside of the establishment, including the ultra-orthodox and Revisionists, became a natural part of Israeliness.

I do not know what Ben-Gurion would have said had he chanced upon our times. But such a person is unable to end his life satisfied. He lived with a feeling of urgency and mission. He required from himself and from his people further efforts, further achievements, and further struggle. Satisfaction was foreign to his character. Otherwise, it is doubtful if he would have become the greatest achiever in the history of the Jewish people in modern times. It is doubtful if he would have been such a fascinating man even in the waning of his years.

ACKNOWLEDGMENTS

Over the years of my research, writing and the translation process I have enjoyed working with some professionals who have contributed to this publication. I'm grateful to all of them. Thanks to my agent, Linda Lengton, editor Marie-Claire Antonie, translator Naama Zohar, The editor of the Hebrew version, Professor Eli Shaltiel, Professor Ronald Zweig, director of the Taub Center For Israel Studies at NYU, who hosted me as post-doctoral fellow, to Professor Itamar Rabinovich, President of The Israel Institute, and to Professor Allan Arkush who have contributed from his experience. Finally, to my beloved family, Lior and Itamar.

NOTES

1. List of interviewees: Shimon Peres, Amos Degani, Mordechai Ben Porat, Zalman Shoval, Ben-Gurion's security guard Aharon Eldan, his doctor Bolek

Goldman, his grandson Yariv Ben-Eliezer, commander of the army company that guarded him, Dr. Zvi Shiloni, director of Midreshet Sde Boker Avraham Tzivion, Gen. Dov Yirmiyah, historians Zeev Tzahor, Tuvia Friling, Michael Bar Zohar, and Avi Bareli. I also used dozens of testimonies given by people from the Ben-Gurion Archive after Ben-Gurion's death, some of which were not taken into account in studies done about him, including testimonies by Binyamin Gibli, Yehuda Erez, Meir Avizohar, Yitzhak Navon, Teddy Kollek, Matilda Gez, Mordechai Surkis, his security guard Aharon Tamir, his children, and others. All these names are listed in the bibliography.

2. Many fascinating books and articles concerning Ben-Gurion are listed in the bibliography. I shall note here only a few of the biographies and monographs that influenced me in my writing: Michael Bar Zohar, *Ben-Gurion* (three volumes) (Tel-Aviv: Am Oved), 1975, and the abbreviated edition, 1980; Shabtai Teveth, *Kin'at David: Hayey Ben-Gurion* [David's Jealousy: Ben-Gurion's life] (Jerusalem: Schoken), 1977, 1980, 1999, 2004 (Vol. 1: The Young Ben-Gurion; Vol. 2: Ben-Gurion—Man of Authority; Vol. 3: The Ground is Burning; Vol. 4: A Man of Strife); Shlomo Aharonson, *David Ben-Gurion: Manhig ha-renesans she-shaka* [David Ben-Gurion: renaissance leader and the waning of an age] (Jerusalem: The Ben-Gurion Institution and Ben-Gurion University), 1999; Tuvia Friling, *Hetz ba-arafel: David Ben Gurion, hanhagat ha-Yishuv ve'nisyunot hatzala ba-shoha* [Arrows in the Dark: David Ben-Gurion, the *Yishuv* Leadership and Rescue Attempts during the Holocaust] (Jerusalem, Sde Boker: Ben-Gurion Institute and The Hebrew University), 2001; David Ohana, *Meshihiyut u-mamlachtiyut: Ben-Gurion ve-haintelektualim, bein hazon medini le-teologya politit* [Messianism and statism: Ben-Gurion and the intellectuals, between political vision and political theology] (Sde Boker: The Ben-Gurion Institution), 2003; Zaki Shalom, *Ka-Esh be-atzmotav: David Ben-Gurion u-ma'avakav al dmut ha-medina ve-hanhagata 1963–1967* [With heart aflame: David Ben-Gurion and the struggle for the image of Israel and its leadership, 1963–1967] (Sde-Boker: The Ben-Gurion Institution), 2004; Zeev Tzahor, *Ha-Hazon veha-heshbon: Ben-Gurion bein idiologya u-politika* [Vision and Reckoning—Ben-Gurion: Ideology and politics] (Tel-Aviv: Yedioth Aharonoth and Sifriyat Po'alim), 1994; Michael Keren, *Ben-Gurion veha-intelektualim, otzma, da'at ve-carisma* [Ben Gurion and the intellectuals: Power, knowledge and charisma] (Sde Boker: Ben Gurion Institute), 1984; Avi Bareli, *Mapai be-reshit ha-atzma'ut 1948–1954* [*Mapai* in the first years of Israel: 1948–1953] (Jerusalem: Yad Ben Zvi Press), 2007; Meir Bareli, *Lehavin et Ben-Gurion* [Understanding Ben-Gurion] (Tel-Aviv: Yedioth Aharonoth), 1986; Yosef Almogi, *Ha-Maavak al Ben-Gurion* [The struggle over Ben-Gurion] (Tel Aviv: Idanim), 1988; and two doctoral dissertations: Paula Kabalo, "Ben-Gurion: Ra'ayon ha-halutziyut ve-nosav [Ben-Gurion: The idea of halutzyut]," Tel-Aviv University, June 2000; Yigal Donyetz, "Ha-Ideologiya ha-le'umit shel Ben-Gurion, 1930–1942 [The national ideology of David Ben-Gurion, 1930–1942]," Hebrew University, April 1988.

3. Zeev Tzachor, "Ben-Gurion kotev otobiyografiya [Ben-Gurion is writing an autobiography]," *Keshet* 65 (1974): 144–56. The editor of Ben-Gurion's last books, Yehuda Erez, responded to the article with a critique, "Ben-Gurion eino kotev otobi-yografiya [Ben-Gurion is not writing an autobiography]," *Keshet* 65 (1975): 151–65.

4. Ben-Gurion in a conversation with an unidentified *Mapam* leader, 1969, IDF Archives, file 240791.

5. Mountains of words have been written about Bus 330 Affair and Harpaz Document, and we can't describe them in details here. Generally, though, they shared some traits with the Lavon Affair. In Bus 300 Affair, it was discovered that *Shin Bet* personnel hid the truth, and even falsely blamed an IDF officer, while the politicians avoided a head-on investigation in order to hide their own involvement in the affair. The Harpaz Document Affair revealed intrigues and document falsification between the chief of staff office and the Defense Ministry.

6. Eli Eilon, *Yetsira atsmit: Haim, adam ve-yetsira al pi Nietzsche* [Self Creation: Life, man, and creation according to Nietzsche] (Jerusalem: Magnes), 2005.

7. For further reading see: Yaacov Shavit and Yaacov Goldstein, *Lelo psharot: Heskem Ben-Gurion-Jabotinsky ve-kishlono* [No compromises: The Ben-Gurion-Jabotinsky agreement and its failure] (Tel-Aviv: Hadar), 1979.

8. Tzahor, *Ha-Hazon veha-heshbon*, pp. 130–47.

9. "Ani ma'ashim [I blame you]," *Davar*, July 7, 1933.

10. Ben-Guryon in a conversation with Mark Segal, March 19, 1972, Protocol Collection, BGA.

11. "Ani ma'ashim [I blame you]," *Davar*, July 7, 1933.

12. Ben-Guryon in a conversation with Mark Segal, March 19, 1972, Protocol Collection, BGA.

13. David Ben-Gurion, "Al hatmadat ha-halutziyut [About the persistence of pioneerism]," a speech at Mapai convention, August 18, 1950, Hazon va-derech, Vol. 2 (Tel-Aviv), 1971, pp. 263–69.

Part I

Chapter 1

The Last Dance

PREFACE

David Ben-Gurion was about to celebrate his eighty-seventh birthday on October 16, 1973. Since retiring from the Knesset over three years previously, he warned again and again that his father had died at the same age. His handful of stalwarts planned on holding in his honor a big event in his home on *Keren-Kayemet* Boulevard in Tel-Aviv. Although he preferred living in his cabin at Sde Boker, most of this year he stayed in Tel-Aviv to be close to his doctors and his hospital.

Ten days before his birthday, at noon of Yom Kippur, a warbling siren shocked the populace. Israel's worst war suddenly erupted.

Since retiring from the premiership ten years before, his public stature had diminished. Interest in him and in his words waned in a cruel process characterizing life's end. But the grief and shock that gripped the Israelis now that they were facing war and its terrors, as well as the fierce disappointment over the leadership's weakness, renewed the wish to cling to him, to bring him back from the depths of oblivion. The original birthday celebration had been canceled due to the fighting, but his handful of disciples were adamant to gather in his house to mark the occasion. It was as if his mere presence was enough to ensure goodness, to be a shield from the horrors of war. They wavered between wanting to show their esteem and an undisguised hope to be comforted by the words he might utter.

Ben-Gurion waited for them in a gray suit, reclining in his armchair, his almost-loud breath rising and falling. His white eyebrows were entwined in his tousled hair, his gaze radiating concern.[1] The Old Man had not been at his best when the fighting broke out. He understood that something terrible was happening, but was no longer strong enough to be fully briefed.[2] In the weeks before the war there had been a marked decline in his health: his power of speech weakened, his eyes dimmed, his thoughts were frequently fogged. A shadow was cast over his features. He was mostly enclosed in the small bedroom that used to be Paula's.

A festive wreath on the living room table welcomed the visitors, as if in protest of the awful mood. It was cold in the gloomy Tel-Aviv Boulevard outside. Little by little they began to gather inside, those few that still wanted to grasp the Old Man's mythic power: former *Rafi* MKs Matilda Guez, Mordechai Ben Porat, and Mordechai Surkis; Minister of Communications and Transportation Shimon Peres; Ben-Gurion's doctor Bolek Goldman; members of his family and his security detail.

Since his right hand was afflicted, it was hard for him to shake their hands. He merely tried to smile wanly at his well-wishers. His doctor read him a greeting from his war-weary protégé Moshe Dayan, who was unable to come. Peres insisted on raising some optimism despite everything. He read a short message from Prime Minister Golda Meir. "We are sure of our ability to withstand an attack by the Arab countries. And you had a crucial part in building our capability."[3]

All awaited Ben-Gurion's words. But it was apparent that he was unable to express all his thoughts. On his eighty-seventh birthday this was no longer Ben-Gurion, the strong and accomplished leader; neither was this the latter-day Old Man, who, despite the waning interest in him, still wrote, advised, and planned.

The biblical allusion was in the air: the founding father's handiwork was drowning before his very eyes, which were too dim to see details. And they, his stalwarts who always awaited his utterances, his analyses, his leadership, were feeling the lapse of his power, imagining that this was the decline of an era, fearing that there was to be no recovery.[4] This birthday gathering was an occasion for a prayer—a secular prayer of Jews in distress.

Surkis tried to prod him into talking: "It's going to be fine; it's going to be OK."

"How do you know that?" Ben-Gurion asked suddenly.

"Ben-Gurion, we know the IDF. We know we shall yet prevail. Don't you believe in the IDF?"

"I do, but the situation is severe," he answered succinctly.[5]

After about half an hour the participants began to disperse. Those seeking encouragement were disappointed. It was a sobering experience.[6] The mutual grief over the mounting number of casualties cast a further veil of sadness over the already glum meeting. "I never hated old age more than in that moment"[7] summed Peres in his diary on his return home.

1

The gathering on Ben-Gurion's eighty-seventh birthday was a terrible finale to a glorious life. His decline as a leader had begun a decade earlier, when he grew weary of his post. "It is better to flay carcasses in the market place—than being a prime minister"[8] he commented in his bureau after another political confrontation with people of the *Herut* party over the strengthening relations and military ties with West Germany. In those days, early in 1963, there was no doubting the revulsion he felt toward the post he held about fifteen years (apart from a break he took between 1953 and 1955, when Moshe Sharett replaced him).

He had borne a heavy burden in the decades of his leadership since the day he stood at the head of the *Yishuv*. The external and internal political struggles, the personal rivalries—all these exhausted him. But that was not the whole picture. After all those years of deciding crucial issues—building up the *Yishuv*'s institutions, establishing the state, the War of Independence, the big waves of immigration, accomplishing national education, the Sinai Campaign—it was apparent that since the beginning of the 1960s he had lost interest of leading the nation in a time which had paled into insignificance.[9] He frequently seemed bored in government meetings. In November 1961 he handed over to Levi Eshkol the task of forming his last government, the Tenth Government, as if he no longer wanted to play a direct part in politics. He was mostly occupied with completing the nuclear enterprise at Dimona and further defense matters. On many occasions he said that he preferred reading philosophy and history over further activities in the political arena.

Nevertheless, on the morning of June 16, 1963, even the people of his bureau were surprised to hear that he was laying down his sword and intending to send a letter of resignation to the president, two years before the end of his term. At first, his followers hoped that this was yet another angry outburst, the daily bread of the leader who defined himself as a "man of strife and contention." Moreover, he gave no concrete reason for the resignation. His bureau announced that the seventy-seven-year-old Ben-Gurion was retiring due to "personal issues,"[10] but what these "issues" were was not clarified. "Much to my regret, I can't continue" was all he said.

The IDF general staff was amazed as well. Deputy Chief of Staff Yitzhak Rabin found it hard to accept the news. Together with General Meir Amit he came to his house and, with uncharacteristic emotion, declared "indeed, the army does not involve itself with policy, it is not a factor and should not apply pressure," but the resignation was a "disaster." Rabin added that he spoke not only for himself: "All the generals said this was impossible, and do not see how it would be possible without Ben-Gurion."[11]

According to the statism patterns that Ben-Gurion worked to implement in the young state, he should have told the generals that the identity of the prime minister was none of their concern. But the Old Man, morose and stretched to his nerves' end, remarked in his diary: "I was barely able to hold back my feelings and my tears."[12]

Clearly he was not wholly decisive about retirement. Why then did he choose this way? It is hard to disconnect his decision from the conflict that broke out between him and Foreign Minister Golda Meir on the eve of delivering the letter of resignation. Their argument, which lasted until late in the night, was over a news item published in the world press, according to which Israeli soldiers were undergoing training in West Germany. Golda was shocked by the disclosure of cooperation between the two states. She considered that public opinion in Israel was not yet ready for this and demanded to censor the news in order to avoid "unnecessary trouble."[13]

Ben-Gurion and Golda had followed the same path for many years. Ben-Gurion praised her contribution to the War of Independence: the fund-raising enterprise she managed in the United States. He nurtured her status in the party, and a short while before the Sinai Campaign in 1956 he nominated her as foreign minister, instead of the ousted Sharett. On her part, Golda never hid her admiration for him. "If Ben-Gurion asks me to jump from the fifth floor, I'll do it right away,"[14] she described in the 1950s the nature of their relationship.

In their meeting on June 15, 1963, none of this was apparent. Golda exploited the published news item to rebuke Ben-Gurion that tightening the ties with West Germany was morally wrong. She objected to the Old Man's term "the other Germany" by which he tried to differentiate between the relations with West Germany and the attitude toward members of the Nazi regime.[15] But not only moral issues lay at the heart of the dispute. Golda feared that a public debate on the relations with Germany, more than a decade after the violent demonstrations protesting the Reparations Agreement, would undermine *Mapai*'s public status.

Ben-Gurion, on the other hand, now nearing eighty after some thirty years when he stood at the head of the *Yishuv* and the state, was not so much concerned about *Mapai*'s status. In any case, he was fed up with political wheeling and dealing, which he himself had done so well over the years, and since in his opinion the relations with Germany were necessary both economically and militarily, he not only objected to concealing the military relations, but even favored publicizing them.

It was not only a pragmatic consideration that stood at the base of his attitude toward Germany, but also an echo of his fundamental approach to the difference between Diaspora and independence: he preferred sidelining the public memory of the Holocaust, the tragic crest of the Jewish helplessness in the Diaspora, and to base Israeli public life on the myth of power and valor.[16] Another reason for objection to concealing the military relations with Germany was his desire to convince the Israeli public and leadership of the need for a strategy of *realpolitik*—considering political interests according to the current assessment of the situation—instead of being influenced by historical feelings of Jewish victimhood and persecution. And since the present interests were incompatible with a political grudge against the new German regime, it should be differentiated from that of the past.[17]

His reasoning of the moral dimension regarding the swift reconciliation with the Germans was philosophical: to hold the present German generation responsible for the actions of the former one meant taking essentialist view—attributing negative genetic characteristics to the German people.[18] "He who declares another unfit only because he belongs to the German people, is tainted with a Hitlerian odor—or to say more delicately—with racism,"[19] he wrote.

But in the argument with Golda, Ben-Gurion did not take the time to enlarge upon arguments from the philosophy of morals, but gave a technical, almost provocative explanation; he ingenuously claimed that he had no authority to tell the censor which news items to suppress. Golda would not be convinced. Toward midnight she left for her home, grumbling angrily.

This night-time confrontation with the foreign minister, who was considered to be close to him, was only one of many he had those days with his intimates. Isser Harel, head of the Institute for Intelligence and Special Duties (the Mossad) since 1952, considered a close and absolute confidant,[20] objected to deepening the ties with West Germany. He even thought that Ben-Gurion was giving undue weight to the German military and economic aid. The controversy between them had intensified since later in 1962, when Israeli Intelligence discovered that German scientists were helping the regime of Egyptian president Gamal Abdel Nasser to establish the infrastructure for developing nonconventional missiles. Harel wanted to promote intensive secret measures for thwarting their work.

Ben-Gurion assessed that the danger was not great. Contrary to the Mossad's position he adopted the assessment of Military Intelligence, AMAN, that this enterprise had no chance of being carried out. Harel suspected that the background to the Old Man's disparaging assessment of the German-Egyptian initiative was his fear of damaging the relations he fostered with Germany. On April 1, 1963, following Ben-Gurion's forbiddance to intensify the campaign against the German scientists, Harel resigned. The retirement of Ben-Gurion's confidant in critical defense matters exacerbated the Old Man's feelings of alienation and loneliness.

2

While Ben-Gurion was skeptical regarding the presence of German scientists in Egypt (later, it would become clear that Ben-Gurion and AMAN were right, and the venture was futile), he was seized by anxiety when it came to the establishment of the Arab Federation uniting Syria, Egypt, and Iraq, which was announced in April 1963. Nasser's warnings regarding the Federation's intentions to "liberate Palestine" drove him to launch a quick, intense diplomatic campaign: Ben-Gurion sent letters to fifty of the world's leaders, demanding them to take a stand and protect Israel in light of the threats against its existence.[21]

Ben-Gurion's political campaign was short lived. The world's leaders turned a cold shoulder in the face of his anxieties. The president of the United States, John Kennedy, rejected Ben-Gurion's proposal to establish a defense pact between the two states. He even delivered a cynical response, arguing that according to the US estimates, the IDF is capable of defending the state.[22] The Arab Federation, however, crumbled shortly after its establishment due to disputes between the different parties. Ben-Gurion gained a negative image in the eyes of foreign governments as well as the Israeli Foreign Ministry staff, who perceived his letters as an expression of excessive panic. Later, Golda explained that she had refrained from stopping the political campaign out of respect for the prime minister. "We admired Ben-Gurion [...] but we were wondering."[23]

Why was Ben-Gurion so quick to launch this excessive political campaign? Michael Bar-Zohar, one of his biographers, suggests that his anxiety was the result of a human weakness, which affected him in an old age, after decades of exhausting public activity. In hindsight, it seems that the truth is more complex than a simple psychological explanation. One possible reason was that Ben-Gurion feared the federation would try to bring down Jordan's Hashemite regime, even if it wouldn't initiate a war against Israel. He believed that if they were to succeed, King Hussein would be removed from power, Israel would have to get involved and eventually find itself controlling hundreds of thousands of Palestinians in the West Bank. Since Ben-Gurion based Israel's security strategy, among other things, on the demographic aspect and securing a Jewish majority, he wanted to avoid this kind of consequences. As early as 1958, following the coup in Iraq, when there were estimations that the Jordanian regimes was about to collapse as well and there was a real chance of conquering the West Bank, Ben-Gurion warned against "the danger of adding a million Arabs to a state of 1.75 million Jews [...] once again, we will be surrounded, we will have an 'Algiers' in the midst of us, which could undermine the entire state. Our critical problem is the lack of Jews and not the lack of territory."[24]

Another possible option was that Ben-Gurion had wanted to use the federation's threats in order to demonstrate to the American administration the existential danger experienced by Israel, and thus to avoid the administration's demand for a more strict supervision over the development of Dimona's nuclear reactor.[25] Ben-Gurion never verified this version in writing, but it coincides with the fact that since Kennedy's arrival to the White House, in January 1961, Ben-Gurion was constantly fighting off pressures from the administration, which strove to prevent Israel from developing nuclear weapons as part of their global antiproliferation efforts.

The tensions between Kennedy and Ben-Gurion lasted for a considerable period of time. At the beginning of 1963, the prime minister tried to set up a personal meeting with Kennedy. When it didn't work out, he sent Shimon Peres to the White House in April. A meeting between the US president and a low-level official such as Israel's deputy minister of defense was a rare occasion—a fact that testifies to the significance of this meeting. At the meeting, which was arranged haphazardly and lasted for about twenty minutes, Kennedy went straight to the point: "We follow with great interest any occurrence of the development of nuclear capabilities in the region. It creates a high-risk situation. Therefore, we were adamant on keeping in touch with your effort in the nuclear field. What can you tell me about it?"[26]

Peres was undeterred, promising: "I can only tell you clearly that we won't bring nuclear weapon into the region. We definitely won't be the first to do so. Our interest is exactly the opposite. We are interested in a complete disarmament."[27] The deputy minister of defense had managed to avoid Kennedy's pressure, but whether Ben-Gurion himself could afford to directly mislead the president was doubtful, especially since the president ordered his intelligence agencies to follow the Dimona operations.

Kennedy-Ben-Gurion's relationship was never based on mutual appreciation, even in its early stages. This fact probably affected Ben-Gurion's fear of jeopardizing the atomic venture, which he perceived as a cornerstone for ensuring Israel's survival in a hostile environment. Kennedy and Ben-Gurion first met in 1960, when Kennedy was still a senator from the state of Massachusetts, and a democratic candidate for presidency. At the end of the meeting, on their way to the press conference and in Kennedy's presence, Ben-Gurion suddenly wondered: "Why would such a young man wish to be a president?" This was a sensitive issue for Kennedy, as his Republican rivals presented his young age as a weakness, and he responded sharply: "It is surprising that the leader of such a young and vivid state would raise such a question."[28] Ben-Gurion mentioned the encounter in his diary laconically, and expressed no appreciation whatsoever.[29]

Even after Kennedy was elected as president, Ben-Gurion was not impressed. At the personal level, Ben-Gurion saw Kennedy as the epitome of modern-age damaged leadership, which was too dramatic and television oriented; at the political level, he was disappointed by Kennedy's decision to reconsider the administration's approach toward Nasser regime, and soften their policy toward it.[30] Following their meeting, Ben-Gurion told his assistants that he was surprised when, toward the end of the meeting, Kennedy asked his advice regarding the Jewish electorate in the United States. He felt that Kennedy was treating him like the head of the Jewish American lobby rather than Israel's prime minister. "You should do what's best for the United States," was his short response.[31] On his way back to the hotel, the Old Man told his assistants: "He seems like a 'politician' [emphasizing the word in English]."[32]

Ben-Gurion's disappointment from the president grew in the face of his Middle East peace proposal. In his initiative, Kennedy demanded that Israel would absorb 10 percent of the Palestinian refugees, while the rest would be gradually absorbed in Arab states within a decade. Ben-Gurion rejected the proposal flat out. As mentioned, one of the cornerstones of his security concept was based on preserving the demographic ratio between Jews and Arabs in Israel. In order to maintain the Jewish majority, he wished, on the one hand, to increase the Jewish immigration to Israel and settle Jews in empty lands in the Negev and in the Galilee, and on the other hand, he called for a complete rejection of the Palestinian "right to return."

While he accepted the absorption of a limited number of refugees, based on the humanitarian policy of family reunion,[33] he refused to accept responsibility for the refugee problem as a whole. His justification was that they fled on their own free will during the combats of the War of Independence. Furthermore, the Palestinian right to return was perceived as leading to a strategic damage to Israel. Hence, he was adamant that any compromise would include a guarantee that this issue would not be raised again. Otherwise, he explained, Israel would find itself "in the same stage of the negotiation, but having already absorbed 100 thousand."[34] He was also disappointed by the refusal of Kennedy's administration to proliferate Israel, against his hopes. Two and a half years after the beginning of the American president's tenure, he wrote in his diary: "I still haven't figured out Kennedy's nature. The US' approach is friendly, but for some reason, they still refuse to sell us weapons."[35]

In light of the bad blood between the US president and Israel's prime minister, Prof. Yuval Ne'eman, one of the senior officials at the Negev Nuclear Research Center at the time, suggested another reason that might have driven the Old Man to resign: "Realizing he could not fight off the president's pressures concerning the reactor's supervision, he opted to be replaced by Eshkol, the master of compromise, assuming that he could find the way to ensure to continuant activity of the reactor without entering into a collision course with the United States."[36]

3

Ben-Gurion's concerns prior to his resignation were not focused merely on the political and nuclear contexts. Internal political developments were bothering him as well. The tightening connections between members of *Ahdut Ha-Avoda* and *Herut*—two political parties that supported the Greater Israel ideology and opposed the relationship with Germany—raised his concern that Menachem Begin was soon going to lead a political block that would become the dominant one. Ben-Gurion recognized the fact that wide public sectors identified with Begin's arguments against the relationship he created with Germany.[37] Thus, on the day of his resignation, he expressed his concerns regarding "the growing power and great *Hutzpa*" of "The Leader"[38] (his nickname for Begin, which insinuated the fascist nature, in his eyes, of the Revisionist Movement).

Another, more intimate development, horrified him as well. At the age of seventy-seven, Ben-Gurion's sharp memory was beginning to play tricks on him. While it wasn't enough to affect his performance, there were times when he struggled to remember the name of a past acquaintance or a place, and he was terrified by this growing phenomenon. "You can renew many cells in the human body, but not memory cells,"[39] he said worriedly.

Hence, in light of his political and security-related anxieties, his disappointment with his loyal followers in the political arena, additional health problems that took their toll on him (in 1962, he was bedridden for weeks due to pneumonia and back pains), and the years-long mental stress—he came to a decision and announced his resignation before the end of his tenure.

The massive excitement around his retirement, the admiration of the masses who gathered to watch the farewell ceremonies, the greetings of world leaders all created a somewhat sentimental, historic atmosphere around his decision to abandon the battlefield. The reasons for his decision, as well as the fact that he was concerned and worried at the time of his retirement, were all blurred.

If there was any doubt regarding his declining status in the political arena, it was evident in the lukewarm responses to his retirement announcement by the leaders of his own party, *Mapai*. At the eve of his early retirement, when he left for Sde Boker in 1953, one of the party's senior leaders, Zalman Aran, wrote: "I beg you, don't do it. This miserable people and this tragic state could not bear it."[40] It was a typical letter. This time, *Mapai*'s secretariat was quick to convent the day after his resignation and hand the task of forming the government to Levi Eshkol, the minister of finance.[41] Eshkol was chosen with the support and encouragement of Ben-Gurion, but the quick adjustment of the *Mapai*'s leaders to the reshuffle supports the assessment that to some extent, Ben-Gurion retired when even his own party members begged him to put an end to the saga.[42]

4

Albeit his retirement, Ben-Gurion had no intentions of abstaining from leading the state toward his own vision. He wanted to pass on the king's throne
to Eshkol, while sewing for himself the cloak of the profit, the king's mentor.
He was tired of running the state's ongoing affairs, but believed that now,
especially now, in light of the waves of mass immigration and the demographic changes created by them, the spirit of the nation should be reshaped,
in order to maintain the combination of pioneering and statism he envisioned.
He wished to educate his successors as well. A short while before his resignation, he wrote an article explaining his worldview in regard to the desired
policy for Israel:

> The member of an independent people, and equal member of the family of
> nations, is not bounded by the Ghetto perspective, which suggests that there
> are two kinds of people in the world: Jews and "gentiles," and that anyone who
> doesn't treat us with the utmost justice is Anti-Semitic, and thus, a Jew hater.
> I believe that the Jewish people can and should be the Chosen People and the
> Light unto the Nations, and I presume any people may perceive itself in the
> same way. Obviously, no two nations are the same, just like no two human
> beings are the same. No nation sympathizes with another, even when they are
> on friendly terms. Any nation has its own considerations, needs and approach.
> They could be wrong, but they are nevertheless its own, and they guide it; and
> its actions are not always perceived in a positive light by others. [...] If I see
> that this or that nation takes actions that harm us, or avoid taking actions that
> would have benefited us—I don't assume they do it because they hate Israel,
> but because they have—or so they think—needs and considerations that are dif-
> ferent of our own. Similarly, I don't believe we must comply with the demands
> of a foreign government, be it the greatest and friendliest state in the world, if
> this demand jeopardizes, according to our view, a matter that is crucial or fatal
> for the people of Israel.[43]

Not in so many words, Ben-Gurion's approach to the two main political
issues bothering him before his retirement resonated in his article: The dispute with the United States regarding the supervision over the reactor ("I also
don't believe we must comply with the demands of a foreign government,
be it the greatest and friendliest state"), and the tightening connections with
Germany, despite the still-fresh memory of the Holocaust ("The member of
an independent people, and equal member of the family of nations, is not
bounded by the Ghetto perspective"). This was the spirit he expected Eshkol
and *Mapai*'s leadership to act upon.

On paper, Ben-Gurion had no reason to doubt his designated division of
labor with Eshkol. The ex-Minister of Finance was a known follower of his

for many years. Their contrasting traits of character—Eshkol was perceived as kind hearted and tending to compromise—were even considered to be a political asset, which would help them promote previously-agreed-upon political goals. Indeed, at the beginning of his tenure, Eshkol generously named his new government "a follow-up government," and Ben-Gurion was nicknamed "Israel establisher," as if Eshkol was trying to prove he would follow the Old Man's footsteps.

But a series of events and decisions only a few months later proved that the person who followed him up until lately was now trying to rule in his own way, to disown his predecessor. Ben-Gurion was angry that Eshkol was willing to forego the demand for a new electoral system in return for *Ahdut Ha-Avoda*'s willingness to unite with *Mapai* for the 1964 Knesset elections (the *Ma'arach* in its first version).

The recurring political splits seemed to Ben-Gurion like another disease from the period of exile, when Jews got used to treat the regime irresponsibly. Since the establishment of the first Knesset, which was actually a constituent assembly, meant to be dispersed after the establishment of a constitution, Ben-Gurion demanded to change the electoral system (and after failing to gather the required majority, he tried to raise the electoral threshold to ten seats).[44] He wished to create two nationally responsible political blocks, like in the British system.[45] This was the only way, he argued, to moderate the divisive tendency of the Israeli parliament, which he perceived as a cancer eating away the nation's body and undermining the political responsibility of the smaller parties. If members of the opposition would know they had a better chance to rule, they would be committed to a more responsible behavior. Ben-Gurion wished to create a different situation:

> One party that wishes to maintain the status-quo, with some tweaks here and there, and perceives private capital and free initiative as the key means of development; and the other, which would strive to transform society through the companionship between laborers, and which would encourage and offer every opportunity for those who have the physical and emotional ability to develop the state.[46]

In the spirit of Jean-Jacques Rousseau, he distinguished between the general will and the will of all.[47] The current system in Israel, he explained, was causing each party to look after its own interests; thus the will of the majority, which is combined of citizens' contrasting wills, was overcoming the general will. He wished to express the integration of the wills of the entire citizens in order to achieve common goals.

Levi Eshkol had no principle dispute with him. But since *Ahdut Ha-Avoda* opposed the change in the system, he had no political choice. Furthermore,

Eshkol believed that his willingness to give up the section regarding the electoral system change would eventually reinforce the labor parties and create a single block. Ben-Gurion, who was already fed up with political compromises, by which he was also bounded as long as he was in office, declared that Eshkol was wrong to prefer the partisan interests over the state's interests. He demanded that Eshkol would be persistent, and when his demand was turned down, he furiously announced his intention to retire from *Mapai*'s central committee.[48]

His anger intensified when Eshkol refused to approve his meeting with the Chancellor of West Germany, Konrad Adenauer, in Italy, aimed to strengthen the connections between the two states.[49] This time, Eshkol was representing the state's interests. He believed that a former prime minister who represented the government in meetings was not a proper administration practice, and argued that Israel mustn't "chase" Adenauer.[50] Ben-Gurion couldn't refute Eshkol's statehood consideration, but still had a hard time accepting it. A few months before, he was the leader of the nation. Is it possible that Eshkol, his prodigy, had no more appreciation for his political wisdom? Could he not understand that the personal links he created with the chancellor must be used for the benefit of the state?[51]

In 1964, Ben-Gurion was disappointed by Eshkol again and again. In the spring, when he was vacationing in Tiberius "Galey Kinneret" Hotel, the prime minister was kind enough to honor him with a visit to his room, seeking political advice. The conversation was pleasant, very pleasant; but a few days later, in the first government meeting after their conversation, Eshkol announced that the bones of Zeev Jabotinsky, the leader of the Revisionist Movement, would be reinterred in Israel. He didn't bother to update Ben-Gurion on this matter. Indeed, Teddy Kollek, his former chief of staff (who continued to work in the same position under Eshkol for a while longer), told him about the plan, but he officially learned about it by listening in on the radio.[52]

Ben-Gurion had avoided this step, of reinterring Jabotinsky's bones in Israel, for years (Jabotinsky ordered that his remains would be brought to Israel only when approved by the government of the future Jewish state he envisioned.). His most blunt argument was that the state is in need of live Jews and not the remnants of the dead ones. The only exception to this rule for him was Theodor Herzl, the state's visionary. His speech in the Knesset at the day when Herzl's remains were brought to Israel were clear: "Not a funeral procession of bringing Herzl's remains to be reinterred in Israel, but a victory parade, the victory of the vision that was realized."[53] He even emphasized the fact that only two people in the history of the Jewish people were honored this way: "Joseph, the first Hebrew man," and "Herzl, the great visionary."[54] Undoubtedly, he would not insert Jabotinsky between those two in the Jewish mythology he wished to instill.

The untold reason for Ben-Gurion's objection to implementing Jabotinsky's will had to do with his ambition to politically marginalize the Revisionist camp and delegitimize it among the general public. The key motive of his struggle against the Revisionist Movement, the *IZL*, and then *Herut*, after the state's establishment, was his argument that their contribution to the Zionist project was limited. He used every opportunity to make fun of the *IZL*'s historiosophy, and marked Menachem Begin, Jabotinsky's successor, as a danger to democracy. In May 1963, a month before his resignation, he wrote to the poet Haim Guri and warned that Begin should not be treated as a legitimate leader:

> Begin is a pure Hitleristic type, racist, willing to destroy all the Arabs in order to maintain the land, justify all means by marking the holy goal—absolute control, and I see him as a grave danger to the internal and external situation of Israel [...] all those [his actions] are not few and far between; they reflect a pattern, a character and an ambition. Begin would replace the army and police commanders with his goons, and will rule like Hitler ruled Germany—he will oppress the Labor movement, forcefully and cruelly, and will ruin the state with his political adventures.[55]

In order to avoid this danger, he opposed any ceremony that entailed recognizing the Revisionists' contribution to the establishment of the state.

Levi Eshkol, on the other side, believed that the residues from the *Yishuv* period were the ones jeopardizing the Israeli society. Unlike Ben-Gurion, he believed that now, when Israel had been established and the great immigration waves had been assimilated, the public was entitled to a relief; they could have more "normal" life and shouldn't be pressed to make an additional effort. Bringing Jabotinsky's bones to Israel was a necessary attempt, in his mind, to put unnecessary tensions to rest, in addition to reinforcing his position as prime minister, who was deemed acceptable by the majority of the public.

After the suggestion to bring the Jabotinsky's bones to Israel was approved, Ben-Gurion was pushed into a proverbial corner. In order to maintain his objection to the ceremony, as he did in the past, he would have to confront *Herut* as well as his own party, *Mapai*. His frustration was expressed in his diary: "*Herut* had a double reason for celebration yesterday: Jabo's bones and the establishment of *Tchelet Lavan* faction within the *Histadrut*, which was meant to take down the red banner."[56]

The Old Man was also furious about the procedures regarding the historic visit of the Pope, Paulus the Sixth, who came to Israel in January 1964. Prior to his visit, the Pope's staff had already announced that he would refuse to take part in an official reception in Jerusalem. The justification was the lack of diplomatic relationship between the Vatican and Israel.[57] But a fundamental theological dispute was hidden in the background: According to the Catholic perception, the proof that God prefers the teachings of Jesus over those of the Jews lies in the Jews' exile from their homeland, as they were punished for their sins; thus, recognizing Israel and the Jewish sovereignty might have been interpreted as contradicting the Catholic claim of moral and religious superiority.[58] Eshkol prioritized the practical aspect over the religious one, and attributed great significance to the visit of the world's highest Christian authority. Hence, he accepted the compromise that was suggested by Paulus' representatives: To accept the Pope in Megiddo. Ben-Gurion saw it as a violation of the spirit of Judaism and an undermining of Israel's sovereignty.

A similar confrontation, which further inflamed Ben-Gurion's rage, was raised in light of Eshkol's decision to hold the military parade of Israel's 16th Independence Day in Beer-Sheva instead of Jerusalem. Eshkol was scheduled to meet the US president around the time of the parade and gave way to the pressures of the American administration, asking him not to provoke the Arabs by holding the parade in Jerusalem. In return he hoped, among other things, to soften the administration's position in regard to the supervision of the Dimona reactor.[59] Ben-Gurion was not aware of Eshkol's considerations, and he perceived his decision as another unnecessary surrender. As the mastermind behind the idea of the military parade, who insisted on holding it as early as the state's first Independence Day, while the sounds of the bombshells from the War of Independence were still echoing, he believed in the historical meaning of holding the parade in Jerusalem.[60] He systematically believed in instilling symbols as a way of educating and creating a renewed, pioneering Hebrew nation. Indeed, intellectually, Ben-Gurion could definitely be categorized as belonging to the rationalist faction of the modern Western philosophy (he was inspired by the writings of Aristotle, Spinoza, and Rousseau). But as far as the significance he attributed to the symbolic aspect is concerned, he was a postmodern leader who believed that the shape was also a type of content, in the spirit of Roland Barthes. Eshkol, he maintained, manhandled both the shape and the content he was trying to design for Israel.

If there was any doubt left in the Old Man's mind regarding the change that Levi Eshkol was making in the state's management practices, all he had to do was to watch the annual cinematic diary summarizing the events of 1964. The diary reviewed the dozen most important public figures in the state. Ben-Gurion was mentioned only briefly, over images of Jabotinsky's bones reinterring ceremony. The announcer even added sarcastically: "This year, we've managed to overcome hatred and hostility that were rooted in the past."[61] Thus, with a stroke of a sentence, the principles of the founding father were presented as reflecting an outdated attitude, which should be revoked. No one had to tell Ben-Gurion who gave the orders to the editors of radio shows and cinematic diaries.

At the end of his first year outside of the prime minister's office, Ben-Gurion was forced to agree with no other than the editor of the magazine he hated most of all, *Ha-Olam Ha-Ze*: Uri Avneri was not wrong when he described Eshkol's policy as "De-BenGurionization."

5

Indeed, the deterioration of the relationship between the predecessor and the successor was quick and unavoidable. But all the disputes described above were but an exposition compared to the decisive confrontation over the Pinhas Lavon Affair (initially named in Israel "The Unfortunate Affair"— *Ha-Esek Ha-Bish*), which split *Mapai*.[62]

The Affair, with its entangled story lines that have since filled multiple books and researches, started in 1954, while Ben-Gurion was vacationing in Sde Boker. Moshe Sharett was then the prime minister, and Pinhas Lavon was the minister of defense. Lavon's appointment was Ben-Gurion's idea. He admired Lavon's activism in security matters, was impressed by his clarity of thought, and identified with his aggressive speeches against *Herut*.[63] The appointment of Moshe Sharett, on the other hand, was imposed over him by *Mapai*'s leaders: He preferred Eshkol as his successor, but in 1953, Eshkol was still avoiding from taking control.

Anyway, in 1954, it was found that the Israeli intelligence ordered its people in Egypt to carry out terrorist attacks against British and Western institutions, posing as an Egyptian nationalist underground group. The objective was to undermine Egypt's internal security and force the British, who were about to withdraw from the Suez Canal area, to stay put, realizing they couldn't trust the Egyptian anti-Western regime. This was an attempt by the Israeli security system to prevent a situation in which Britain would withdraw and the Canal would be closed to Israeli vessels.

Jewish-origin Egyptians were recruited for this mission. But the network was exposed after two attacks. The devious plan was found to be reckless and irresponsible. In light of the failure and the political fallout, accusations were thrown back and forth between senior security officials concerning the responsibility for approving the plan. The head of the military intelligence at the time, Binyamin Gibli, claimed that the order was given by Pinhas Lavon, while Lavon argued that Gibli acted on his own accord. He pointed out Ben-Gurion's prodigies, the Chief of Staff Dayan and the Ministry of Defense's CEO Peres, and accused them of being involved in a conspiracy to put the blame on him. Dayan argued he had been abroad when the plan was approved, and wasn't updated.[64] Peres denied any foreknowledge about it as well.

The Prime Minister Sharett ordered the establishment of an investigative committee, headed by the Chief Justice Yitzhak Olshan and the former Chief of Staff Yaakov Dori. The committee concluded its inquiry at the beginning of 1955, but failed to reach any conclusive evidence. Lavon felt he had been wronged and resigned in protest. In February 1955, dissatisfied with the way Sharett's government had handled the problem of the infiltrators (*Fidayun*) from Egypt and Jorden, Ben-Gurion returned to the political arena and replaced Lavon at the Ministry of Defense. In May, he was reappointed as prime minister, instead of Moshe Sharett. Lavon hoped that Ben-Gurion's return would mark the end of the chaos in the security system. In a personal meeting, he asked to clear his name off the allegations made against him. Ben-Gurion refused, arguing that he wasn't a judge. An additional military committee that investigated the matter supported Lavon's arguments and even stated that the documents presented in front of Olshan-Dori committee were counterfeit. Yet, the committee didn't point out the culprits.

Out of distress, Lavon started a campaign of his own for clearing his reputation. Lavon's campaign was unprecedented in 1950s Israel, especially since he was part of the security system and fought against the institution of which he was a member. His campaign included leaking information to journalists, threats to expose national secrets that would embarrass officials, and accusations concerning moral defects deep within the military and political systems, which were tightly involved with each other as long as *Mapai* was in power.

In 1960, Lavon took a step further. He testified in front of the Foreign Affairs and Defense Committee about a conspiracy that was formed against him in the IDF, while exposing protocols and documents and allowing *Mapai*'s rivals within the committee to use the Affair for political attacks.

This step provoked Ben-Gurion's rage.[65] Lavon was actually slandering the security system, which was Ben-Gurion's own creation. Up until then, no one from within the system ever dared to defame it in such fashion, and the Old Man deducted that the significance of the Affair was greater than Lavon's personal fate. He came to dislike Lavon for jeopardizing his basic objective: to create a civil commitment to the state's institutions among the Israeli society. When he retired from his role as prime minister, he already harbored a wish to lead the people in the spirit of statehood; the Affair and its aftermath were an opportunity to complete the historic journey, which should have educated the Israeli Jews about proper citizenship.

Ben-Gurion was not naive, and he knew there might be some truth in Lavon's claim, that he was falsely accused by some senior security officials. In a speech he gave in 1950 about the army's future of the War of Independence, he had already admitted that there were some moral defects within the army.[66] But in the society he aspired to create, the citizens—every citizen, but specifically those who headed the security system—were required to be committed to the collective, even when their personal reputation was damaged. The collective commitment was not supposed to dismiss private justice and the search for the truth. In the spirit of this commitment, Lavon should have demanded justice in a more moderate way, using the law alone, and not threaten the establishment with exposure of military and personal secrets, while using *Mapai*'s political rivals. Ben-Gurion stated that truth and justice should not be chased through "the easy and futile mission of searching for the sins of the other," but by "official tools which were meant for this purpose—we have a Knesset, we have the State Comptroller, we have a police, we have judges."[67] Lavon's approach violated, in his mind, the rules of the game, which were the foundation of the political system he tried to establish. He wanted Israel to adopt the British norms of governmental ethics, which prevent public officials from slandering the establishment, motivated by their personal or partisan interest, as just as it may be.

Ben-Gurion demanded that the course of events would be investigated by a legal investigative committee, which would be based on judges and present strict conclusions. But most of the ministers voted for a different committee, "The Seven's Committee," which was comprised of seven ministers. They assumed that unlike judges, the ministers would take into consideration the need to maintain *Mapai*'s status, since most of the people involved in the Affair were members of this party.

Ben-Gurion abstained and waited for the investigation's results. On December 25, 1960, the committee ruled that Lavon did not give the order. Gibli resigned. The government accepted the conclusions. Prime Minister Eshkol hoped that Lavon would be satisfied and the Affair would finally be put to rest. As compensation, Lavon was appointed to be the general secretary of the *Histadrut*.

Ben-Gurion protested. He criticized the establishment of a procedural committee, which was not authorized to offer conclusions, since the executive branch could not function as the judicial branch in a civilized country. Therefore, he insisted on reinstalling the judicial investigative committee. At the same time, he persecuted Lavon and forced the members of *Mapai*'s central committee to vote him off his position in the *Histadrut*'s secretariat.

Lavon was dismissed and he left *Mapai* in 1961. He was bitter, and established the group *Min Ha-Yesod*, named after a neosocialist magazine that opposed Ben-Gurion and his way. The group members argued that Lavon's persecution and the Old Man's refusal to accept the conclusions of the "The Seven's Committee" suggested that his ruling patterns were partly totalitarian in nature.

A while later, Lavon's health deteriorated. Yet, his disease and dismissal never soothed Ben-Gurion's rage, and he continued to require the establishment of a judicial investigative committee. During one of the sessions, Paula embarked on his room and noted: "But Lavon is sick!" After a short reflection, Ben-Gurion answered: "What am I to do? I can't change a principle and official position over that."[68]

By 1964, Lavon was away from the political arena due to his disease, and Ben-Gurion had already retired from his position as prime minister. But his demand to establish a judicial committee was not forgotten, and he even pushed it further. He presented Eshkol with the demand that the judicial committee would include the discussions and conclusions of "The Seven's Committee" in its investigation. Eshkol refused, wanting to push the Affair away from the public agenda. He believed that the intrigues discovered were nothing but human weaknesses. He found no use in opening this Pandora Box, which would smear *Mapai*'s reputation and cause further internal disputes.

The same way Ben-Gurion fought the dissident organizations *IZL* and *Lehi* before the state was established, not just because he morally and fundamentally opposed the violent struggle against the British, but mainly because they defied the authority of the national institutions; the same way he decided to liquidate the *Palmah* after the War of Independence, despite its military achievements, because he was afraid their commitment to *Mapam* would overcome their commitment to the state; and the same way he fought after the state's establishment to implement the State Education Law—he tried to use the Lavon Affair in order to educate toward the construction of the state's authority and dictate the ethical rules for governmental institutions. Ben-Gurion feared that Lavon, who he nicknamed "the hypocrite vulture,"[69] had laid the foundations for a new era. His list of traits for the "pioneering personality" required from the state's citizens included role model behavior, service, and commitment.[70] He assessed that Lavon's struggle against the establishment was paving the way for a post-pioneering careerist era,[71] the one he was afraid of, knowing that revolutions are destined to sag and can't be maintained forever.[72]

Ben-Gurion's approach sparked resentment not only among politicians, but also among prominent academics in Israel. The latter identified antidemocratic elements in his approach, which required society to sacrifice individual freedoms in favor of institutional interests. Martin Buber, for instance, argued that in trying to squash Lavon and his claims, Ben-Gurion was sacrificing the individual in favor of a "bureaucratization" of society and positioning the state's institutions above the citizens.[73] Buber explained that Ben-Gurion was creating a violent version of democracy, where the establishment represses the individual's right to fight for his own reputation while trying to dictate ideas and ways of thinking for the public through governmental tools. Buber, along with other intellectuals, led the camp that perceived Lavon's struggle against the security institutions as a given right, and even a civil duty.

Ben-Gurion's soft spot when it came to security personnel was never a secret. For him, they embodied the vision of the "new Jew," the fighter and farmer. Without them, he wrote, the Zionist project would not have survived.[74] "I treasure the army more than anything else," he admitted on the day of his resignation, emphasizing that it wasn't because he was "a militarist, but rather because this is the most pioneering institution among our people."[75]

Obviously, it was easier for him to defend the military establishment rather than Lavon as a person. Yet, as mentioned, his struggle against the acquitting conclusions of the committee should not be explained solely by his attempt to defend the military establishment. On the contrary, the judicial committee was supposed to investigate further into the establishment. He believed that if, indeed, the conclusions of "The Seven's Committee" were true, and grave conspiracies were taking place within the security establishment, there should have been a thorough investigation into the holiest patch of Israeliness, and not by ministers, who are motivated by short-term political considerations.

Ben-Gurion also tried to leverage the Affair for a complete transformation of the state's mechanisms, before they would be conquered by decay. What Buber saw as a totalitarian version of democracy was, in Ben-Gurion's mind, the highest model of proper civil conduct. According to him, individuals in a democracy should also see themselves as part of society, like the ant would prefer the interests of its swarm before its own. Individuals must accept their duties to the public, after these duties were set by the majority-elected government. Otherwise, Ben-Gurion feared, Israeli democracy would deteriorate into anarchy, and the social cohesion would be lost.

This fear was another derivative of his negative attitude toward the exile mentality brought to Israel by the Jews after 2,000 years of nonstatehood life. In his speech before the establishment of the state he warned:

> These Jews, like all the Jews in exile, were not citizens for the last 1,800 years, because people cannot be citizens unless it's in their own country, their own land. These Jews have no sense of citizenship, particularly those who know what was done to them by their states in Poland, Germany, Lithuania and the rest of the countries, which were transformed into cemeteries. Strong are the anarchist instincts in the Jewish life. Citizenship is a deeply embedded personality trait [...] I fear it is not found in this room. [...] In Europe, the Jews only make demands [...] this sense of citizenship means that [people] must recognize their duties first and foremost, must know that collective can only have what it is given by individuals.[76]

Ben-Gurion's problem was the complexity of his arguments rather than their quality. His image, of a vengeful, all-encompassing leader, was also held against him, and this image even grew stronger in light of his blunt style in

handling Lavon and The Affair. Moreover, the political system and the public
as a whole were fed up with Ben-Gurion's attempts to educate them. The state
was less than twenty years of age, and its citizens wanted some relief from the
constant effort demanded by the founding father. Prime Minister Levi Eshkol
was aware of that, as mentioned before, and wanted to grant the public some
relief after decades of constant effort. But in Ben-Gurion's mind, Eshkol's
compromising policy was constructing the activation code of future generations. His criticism on Eshkol's tendency to put the Affair to rest without a
thorough judicial investigation was one of the reasons for his reproach:

> [Eshkol] sins were against statehood, the kind of sins that damage the state,
> lower its stature and create a reputation of uncivilized state. Pakistan could
> exist for centuries without an international moral status. Mexico could survive
> for generations with a completely rotten regime. There, as you know, the Presi-
> dent starts his tenure with empty pockets and walks away as a millionaire. This
> doesn't hurt Mexico. It can still exist. But not Israel. If we are not a role-model
> people and a role-model state, we wouldn't survive for many years.[77]

As in anything related to Ben-Gurion's actions in the 1960s, some point
out the nuclear context even in regard to the Lavon Affair. Ben-Gurion might
have feared that Lavon's claims of corruption within the security system
would be fixated in the public mind, thus weakening the status of Peres and
his people, who were accused by Lavon of being involved in the Affair; a
damage to the people who were appointed by him to manage the nuclear
project might have meant a damage to the project itself, which was raising
controversies regarding its necessity and implementability.[78]

6

The nuclear project was unaffected by the Affair, but Ben-Gurion's image
was not: His objectives were too complex to be explained in laymen terms,
too exhausting to be accepted, and he was seen as someone who tries to
enforce his own will at all costs. The public and the political system didn't
feel he was fighting for his principles; they thought he couldn't hold back,
even though his time was up. This feeling turned into antagonism toward the
founding father, with the active contribution of Eshkol, who deviously tried
to pass on the message that Ben-Gurion was responsible for the continuous
splits and confrontations within the state and within his own party.[79] The
result, from Ben-Gurion's point of view, was gloomy: He hoped that by leaving the prime minister's office he could avoid internal partisan disputes, pave
the path for society, and be remembered as a person who could put an end to
his own political career—but he achieved the exact opposite.

Toward the end of 1964, more than a year after his retirement, almost all of the leading figures in *Mapai* were already united against his investigative committee campaign. Yigal Alon, the minister of labor, even offered to order the police to investigate Ben-Gurion under the suspicion he had confidential materials related to the Affair in his possession (Ben-Gurion used these materials to investigate the matter on his own and publish his conclusions in a book). In public interviews, Ben-Gurion had no choice but to support Alon's position. He admitted that good governance practices can't grant an ex-prime minister any privileges regarding the possession of confidential materials. Yet, he felt that Alon was trying to humiliate him, rather than supporting the state's interests and good governance.[80] His supporters felt he was crucified for no reason at all: Should he, the man who knew the state inside out, be investigated for reading confidential materials? Was there a secret he did not create himself?

The decline of his status affected his family as well; Geula, his oldest daughter, started crying when she said that during English class, when the teacher taught the students the word "mission," she gave the following example: "Just like Ben-Gurion's mission is to harass Eshkol."[81]

Ben-Gurion himself was distraught during this period. He was aware of his declining position, and the events and struggles around the Affair, big or small, pushed him into feeling that he was attacked for no reason, no justification, particularly after he left the power center on his own accord. Strolling with his bodyguard through the pavements of the Kibbutz, he said that Alon was "a disabled person" and explained that the key problem of the *Palmah*'s ex-commander was the excessive influence of Arab culture on his upbringing.[82] In a way his struggle against Lavon trampled individual rights and he was trying to avenge the establishment's insult by hurting a defense minister with a civil philosophy, who declared that "The army is not the cause, it's the mean." In fact, his struggle was a complete mirror image of Lavon's, but he never noticed it.

Anyway, after their disagreement over the establishment of a judicial investigative committee, Ben-Gurion and Eshkol went on to get ready for the *Mapai* convention in February 1965, leading two opposing camps. The convention's declared goal was to decide whether or not to establish a judicial investigative committee, and whether or not to support the union with *Ahdut Ha-Avoda*. But beyond the declared agenda, there was a fundamental struggle about worldviews, political philosophy, and different approaches regarding the Israeli society. In addition, there was, probably, an instinctive struggle between the man who was used to ruling and realizing his wills and his successor who had a natural desire to rule in his own way.

Eshkol enjoyed the support of the party's seniors, like Golda Meir, Moshe Sharett, and the other members of the *Third Aliyah*, while Ben-Gurion was supported mainly by the younger generation, like Moshe Dayan, Shimon Peres, and Yosef Almogi.

Eighty-one-year-old Ben-Gurion was upset, bitter, and frustrated when he came to the convention. He was aware of the fierce fight awaiting him, but he didn't expect that the hatred and grudge accumulated against him among *Mapai*'s seniors during the years of his absolute reign would break out in such a force.

The first speaker against him was the former prime minister and current minister of foreign affairs, Moshe Sharett. Ben-Gurion decided the political fate of Sharett ten years before, in May 1955, when he practically dismissed him from his premiership, feeling that Israel's security was deteriorating under his leadership. Ben-Gurion believed that Sharett had failed because he objected the reprisals, tried to achieve a massive compromise in order to ensure peace with Israel's neighbors, and strove to tighten the links with the United States, while Ben-Gurion put his faith in the alliance with France.[83] After replacing him as prime minister, he also made sure that Sharett would be dismissed from his duties as the minister of foreign affairs and replaced by Golda Meir. Sharett believed that Ben-Gurion's activist policy was pushing further away the possibility of peace, which was the only way to ensure the state's survival, and now, at the convention, he was reciprocating Ben-Gurion's treatment from the past.

Although cancer was already eating away Sharett's body, and he was nearing the end of his life, he came to the convention in a wheelchair, determined to take his revenge at Ben-Gurion with whatever powers left in him:

> A leader cannot focus all his might on what happened eleven years ago, or what happened 4–5 years ago, while neglecting future thoughts and concerns [...] the movement should be inspired by the leader, but the leader cannot outweigh the movement, freeze its thought and enforce his own personal opinion, relying merely on his enormous authority [...] with his insistence, he desecrates leadership [...] he undermines the prestige of this state.[84]

Sharett's accusation against Ben-Gurion was, in fact, the same one pronounced by Ben-Gurion against *Mapai*'s leadership—putting the personal interest before the statehood's one. He particularly mocked Ben-Gurion's famous qualities as a leader: His ability to foresee the future, plan steps ahead, and respect statehood.

Ben-Gurion couldn't understand how Moshe Sharett had dared to discredit him like that, particularly since he knew that Sharett was not fond of Lavon, who undermined him when he was the minister of defense. Therefore, he argued that Sharett's speech was hypocritical. Ben-Gurion's one-dimensional judgment of Sharett's speech reflected one of his greatest weaknesses:

his obliviousness to the depths of the human sole. Just like he couldn't understand Eshkol's motives, when he naturally tried to spread his own wings upon being appointed as prime minister, he refused to acknowledge Sharett's ongoing pain after being dismissed from his positions.

Ben-Gurion expected his fellow leaders to treat themselves the same way he treated himself: as a tool; an instrument serving the idea, the state, the people. But this demand was almost superhuman. Every person has his or her own sensations, feelings, frustrations. Ben-Gurion's expectation—that Sharett would accept that fact that he was dismissed for the common good and give up his personal worldview—was excessive, extreme, blind. Furthermore, he ignored the fact that personal impulses had affected him as well in many of his struggles.

Some saw a poetic justice in Sharett's speech and the anti-Ben-Gurion feeling it had created. When Ben-Gurion dismissed Sharett, who was considered to be his natural successor, he already signaled to the rest of the ministers that their positions were at stake, thus undermining their loyalty toward him. None of his men would tell him directly during the hectic days of the conference; but in hindsight, this period—when he was at the pick of his glory, at the highest position of his life, after returning to premiership in 1955 and leading the IDF to a victory in Sinai Campaign in 1956—was the beginning of his political end: the seeds of rebellion within his party were planted back then.[85]

At the end of Sharett's revenge speech, he was approached by Golda Meir, who kissed him on his forehead. It was a human gesture in the face of the heart-wrenching gap between Sharett's furious words and his feeble physical appearance. It was a scorpion's kiss for Ben-Gurion. The following speech by Golda Meir, who also supported Eshkol's position, was unbearable to him, and he rushed home. "The ugliest thing in the entire convention was Golda's poisonous speech," he wrote in his diary. "I was sorry to listen to her speaking like that, full of hatred and venom. Where did it come from, and why?"[86] He couldn't understand her natural choice to maintain her loyalty to the new prime minister and the position of her party, which she didn't want to drag back into the Affair.

Ben-Gurion's insistence on his one and only truth, as well as his feeling of betrayal, blurred his vision and prevented him from seeing things as they were. After all, this was Golda—"the greatest gift given to us by America Jewry,"[87] as he wrote in the 1950s with unmistakable feelings. How could she have attacked him like that? The pain caused to him by her attitude was even greater than his disappointment from Eshkol or Sharett, due to their delicate relationship prior to this confrontation, which had a father-daughter quality.[88] Instead of exploring the real reasons for her changed approach toward him, he started suspecting that even when she was loyal to him,[89] her considerations were opportunist. He noted in his diary that he should check whether her current attitude was "new or not."[90]

Still, he tried to win back *Mapai*'s members in his speech, using his renowned charisma, and said: "I have no idea what the people wants, I just know what it needs." The sentence, which later became an idiom for describing unpopulist leadership, was not liked by the audience. It was perceived as another proof of his totalitarian leadership pattern. Unsurprisingly, most of *Mapai*'s members refused to believe Ben-Gurion was holding monopoly over the interpretation of the truth, and Eshkol won the majority of the votes.

Ben-Gurion's struggle against *Mapai*'s leadership was perceived by many as a predestined failure. How could he expect the members of the dominant party to risk their position for another investigative committee of an event that no one never really understood properly, because the details were obscured by censorship? His insistence to fight, at the age of 81, against the partisan mechanism that was his own creation raised questions regarding his quality of judgment; and some even thought his actions might have had an unconscious masochist element in them. Yitzhak Ben-Aharon was one of them. He believed that Ben-Gurion knew he was drowning in a struggle in which he had a small chance of winning, but was trying to punish himself as well, because the shame of the military system, as portrayed in the Lavon Affair, was also his failure—they were all his sons.[91]

7

Ben-Gurion was never open minded enough to analyze himself psychologically. He was a man of action. After losing the vote, he joined another struggle. In June 1965, he even requested to be reassigned as *Mapai*'s candidate for premiership. He was outvoted again. Desperate, during a meeting with the members of *Min Ha-Yesod* group, he mentioned when talking about the meaning and significance of the leader in history: "History is created by the people and not by public figures,"[92] though he believed in the power of a leader to make a difference. He started a campaign in various platforms and private conversations, throwing accusations against *Mapai* and Eshkol for committing "sins against statehood" and insinuating that some are related to still-kept state secrets. His words referred probably to three main issues: First, a compromise of sorts on Eshkol's side concerning the White House's demand that American supervisors would be allowed into the Dimona reactor.[93] Second, the approval given by Eshkol to the Mossad, at the request of the Moroccan government, to assist in murdering the opposition leader Ben Barka in French territory; according to Ben-Gurion, the revelation of the Israeli involvement in the murder contributed to the decision of the French president, Charles de Gaulle, to reconsider France-Israel relationship. The third issue was the cancellation of the development venture of medium-range missiles, meant to carry the weapons that were supposedly developed in Dimona.[94]

Ben-Gurion's hostility, frenzy, and the power of the accusations toward Eshkol were difficult to overstate. The question was, was this criticism based on facts, or maybe Eshkol knew how to preserve Israel's security interests in his own way?

Researches that were conducted over the years suggest that Ben-Gurion was overreacting. Indeed, Eshkol canceled the development venture of medium- and short-range missiles, which was agreed upon under Ben-Gurion, for financial reasons,[95] but regarding the continuation of Dimona's activity, he followed Ben-Gurion's footsteps, albeit in his own way: He managed to ensure the continuing operation while preventing a confrontation with the American administration, although he might have agreed to slow down the development rate.[96]

The Old Man was too harsh in his criticism regarding the Israeli involvement in Ben Barka's murder as well. Although Israel's involvement was obviously not conducive to the Jerusalem-Paris relationship, de Gaulle started changing France's policy toward Israel as early as 1959, based on his own assessment regarding France's interests in the Middle East.[97]

Thus, Ben-Gurion's accusations against Eshkol originated from his personal frustration as well. It was but natural. Should he have even hoped he could pass the crown on to Eshkol while maintaining his dominance at the same time? Was there any leader in history, even among the most glorified and significant ones, who managed to retire on his own will, while in his prime, and continue to pull strings without fulfilling any official position? Was there ever a person who was able to rise above the circle of life—rising, declining, and withering—and end his life exactly as he planned? It seems that Ben-Gurion's revolutionary, Promethean, basic approach gave him superhuman false hopes to begin with, and a faith he could escape mortal fate and continue to rule even when his time was up.

As a leader, Ben-Gurion could identify public trends and use them in order to advance his goals. Following the murder of Haim Arlosoroff, the head of the Jewish agency's political department in 1933, for example, he used the bad blood in the *Yishuv* between the Revisionist and Labor camps and strengthened his political power in the eighteenth Zionist congress elections. Yet, as a person, particularly in his later years, he struggled to understand his colleagues' motives. As someone who never read fiction, and dedicated his time to thousands of nonfiction books, he missed out on the human aspect, which should have tipped him regarding future developments in the dispute between him and his successor. Instead, he continued tirelessly to complain about Eshkol's ideological, political, and strategic mistakes. As if their dispute was solely based on principle difference of opinions and not on a human gap, which was almost unavoidable, between past and current leaders.

In hindsight, Ben-Gurion's political end seems to have been written by the ancient fathers of Greek tragedy: After decades of leading the *Yishuv* and the state, Eshkol and the political establishment might have still needed his advices, but more than that, they were trying to free themselves of his long, threatening shadow. Only the "murder of the father" could have released them from his mythical presence, which prevented them from stirring the ship into a new era.

Chapter 2

By All Means

1

Shortly after Ben-Gurion's request to return to his position as the party's leader was rejected by *Mapai*'s central committee in June 1965, his supporters within the party were gathered by his youngest and most active follower, Shimon Peres. Peres announced that the wisest way to fight Eshkol was from within the party, and those who were talking about a split were politically wrong.

Ben-Gurion was not invited to the meeting that Peres arranged for him. Paula, who was suspicious even toward her husband's followers, urged him to leave the house and go to the meeting. The Old Man entered the conference room, which was filled with his supporters, during Peres's fiery speech.[1] Without hesitating, he stopped Peres mid-sentence and announced in a determined, loaded, and angry voice that he intended to retire and form an alternative party. Peres's face turned white. But he recovered quickly, announced that his proposal was not going to be voted on anyway, and left the stand. Ben-Gurion had known that Peres, like Dayan and the majority of his followers, were not interested in a split.[2] But even at the age of seventy-nine, he did not hesitate to present them with a done deal.

The fact that Ben-Gurion could afford to barge into Peres's words and contradict them was not an accident. He knew well enough that Peres would not dare to defy him. Indeed, despite his objection to the idea of a new party, Peres drafted the news release announcing its establishment at the end of that meeting. The name chosen for the party by the Old Man, *Rafi* (*Reshimat Poaley Israel*, Israel's Labor Party), pointed out its main objective: to hurt *Mapai*. As a matter of fact, *Rafi* was established to provoke *Mapai*—the Party of Israel's Laborers. Ben-Gurion dictated the principle, and Peres quickly became his ideological and operational branch. He wrote most of the platform, ran around haphazardly between established local offices, and immersed himself in Ben-Gurion's political initiative, as if he had never objected it.[3]

Moshe Dayan, a tough nut to crack, who was loyal mostly to himself, was not persuaded as easily. While he was also considered to be one of Ben-Gurion's young supporters, Dayan thought that the Lavon Affair should be put to rest and not delved into any further.[4] When the Old Man tried to urge him to join the new party, Dayan reminded him that he, Ben-Gurion, was the one who appointed Lavon to be the minister of defense, and that he was the one to resign a decade later and support Eshkol's appointment as prime minister. Therefore, Dayan argued, Ben-Gurion should bear the consequences. Faced with the Old Man's angry expression, Dayan snapped: "You can't milk this ram any more, Ben-Gurion."[5] Ben-Gurion was not used to hearing such harsh words within the intimate circle of his followers, nor was he able to ignore the clear albeit gloomy mirror presented to him by Dayan. Yet, when Dayan realized *Mapai*'s members considered him to be one of the Old Man's followers anyway, he joined *Rafi* after all.

The establishment of *Rafi*, although it involved an inherent air of provocation, spiteness, and personal frustrations, was also Ben-Gurion's last important political act. By deserting *Mapai* after more than thirty years of leading it, he also tried to demonstrate his position of statism: The state and its institutions were more important than any partisan loyalty. Precisely because he was one of the creators of the partisan mechanism, he was repulsed by what he perceived as the corruption of the mechanisms over time. As a leader whose ruling patterns were mainly based on his charisma, he tried to establish his power anew based on the people's choice.[6]

Rafi, the first party in Israel that did not belong either to the political right or left, was not only a political conspiracy meant to undermine *Mapai*'s dominance. As an openly nonsectoral party, it was also meant to offer an alternative to the multiplicity of parties in Israel, which, as mentioned above, was perceived by Ben-Gurion as an obstacle, which was limiting governability and the state's development. During one of *Rafi*'s first meetings, he even offered to join hands with some of the veterans of *Ha-Zionim Ha-Klaliyim* in an ad hoc list, which would run on a single-section platform: An electoral reform. He believed that the election results would make the ad hoc list an inseparable part of any coalition, and then the Knesset would be dismissed and its members would be reelected based on constituency elections.[7] "In Israel," he explained, "the Knesset members are chosen by partisan committees and not by the public. The citizens have no idea who they vote for, and the Knesset members don't know their electorate."[8] He reneged on his radical proposal only in light of Peres and Dayan's vehement opposition, just like he managed, throughout his whole life, to ignore radical ideas thrown in the heat of the moment, as if they were never heard (and yet, he still believed the electoral system must be replaced; in his later years he once said that the only mistake he had made when he had drafted the Declaration of Independence was his failure to mention constituency elections, since they were "a basic element of democracy"[9]).

Rafi's platform included many promises for transformation in the political system, including "a car for every laborer" and a technological advancement of the government mechanism (state scientification). Concerning the economic aspect, the term "socialism" was absent from the platform, and the party presented an activist approach regarding foreign and security affairs.[10] Politically, *Rafi* could be positioned on the left side of *Gahal*—the newly created union between *Herut* and the Liberal Party—and on the right side of the *Ma'arach*, which was based on a union between *Mapai* and *Ahdut Ha-Avoda*. This was *Rafi*'s ideological background. In fact, the party's main feature was the Old Man's fierce spirit.[11] In his speech during the party's founding conference he sounded raged, and particularly defying: "What do we want to renew? We want to uproot corrupted novelties within the party, fear and deceit."[12]

Toward the sixth Knesset election, the different parties started to use US-imported patterns, including the use of public opinion polls. Ben-Gurion was undeterred when the polls predicted that *Rafi* would win only ten seats. Those who were worried got a response with his typical impatience: "I will continue my campaign for truth and justice even when I'm all alone. [...] I have no fear of pessimists' prophecies."[13] He hoped that *Rafi* would get twenty to twenty-five seats, which would make it an essential part of *Mapai*'s coalition.[14] In turbulent moments, he was even willing to marvelously exaggerate the chances of success: Even sixty-one seats were an option.[15]

2

The sixth Knesset election was characterized by defamations and struggles, which were sometimes violent. Despite the hatred he encountered in among *Herut*'s supporters and in the left-wing Kibbutzim during previous campaigns, Ben-Gurion had never before got spit in his face, like in *Rafi*'s convention in the city of Ashdod. The offender, a *Histadrut* activist, claimed he was affected by publications in *Davar*, *Mapai*'s newspaper, which reported that Ben-Gurion had dismissed Moroccan Jews in an interview to *LOOK* magazine.[16] Ben-Gurion and his followers blamed Eshkol and *Mapai*'s PR department in manipulating his words.[17] But Ben-Gurion was not worried because of this particular interview. Like any other public figure, he was used to quotes taken out of their context. He was furious because he realized that these publications were the first to challenge the "melting pot" concept from within the system.

In the spirit of this idea, Ben-Gurion had boasted that the newcomers from Morocco were shedding their unworthy exile culture and gradually becoming new, Israeli-born Jews. As early as 1950, he described newcomers from third-world countries as "riffraff" (*avak anashim*)—a term that would later be used as a proof of his condescending approach.

> The ingathering of the exiles is the message on which our strength is built; our state will be based on it, and our independence will prevail in it. First, we must lay the foundation. This foundation is not made of rocks or trees or steel, but rather of people. The people who come here—they are riffraff of the most secluded, poor, humiliated and vile countries. We will welcome the Jews coming back to us, whatever country they were expelled from, even if it's the most underdeveloped and unworthy. The sons of Israel are all kings, the sons of Abraham, Yitzhak and Jacob. We will welcome them with love, extend our faithful hand and brotherly assistance, so they can put down roots in our homeland, culture, language, life, and benefit the IDF as well.[18]

Through the "melting pot," Ben-Gurion wished to replace the cultures brought by the newcomers from their countries of origin with a local Israeli culture, which included Hebrew as a native tongue, knowing the land and its heritage, and adopting a secular-national agenda.[19] The process required uprooting centuries-old traditions and customs, violating the dignity of newcomers from various countries, and sometimes even breaking traditional familial structures. Yet, in his mind, this process was necessary in order to realize his ambition of creating one unified people in its own land out of the separate religious groups. While the "melting pot" is perceived as colliding particularly with the culture of Jews from Eastern and Islamic countries, the truth was that Ben-Gurion wished to reshape all Jews. Therefore, in his own mind, the "melting pot" was not condescending over Eastern Jews. On the contrary, during this period, he noted in his diary with disappointment and defiance that the *Histadrut* was still led by Ashkenazi Jews.[20] He believed that the reshaping process did require effort, but its purpose was to create equality between all the Jews in Israel.

This was another reason, out of many, for his bitterness toward Eshkol's era: He realized that Eshkol's rise marked the end of the "bill of duties" era, in which the citizens were required to make an effort; from now on, Israelis will strive to realize their "bill of rights" according to the American model—a process that was accelerated later, when the Likud party became dominant and, under Menachem Begin, specifically wished to "treat the people well" instead of presenting demands.[21]

Anyway, the public uproar regarding the spitting act and the following public debate regarding the melting pot concept was just one of many disputes during this election campaign, which was described by Ben-Gurion as "the ugliest election campaign ever seen in Israel."[22]

Regardless of the preelection disputes, the results were also disappointing. *Rafi* won merely ten seats, as predicted in the polls. This was a testimony of the fact that while the public still respected the Old Man, most of them couldn't understand how the man who created the establishment with his own two hands was now leading a revolution against it.[23] Ben-Gurion was forced to discover that the *Mapai* mechanism was stronger than him: *Rafi* couldn't stop Eshkol from forming a coalition.

3

In many ways, despite its failure, by establishing *Rafi*, the Old Man was actually ahead of his time. The challenge against *Mapai* was the first link in a chain of events that removed *Mapai* from its leading position a little more than a decade later. Furthermore, *Rafi* was an innovative political attempt to establish a nonsectoral party, which would undermine the hegemony of the main left and right parties. Since then, the political center in Israel has seen the rise of more and more parties: Yigael Yadin's *Dash* in 1977; *Mifleget Ha-Merkaz* headed by Yitzhak Mordechai in 1999; Tomi Lapid's *Shinuy* in 1999; Arik Sharon's *Kadima* in 2005; Yair Lapid's *Yesh Atid* in 2012. In fact, since 1965, the major political parties in Israel have tried to position themselves in the political center during every election campaign, blurring any leftist or rightist explicit ideology.

But this can be said only in hindsight. At the time, *Rafi*'s failure was painful. For the first time since the state's establishment, and two years after resigning from premiership on his own accord, Ben-Gurion became a member of the opposition. The man who was seen as the greatest practitioner in the modern history of the Jewish people, of whom Zalman Aran, one of his ministers, once said he trusted Ben-Gurion's intuition more than his own opinion,[24] had to adjust to his status as a person who interrupts parliament speeches. While he was a realist, and aware of his achievements, which were almost unprecedented among world leaders in the twentieth century, his marginalization left him hurt, bitter, and frustrated from the turn of events in his life.

He could lead against public opinion, and even excelled in it, but the love of the masses was still important to him. Once, at the pick of his glory during the 1950s, he pointed out the tension between the need to act according to his own discretion and the need for public approval, using the Chinese parable.

"Confucius was asked, who should be elected to lead the people. Should it be someone that everyone loves? He said: No. They asked again: Should it be someone that everyone hates? He said: Of course not! They asked for the third time: Who, then? He said: You must choose someone that's loved by the good people and hated by the bad ones."[25] But after the people made their choice, he could no longer argue that only the "bad ones" were against him. The majority of the public voted in favor of *Mapai*'s rule.

After the elections, his confrontations with *Mapai*'s leadership became pettier—to the point that Golda ordered the employees at *Mapai*'s archives to prohibit him from copying protocols that were kept there from the party's early years. Ben-Gurion, who needed the protocols in order to write his memoirs, was offended. The day he heard about the birth of his grandson, he gathered his followers and wondered painfully: "Did Berl and Golomb decide to expel me from 1930 *Mapai* as well? Why won't they let me observe materials from that period?" Only then did he share his joy over the birth of his grandson.[26]

Yosef Almogi tried to mend the relationship between Ben-Gurion and Golda, and even managed to persuade them to meet with each other. Ben-Gurion's excitement before the meeting, which was secretly held in a Tel-Aviv hotel, seemed to Almogi like the excitement of a man who was going to meet the girl who broke his heart after a long period of separation. But at the end of the meeting, Ben-Gurion was angry. "She doesn't believe that Eshkol is a liar," he snarled. Almogi turned to Golda, and she desperately reported that Ben-Gurion demanded that she would declare publicly Eshkol was a liar. "Come on, could I do that for him?"[27]

Almogi never repeated his attempt.

Chapter 3

A Gloomy Victory

1

On May 15, 1967, while the ceremonies of Israel's Independence Day were held, Egyptian military troops were entering the Sinai Peninsula. The Israeli security system was caught unprepared. Yitzhak Rabin, the chief of staff, got an update while watching the military parade, and reported to Prime Minister Eshkol, who was sitting next to him. Eight days later, Gamal Abdel Nasser, the president of Egypt, ordered his troops to block the Straits of Tiran. The Egyptian action further enhanced the tension that had been going on for months between Israel, Egypt, and Syria, along with threatening decelerations regarding the nearing end of the Jewish state. These were difficult days for Israel: The economy was still recovering from a long recession, France was no longer a guaranteed ally, and the anxiety was further enhanced by Eshkol's image as a hesitating leader, who can't lead the people in the crucial fight.[1] Senior officials in the IDF General Staff were starting to understand that if Israel wanted to win what seemed like an unavoidable war, it would have to send the first blow. Eshkol and the political leadership continued to weigh other options.

During the waiting period, Ben-Gurion gave many interviews and his warnings against the prime minister's mistakes were getting graver, contributing to the rising flames of public panic. He believed Eshkol was wrong when he authorized, in November 1966, the IDF's operation in the Jordanian village of Samo'a. Ben-Gurion thought it was an unnecessary operation, which undermined King Husain's prestige and negatively affected his basic tendency to avoid war. After his sovereignty was jeopardized, Ben-Gurion assessed, King Hussein had no other option but to demonstrate his power and tighten his alliance with Nasser.[2] Ben-Gurion thought that the Israeli recruitment of reserve forces during the waiting period was generating escalation. He argued that Israel must guarantee the superpowers' support for any act of war; otherwise, it would have to face a difficult political campaign. And he still stuck to his firm belief that France's support was essential.

The chief of staff, Yitzhak Rabin, was also concerned by the turn of events, despite his support of a preemptive strike. Rabin-Ben-Gurion's relationships went through crises over the years, but they were still based on mutual appreciation. One of Ben-Gurion's final requests from Eshkol before he left premiership was to keep his promise to Rabin and make him chief of staff. The promise was kept in December 1963. The Old Man favored Rabin since he had been a teenage boy,[3] when he was a friend of his parents, Rossa and Nehemiah Rabin, who came to Israel during after World War I. In his diary he referred to Rabin fondly as "Major Rabin."[4]

Alongside his appreciation, he believed that Rabin was "a little bit over-cautions."[5] This notion originated during the 1948 War, when Ben-Gurion wished to ensure that Jerusalem would not be conquered by the Arab Legion and demanded the IDF to complete "Yoram Operation" and get a hold of Latrun. The operation was designed to protect Jerusalem, even at the price of multiple casualties. Rabin, the commander of Harel Brigade at that time, believed that the operation was wrong and unnecessary. He and Yigal Alon, the *Palmah* Commander, argued that the price, in the form of many lives, some of them Holocaust survivors who were sent to the battlefield straight from their ships, was too heavy. They offered an alternative: to pave Burma Road in order to assist Jerusalem. Alon had sent Rabin to persuade the Old Man. Only after a fiery argument did Ben-Gurion give his consent to the alternative offer. According to Rabin, Ben-Gurion yelled during the argument: "Yigal Alon should be shot at," because his approach was verging on disobedience.[6]

Rabin and Ben-Gurion had another disagreement after the war had ended. This time it was due to the Old Man's decision, in October 1948, to desolate the *Palmah* and disperse its soldiers among the various IDF units. Rabin thought that Ben-Gurion's concerns regarding the left-wing parties influencing the *Palmah* as a single unit were exaggerated. But he didn't confront Ben-Gurion about it, because he accepted the statism principle: Israel should have only one military institution, authorized by the government.[7] Rabin refused to accept only one symbolic demand: He was adamant he should be present in the farewell ceremony for the *Palmah* members. His absence would be a grave insult to the value of friendship, and he did it out of "a deep psychological need."[8]

For Ben-Gurion, the fact that this farewell ceremony was even held was a provocative act. In order to transform the distributed *Yishuv*—Jews that were not used to obeying—into the citizens of the newly established unified state, he believed that any expression of political independence within a military brigade should be avoided. Therefore, he wished to test Rabin's loyalty as his follower. He invited Rabin to a meeting at his home, a few hours before the ceremony was scheduled to start. Rabin came on time. During their conversation, Ben-Gurion avoided the topic of the ceremony, ignoring it completely. Rabin was the first to lay his cards on the table. He wondered why the Old Man was insisting on preventing him from making this human, friendly, natural gesture. Ben-Gurion responded by an invitation for Rabin to dine with him that evening and discuss the matter. Rabin refused politely. He realized that Ben-Gurion was trying to stall him, rushed to the ceremony, and arrived late. Eventually, his presence at the ceremony of the *Palmah*'s desolation resulted in a reprimand in his personal file. Ben-Gurion never expressed understanding for Rabin's motives, but the fact that he supported Rabin's appointment as chief of staff sixteen years later spoke for itself.

Yitzhak Rabin, in turn, never doubted Ben-Gurion's judgment and leadership skills. Against the tension of the waiting period before 1967 war, and the disappointment of the IDF's higher command from Eshkol hesitancy to declare a war, Rabin turned to the Old Man in late May 1967 and asked to consult him and listen to his assessment.

The chief of staff was tensed and angry when he arrived to the meeting. It was obvious he yearned for some encouraging words from the founding father. He didn't know what Dayan and Peres already knew: That Ben-Gurion was skeptic about the need for preemptive strike; he assessed that the war could go on for weeks and argued that Israel should not attack without the support of the Western powers. One reason for Ben-Gurion's pessimism was the fact that he was, for the first time since the state had been established, detached from the decision-making process. He didn't know, for instance, that while he continued to believe in the essentiality of France's support, Israel was actually trying to coordinate its moves with the United States.[9] Ben-Gurion was convinced that Levi Eshkol was responsible for the escalation, and repeated his assessment that the operation in Samo'a and the recruitment of reserve forces were mistakes. While he noticed Rabin's tension—"Yitzhak was depressed,"[10] he noted in his diary—he didn't spare him, believing that "a war should be avoided at all costs."[11]

For years, Ben-Gurion feared that the Arab armies would focus on Israel's weakest link—the population centers—being aware of the IDF's qualitative advantage in the battle field. "If there's a war, it won't be against the armies of 1948," he said. "Although I'm convinced we would win, we will suffer many fatalities, including citizens, particularly in the metropolitan I have no other name for other than Tel-Aviv. But not only Tel-Aviv [...] such small people and state cannot sustain so many casualties [...] we need a deterrent force."[12]

During his meeting with Rabin, Ben-Gurion mentioned that the Sinai Operation was launched only after he reached understandings with France and Britain, that they would defend Israel in the case of an air strike. In comparison, he said: "we are currently in distress, completely lonely, unlike the past."[13] The impact of the conversation on Rabin's mood was grave. While we can't determine the exact cause, and we may assume that Rabin was probably preoccupied by the menacing developments, we do know that Rabin collapsed shortly after listening to the Old Man, and had to be treated with tranquilizers.

The end of May 1967 saw fascinating developments in the political arena as well. *Herut*'s leader, Menachem Begin, who was also concerned by what seemed like a government that would struggle to stir the state in stormy seas, decided, against the judgment of his party members,[14] and encouraged by Peres, to call for the reinstating of Ben-Gurion as prime minister, or at least as the defense minister. This was historical irony at its finest: While Ben-Gurion's glory had already lost it charm in the eyes of *Mapai*'s members, it was *Herut*'s leader who was still captivated by it.

Begin's suggestion included a political consideration as well. He hoped that Ben-Gurion would establish a new, national-unity government, which would include *Gahal* for the first time and grant him his much desired legitimacy. But when he met with Ben-Gurion, Begin was disappointed. As he stated in front of Rabin, Ben-Gurion explained to Begin that Israel should avoid a preemptive strike without coordinating it with the superpowers, and blamed Eshkol's government for the escalation. The offer to rejoin the government was left with no response.

Despite Begin's disappointment with Ben-Gurion's position regarding the war, he continued to believe in Ben-Gurion's ability to lead the nation during a crisis. Though he knew that Ben-Gurion's return would be strongly opposed by *Mapai*'s members, particularly Eshkol and Golda,[15] he tried to convey the necessity of the move to Eshkol. Against his hesitant image, Eshkol was adamant when it came to Ben-Gurion. He announced: "These two horses could never pull the cart together."[16]

Shimon Peres was typically undeterred, and presented a new proposal: a national-unity government with *Rafi*, *Gahal*, and the *Mafdal*. Moshe Dayan—who declared his willingness to return to the IDF as the chief commander of the Southern Command—would be appointed as the minister of defense. Eshkol objected again. But due to the *Mafdal*'s insistence and the atmosphere of an almost generals' uprising within his party, he gave his consent. On June 1, after a meeting of *Mapai*'s secretariat, the conditions for a national-unity government were finally settled.[17]

Now, Peres was supposed to convince Ben-Gurion to support *Rafi*'s integration with the new government under Levi Eshkol. Ben-Gurion was dissatisfied with the political plot. He continued to demand that Eshkol would be replaced. His rage was directed at the messenger: "I thought you were a friend, but you are not. I thought you were a politician, but you are not. I thought you were a man of principle, but you are not."[18] Peres felt he was on the verge of "fainting."[19] The Old Man conceded only after a few hours. He admitted to Peres that he was right arguing that security considerations were first priority, and granted his consent for *Rafi* to join the government. But before he sent Peres to announce his decision to Eshkol, he added one final condition. He coerced Peres to say that the fact that *Rafi* would join the government doesn't mean they recognize Eshkol's ability to lead, and that *Rafi* will continue to try and dismiss him from his duties. Peres, who was shocked but still loyal to his mentor, promised to repeat the words. Shortly before he left Eshkol's chambers, after they both verified the details of the agreement, he requests, "pale as a sheet,"[20] to add another important statement. He repeated Ben-Gurion's declaration in a low voice and waited for Eshkol's response. "Younger man [said in Yiddish], I know Ben-Gurion asked you to say that," Eshkol smilingly tried to alleviate the tension.[21] Peres wanted to take advantage of Eshkol's good mood and proposed, without consulting Ben-Gurion first, to send the Old Man to the United States for political consultations. Eshkol requested time to think about it. A few hours later he said no.[22] Peres chose not to tell Ben-Gurion about the rejected proposal.

Ben-Gurion himself was already focused on his desire to impact the new defense minister. Moshe Dayan, with his sly grin, sharp tongue, and independent personality, seemed like he was tailored according to Ben-Gurion's vision of the "new Jew," a successor of Biblical warriors, with intense expression, who can handle a spade and a rifle with the same level of skill.[23] Ben-Gurion fostered Dayan his whole life: He appointed him to be the commander of the Southern Command after 1948 War, put him in charge of the IDF shortly before his first resignation in 1953, and promoted him in *Mapai* after he left the military. Ben-Gurion had no doubt that Dayan was the best "war commander" that has ever been in the IDF.[24]

Dayan, in turn, perceived the Old Man as a role model of fearless leadership. In his arrogant style, he explained that Ben-Gurion was the only one from whom he cared to hear "a good word."[25] He believed that Ben-Gurion resembled, "in many ways, King David, who could also remember and bare grudge."[26] In the same sentence, consciously or not, he also glorified David's minister of war, Yoav Ben-Tzruya. Dayan never explicitly compared his relationship with Ben-Gurion to those of David and Yoav, but the comparison was hardly avoidable; it is well known that Yoav had served David faithful, but also frustrated him to no end and acted against his command.

Indeed, a comparison between Dayan and Ben-Gurion's diaries from those days presents an almost cruel deterioration in the Old Man's position.

Ben-Gurion wrote: "[Dayan] demanded that he would be close to me," that is, he would consult him,[27] while Dayan had already known he would have to trust mainly himself in this war.[28] Knowing the Old Man's concerns regarding a war, he said: "Ben-Gurion lives in the past. He admires de Gaulle, overestimates Nasser's power, and can't appreciate the IDF's full power."[29] Therefore, he decided before the war, in his own alienated style, to ignore him.

Ben-Gurion knew nothing about Dayan's intension. He left his cabin in Sde Boker and got settled in his house in Tel-Aviv so he could be close to the IDF's central command. On the morning of June 5, he was waiting for an update meeting with the new defense minister. When he heard a knock on the door, he was quick to open it himself. Surprisingly, he found there the gloomy face of Dayan's assistant, who said that the minister was busy, but would be willing to meet Ben-Gurion later that day "for five minutes tops." Angry and disappointed, Ben-Gurion responded that if this was the case, Dayan "shouldn't bother, because five minutes are not enough to clarify the situation."[30]

This was definitely one of Ben-Gurion lowest moments as a retired leader. Dayan's cold shoulder was exceptional: It is worth mentioning that Yitzhak Rabin, despite the harsh words he heard from the Old Man during their pre-war meeting, couldn't refuse his request to meet with the commanders of the Southern Command. Despite his objection to this meeting, he responded reluctantly: "I won't refuse you." Ben-Gurion took the hint and decided to let the matter go.[31]

But during these stressful times, Ben-Gurion had no time to reflect on Dayan's betrayal and the stinging feeling that his prodigy was alienating him. Practical as ever, he wasn't going to wait idly. In the afternoon of June 5, after the airstrike against the Egyptian air force bases, he appeared, uninvited, in the Air Force Command at the Kirya in Tel-Aviv. The success of the strike had already been felt throughout the offices. The presence of Ben-Gurion, who listened to the briefs, intensified the excitement, although it also created an uneasy feeling among the senior officers, who didn't know how much information they should provide to a person who had no official position.[32]

As the war progressed, Ben-Gurion never tried to contact Dayan. Except once, when he couldn't help himself. On June 9, after hearing in the radio that the cease-fire between Syria and Israel, which was declared by the UN Security Council, was breached, Ben-Gurion called Dayan and asked what happened. Dayan refused to provide details. Ben-Gurion concluded that Israel was responsible. With no one to listen to his advice, he vented his frustration in his diary. "The Golan Heights are useless to us, because we are not going to stay there [...] we said yes to a cease-fire but continued to fight. Particularly since it is unnecessary for us and might also harm our reputation and damage the communities in the North."[33]

His approach to the occupation of the Golan Heights, as well as the entire war, was affected by the trauma he had carried with him from the Sinai

Operation. He feared that like in the previous constellation, Israel will be forced to give back the Occupied Territories, particularly after it turns out that Israel was the one breaching the cease-fire.

Ben-Gurion was wrong. The war ended after six days with a quick occupation of the West Bank, Jerusalem, the Sinai Peninsula, Gaza Strip, and the Golan Heights. Such a decisive victory had not been seen in the Middle East since the El Alamein battles. Despite the concerns regarding a political campaign that would eliminate the military achievements, the United States was backing Israel behind the scenes.[34] In fact, the "special relationship" between the global superpower and the Jewish state was pushed further by the Israeli achievement, and the era in which Israel relied on France became a history that no one wished to recreate.

At the end of the war, before its historical meanings could be assessed, the Old Man was also carried away by the national wave of celebration. In the heat of the moment, he reported that he was even more excited than in the day of the state's announcement:

On the fifth of Iyar 5708 I was completely focused on a single issue: How can we overcome the dreadful challenge of the invasion by the Arab armies [...] Last week, however, I was full of joy—this word doesn't do justice to the deep and celebratory sensation that filled my entire being in light of the quick and amazing victory given to us by the IDF. The only other time when I felt such a deep experience was during the first night when I came to Petah Tikva, and heard the jackals howling and the donkeys braying and knew I was in our revived national homeland and not in exile, on a strange land.[35]

The fact that his prewar assessments were refuted was cast aside. Ben-Gurion was not used to justify himself or beg for forgiveness. But he did wish to atone for one thing he did during the waiting period: A few days after the war had ended he requested to meet again with Rabin, who was now a glorified and victorious leader, in the Ministry of Defense. Unlike their previous meeting, this time around Ben-Gurion found it difficult to restrain his feelings: Even before Rabin could tell about his experiences, the Old Man hugged him long and hard and "mumbled some fragmented words,"[36] according to Rabin. Fragmented words in which he expressed his apology and the turmoil of the personal and national story that was in the background in those days.

2

Historical irony: The war that ended with the greatest victory in the history of the state marked the final decline of the leader who announced its establishment. His dismissal from *Mapai* and *Rafi*'s electoral failure didn't damage his position as the state's greatest politician like the results of 1967 War. Until then, despite the reduction of his political power, he was still considered to be the final authority in matters that were crucial to the state's fate. It was no accident that both Begin and Rabin tried to lean on his leadership skills during the days of anxiety, even though he had already lost some of his political weight.

But after his fears regarding the war and his assessments regarding its results were refuted, the time when the chief of staff was consulting the former prime minister and no one wondered about it was finally over. This was the first war in which the political and security institutions acted on their own, without their leader, and did it well. The success gave a greater momentum to Levi Eshkol's desire to lead the people, away from the threatening shadow of the founding father.

Ben-Gurion never publically recognized this fact, but it might have been more than a slip of the pen when he wrote in his diary, two years after the war, that in fact, his final resignation from his national duties was in 1967, "and I made my mind never to go back."[37]

Ben-Gurion's mental state after the war was funny: The war was won by his own boys—Chief of Staff Rabin and Defense Minister Dayan—but they did it against his advice, and despite his warnings. At the age of eighty-one, he realized that things had changed. Gradually, he let go of his control over *Rafi*. He managed to overcome his feelings and embraced his followers who spread their own wings, as a man who understood that this was life's natural course. But he knew that many people were gossiping, saying he was wrong and no longer relevant, and this knowledge weighted upon him and tortured his soul.[38]

3

As for the victory's implications, Ben-Gurion had no doubts. He alerted that Israel should be ready to give back the territories—apart from the Golan Heights, Jerusalem, and Hebron—in return for a genuine peace. He was interested in keeping the Golan Heights for security considerations:

> The plateau of the Golan Heights towers over the lower territories of the Galilee, and the Kibbutzim over there will always be exposed to attacks by Syria. Furthermore, not one Arab was left there besides the Druze, with whom we have good relationship, and the Syrians have no use of these lands: they have huge, fertile and unpopulated areas.[39]

Jerusalem and Hebron created, in his mind, a direct and tangent link between the Israeli era and the cradle of Jewish history. His requirement to hold on to these two cities originated from his desire to preserve heritage values for future generations. These were also the two cities he was quick to visit after the war. He visited the Old City of Jerusalem with the mayor, Teddy Kollek, and the generals Ezer Weizman and Mordechai Hod. He noticed a sign close to the Western Wall saying that this was the place where Prophet Mohammad met one of the Angels, and called loudly: "Erase it!" One of the enthusiastic soldiers was certain this was a command, and slashed the sign with a hammer.[40] Ben-Gurion demanded that the city would be united and its Eastern parts settled by Jews, and kept pushing Kollek, who was elected as mayor in 1965, to carry out this mission.[41]

The historical context, which anchored his attitude toward Jerusalem, brought him to raise many different propositions after the war. One of them was to destroy the walls of the Old City. Since the walls were built by the Ottoman Empire to protect the city against bandits, he said, they were no longer needed now, that the IDF was defending the city.

> Whenever a wall was built in Jerusalem, it was always built around the whole city. This was true during the time of Ezra and Nehemiah, as well as in the time of the Ottoman Sultan Suleiman al-Kanuni, who built the existing wall. The Jews of our time—less than a century ago—emerged from within the walls and built New Jerusalem. Now, we must turn the New Jerusalem and the Old Jerusalem into one city, united forever. We have no need of a wall that would separate one part of the city from the other. As far as I know, there is no European or American city which is currently surrounded by a wall—the IDF is the contemporary wall of Israel.[42]

Alongside Jerusalem, he glorified the significance of Hebron as well.[43] In an article he wrote, titled "The sister of Jerusalem," he emphasized the fact the Hebron came even before Jerusalem:

> The city of Jerusalem, which has become over time, since King David's age and to these days, not just the most holy and sacred city in Israel, but also one of the most revered cities in the whole world, was never mentioned in the Torah. We mustn't forget: The greatest king of Israel, David, started his reign in Hebron. He ruled there for seven and a half years, and this is the city to which came the first Hebrew man, about eight hundred years before King David—it will be a terrible mistake not to settle in Hebron, Jerusalem's neighbor and predecessor, and create a Jewish community immediately. This would be a blessing for the Arab neighbors as well. Hebron is worthy of being Jerusalem's sister.[44]

After the war, he used to tell that during the final stages of the War of Independence, in September 1948, after the Jordanians had blown up Latrun water pump and damaged the supply line to Jerusalem, he suggested that the government would launch an attack in the area between Ramallah and Hebron, which would end with the conquest of Jerusalem and Hebron provinces. The ministers rejected his proposal, and it was, so he said, "a historical mistake."[45] In a personal letter to Ezer Weitzman he took responsibility for the rejection of his proposal. He claimed that he didn't invest enough efforts in convincing his ministers to support the proposal before presenting it to the government.[46]

There is no way of knowing whether or not he really planned to conquer Hebron and Jerusalem in 1948; maybe he just wanted to send a message via this myth: These cities shouldn't be abandoned, not even for peace. His claim that the ministers rejected his sincere will to launch a military campaign is inconsistent with what we know about his power at the time, and his skill of fulfilling his political ambitions through political maneuvers (just like how he got the green light from his government at the eve of the Sinai Campaign without sharing the details of his agreement with French and Britain[47]). Another reason to doubt his version of the events arises from the fact that during the government discussion, in which he supposedly proposed to conquer Jerusalem and Hebron provinces, he also said: "If we could get the minimum through an agreement with the Arabs, I would do it, because I'm terrified of the militarization of the youth in our country. I can already see it in the souls of these children. This is not the people I've dreamed about, and I don't want it."[48]

Anyway, the rest of the West Bank territories were definitely redundant in his view. Two days after the war had started, he already said worryingly: "There are million Arabs in the West bank of the Jordan. We don't need them to be added to the Israeli Arabs. There are also about two hundred thousand Palestinian refugees in Gaza Strip. They won't be easy to get rid of."[49]

The deciding factor in his strategy for ensuring Israel's security was based on increasing the number of Jews and spreading them across the Negev and the Galilee. Therefore, he preferred to focus his efforts on educating and encouraging immigration of more Jews to Israel rather than in territorial expansion.[50] Ruling the Palestinian population was perceived by him as a demographic burden, but he never referred to the moral issue of controlling another people, since he didn't recognize the Arabs in the Occupied Territories as members of the Palestinian people. "A bluff designed to defame Israel,"[51] was his description of the arguments regarding the existence of a Palestinian people. The appropriate model for the conflict's resolution was, according to him, an autonomy, which would create a linkage between the population in the Occupied Territories, Jordan and Israel: "The population in the West Bank should be granted an autonomy, which would be economically tied to Israel, and Jews could settle there at their will."[52]

When the settlements in the Occupied Territories started to emerge, he believed they were not posing an obstacle for peace, since they could remain in their location under Arab rule when the time comes:[53] "If there was an option for peace, that is, friendly and cooperative relations in the political, economic and cultural fields, I would support giving back Sinai and the West Bank. [...] Seeing that such a change is unlikely to occur in the near future, we must settle around Hebron and in Gaza Strip, and possibly even in Salomon Bay (Sharm Al-Sheik)."[54] It is worth mentioning in this context his inconsistent approach to Gaza Strip. At some point, he wanted to relocate its population and send them to the West Bank, hoping, so it seems, to annex the empty strip.[55] But this plan was quickly abandoned and was never mentioned again.

4

After the war, when *Rafi* had already joined the government, Ben-Gurion's political struggle against the leaders of *Mapai* was marginalized in the public mind, like an old, long forgotten memory. The Israelis focused on the fruits of victory. *Rafi*'s alternative, as presented in the election, seemed unnecessary. Like all politicians, the members of *Rafi* quickly sensed the change in the public opinion. On December 12, 1967, about six months after 1967 War, the party's central committee gathered to decide whether or not to join the *Ma'arach* (in its first version) and turn into a new political group—the Labor Party (*Avoda*).

Ben-Gurion objected. Although the vision of a united labor party was one of his goals as prime minister,[56] he believed that the current union was not carrying an ideological innovative message. His reservations were mainly focused around the fact that the unification did not promise any action regarding changes in the electoral system, and had no pioneering message. He warned for years against the "consolidation of a bourgeoisie," which would lead to a more civic and less pioneering and mobilized society.[57] The Labor Party was perceived by him not as a renewed attempt to establish a pioneering, idealistic party, but rather as an opportunistic framework, which represented the decline of the *Yishuv* ideals. The party, for him, was a "deceit."[58] But being in the ninth decade of his life, recognizing his declining status, he chose to abstain. As expected, most of his party members supported the return to *Mapai*.

By joining the Labor Party, even the last of his followers closed the door on the option that he would continue to be an influencing political element in the country. For the first time in their political career, even the most devoted followers of Ben-Gurion—Shimon Peres, Yosef Almogi, Yitzhak Navon, Moshe Dayan, and others—renounced their historical patron. He saw it as ingratitude on their part, although he tried to keep his feeling to himself.[59] Despite his disappointment, he was realistic enough to recognize the fact that he no longer had the power to mobilize his followers for his own struggles. He announced he would accept the decision, but won't join the party with them.

Seeing the party's founder on his own, without friends, Almogi and Peres began to have scruples. As a sign of solidarity with his situation, they chose to stay away of the first few meetings of the Avoda Party, despite being its members. The Old Man was not fond of this kind of gestures. In a letter full of irony, sadness, and rage, he wrote:

> I read in the papers yesterday that you refuse to sit together with the Avoda members because of me. I believe you are making a grave mistake. a. I am not afraid to sit in the Knesset on my own. b. The main point—you can't say to members who accepted the union and signed it—not to act like other members of the party. I am (still) not the greatest favorite of the Avoda party. Its leaders (for now, anyway) have not changed, and I'm not sure they ever will. But your opinion is different, and it was the reason (so I think) that you united. It is not good to start it by worrying and hesitating because of a man who is not part of this party. If the word *Haver* [in Hebrew—can be both "a member" and "a friend"] is reserved only to the members of the same party, let me use a different word—Yadid [Friend]. I implore you, as my personal friends, not to do this mistake, and to act like party members. I cherish your concern for me. But despite my very old age, I can still stand on my own two feet without any support, and even on my head (which might be even more important than standing on your feet).[60]

5

The unpleasant separation from his friends at *Rafi* was combined with Ben-Gurion's personal miseries. His wife, Paula, was hospitalized at the beginning of 1968. Her condition quickly deteriorated. Ben-Gurion went to visit her, anxious and tensed. By pure fate, when he left her room on his way to the elevator, he met Golda Meir, who had also come to check on Paula. Golda, who was aware of the Old Man's rage, nodded her head in recognition. It wasn't the time, she thought, for political rivalries. Ben-Gurion looked away and ignored her.[61]

A short time after she was hospitalized, on January 29, 1968, seventy-six-year-old Paula passed away. They had been married for more than fifty years. She had taken care of all his personal needs, run the household, and raised their children almost by herself. During his bitter years, after Ben-Gurion retired from premiership, she would comment to the visitors, who no longer came very often: "It doesn't matter if he's the prime minister or a driver. He is Ben-Gurion, which is much more than a prime minister."[62]

Her gravesite was chosen by Ben-Gurion in a time of bitterness and absent-mindedness, during one of his last visits to her hospital room.[63] He managed to tell her he chose a plot for both of them, and when he came back to Sde Boker, he pointed out an area close to the *Midrasha* (the local college), not far from their cabin, above the Tzin Valley.[64] He defined her death as "Paula's catastrophe."[65] But actually, it was his own catastrophe. In his eulogy over her grave, he expressed a half-mouthed apology for the lifestyle he created for her, for often putting his family aside and preferring his public activity: "Go, and cry in the ears of Jerusalem, saying: I remember for thee the affection of thy youth, the love of thine espousals; how thou wentest after Me in the wilderness, in a land that was not sown" (Jeremiyah, 2:2).[66]

Alone, grieving for his wife, frustrated by his failed struggles, and so very tired, he spilled his heart in a letter to a friend. "I was convinced that Paula will outlive me, because most women outlive men, so I told her where I wished to be buried. It never occurred to me that she would get there before me."[67] About a year after her death he confessed: "I was deeply depressed for months after Paula's death."[68]

6

The tragic familial turn of his life story left Ben-Gurion with no intimate shoulder to lean on, at a time when he was nothing but a lonely, frustrated, and bitter Knesset member. Deep in thoughts, he tried to project global developments, as a kind of comfort, and documented his projections in response to the request of the Knesset member Shlomo Zalman Shragai (*Ha-Poel Ha-Mizrahi*):

I imagine the world in 1987 as thus:[69]

1. The internal pressure of the ever growing Russian intelligence for greater freedom and the masses demands to improve the standard of living might [so he wrote] bring about Russia's democratization.
2. Western and Eastern Europe will become a federation of autonomic states with social and democratic regimes.
3. Science and technology will find an inexpensive way to desalinate sea water, allowing cheap irrigation in Asia and Africa deserts and improving the standard of living in these two underdeveloped continents.
4. Science will discover a way to manufacture massive amounts of inexpensive power, and create equal standard of living throughout all the continents.
5. Birth control pill will slow down the natural population growth in China and India, and stop the overpopulation which is so feared by today's biologists.
6. Biochemistry will develop a shot that will change the skin color of a person from black to white and vice versa, thus eliminating the segregation in the US and in other countries.

7. Except for the USSR, which will remain a federative state according to the European tradition, all the other continents will become federations of autonomic states, united in eternal ally, which will have a police [designated] to maintain a global block, and armies will be dispersed.

8. The UN will build a monument in memory of the prophets in Jerusalem, and next to it will be a hall of the human race Supreme Court, which will settle any dispute between the federative continents.

9. Global air conditioning will provide moderate climate throughout the globe, and people will be able to settle in any part of the Earth, including the North and South Polls.

10. Absorption of cosmic dust will enable settlement on the moon and on Mars and the rest of the close-by planets.

11. Average life expectancy will be raised to 100 years.

12. Scientific research will focus on efforts to understand the activities of the mind and the source of thoughts, and biologic technology will upgrade the brain's skills to a much higher level.

13. Higher education will be the right and privilege of every person, men and women, in our world.

This was his projection, written in 1968. In hindsight, it almost looks like a prophecy. The USSR was dissolved in 1991. While the former-USSR state did not remain in a federative structure, they did go through a democratic revolution. Most of the European states were indeed joined in a federation, as part of the European Union. Desalination factories thrive all over the world, which is gradually becoming a global village, and the birth control pill is one of its most popular products on Earth.

The international tribunal in The Hague is the embodiment of his vision of a Supreme Court for the human race, although Ben-Gurion hoped it would be established in Jerusalem (interestingly, this section of his projection is sometimes used today to justify anti-Semitic arguments regarding the Jewish desire to rule the world, and it appears, out of context, in various websites[70]). As for air conditioning, the right for higher education, and life expectancy, there's no need to state the obvious. Even his most extreme projection, regarding a shot that would change people's skin color, is currently developed for pigment removal treatments.

7

Despite his predicting skills, and perhaps because of them, he refused to acknowledge the existence of a Palestinian people as a legitimate, solid national phenomenon. He shared Golda Meir's view on this issue. Just like her, he thought that the Palestinian nationality was an unfounded historical fabrication. Yet, he did understand that the international recognition of the Palestinian people will grow globally and locally, and looked for ways to handle this challenge.

Like many of the Jewish immigrants who came to Palestine between the two world wars, his basic attitude to the local Arabs was complex, due to the tension arising from the combination of socialism and the national aspect. After his arrival, he realized he had not come to an empty land; he believed that the Arabs in Palestine could be persuaded that the Zionist project will entail financial benefits for all the local residents, and hoped to create class-based cooperation.[71] The hope to solve the Jewish-Arab dispute over the Land of Israel through united socioeconomic interests was shattered when he was forced to realize that the national aspirations of both parties were stronger than any class consciousness.[72] The scope of the conflict, so he used to say, was internalized during World War I, when he was charged with political subversion and deported from Palestine by the Ottoman regime. He wished to share his distress with Yahya Effendi, an Arab friend who was his fellow student in the law faculty in Constantinople. He was surprised by Effendy's answer: "As your friend—I feel your pain. As an Arab—I am glad." This was a confirmation of the fact that the dispute over the Land of Israel was rooted in fundamental contradicting aspirations.

> His words amazed me. I said to myself: If such an honest and decent man honestly feels sad for my deportation, but is glad as an Arab—what would others say? Less decent Arabs, who are not my friends? And beyond their words—what would they do? His words left a harsher impression than any other encounter we had with the Arabs until then. I was beginning to see what might happen, and indeed, it happened.[73]

But he didn't let go, even after his conversation with Effendy. After being elected as the Head of the Jewish Agency, he negotiated in 1936 with Musa Alami, the delegate of the Arab Higher Committee and a leader of the Palestinian national movement. Ben-Gurion tried to convince him as well that the Palestinians would benefit from the Zionists' socioeconomic contribution to the development of the land. But Alami's response was similar to that of Effendy: "I would prefer that the land will remain poor and empty for another century, until we, the Arabs, will be able to develop it ourselves."[74]

Ben-Gurion was disappointed, but appreciated his honesty. He perceived Alami as an authentic leader, who rightfully represented the national aspirations of his people. Based on his previous negotiations with other Arab leaders, he told later, he had learned to beware of trying to achieve an agreement with a leadership that was detached from the public. A regime "that can be bought with money," he said, would propose an empty agreement, which would be shot by the dissidents' bullets.

Since the late 1930s, after realizing that a Jewish-Arab conflict would not be resolved any time soon, he focused his efforts on creating a Jewish defensive force. This continued to be his guiding principle after the state was established. Alongside his initiative for building the Dimona nuclear reactor, he strove to establish military industries and initiated requisitions and other means of action in order to strengthen the IDF, based on his assumption that peace agreements would not be reached in the foreseeable future. We could say that politically he actually accepted Jabotinsky's approach to the conflict, as presented in his renowned Iron Wall essay.[75]

Jabotinsky argued in this essay that the Zionist movement should get rid of the illusions of a political settlement and realize the powerful national aspirations of the Arabs in the Land of Israel and around it. His estimation was that a resolution would not be achieved by promises of improving the Arabs' financial situation or in return of a territorial compromise. Therefore, he argued, the Jews must develop their military power, an "iron wall," which would convince the Arabs that the Jews could not be overpowered by force. The essay did not end in a pessimistic note. Jabotinsky believed that once the Arabs would acknowledge the Jewish power, a more moderate leadership would emerge, one that would accept a mutually binding compromise, which would bring both parties to relinquish some of their demands. Ben-Gurion's modus operandi was actually following Jabotinsky's outline. The key difference, however, was that the Old Man chose to act in the spirit of the Iron Wall without a public declaration and take political and military steps while at the same time continually calling for peace.[76]

Alongside the construction of a military force, Ben-Gurion realized that the Israeli-Arab conflict could be solved in the long run only through compromise. In his future vision, he perceived Israel as part of a Jewish-Arab ally, which would retrace the glory days of the ancient Middle East, and believed that the Israeli Arabs could serve as a bridge in creating this ally.[77]

Yet, during most of his tenure as prime minister, he distinguished between vision and practice. Furthermore, he made no effort to get to know the Israeli Arabs and their interests beyond the theoretical level. Interestingly enough, he visited an Arab village only once: it was a visit to Baqa al-Gharbiyye before the 1959 election.[78] He believed that the Israeli Arabs were naturally inclined to support their people, and until the situation changes dramatically, they had to be put under the limitations of a military regime (surprisingly, it was Begin's *Herut* party that demanded to eliminate the military regime, claiming that an army cannot control citizens in a democratic state[79]). The military regime of the Israeli Arabs was eliminated only in 1966 by Eshkol—another decision that was disputed by Ben-Gurion.

In fact, in the political context, Ben-Gurion distinguished between two time aspects. Regarding the Jewish state's military power, he acted under the assumption that time was short, and it should be rushed. As for peace agreements, he acted like a man who assumed that we must allow time to soften future generations. Indeed, he believed that until there is a real constellation for peace, the conflict might carry a few benefits:

> It is very possible that historically, the Arab hostility has proved itself as an advantage for Israel. I wasn't interested in the War [of Independence]. But when it was forced on us, it was discovered that we were a stronger nation than we would be if we weren't forced to fight. I didn't welcome the Arab boycott, but when it was declared, we were forced to create sound and healthy foundations for our economy and society.[80]

He also mentioned that Tel-Aviv Port was established due to the fact that Jaffa Port was closed to Jews during the Arab Revolt in 1936–1939; the struggle for Jewish labor intensified in light of the Arabs' rejection of class-based cooperation; and he also estimated that the ability to convince newcomers to settle in the periphery would be lower under circumstances of peace.[81]

8

When *Rafi* was dissolved, however, Ben-Gurion was suddenly inclined on renewing his relationship with Musa Alami, who had been moving back and forth between Aman and Europe since 1948. Finding Alami was not an easy task. Ben-Gurion shared his efforts to renew this relationship only with a few people. When he found out that Alami was staying in London, Ben-Gurion tried to contact him through the Israeli embassy. The embassy staff members were skeptic. Indeed, the initial attempts failed. Simultaneously, Ben-Gurion tried to approach Alami through a private channel of a mutual acquaintance, who tried to persuade Alami to meet Ben-Gurion after all. In June 1969, the embassy staff in London were surprised when they received an unusual message: Alami was in town and was willing to meet the Old Man. The ambassador in London reported to the foreign ministry in a top secret document: "Amazingly, Alami was happy to accept the offer and agreed to come to Ben-Gurion's hotel room."[82]

Ben-Gurion and Alami were both no longer relevant as leaders (by 1969, Yasser Arafat had already leading been the national Palestinian movement as the leader of the PLO). But the Old Man believed they could find a path for a future settlement, specifically because they were no longer tied to the political systems of the time.

The meeting was a strange spectacle. On the one hand, Ben-Gurion and Alami prepared like it was a highly important summit. On the other hand, when Alami entered Ben-Gurion's room and showered him with hugs, they seemed more like two veteran soldiers in a nostalgic reunion than like negotiators dealing with a complicated dispute.[83]

After reminiscing and exchanging views on books they had read recently, Ben-Gurion and Alami approached the issue at hand: Could there be a way to make peace between Israel and those called "the Arabs of the Occupied Territories" by Ben-Gurion and "Palestinians" by Alami, and was there any hope for a settlement between Israel and one of its neighbors?

Alami assessed that any settlement between Israel and any Arab country seemed unreasonable in the near future. He offered to focus their efforts on the Palestinian front and presented an actual political plan: As a first step, Israel would organize an election process among the Palestinians in the Occupied Territories; then, when there is an elected Palestinian leadership, the Israelis would agree to include diaspora Palestinians in the Palestinian delegation. Alami assured the Old Man, based on his familiarity with the territories, that the moderate elements would win, and that the diaspora's representative won't be extremists as well. In exchange, Alami asked that Israel would entrust the administration of the Occupied Territories into the hands of the UN Security Council before the end of the negotiation, which would result in the establishment of a Palestinian-Jordanian confederation or a Palestinian autonomy.

Ben-Gurion never expected such a concrete offer. He thought that the meeting would revolve around general outlines of possible political options. He took the wind out of Alami sails saying that he was not an official representative of the government, yet he didn't reject the offer completely. He offered a second meeting, after he had time to console, in order to discuss details.[84]

Two months later, Alami announced that he was ready for another meeting. Ben-Gurion mentioned in his diary, using the code name Musa, that he would clear his schedule immediately and fly back to London.[85] I found no documentation of the details of this second meeting in Ben-Gurion's diary or in his archive; such a document could have shed light on his solution to the Palestinian problem.[86]

In any case, the significance he attributed to his conversations with Alami, and the fact that Ben-Gurion didn't reject Alami's suggestions outright, proves that his persistent renunciation of a "Palestinian people" wasn't the result of a political blindness, but rather was an attempt to instill the Zionist historical narrative in the young generations. He insisted on the fact that the national movement of the Arabs in Palestine was nothing but a late reaction to Zionism, and was never based on the idea of a Palestinian people, but rather on the centuries-long existence of Arabs in the Land of Israel. Hence, before and after his meeting with Alami and until his death, he was outraged by any mention of a Palestinian people. "There never was a Palestinian nation nor there has been such a state. The Romans didn't want to call the Land of Israel by the name of Judea, so they called it Palestine, but they referred to the Philistines, who came from various islands in the Mediterranean Sea. The whole idea of a Palestinian entity is a current-day invention."[87]

His refusal to acknowledge the Palestinians as a nation was impacted by the requirement derived from such an acknowledgment: To take responsibility for the refugee problem created by the War of Independence. (According to UNRWA records, some 700,000 Palestinians ran away or were deported during the war.) "This is a bluff, this whole business with the refugees. Where did one million and two hundred thousand refugees came from? This is one of their arguments that were meant to damage Israel's reputation, to destroy Israel. It is true that the Arabs have lived here for 1,300 years and have a right to live here. But the Land of Israel belongs to the Jewish people as a whole and to the Arabs residing in it,"[88] he stated.

Until the end of his days, Ben-Gurion insisted that the IDF did not deport anyone during the War of Independence. Indeed, such a written order or instruction on his behalf was never found. Yet, according to the testimony of Rabin—who signed the deportation order for the Arabs of Lod[89]—when he and Yigal Alon asked the Old Man, at the height of the war, what should they do about the Arabs in Lod after the city was occupied, Ben-Gurion responded with a hand gestures, which they interpreted as an order to deport them.[90]

9

Ben-Gurion's meeting with Alami suggested that even at the age of eighty-three, after he had already accepted his political status, Ben-Gurion was not yet willing to stop being active. His desire to generate a change in the coalition—even with no partisan backup—was also still alive, although his ability to realize it was not.

In January 1969, he wrote a twenty-five-page letter, in which he presented his grievances against Eshkol's government. The letter was addressed to Golda Meir. When he finished writing, he turned to his diary and wrote in a desperate tone: "Will she listen to me this time?"[91] In her answer, Golda Meir tried to soothe his rage a little, and reminded him his days of cooperation with Eshkol. But Ben-Gurion refused to calm down: "I thought he agreed with me not because I was Prime Minister, but because it was his own opinion, and I thought he put the state as priority before any partisan or personal consideration,"[92] he wrote.

When his hope to affect Golda and drag her away from Eshkol was relinquished, he turned to the right-wing members of the government. In a nostalgic letter to Begin he stressed:

My Paula admired you, for some reason. I opposed your path, sometimes vehe-
mently, before and after the State was establishment, just as I opposed the late
Jabotinsky's path. In 1933, when I was elected for the Zionist Directorate, I
tried to get in touch with him and we became friends, although my colleagues
rejected the agreement we'd reached together at the end of 1934. I rejected
some of your positions and actions after the State was established, and I have no
regrets, because I believe I was right, and any man can make a mistake unknow-
ingly. Personally, however, I never bore any grudge against you, and the better I
got to know you over the last few years, the more I cherished you, and my Paula
was happy for that.[93]

Ben-Gurion's compliments for Begin were drafted carefully. They did not
suggest any significant transformation in his attitude toward Begin, only his
acceptance as a legitimate player in the political field. Ben-Gurion was definitely struggling, and it was no coincidence that he used Paula's name twice,
instead of his own, when praising the leader of *Gahal*.[94] At the core of his
letter stood explanations, which were meant to convince Begin that he should
leave Eshkol's government (he also included a copy of his letter to Golda).
But he didn't foresee the result: Begin was not convinced, and later was even
willing to publish the letter, in order to prove that Ben-Gurion had changed
his attitudes toward him in his later years, leaving out the political context in
which it was written.

Anyway, in February 1969, not long after the letters were sent, Ben-Gurion
left for the spa in Tiberius, to take care of his back and wrists. And then he
got a call from the President Zalman Shazar: The prime minister, Mr. Levi
Eshkol, had passed away.

In a shocking decision, which combined insensitivity, stubbornness, and
rare honesty, Ben-Gurion was quick to announce that he wouldn't attend the
funeral. Even if he was sorry for the death of the man, he said, he could not
be sorry for the loss of a leader.[95] Outbursts, blatant statements, and turmoil
characterized Ben-Gurion throughout most of his life. During the *Yishuv*
period, at times of crisis, he didn't hesitate to threaten the entire British
Kingdom; when he realized it was too much, he could dismiss his previous
outbursts as if they were nothing. This time, he refused to change his mind.
He insistently rejected any arguments raised before him until the time of the
funeral. "I knew people would curse me if I don't come to Eshkol's funeral. I
don't care," he unloaded his anguish. "I will not come to pay my respects to
a criminal, a cheater, who might disgrace his own people. [...] Do you want
me to praise him now, when he is dead?"[96] In a private conversation with
Mordechai Ben-Porat from *Rafi* he was even blunter: "Just like I wouldn't
want him to come to my grave, I won't come to his."[97]

Ben-Gurion was a man of extremes, of decisions, of fearless belief. When
he hated—he despised; when he appreciated—he respected. Moshe Dayan

summed up his character in this regard better than anyone else: "I don't know what Ben-Gurion felt when Eshkol died, but he was no hypocrite."[98] After Eshkol's death, Ben-Gurion offered another explanation, which he didn't dare to write or present publicly, for his relationship with Eshkol: Talking with his bodyguard, he blamed Eshkol's young and third wife, Miryam, for deflecting Eshkol against him. He even admitted that before becoming prime minister, Eshkol did his job properly ("great at execution") as long as there was someone to guide him.[99]

10

About two months after Eshkol's death, Golda Meir was chosen to replace him. The political system was preparing for the 7th Knesset election, which was scheduled for October 28, 1969.

The Labor Party, with Golda as its leader, prepared as well. *Mapam* party joined it in creating a new labor party, the *Ma'arach* (in its second version). The *Ma'arach*—a combination of *Mapai, Ahdut-Ha-Avoda-Poaley Zion, Rafi,* and *Mapam*—was also rejected by Ben-Gurion. He maintained his position that the union carried no ideological innovation, and was merely a political framework. Yigal Alon's dominant role in creating the *Ma'arach* was not a positive point in Ben-Gurion's eyes.

The hostility between them had formed earlier, before Alon offered to investigate Ben-Gurion for holding on to top secret material relating to the Affair. The negative feelings between them were rooted in the War of Independence. At that time, toward the end of the first truce, when the acting Chief of Staff Yadin wanted to appoint Alon as the commander of the central front, Ben-Gurion objected. Some believed that his objection was based on a political consideration—but the Old Man maintained differently: Dayan had a superior military education and Alon's discipline was lacking.

The Yadin-Ben-Gurion argument regarding Alon's promotion almost caused the disintegration of the newly born military; a compromise was finally reached, only after all the parties involved threatened to resign: Alon was appointed as the commander of Operation Danni, but did not get the coveted title.

When the war progressed, and Alon was leading the southern front, he raised Ben-Gurion's rage when he progressed with his forces to Al-Arish without authorization. Ben-Gurion had to deal with the pressure of the American administration and retreat quickly; he saw it as another proof of Alon's rebellious nature.[100] Later, he compared the magnitude of stopping Alon's dashing into the Sinai Peninsula to that of the Altalena affair and the *Palmah*'s disintegration. It was one of his decisive actions, meant to stabilize the regime in Israel and instill statism disciplinary values in the military leaders.[101]

Yigal Alon, in turn, had his share of grievances against Ben-Gurion. After the state was established, he believed that the enforcement of statism and the requirement of complete loyalty to the state's institutions were harming the pioneering aspect of the Israeli society, which was still being shaped. Alon thought that Ben-Gurion's attempts to impose his authority and a monolith social direction reflected in the disintegration of the *Palmah* and in enacting the State Education Law, which eliminated the different factions of the education system, created a society "which was indifferent to critical political and social questions." He blamed Ben-Gurion, in various occasions, for blocking the development of initiatives and unique qualities of individuals and groups that deviated from his own line of thought.[102]

Ben-Gurion insisted on arguing that Alon was not after pluralism, but rather was representing a different phenomenon: The spoiled Jewish nature, which was designed in exile. Many times, he complained about the factional tendencies of Jews, their tendencies to take part in personal disputes disguised as struggles over noble ideas, and explained that this was the result of centuries of existing under foreign, hostile regimes. This pattern of behavior, he argued, seeped into the political system, and contributed to the fact that he was cheated by many over the last few years.[103]

11

As usual, Ben-Gurion was not content by presenting his complaints. He wished to disintegrate the *Ma'arach*, and after Golda and Begin had failed him, he invited to his cabin, at the beginning of 1969, one of *Mapam*'s leaders, whose name was not mentioned, for a heart-to-heart talk.

During his tenure as prime minister, *Mapam* was an adversary, untamable party—the main opposition of his government. His decision to establish the first Israeli coalition with the religious parties instead of *Mapam*, who was the second largest party at the time, carried crucial historical implications over Israel's future shape and nature. He continued to resist *Mapam* as the leader of *Rafi*. He defined it as "a semi-communist cult"[104] and declared that this party was "tied to old dogmas, which were based on Stalinism."[105]

Now he sounded completely different. "I'd rather stay away from politics and dedicate my time to writing in the few years I have left," he said. Yet, he was forced to get involved in politics because he had "no one to vote for. *Mapai*'s leaders are leading the state to destruction. The leader of this party only thinks of one thing: Another term. The closest party to my way today is actually *Mapam*. If they wouldn't join the *Ma'arach*, I might have given up [his attempts to disintegrate the *Ma'arach*]."[106]

His sudden sympathy with *Mapam* is bewildering. Not just because of his previous declaration, but also because he was drifted further from his socialist roots over the years. Actually, Ben-Gurion was never a real socialist, in the fullest, deepest sense of the word.[107] In fact, the socialism he believed in was basically a tool to promote the Zionist idea. He openly admitted in the 1920s: "Constructing the state only through capitalism will not bring about the realization of Zionism. A completely capitalist settlement will lack Hebrew labor, and the land will not change hands and be occupied by the Jews. Without Hebrew labor and Hebrew land, Zionism will become a mockery and remain a mere fantasy."[108] Socialism, it seems, was a historical necessity, in order to create the "new Jew," who returns to manual labor and rejects trade and religious interpretive deliberations, which characterized Jews in exile. The socialist idea, however, was merely a mobilizing myth in the service of national aspiration. After the state was established, socialism was marginalized even more in favor of statism, and Ben-Gurion prioritized the state's institutions and objectives over any other social institution.

About a year and a half after the state's establishment he even blamed the Kibbutzim, in an almost cruel speech, for not contributing enough the efforts to absorb newcomers, and added that he was "ashamed" that during the War of Independence "there were almost no volunteers [among them], only those who were drafted, came to fight."[109] The political context of these words must be noted—at that time, he tried to undermine the power of *Mapam* as an opposition. Yet, he was generally reserved about the idea that equality can be imposed on people of different nature. Philosophically, he explained, he even rejected the concept of "equality," and preferred the concept of "sharing."[110] "I see it as a grave mistake, both theoretically and practically, to highlight equality as the main and principal value of the group," he wrote. "I believe—and I may be wrong—that the main thing is settling the land and working in agriculture, and I am mortified when I listen to members of the Kibbutz who blur these fundamental values when explaining the logic behind of the group."[111]

His resentment was also rooted in personal experience. When he had joint Sejera in 1908, he was the only one who hadn't joint the commune, and preferred working as a farmer's salaried employee. His choice to live in Kibbutz Sde Boker shouldn't be taken the wrong way either. When he settled there, in 1953, it was an independent settlement, an agricultural cooperative with no partisan affiliation. The first settlers were idealist pioneers, some of them adventurers and outdoor people; others were *Lehi* former members, who didn't like to discuss communism or socialism. They settled the desert based on pioneering, Zionist ideas. Even in 1955, when most of Sde Boker members decided to join the Kibbutz Movement based on considerations of financial survival, Ben-Gurion was one of the few members who opposed it.

This position was strengthened now. He even called to ban by law a workers strike of a few occupations, such as: "Teachers, doctors, nurses and maybe also port workers, although I am not certain. Because their role is related to statism."[112]

What did he mean, then, by saying that *Mapam* was his political home now? Beyond the political consideration, which was his desire to befriend his listener, we must remember that his interest in the financial-class issues was reduced anyway after the state was established. He expressed general objection to Soviet capitalism and to extreme American capitalism, and that was it. He prioritized issues of security, statism, and pioneering over any other economic question. Indeed, Ben-Gurion explained his tendency toward *Mapam* in the party's political transformation, and its drifting further away from the Soviet Union since 1967 War. Without the communist notion, Ben-Gurion explained, *Mapam* remained the most pioneering party, the one that realizes the need to settle frontier regions. "I never doubted their Zionism. They were always great Zionists. Pioneers, practical people. [...] They were communists for many years, but ceased to be in recent years."[113]

Even if his interpretation of *Mapam*'s transformation was exaggerated, a change in the political approach of the party's leaders did happen after 1967 War. Yaakov Hazan even explicitly supported the settlement in the Golan Heights.[114] Ben-Gurion's appreciation of *Mapam*'s leaders was also based on his assessment that they weren't chasing honors (*Mapam* prohibited its leaders from being ministers, and its ministers were not Knesset members). And yet, beyond any other explanation, we must consider his tendency toward *Mapam* as a testimony of his resentment against *Mapai*, which became, in his mind, a decadent party. At times, he considered the decadence to be a natural development of old revolutionaries. At other times, he described it as an ugly breakout, which twisted the party's original path. Anyway, his rage caused him to eliminate all of *Mapai*'s achievements since the state was established: "Until then, it was a fine party. It was focused on service and not on dominance. When the state was established, I slowly started to realize that the party was becoming a ruling tool. Ruling became their main purpose."[115]

Therefore, he commented to his anonymous partner that he was pessimistic as long as *Mapai* was still in power.

Israel needs a moral leadership, which would save it from the eminent danger of destruction. It might happen. The IDF won three wars, because, among other reasons, it emerged from the ground of a state based on truth, justice, and honesty. If the state of Israel won't free itself from a leadership based on non-truth and non-ethics, the IDF will inevitably be the same. An army like that cannot fight and win, and the state will have no allies in the international community.

Therefore, I shall keep shouting, telling the truth. Only if the people see clearly the danger threatening them and their country, if they choose a different leadership, they will try to change things. Unfortunately, I cannot say the whole truth. I am afraid to say the whole truth. And sometimes I see myself as a coward. But what I do say is enough for the people, so they'll know what they have to do.[116]

The conversation went on for about an hour. The Old Man was agitated and almost couldn't be stopped for questions. He talked like a master to his disciple. Particularly, he wanted to bring back the internal fortitude and social cohesion to the top of the priority list. He offered a comprehensive overhaul in the administration and return to the pioneering foundations. In fact, he wanted to change the electoral system, replace the prime minister by a more poised and ideological authority, and declare that *Mapam* will not join the *Ma'arach*.[117] His partner listened, but was not carried away. After daring to recall old memories from the state's early days, he said that the political constellation was "complex," not black and white, and made Ben-Gurion understand that he was not convinced.

Ben-Gurion's failing attempts to fight against *Mapai*'s dominance portray him, at this stage of his life, as sharing a fate with the statue looking at him from his desk: the statue of Moses. Just like Moses, he was left outside of the camp in his final years, looking at the land, but cannot get in. This wasn't just a natural subjective feeling of a person who used to carry the burden and was suddenly thrown out. In many ways, when his suggestions were overlooked, we might say that Ben-Gurion was unofficially dismissed from his role as the greatest politician of his generation. His insistent struggle against this dismissal only added a tragic aspect to his ordeal.

The scars of rejection cut deep. After all, he was a human being, flash and blood, not a Messiah, although he was treated like one only a few years ago, in the height of his glory.[118] One night, he woke up in terror—he dreamed about Golda, who refused to listen to him and ignored his advice. As always, he revealed his distress in his diary.[119]

Endless comparisons between Ben-Gurion's career and the ending political career of Ramsay MacDonald, the revered leader of the Labour Party in the early twentieth century, were common in *Davar* newspaper and among the members of his ex-party. MacDonald, who led the Labour to their first electoral victory in 1924, later made an ally with the Conservatives, adopted some of the free market principles—like cutting government spending, approaching employed and unemployed people, and causing his party to split. At the end of the political process, he was left merely with the support of the Conservatives, who weren't particularly loyal to him. After becoming the most hated person by the Labour as well as the Conservatives, he was dismissed from his position as prime minister. His doctors ordered him to have some mental rest. In 1937, he sailed to sea on a ship and died.

Ben-Gurion rejected this comparison more than any other. After all, MacDonald split the Labour because he wanted to remain in his position, while he was dismissed by his own party based on an ideological-national dispute, having given up his position on his own free will.[120]

He recognized the public image created around him and sometimes felt uncomfortable when dealing with the public. Once, when he visited Galy Kinneret Hotel, he accepted the request of the hotel managers and dined with the rest of the guests, instead of dining in his room, as he usually preferred to do. When he took his sit at the table, he was welcomed with applause and intrigued looks. He was well adjusted to crowds from his years as prime minister. He usually smiled.[121] Some days, he even enjoyed assessing the level of the applause he got.[122] Now he was discomforted by the crowd's interest, because he believed they were gossiping behind his back. Going back to his room, he turned again to this diary and wrote down his distress: "I decided never to go back there again. I felt very uncomfortable and resolved to dine only in my room."[123]

12

But still, some people tried to drag him back to the spotlight. His reservation against the *Ma'arach* encouraged some of *Rafi* members, who didn't join the coalition, among them Meir Avizohar and Yigal Horowitz, to recruit him for establishing a new party for the seventh Knesset election. Despite his desire to continue his fight against *Mapai*, at this point, Ben-Gurion was skeptic about the move. He encouraged his followers to continue their protest against the government, but admitted that he no longer saw himself fit to do it. He promised that if the party will be founded, he "will join the party" but "only in the lowest place on the list."[124]

Soon, however, it turned out that the ancient fathers of the Greek tragedy were right when they said that a man's character was his destiny. When they pressured him and said that the new party will have no chance of attracting voters without him, and when they argued that he must grant the request of his remaining followers for moral reasons, he seriously began contemplating the possibility of leading a new party.[125] Yet, in light of the failure of his latest political adventure, he wanted to find out first if the public was interested in a new party. He suggested asking newspaper readers about the need for a new party.[126] In another meeting, he was presented with data saying that 30,000 of *Rafi* voters would like to see him continuing his public struggle. Tired, but also equally affected by his still-burning Promethean passion, he said: "Try it."[127] Thus, in a strange maneuver, which caused people to question his political wisdom, in which he was dragged more than leading, and without clearing out the new party's platform first, he gave his blessing for its establishment. He explained in his diary that he was going to run so he could continue explaining to the public why he left *Mapai* and the dangers that lay in "the decadence prevailing in the dominant party."[128]

His decision was definitely a testimony of the frustration and stubbornness left in him, and his inability to detach himself from politics. The establishment of a new party was not based on a knowledgeable political assessment. But only a few dared to confront his frustration and tried to persuade him that he would be better off putting his weapon down and observing from the sideline.

In the summer of 1969, the establishment of the new party, *Ha-Reshima Ha-Mamlachtit*, headed by David Ben-Gurion, was officially announced. The party's platform was less impressive than that of *Rafi*. The focus, again, was on a reformation of the electoral system, an activist approach on security-related issues (but no reference to Israel's future borders), and support of free economic enterprise.[129] In fact, in many ways, there was an ideological gap between Ben-Gurion and his fellow members of the new party: Many of the members in the new party supported the Greater Israel ideology, as well as liberal economy in its wider sense. But Ben-Gurion, who was a revolutionary through and through, even if his revolution was somewhat messed up and tinted with old age, believed that retiring from the political system was surrendering. His decision to lead the *Ha-Reshima Ha-Mamlachtit* was an inevitable defiance, a judgment of *Mapai* leadership as well as a provocation against it and against his fate in his final years. It was, in fact, his last "Ben-Gurionist" act, his final attempt to go against the flow, against all odds, against reality.

During the election to the seventh Knesset, Ben-Gurion ran not only against the *Ma'arach*; he seemed to be fighting against technological developments as well. Television screens were already common in 1969 Israel, and election broadcasts were presented in movie theaters. Ben-Gurion's grandson, Yariv, as well as the media professional Moshe Theomim, briefed him before his appearances on the collective radar. He was asked to keep his sentences short and his voice lower. They thought he had a TV potential, although it was evident that in his age of eighty-three he wasn't going to make any special effort in order to become a talent. His main reservation was the requirement to record his words over and over again.[130]

At one point, he was overcome with enthusiasm about his political adventure and expressed his hope that Shimon Peres and Moshe Dayan will recognize the error of their ways and rejoin him. He wrote in his diary: "Shimon is depressed, he feels he made a mistake by going back to *Mapai*," and made a note to himself to talk to Dayan.[131] It was a false hope. Instead, he found some comfort when Isser Harel joined him.[132] On paper, it was a reunion of two giants. In fact, at this stage of their lives, it looked more like an ally between two has-beens.

When some people noted that Harel was joining Ben-Gurion only because he had no other choice, and reminded that when Harel retired from the Mossad he was appointed as Eshkol's advisor, the Old Man requested them "to forget things," although he didn't say what they were.[133] At this point, he needed any support he could get.

Ben-Gurion tried to do his best for his new party. He encouraged voters to give their voice to his party in interviews, although he mostly attacked *Mapai* and its leaders instead of reasoning the need for this new party.[134] He even claimed that *Ha-Reshima Ha-Mamlachtit* was, in fact, the true *Rafi*. "Indeed, I was left alone in the Knesset, but there are many members who decided not to go back [to *Mapai*] [...] I will remain a member of *Rafi*, and all those who wish to rob me off this name can get lost."[135] And here lies the whole story in a nutshell: "They can get lost." This was, so it seemed, the key mental motivating element behind his continuing struggle. To show them, to defy them, to prove there was a chance, and he would hold on to it, even well into the ninth decade of his life.

Toward the election, which was scheduled for October 28, 1969, he sent letters to hundreds of citizens all over the country, urging them to vote for him.[136] There was no public roar. And why should it be? In the fall of 1969, four years before the Yom Kippur War, Israel was enjoying some good times. The great victory of 1967 War was still echoing. The frequent armed confrontations in the Egyptian front were still not recognized as another war, the *Hatasha* War (War of Attrition). The economy was robust, and tourists came from all over the world to witness the miraculous Jewish revival. The defense minister, Dayan, instituted a policy that encouraged trade and work relationship between Israel and the Occupied Territories. Many Palestinians were willing to work in manual labor inside Israel. On weekends, many Israelis would take the opportunity to visit the Territories, march with pride in a land that was marked by their historical past, and negotiate prices of products in the local markets. On the surface, it seemed that the two peoples were adjusting to their situation. Even the football national team excelled and managed to qualify, for the first time ever, to the FIFA World Cup games in the summer of 1970. It seemed like the young country, which was only twenty-one years old, had already reached some peace and tranquility. The Old Man's bitter prophecies and his requirement for another pioneering effort and a transformation of the electoral system seemed like a groundless threat and as outdated demands.

When the results of the seventh Knesset election were announced, it turned out that *Ha-Reshima Ha-Mamlachtit* won only four seats. The Old Man was ostentatiously indifferent. He had no illusions regarding his recent political struggle—it was significant mainly because it happened.[137] He briefly presented the results in his diary, and the next day he was refocused on the need to get ready for writing his memoire.[138] Only three weeks after the election he expressed a renewed interest in his party: He was looking at the vote's distribution in his Kibbutz. Among the fifty-two voters, only five had voted for him—only one voice more that Menachem Begin had got. Most of the voters, forty of them, had elected the party he was constantly slandering—the *Ma'arach*.[139] This was an unpleasant surprise in a Kibbutz that was established by a group of independent settlers with no partisan affiliation. He didn't express his surprise in his diary, though later he mentioned that "about 60,000 votes were disqualified,"[140] as if trying to suggest that there were other explanations for the low numbers of voters.

Ha-Reshima Ha-Mamlachtit was not particularly noticeable in the Knesset. Ben-Gurion skipped most of the meetings. Without him, the rest of the members—Isser Harel, Meir Avizohar, and Yigal Horowitz—had little to offer. Ben-Gurion and Harel were already past their prime, and Avizohar and Horowitz were not gifted speakers. Even when the Old Man did make an appearance in the parliament, he seemed to feel more comfortable with the members of *Rafi*, and he was whispering secrets in their ears in the cafeteria, rather than talking to his new colleagues.[141]

13

The significance of the final period in Ben-Gurion's political career, if there was one, lies in his last speech as a politician, given in April 1970. He was almost forced to carry out this speech. Most days he would sit in his cabin, organizing his archive and preparing to write his memoir. Even when he went out of the Kibbutz, he preferred to meet with journalists, intellectuals, and ex-politicians over joining the party's sessions. He had already witnessed enough of those in his life.

His approach mortified his colleagues. They, his loyal followers, who backed him up until the end, continued to describe him in their party brochures as the "nation's architect" and demanded his guidance. After repeated requests, he reluctantly agreed to appear and present his position. The members of *Ha-Reshima Ha-Mamlachtit* were invited to the big lawn of the Kibbutz on a pleasant spring day in 1970. For a moment, Sde Boker was oozing again this exciting political roar, which was well known from the past—Ben-Gurion was heading yet another political conference. Dozens of the party members wore the traditional white shirts and gathered on the lawn, tasting the peaches that were grown in the Kibbutz, the pride and joy of Old Man, and waiting for him to speak.

Physically he was still strong, particularly for his age. His march to the small stage was vigorous, determined. He didn't wave his hand, creating a businesslike atmosphere, combined with impatience. He knew he was going to say many things, big and small, and decided that one thing would remain undeclared, although in hindsight, he did give some very prominent hints: This would be his last speech as a politician. "I will not touch upon ongoing actions and events, for the simple reason that I don't know about them," he started, acknowledging his current detachment from the government. "Likewise, I am not familiar with the government's ongoing affairs, and I am by no way presenting it as someone else's sin. It is my own sin, since I am currently closer to the members of *Ha-Reshima Ha-Mamlachtit*."[142]

Then, he couldn't help himself and reminded the crowd that he stayed in *Rafi* and did not establish a new party. "I was a member of *Rafi*, and I don't know who has the right to take away the name of my own party. Is there a country in the world where a party takes away the name of another party? I am not aware of such a case. I am a member of *Rafi* to this day, but *Rafi* has ceased to exist, it was deleted."[143]

He was not deterred by the crowd's whispers. Yes, he continued to press the paradox: He was a member of *Rafi*, despite his leading role in *Ha-Reshima Ha-Mamlachtit*. Yes, he was still stubborn and meticulously strict. But even in his weird, petty moments, he was more than that—and when he finished venting his political frustration, he started to preach the advantages of a new political distribution of Israel: "1967 War created new trends, or so-called new: Those who seek peace and those who want Greater Israel. I don't know where I stand in that matter. I supported both all my life, and I've been a member of many parties," he stated cynically. "Those two things, peace and Greater Israel, as long as they were realistic and possible, I supported them wholeheartedly [...] and therefore, I see no contradiction between the two. These are not two separate parties; these are two different situations."[144]

At first, not everyone understood what he was saying. The dispute regarding the future of the Occupied Territories was perceived as creating a wide, significant rift across all parties. But the right-left division around the issue of the territories seemed redundant to him. To demonstrate his position, he reminded people that he was one of the supporters of the Greater Israel vision during the days of Balfour Declaration.

I mentioned the borders of the land [...] which was then a part of Syria and Lebanon, to the Red Sea, but I did not include, and I still don't include the Sinai Peninsula, because I do not know when was it ever a part of the Land of Israel, and I don't want to get into this argument [...]. But it was all common knowledge, until the British Mandate removed the East Bank of the Jordan River from the Land of Israel [...]. I was familiar with the Greater Israel vision, and I supported it when the conditions were right [...]. But if we could have true peace with the Arabs, which I publicly declared a number of times right after 1967 War, I was in favor of giving back all but two [Jerusalem and the Golan Heights] of the Territories, and I still think the same.[145]

He explained that when the Declaration of Independence was drafted, he opposed the suggestion to include the borders of the land, just like the United State, which did not include a definition of its borders when declaring its independence. The deciding principle of the Zionist project was supposed to be based on security-inducing peace agreements. Borders could be changed as part of these agreements. And as long as Israel and the Arab states cannot agree on a concrete proposal for true peace, there is no need to address this issue.

Most of the members of *Ha-Reshima Ha-Mamlachtit*, who supported the Greater Israel vision, were not happy with his statements. His speech, however, reflected the classic Ben-Gurionist pragmatism. This was the key working principle of his political system: "Utopian realism."[146] He navigated between possibilities and impossibilities.[147] This was his recipe for avoiding the paralysis resulting from a policy that would only pursue the achievable, while also avoiding the exasperation resulting from a policy that would pursue only the unachievable.

Another reason for Ben-Gurion's resentment against the ongoing debate about the division of the land was the fact that the debate attracted efforts, instead of turning them toward the realization of the Zionist vision. As a follower of constructive Zionism, he believed that the energy put by Israelis into the political debate should be channeled into developing the land, encouraging Jewish immigration, and reforming the society and the culture. The critical equation regarding territories, he argued, was their ability to contain all the Jews who might immigrate to Israel. In this respect, the pre-Six Day War borders were perfectly adequate.

> I am certain that we could fit into these borders all the Jews we could ever hope to bring into Israel. Belgium's total area equals that of pre-Six Day War Israel, and it holds a population of 12 million [...] I am certain that the majority of the Jewish people, when faced with the choice of peace versus endless expansion wars, would choose peace.[148]

Then, in what seemed like a change of subject, he moved on to talk about the assistance Israel got from the Soviet Union in its early days:

> We had no loyal, hard-working and smart supporter since the UN decision and until the War of Independence other than Russia. America, which knew that

the Arab states had announced they would fight and destroy us, declared an embargo. Indeed, it included both Israel and the Arab peoples, but they didn't need America—they had a safe and loyal weapon source—England. If we didn't get weapons through Russia—I cannot imagine how the war would have ended. I am positive we would have won, but we would have suffered great losses. It was Czechoslovakian weapon, but we got it only because of Russia. Things have changed and the years have passed, but we should never forget what Russia did for us.[149]

Again, his statements raised questions. Not only because they were pronounced right after his reference to the Occupied Territories, but also because most of the members of *Ha-Reshima Ha-Mamlachtit* resented communism and supported further liberalization of the Israeli economy.

During that year, his speeches were scattered and circulatory, and his intention became clear only after quite a few moments. But the link he created between past and present was no mistake. Similar to his attempt to stress the need for pragmatist policy, like he wrote a short time before he retired from premiership, now he used the transformations of the USSR's attitude toward Israel to demonstrate the importance of political realism. His perception was based on the recognition that history is based on changes, and a wise leadership should filter out what's possible out of everything that is desired, and be realistic.

As early as the late 1930, Ben-Gurion stated: "When I come to consider a political matter, I become a calculating machine."[150] And indeed, this was his way along the years of his leadership: Before World War I, he tended to rely on the power of Turkey. After the war, he cooperated with Britain. While after the St. James Conference in 1939, he came to the conclusion that it would be better to gravitate toward the Unites States. And so, despite the heavy burden of the Holocaust, he expanded the relationship with Western Germany, based on his realistic calculation that Israel would need its support for security and financial reasons.

Chapter 4

My Way

In May 1970, about a month after Ben-Gurion's speech, Israel celebrated its twenty-second Independence Day. The man who had announced it celebrated in an almost complete solitude, in his kibbutz, and didn't participate in any official ceremony. He read some things written by the members of the kibbutz and added a bit of his own. None of the ministered bothered to drive south and honor him. It was "a terrible scene," according to his bodyguard.[1] Ben-Gurion kept his feelings to himself, and pretended that celebrating away from the political core was routine for him. A short while before the celebrations, he accepted the fact that he was no longer needed in the political system, and decided to retire from the Knesset. His justification was prosaic: "I just can't come to the Knesset like I used to."[2]

Despite his old age, and the fact he was an exhausted Knesset member, who missed most of the sessions and led an unimportant party, many were disappointed by his announcement. It seems that with regards to Ben-Gurion, people found it difficult to face the facts of life, his natural withering process, as if his presence in the Knesset was some kind of an insurance policy, a testimony to the state's strength, continuity, and survival power.

"Wait a little longer," "This is not the way," "Why are you retiring only a year and a half after your election?" They tried to convince him. Among the most persistent advocates of Ben-Gurion's staying in duty were Teddy Kollek and Haim Israeli, who was described by the Old Man with the following sentence: "If everyone were as loyal as he is, we would be in Heaven."[3] But Ben-Gurion, as always, remained consistent. He wanted to retire immediately. After he make up his mind, some tried to convince him to stay for another month, until late June, when the Knesset session celebrating 100 years for the establishment of Mikve Israel was scheduled. The date was chosen for a reason. Ben-Gurion used to say that the establishment of Mikve Israel in the year 1870 was an important milestone in the history of Zionism, because in this occasion, Charles Netter established the first agricultural school in Israel. Ben-Gurion saw it as an initial implementation of the "new Jew" vision, a Jew who returned from exile to his homeland to engage in physical labor.[4]

He had no decisive reason to expedite his retirement. He was asked to defer his retirement only for a short while, in order to make it more festive. But he was always exceptionally insistent, and this time was no different. On May 5, 1970, the Knesset's summer session was gathered, and David Ben-Gurion, wearing a white, open collar shirt and a gray jacket, presented a laconic resignation letter, which marked the official end of an era. The facts of life apply to him as well.

> For a while now, I haven't been able to attend the Knesset sessions, and I see no possibility that I will be able to attend them in the future. I have no right to be a Knesset member if I cannot fulfill my duties and attend the Knesset sessions. I hereby announce my resignation.[5]

The matter-of-fact laconic description of his justifications for retirement reflected the man who believed in practical Zionism throughout his life; but it also reflected the bitterness of a giant, who had been gradually deteriorating for seven years now.

Even after his retirement, verging on eighty-four years, he had no intentions of ending his business on Earth. He had an additional critical task: To complete his memoir, since the day he was born in 1886 and until his resignation from premiership in 1963. He believed that the myth had the power to unite society and inspire it to act, and since he believed that the Zionist movement did not realize its full vision, even after the state was established, the writing of his memoir was critical for completing his mission of founding the nation.[6] Writing history texts was part of the effort of Zionism founding fathers to revolutionize the Jews' approach to national memory. For him, the religious ceremonies and writings could no longer function as the sole foundation of the shared national myth. Just like he wished to strip the Biblical texts of their holiness and interpret them in the spirit of national-social-moral ideals, he also wanted to instill the memory of the state's early days in future generations, according to his own perspective:

> I do know that historians who will live 30–40 years from today will know a few things that were done in my time and before my time—things I do not know today. But I believe that a few things that happened in the state are known to me more than they are to others—and the youth directing the future must know about the good and not-so-good things that were done here in my time.[7]

His words disclosed his estimation that future historians will compete for a historical revision of his version for the story of the Zionist project, and that his position may be rejected. Specifically because of that, he wanted to present his narrative for future generations to judge.

Another mission made relevant by his resignation was relatively insignificant, but he insisted on perceiving it as crucial as well: He wanted to trim his famous mane of hair. His followers, who believed his hair was a key part of the Ben-Gurionist myth, objected.[8] But he insisted. He must get a haircut. It was as if the hairdresser's scissors were an undermining, reshaping element. Indeed, Ben-Gurion who left the Salon was a completely different person.[9] The hairdresser, out of excitement or overly good intentions, executed the Old Man's instructions to the letter: He trimmed the mane almost to zero.[10] It seemed like a minor event. A haircut. But for Ben-Gurion, who had never wasted his time on cloths and appearances, his alienation toward his growing hair was also a statement. Was there any truth in the feeling of some that the Old Man, who was an advocate of the Bible and its messages, found a way to compare his current situation to that of Samson, who lost his power when his hair was cut?

Part II

Chapter 5

Back to the Cabin

1

The air stood still, like an outside observer. The sheep wandered lazily, crowded under any narrow shade strip offered by their pen's asbestos roof rack. Once in a while, the sound of a stray dog's bark was heard; the squeaking rusty bike chain of the local gardener, a blow of a salty desert wind. But mostly silence. Stable like a siren, climbing from the deep valleys up to Ramat Nafha tents and Sde Boker's sand clamps.

The cabin stood at the far end. Green, authoritative, shining like a treasure box that is no longer needed. On the chest of drawers, in the hot stiffening guestroom, stood a menorah. Next to it stood a statue of Moses, who seemed to return the Old Man's gaze, keeping an important secret. Next to the statue stood the television set, which he hated and almost never turned on. A prominent wooden desk stood at the center of the next-door den, mounted with books and letters he planned on replying. The desk was covered with glass, which held some family photos in place. Along the walls, were carton boxes holding historical documents from his entire career. The bookshelves were on the verge of collapsing. The old radio was turned on every hour for the news broadcast. The next room held a narrow bath, with a window above it and a small stove for the winter. The bedroom was facing east, with a small closet next to it. The kitchen was painted white and included an Amcor refrigerator, a stove, and two small sinks. The coffee set on the shelf above was usually left untouched.

Great leaders were no longer coming to the front door, blocking the narrow entrance roads with their luxurious automobiles. The bodyguards, living in the next-door cabin, were also less busy than before. There was no longer need to hiss the enthusiastic kibbutz children. Rarely, buses unloaded some ecstatic tourists. The bodyguards' attention was focused mainly inside, on the man who was still there, busy with writing his memoirs as promised.

His children—Geula, Amos, and Renana—didn't call much, and visited even less. They lived far away, and the drive to his cabin was rough. They expressed their love in other ways—different, unusual ones. When he asked to make sure they would be present in the screening of a movie that was made about him, he called his assistant and questioned whether "my children all know and will be there."[1] Like everyone else, his family members got to the habit of talking about him as if he was some strange, far away being. As if he was inaccessible even when he was present. Actually, he loved to talk, tell stories, and recreate the past—especially now, when the number of his listeners was reduced—but he almost never exposed his feelings, and of course, he never mentioned his loneliness and being away from his family. "Forget it," he said quickly, waving his hand in an ambiguous gesture; but it was enough to show his distress.[2]

Up until a few years before, he was walking five miles a day—2.5 back and forth.[3] Since he retired from the Knesset, his walking pace and time were reduced. His feet got heavier, but he wouldn't stop walking. Angry and bitter, he continued to circle the kibbutz back and forth, twice a day. The first time was exactly at 8:00 a.m., while the second was at 4:00 p.m., after waking up from a short nap.

His daily schedule remained strict, like it's been for years, but now it was empty and void. He would wake up at 7:00 a.m., eat his breakfast quickly—some yogurt, a cucumber, a soft-boiled egg, some salad, a glass of grapefruit juice, and finally, a cup of coffee with milk, made according to Paula's traditional recipe. "You shouldn't spend more than 10 moments on a meal,"[4] he used to say, and even in this short time he dedicated to his meal, he would alleviate his boredom and use the time to read his newspaper. When he got up, he usually cleaned his plate. Most days, he didn't wait to Mazal, his dedicated housekeeper, who was responsible for house chores. His two bodyguards, who were being replaced every two weeks, stayed in the next door cabin. One of them was also his driver. They were his loyal and close staff members, answering the few phone calls and preparing his meals.[5]

During the morning, he would go over the newspapers he got to his cabin. He read *Davar*, *Mapai*'s newspaper, but preferred the liberal *Haaretz* and went through it more carefully. If he had no meetings, he would be at his desk exactly at 8:00 a.m., like a good soldier.[6] At lunch he would taste some chicken and rice, and his dinner included mainly salad and tea. On rare occasions, he would get a meal from the kibbutz's dining room, which he stopped visiting after Paula's death. He would go to bed late, when everyone else was already sleeping, and always with a book in hand.

Sometimes, when he left his cabin, he would stop next to the sheep or the dogs strolling around the kibbutz, as if trying to learn something from the animals' lifestyle. Every now and then, he tried to describe their behavior:[7]

> I realized there is no real difference between human beings and animals. Some are hardworking and some are lazy, some are smart and some are stupid. I knew everyone with their unique qualities, and they knew me. When I came to them in the morning, they would gather around me, knowing that I will take care of them. I didn't understand it, but I was told they had their own way of communicating.[8]

He believed that animals, like human beings, were spirits embodied in a body, a material form. They were also doomed. He wondered about the depth of their awareness. Do they have feelings? What occupies them?

Household animals and birds must have souls:

> There is a difference between one bird and the other. Each of them behaves differently. I read in a few books—science books, actually—that some animals are smarter than man. I must disagree. But here, in Sde Boker, I was caring for the little, orphan sheep, and it taught me things I never imagined. After ten to twelve days, I already knew each one of them according to its tendencies and traits—and they knew me as well.[9]

Since his retirement, he tended to reflect more about the world's creation, and about the meaning of the world and its creators.

Away from any political activity, he continued to contemplate the way he was marginalized, the way his number of listeners was reduced, the disappearance of those who could carry the extra burden he wished to lay on the public shoulders, and the change he wished to create. Just a few days before, he got a visit from Ezer Weizman, who was appointed by Ben-Gurion to be the Air Force Commander and now was a member of *Herut*. Weizman came to Sde Boker and exchanged a few words with him. But when Ben-Gurion urged him to stay for lunch, Weizman announced he must get back to Jerusalem. Ben-Gurion understood: He was no longer attracting genuine interest.[10]

On the other hand, his bodyguard, Yehoshua Cohen,[11] was always attentive. Cohen was a member of the *Lehi*, the underground that was finally eliminated by Ben-Gurion only in September 1948, after the state was established, following the international scandal that ensued when the organization's members murdered Count Folke Bernadotte, the Swedish mediator appointed by the UN to reach a settlement between Israel and the Arab states. They were furious at his proposal to leave Jerusalem under an international regime and give most of the Negev desert to the Arabs. The members of *Lehi* suspected he was an anti-Semite. While the assassins called themselves "members of the homeland front," it was quickly discovered that they were some of the ex-*Lehi* members. Yehoshua Cohen was the one who pulled the trigger.

Ben-Gurion only learned about it in the late 1960s, when his own biography was written. He wanted to verify it personally. In their conversation, which was not documented in details in his diary, Cohen admitted he did it. They never talked about it again.[12]

They met in 1953, when Yehoshua was a member of Sde Boker, and Ben-Gurion chose to join the kibbutz after resigning from premiership. Their friendship was not easily formed. Initially, Ben-Gurion still treated Cohen as a member of his rival underground organization. Cohen quickly noticed that one of the straying dogs in the neighborhood got the nickname Eldad by Ben-Gurion. While he never provided an explanation for this nickname—there were things Ben-Gurion repeated dozens of times, and others he preferred to leave untouched—Yehoshua felt he was referring to the surname of one of the three *Lehi*'s leaders, Israel Eldad, as if trying to convey the message that he never forgave the past.[13]

Occasionally, Ben-Gurion expressed interest in the worldview of *Lehi* members and their attitudes toward him. Once, he even asked whether they could have murdered him. Cohen said that if they wanted to—they would do it. In such moments, the Old Man was reliving the ancient rivalry. He reprimanded Cohen about the underground's error ways and reemphasized the need to educate Jews to accept authority, a necessary trait of a civilized society. He even teased Cohen about the demand of *Lehi* and *IZL* members, after the state establishment, to take part in the national parade in Independence Days. "You were the dissidents, weren't you? How come we became one out of a sudden?"[14]

The Old Man accused the dissident underground organizations: "They demanded terror for terror and killing an Arab for every Jew killed by an Arab. A horrifying idea."[15] Although, actually, more than blaming them for moral defect, he was angry for their defiance against the *Yishuv* institutions, and the sabotage of his idea of statism. In fact, he wasn't against violent struggle when needed: He authorized *Palmah* and *Hagannah* operations and supported the collaboration with the dissident undergrounds during the periods of the Jewish Resistance Movement in 1946, when the *Hagannah*, *IZL,* and *Lehi* cooperated in their struggle against the British Mandate for a few months. The struggle against the dissident undergrounds was, for him, mainly another chapter in his war against the splitting pattern brought by the Jews from their original countries.[16] And thus, although he wasn't the head of a state yet, he already defined their activities during the *Yishuv* period as "illegal" acts.[17]

Even after retiring from the Knesset, when he observed his life in retrospective, he never regretted his decision to bomb *Altelana*.[18] The affair haunted him for years, because it was one of the cornerstone steps he made in an attempt to fulfill his life's mission—establishing Hebrew statism. In an essay he wrote, he declared that he didn't regret it, despite the casualties, and despite the loss of weapon, which was supposed to assist the *Yishuv* in the War of Independence. The struggle against Altelana was, in his mind, a struggle for the people's spiritual independence, educating it and creating a sense of citizenship.[19] He never forgot that when the ship arrived, "many of the *IZL*'s soldiers, who served in the IDF, ran away from their battalions and came to Kfar Vitkin"[20] to assist in unloading it. Their act held the danger of splitting and spreading the Jewish army, which was finally established, after 2,000 years in exile. Even after he read Menachem Begin's response essay, who argued that the Israeli branch of the *IZL* didn't know about the ship before it set sail (which was historically true[21]), he refused to reach out and seek reconciliation. Answering Begin, he said that the fact that the *IZL* had its own independent branch in June 1948 was breaching the IDF Law, which was enacted on May 26 and defined a single legal army in Israel.

He mocked the Revisionists' "historiosophy" and tales of heroism, and emphasized: "If the *IZL* or the *Lehi* believe they drove the British Mandate away—let them. This 'question' is of no interest to me what so ever."[22] Sarcastic as usual, he added that he wouldn't ask Begin "whether it was true that at some point, *IZL* members betrayed *Lehi* members to the British government"[23] (which was historically correct). He didn't regret the Saisons either—the operation in which the *Palmah* people betrayed the underground members, and particularly *IZL* members, to the British, or arrested them themselves. This operation was orchestrated following the murder of the British minister of state in the Middle East, Lord Moyne, by *Lehi* members in November 1944. The act was not only immoral, Ben-Gurion explained. It also portrayed the national institutions as unable to control their people. And it also projected the national institutions helplessness in controlling the *Yishuv*. It proved that the Jews were still not ready to have their own state. Furthermore, he added, the victim was not anti-Semitic, despite the *Lehi*'s version, which was commonly believed. Moyne, he said, had promised that at the end of World War II, Britain would take hold of part of Germany and support the establishment of an autonomous Jewish province over there.[24]

And yet, he forgave Yehoshua Cohen. Why should he hold grudge against one of his few last loyalists? "The man who could definitely hate," as Cohen defined Ben-Gurion, "was, in 1970, a lion at the winter of his life, a hero who needed support."[25] His anger was directed toward his comrades at *Mapai*. New struggles had already pushed the old ones away. Moreover, Ben-Gurion rejected the *Lehi*'s worldview, but still preferred it over that of the *IZL*. The fact that the *IZL* was linked to the Revisionist party made it a suspect of trying to take over the *Yishuv*'s leadership. Hence, even though the Saisons started after a *Lehi* operation, the persecution was directed mainly against *IZL* members. His aversion to the *IZL* was particularly severe. Four days after declaring the state's independence, during a visit to Jaffa, he was surprised to be greeted by a salute of the *IZL* members he met there. "They look like criminals,"[26] he mentioned in his diary. This sentence was omitted from the version published by the defense ministry when Menachem Begin was prime minister.

The *Lehi* members, on the other hand, partially because of their more diverse political opinions, were perceived by him as heroic warriors, who wrongly believed they could accelerate salvation.[27] While he continued to judge *IZL* members harshly even after the state was established, some *Lehi* members were partially forgiven when he was still prime minister. Thus, for example, he allowed Yitzhak Shamir, who was head of operations in the *Lehi*, to work under Isser Harel in the Mossad. In 1962, he was moved when he read the book *Sipura shel lohemet* (The Story of a Female Warrior), about the *Lehi* member Geula Cohen, and wrote to her: "I have no doubt that this warrior's story will commemorate the brave fighters who gave their lives because they believed in the salvation of the Jewish people [...] this book was written with a sacred pen."[28]

Unlike Ben-Gurion's oral statements, which were often uttered in the heat of the moment, his written ones were carefully crafted. Knowing that, some *Lehi* ex-members believed that his use of the word "sacred" was meant to compensate them for his argumentative declaration regarding the holiness of the cannon that had bombed Altelana.[29] But this was a far-reaching observation. As mentioned above, he never forgave the *Altelana* affair. Concepts of holiness were common in his vocabulary, as part of his political theology[30]— his attempt to apply a spiritual meaning to the state of Israel and an almost-sacred status to its institutions.[31]

This is why he easily befriended Cohen, who was, in his mind, a pioneering role model and avoided politics, despite his past. As for Cohen, when Ben-Gurion was marginalized at a late age, their relationship was strengthened and they created some kind of an ally of underdogs. He even considered asking Ben-Gurion to talk at the memorial ceremony of Avraham "Yair" Stern and announce a historic reconciliation. Eventually, though, he refrained: Knowing the Old Man, he feared that even if Ben-Gurion accepted the invitation, he would have found it hard to avoid criticizing the past, and might have even made a distinction between the *IZL* and the *Lehi* in a way that could drive a wedge between the veterans of the two organizations.[32]

2

Ben-Gurion's frustration level, even after retiring from the Knesset, is demonstrated in his declaration, in response to a request that he would sum up the state's progress: "The State of Israel does not exist yet! No, it doesn't exist! This is still not the state we prayed for. There are not enough Jews in the land, there's no peace, no one settles the pre-Six Day War territories, we are only at the beginning."[33] For him, the establishment of the state was nothing but a stage, an accelerator in the process of rectifying character traits that the Jews had picked up over their years of exile, and he believed they still had a long way ahead of them. "We are not like the English, or like more healthy and quiet peoples. The contradictions among us are mental, not only idealistic. We fuss over good things as well as bad things, we envy, we burn, we have no limits,"[34] he had grumbled in the past, and his final years in the political arena only strengthened this recognition.

His bitterness was revealed even in forums that were not designed to expose his sharp tongue, like his meeting with the youth of the Avoda party, who were not related to his political struggles, and merely hoped to get a general advice from the founding father regarding the state's desired path. There is no such path, he admonished them, at least not as long as *Mapai* was in power. And *Mapai*, so he explained, should be dismantled: "It can't be fixed from the inside."[35] When one of the perplexed boys asked him about his solution, Ben-Gurion rejected him with his dry sense of humor: "A solution? I only have a solution for myself. That's why I left."[36]

His outbursts were not planned. They were just the force of a habit. Throughout his leadership career, he often expressed his feelings and positions without considering the context. But even in moments like that, when his blunt expressions lacked any intellectual justifications, he still had his overwhelming charisma. Now, at an old age, his outbursts created mainly sadness and compassion toward his situation.

He recognized the gloomy transformation of his public image, but couldn't help himself. Generally, he rarely expressed explicit regret for his actions. Such was the case of his surprising retirement from premiership in 1963, which led to his seven lean years. Even now, in his cabin in Sde Boker, he didn't present a single argument that could have shed light on the reasons for his resignation. In one of his letters, he explained that he resigned because of the need to set a principle-democratic precedent, according to which "no one should be in the government for more than 15 years."[37] In another letter he argued: "I retired so I wouldn't be identified with the state itself, but I don't necessarily believe that everyone has to retire after 15 years."[38] The fact that he changed his arguments over and over again is a proof of the impulsive nature of his resignation, as well as his inability to accept what had happened to him since then. As a principle, it seems, he did believe that a prime minister should be replaced after such a long period of time. Personally, however, when left with no official title, he felt that no one could force someone else to turn off his life by decision. No one can tell someone else to being active.

At the same time, he explicitly emphasized the fact that his decision to retire was his own. He was enraged when he heard the rumors that in fact, he was unofficially dismissed from his duties by his colleagues at *Mapai*. When a citizen asked him whether he was "dismissed from the government," he answered:

> Your letter ends with a claim that is the opposite of the truth, as if the government (which one?) took away my throne. I never had a throne—I was merely Prime Minister and Defense Minister, and I left on my own accord, for reasons I have no interest of presenting to you. But no government ever took away my authority as prime minister and defense minister! Were the Sages not strict about telling the truth?[39]

3

His favorite spot in his cabin was his den—where he could dedicate his entire time to his final life's mission, the writing of his memoir, which he wished to achieve as soon as possible. In his old age, he knew there was no indecent aspect more than the passing of time. The autobiography he wanted to write was supposed to spread across five to seven volumes,[40] and he feared he wouldn't have the time to complete it. He often used to mention to his staff, as if telling a secret: "My father passed away at 87."[41] At other times, he used to hit his pocket with his palm and say: "I have eight years missing."[42] His loyalists couldn't bear to hear him talking about end and death. Even though he never mentioned it, the atmosphere at the time of his retirement from the Knesset and his frequent mentions of his father's age at death were painful: The revolutionist was starting to see the end, putting away his weapons.

Although he kept writing in his personal diary, which was his constant companion since youth, you can rarely find in it any sign of feelings or moods that are not related to his self-assigned mission. His emotions are only evident through interpretations. For example, in a consolation letter he wrote to his friend and doctor, Dt. Haim Shiba, after reading a critical article against him:

> Is there a public figure in our midst that wasn't shamed and defamed? Are they any less for it? Are they less respected? Less loved? You should worry more about your own health, so you can continue your activity, which is welcomed, cherished and loved, not just by your friends and dear ones, but also by the masses, who may not even read the tabloids, but know they should cherish and appreciate your life work, which is almost unprecedented in our country.[43]

Did he try to encourage his friend or himself?

No one dared bothering him with issues related to mental distress,[44] and the number of people he might have been willing to confess to was constantly reduced. Paula was gone. Some losses are incurable, he said repeatedly after her death. He didn't visit her grave very often, but he kept writing to widowers among his own generation: "As someone who tasted this loss, it is inconsolable."[45]

He lost his parents a few decades before. His mother, Scheindel, died before his 11th birthday. He said that unfortunately the memory of her face was already lost to him. His father passed away before the state was established. Among his siblings, his brother Michael, "Michel," a vendor at a small store in Nordau Boulevard in Tel Aviv, was the only one still alive, but they never found a common language. Ben-Gurion's last mention of him in his diary was in 1959, when he heard that Michel had had a heart attack: "Michel's wife told me that he was bedridden due to a heart attack. I went to visit him with Paula this afternoon. He is already 80 years old, but his face looks good. I was concerned: Who will take care of the store, which was the source of his livelihood? Could he rent it to another man, who will pay him 300 Lira per month?"[46] Now, after years of separation, he invited his brother to meet him,[47] hoping to renew their relationship, but was disappointed. Their blood relations could not produce common ground in their fields of interest.

4

Since his retirement from the Knesset, his staff members were particularly worried about his ability to adjust to a life with no official position. Indeed, he wasn't the strongest man in Israel for years, since his retirement from *Mapai*, and his stint as an opposition member was no longer what it used to be. Yet, he remained an active player, and headed two new political parties. What will he do now, without a party, without the consultations that occupied him, without politics?

As a young man, he was already famous for not being able to conduct a natural, human, purposeless small talk. He even planned ahead his pleasantries at the beginning of meetings: When it was a woman, he would inquire after the number of her children. When it was a man, he would labor to decipher the source of his surname.[48] When he met with young couples, he would recommend them on having four kids: two as substitutes of the biological parents, and two for the benefit of the Jewish people.[49] Whether or not it was a joke remained unclear.

His deadly seriousness was one of his prominent features. In 1953, he responded to a nice letter from a young girl, writing that "I was happy to receive your letter," but explaining: "[generally], I requested not to be bothered."[50] Another eleven-year-old boy, who sent a letter full of spelling mistakes, was reprimanded by Ben-Gurion: "Don't ask me any new questions until you learn to write Hebrew properly."[51] He never meant to offend, nor did he mean to come across as condescending. On the contrary, his approach to children, teenagers, and old people alike was part of his human nature. He never discriminated anyone, but treated everyone according to the matter at hand. Personally, he was aware of his weakness. "My Poliya understood people better than I did,"[52] he wrote more than once, in different contexts. It was partially exaggerated, of course. Ben-Gurion could never have achieved what he did, reach the summits he conquered, without understanding people. It would be more accurate to say that he understood humanity more than he understood human beings. He could get to the bottom of people's interests, but avoided exploring their souls. The interpersonal channel was a no man's land for him. He sent his messages to the public through other layers of consciousness—political, ideological, moral. Once, he even mentioned in his diary in wonderment that Yosef Sapir had visited him, but presented no specific subject for discussion. "I was certain he came to offer something or demand something—and I was wrong. He just came for a visit." The bottom line of the meeting, for him, was that the two hours were wasted.[53] Even the decision to celebrate the *Shabath* eve together in his kibbutz was resented by him—he could have used this time for working or reading.[54]

His detachment from human conventions was evident in his approach to his family as well. When his grandson, Yariv, was preparing for his wedding, Ben-Gurion summoned him and announced that he wished to consult him regarding the book he was going to get as a wedding gift. But Paula intervened and made it clear to him that the young couple would appreciate something of material value.[55]

"I haven't read fiction for 40 years, and I have no interest in it,"[56] he admitted, in a statement that was less a testimony of his literary taste, and more a reflection of a prominent aspect of his personality: He moved back and forth between practice and vision throughout his life, never allowing time for some human hobbies in the middle. He never even understood the point of wine drinking: "Ever since I worked in a bad winery in Rishon Le-Tzion as a young man, I can't stand the smell."[57] He listened to music only rarely. After visiting the concert hall once, when he was invited by Leonard Bernstein and was too embarrassed to reject the invitation, he felt disappointed. Talking to his daughter, he questioned the listeners' level of understanding concerning the music they heard: "How does the audience know when to applaud? Whether it is good or bad? Is playing aloud a good thing, or should they play quietly?"[58]

5

The lights in the windows of the kibbutz's houses were turned off, but Ben-Gurion kept writing his memoir, as if words could heal. He searched in his archive day after day, collecting the materials he needed and writing, stopping only occasionally for rest, from sunset until the light in his window at sunset became gloomy, like a shade casted upon his life story. Immersing himself in the documents of his memories, he was caught in a fight with his own demons, which came to remind him that the minister of history had already sealed the fate of his final years in politics. The combination of scanning archive materials and his current feelings left a bitter taste, and intensified his rage even further. One day, he found in his archive a document from 1934, in which said that the Revisionists approached one of *Mapai*'s representatives that summer concerning his and Jabotinski's resolution talks. He was angry for not being updated in the matter,[59] as if it was a current act of betrayal, and not an old and irrelevant document.

Facing the archive materials, he was also forced to reexamine his relationship with his family members. Sitting in front of his opened diary, he started a strange calculation: He counted the time he was away from them until the state was established. Summing up his travel time abroad, he figured he was away from them for about three years.[60] The family, he decided, will get its proper place in his autobiography. He decided that the fourth chapter will begin with the renewal of his familial ties and the letters he sent to his younger sister and his father.[61]

Unlike at the height of his glory, now he cherished every family gathering, as if discovering their comforting powers. When Geula and her husband, Emanual, came for a visit in Sde Boker with their grandson, Ehud, they found a transformed Ben-Gurion: He crawled on the floor and played with his grand-grandson.[62] When Geula and her family wished to return home, Ben-Gurion insisted they should stay. Stay a little while longer, just a bit, he asked. Later he wrote proudly that they spent with him "four hours."[63]

When his favorite grandson, Yariv (son of Geula and Emanuel), told him he was going to go abroad for several years, in order to study for a PhD degree in Mass Media in the United States, Ben-Gurion objected. His grandson felt he just didn't want his family members to be away. Ben-Gurion himself, though, provided an ideological argument, as usual: Journalism is not a science that should be learned in the university.[64]

His love-hate relationship with the press was a lifelong one. When he first came to the Palestine, he chose journalism as a profession and published articles in *Ha-Ahdut* newspaper (his essay in the second volume was signed, for the first time, by the name of Ben-Gurion, named after a Jewish hero from the time of the rebellion against Rome). Although he read newspapers obsessively, wrote many essays, and conducted long-term correspondences with various journalists, he made it clear that the press had no real influence, as far as he was concerned. Back in 1951, he told the members of the Journalists Association:

I do not know if the sensational, fat headlines, which shook the readers' hearts day-in, day-out, will ever be worthy of being cherished in the chronicles of our time. I believe that future historian will fill his book with descriptions, reviews and analyzes of actions that were never mentioned in the daily press. The journalist is not at fault here—he is a journalist, not a historian. He must describe the fleeting, noisy incident and not bore the reader with scientific dissertations of chronicle authors.[65]

This was one of his more refined statements in the matter. During a youth meeting in Nahalal in 1954 he called teenagers to ignore press reports. "The 'glamorous,' dirty tabloids, filled with 'treacherous tails,' sensations and pornography, do not reflect this generations, and can only corrupt and pollute those who are already corrupted and polluted."[66]

His perception of the press as superficial and inaccurate did not change in his later years. One night, when he finished reading an essay in the *Herald Tribune* about the Middle East, he wrote in his diary: "For the first time in my life, I found a newspaper that presented an accurate quote of my words."[67] The author's name was Michael Megara.

He remained skeptical, even in face of his grandson's efforts to explain the importance of mass media studies, which were a new academic field in those days. His aversion toward media studies was not only a reflection of his attitude toward the press, but also a reflection of his dismissive attitude toward anything that wasn't natural sciences or humanities. As a person whose personality was shaped during the enlightenment era of the late nineteenth century, he believed that science should present fixed, unchangeable truths, and that there is a reality that can be objectively described. Inspired by the Platonic school, which he often mentioned, he assumed that eternal ideas do exist. Hence, research of social and political matters, he believed, was plagued with the pretension of granting a fixed, "truthful" validation to the human soul and actions. For him, the problem of social sciences, which naturally included varied perspectives of human behavior, was their inability to grasp the "truth," beyond the interpretive perspective. A rather amusing testament of his position can be found in a letter he sent to Prof. Benjamin Akzin, Chairman of the Israeli Political Sciences Association, during the 1950s. He wrote that he did read political sciences articles once in a while, "If there is indeed such science."[68]

6

For a while after retiring from the Knesset, he stopped writing in his diary, feeling, perhaps, that his era of action had ended. The first thing he wrote in his diary when he started writing again was related to his desire to find the suicide letter left behind by Nehemiah Argov, his right hand during the state's early years.[69] He decided to dedicate an appropriate place for Nehemiah in his memoir, as if trying, just when his passion for life was exceeding his ability to realize it, to understand his assistant's reasons for giving up on life as a young man. When he failed to locate the suicide letter, he requested to look for it in the Defense Ministry's archives.[70]

Ben-Gurion and his assistant had a complicated relationship. To Argov, who lived alone in a ground-floor apartment and fell in love with women easily, Ben-Gurion was everything he wasn't: A firm leader, made of steel, a legendary hero who never shied away from a decision. "If I have anything left in my life, it is the fact that I had the right and privilege of being close to this great man,"[71] he wrote admiringly. Ben-Gurion wasn't comfortable with Argov's over sentimentality with regard to himself, but he appreciated his dedication. During the state's early years, Argov was his constant companion in every matter—fetching his coat when he left the office and offering a sympathetic ear when he needed to spill his guts freely. Argov was the only one authorized by Ben-Gurion to forge his signature on general and official documents.

On October 29, 1957, when Moshe Dwek, a mentally unstable man, threw a hand grenade toward the government table during a Knesset session, Argov was away. Later, he was told that the prime minister was slightly injured in his hand and leg by shrapnel. Ben-Gurion took it lightly, and even wrote to Dwek's mother that he forgave him and acknowledged the family's pain caused by the act, which was both "despicable and nonsensical."

But Argov was shocked when he saw Ben-Gurion in his hospital bed. He almost wouldn't budge from Ben-Gurion's bedside, coming and going with various missions in the service of the premiership office. Amidst the chaos in the hospital department, only a few noticed that his already agitated face was covering a deep turmoil. During one of his missions, while driving his car from Tel Aviv to Jerusalem, he lost his focus and hit a bicycle rider, David Kadosh, a father of four. Kadosh was gravely injured. On November 2, 1957, a short while after the accident, Argov charged the gun he was carrying and pointed it at his head. Later, it was found that he experienced an unrequited love around that time. His will included an order to leave his few possessions to the family of Kadosh, who healed later.

His suicide shocked the prime minister's confidants as well, and they didn't want to burden him with another grief while he was still in the hospital. Moshe Dayan, Yitzhak Navon, Shimon Peres, and Teddy Kollek conferred and approached some of the newspapers' editors, asking them to hold the suicide story until the Old Man recovered. The editors agreed. A special edition, minus the report about Nehemiah's death, was printed in the printing

houses and presented to Ben-Gurion in his bed. The rest of the people could
read about the suicide in the actual edition. Ben-Gurion was updated about
Argov's misfortune only two days later, and was handed the letter he left
behind.

> Just as you are strong, you must want the employees [around you] to be strong
> and undeterred by the many ravages of life, which we encounter daily. Forgive
> me for this weakness and don't be sorry for it, for I do not deserve it [...] be
> strong and healthy, because this people needs you, even those who wouldn't
> admit it. Love, Nehemiah.[72]

Ben-Gurion read, turned his back to his assistants, and when they left the
room, they heard him weep.

Argov was the first person mentioned in Ben-Gurion's diary after his
retirement from the Knesset. Now, more than ever, he needed Argov's loyalty, dedication, and honesty. He also bit himself for not being more attentive
to his assistant's mental distresses.[73]

7

While searching through his archive, Ben-Gurion was surprised to find,
among other things, what he called "revelations"[74]—letters he had sent
to Paula and his children, which he and didn't remember to be still in his
drawers. He went over them again and again, and decided to leave them
unexposed. While he did publish, in the year following Paula's death, a collection of letters he had sent to his family,[75] he censured many that were more
intimate ones. In a letter to his friend, Haim Hazaz, he admitted:

> I was exceptionally lucky. I got married in America, when I was in exile, with
> no sympathy to Judaism, Zionism and The Land of Israel. While I wouldn't dare
> saying that there was never a girl who loved her man like her, throughout my
> life experience, I've never met, in literature or in real life, such a deep, almost
> infinite love, not just to the man, but also to his life's ambition, which she was
> completely estranged of [...] and I am not convinced I expressed it fully in my
> letters to Paula.[76]

He was moved by a letter he sent to Paula from London in September 1933,
a letter he didn't remember writing, and was quick to mention it in his diary.[77]
Despite so much love and tenderness he sent her way as a young man, and
so cruel was his attitude later on. He uprooted her from her natural surroundings, a city girl from New York who became a revolutionist's wife against
her will. After many years of dedicating himself to the *Yishuv* and the state,

and neglecting his own family, it was too late to get soft and expose himself through the letters he had sent her as a young man. He read them and put them back into the box, as if kissing his past goodbye.

They met in 1915 when Paula, an American Jew from a non-Zionist middle class family, a nurse, agreed to assist him in reading and writing English documents at the library. Two years later, they got married in the New York City Hall. Their wedding was simple and unceremonious—he paid two dollars for two witnesses who declared they were single, and they were registered as a married couple within fifteen minutes. Right after the wedding he was quick, as usual, to go back to his business. With his dry humor he now recreated his wedding day. "I was late for a meeting. When I was asked for the reason, I said: 'I got married.'"[78] He already knew that Paula's life beside him was not going to be an easy one.

They were married for more than fifty years. She dedicated herself to taking care of his needs—those he acknowledged and those he didn't. She was the one who took care of his health, food, clothes. Raising his children was another one of her assignments—he wasn't always sure about what grade they were at school, and remembered their birthdays only because he wrote them in his diary.[79] During the *Yishuv* period, he was so busy he didn't even sense his family's financial distress. At times, Paula would give up her meal so he could eat properly. She would tell her children that she wasn't eating because she waited for their father, and Ben-Gurion was told she didn't eat because she already ate with her children.[80] No one noticed she was hungry.

His decision to settle in Sde Boker at the age of sixty-seven was not the best one for her either. "What does he want from me? He uproots me from my home, where I've lived for decades, takes me away from my friends and rips me away from my children. I mean, there is not even a telephone there, so I could call my children!"[81] She unloaded her distress. A telephone line was installed in his cabin only in 1958. To diffuse her loneliness, his bodyguards would ask the local women to play Poker with her once in a while. Once, after retiring from premiership, he joined the game himself.[82] But most of the time he wasn't there for her. In a justifying letter to a friend, he wrote that when he decided to settle in Sde Boker, he was attentive to her distress, and therefore proposed that she would stay in Tel Aviv, close to her family and friends. He wanted to let her continue enjoying the city life, and meet her at a fewer occasions, but Paula, he emphasized, was the one who insisted on staying by his side.[83]

Only once, in the 1940s, she reached the verge of a breakdown. Talking to close friends from Jerusalem, she threatened to end her own life when she suspected her husband was not loyal to her.[84] Her friends managed to restrain her rage, arguing, among other things, that his activity was too important to the Jewish people, and it couldn't be disrupted by a family crisis.

Her dedication had deepened since that day. Throughout their years of marriage, she even moved to a separate bedroom, wanting to allow him the peace of mind he needed.

She was the sole person responsible for the household: starting with the arrangements she made to get an effective generator that would heat the cabin in Sde Boker—an air-conditioner was installed only in the late 1960s—and ending with instructions to his visitors to take off their shoes when they entered the house, so they wouldn't get dirt in.[85] Sometimes, she even helped him to avoid political mines. For example, in the late 1950s, Ben-Gurion rejected the party members' request to hang the red flag over their house for May 1st events. He explained that the flag symbolized the Bolshevik revolution, and it should be renounced in light of the current events in the USSR. Paula decided to take action and prevent an unnecessary conflict. She climbed the roof by herself, and hanged the flag. Ben-Gurion, she assumed, wouldn't notice. And she was right.[86]

This wasn't the only time when Paula took an independent stand. When she believed she was right, she could reprimand his guests, throw remarks at his assistants, and bother him at meetings. Throughout their life together, he often resented her tendency to reprimand his guests, although he usually managed to restrain himself and keep silent in face of her outbursts, waiting for her to calm down on her own.[87] He never forgot her behavior during the visit of Dag Hammarskjöld, the UN General Secretary in the 1950s, to his cabin in Sde Boker. Against the backdrop of the common allegations in Israel regarding the UN hostility, and the rumors concerning the secretary's sexual orientation, she could not resist the urge and snapped during lunch: "You should get married. When you get married and have a wife, she will make your life miserable and then you'll leave us alone."[88] Their oldest daughter, Geula, felt that outbursts of this kind were also derived from Paula's desire to assert her own presence in their relationship. Despite the inconvenience caused by her, it was, in fact, a feminist act in a chauvinist era, and she was proud of it.[89]

Ben-Gurion missed Paula's constant honesty. While his bodyguards did everything in their power to replace her—including offering his cup of milk with honey at 10:00 a.m. exactly, like Paula used to do[90]—they couldn't recreate her presence. In the 1950s, when he was in his cabin for a week while she remained in their apartment in Tel Aviv, he wrote some sentimental words: "Our cabin is empty and hard without you [...] when will you be back?"[91] The rib from which God had made Eve was missed now more than ever before. After she passed away, he left her stuff untouched: The radio in her bedroom, the closet, and the electrical refrigerator, whose content was the source of her eternal ranting.[92] But without her, they were only half present. Ben-Gurion was never the romantic type, but, as some kind of a hindsight gesture, he continued eating this weird compote, "Kuch-Much," a mixture of raspberry juice and yogurt, which Paula used to make, arguing it was good for his health. When his grandson, Yariv, wondered about his loyalty to the not-so-tempting food, he said: "But Paula used to make it."[93]

8

The memory of Nehemiah and Paula was the focus of his diary entries after retiring from the Knesset, and not by coincidence. Throughout his life, he knew many people who dedicated themselves to an idea. But only a few could dedicate themselves to a man, without asking anything in return, without holding back. They kept appearing in his responses to citizens' letters, despite the fact that he had other loves in addition to Paula, but he refused to mention them, in order to protect her honor.

The truth was that the love of his life had failed him. Her name was Rachel Nelkin, a beautiful girl with dark almond-shaped eyes, who was supposed to be his companion for life. Like him, Rachel was born in Plonsk. She was five years his junior and one of the three "most beautiful girls among the Second Aliya immigrants,"[94] as he once wrote passionately. In 1906, they boarded the same ship to Palestine and never left each other's side throughout the journey. On their way to Palestine, during the last leg of the journey on board of a Russian ship, Rachel's mother decided to sleep between them, to make sure they would maintain their purity.

Unlike Paula, shy and fragile Rachel couldn't handle the other passion that motivated Ben-Gurion since youth, the Zionist passion, who took over the other, intimate one. When they worked together in Sejera, he often reprimanded her for not fitting into the pattern of an agricultural worker, as a Zionist girl was required to do. She drifted away in a swift and cruel process, and married a man who could dedicate himself to her like she needed, Yehezkel Beit-Halahmi, who was also their childhood friend from Plonsk. Ben-Gurion was invited to the wedding, but he chose not to attend. His friends were there, dancing and celebrating, while he carried away with him for years the feeling of a missed opportunity.

Now he was ready to open up his heart just a bit and tell about his childhood sweethearts: "My poetic tendency was born out of love," he admitted concerning his attempts at poetry as a young boy. "The problem is, I don't remember who I loved, but it went on for one year only."[95] The truth was he remembered her clearly and knew her name, but when these words were written he was already a national symbol, Paula's husband, and he had no interest in disrespecting her by mentioning ancient love stories with no future prospects.

He was enormously sensitive to the way future historians would describe him, both the in national and personal aspect. He refused to part with a postcard he once sent to a girl as a teenager—"I'm writing to you with my hand, expressing a small part of what my heart feels towards you [...] May God grant you a blessed year, a happy new year, in which you will find endless content and happiness." He hid the postcard in his archive, but cut out the name of the addressee, as if he was afraid of it being found by his future biographers.[96]

9

Alongside dealing with past memories, Ben-Gurion wished to expand his encounters with young people, talk with them, and understand their state of mind. But the gap between him and the 1960s Israeli youth was rapidly expanding. He still imagined them as his young friends in Plonsk, the members of the Second Aliya, and hoped to find in them the ancient Canaanites, as expected of the generation of the state's builders. But young people were no longer gathered around the barn to talk about the state's future on Friday nights. They were going out to dance in urban clubs, opening up to the Western culture and freeing themselves of the heavy burden of the Zionist mobilization project. The gap between his perspective of what he called "youth" and reality was evident almost in any conversation with the members of these generations.

Thus, for example, during a meeting with young people who were about to join the army, he was asked about his opinion concerning the "disco club youth." In response, he wondered: "What are the disco club youth?" When he got an explanation, he revealed his dry sense of humor, which was sometimes surprising: "Well, I have no opinion about them. But I do hope you are not one of them."[97] A similar dialog with the young generation developed after a talk he gave at a Kiryat Motzkin high school. One of the students inquired about Ben-Gurion's opinion concerning pop music, and Ben-Gurion, serious as always, turned to his companion, the Labor Minister Almogi, and asked for an explanation: "What is pop music?" Almogi, who wasn't a frequent visitor of disco clubs himself, did his best to explain. Ben-Gurion, who never tried to flatter the audience or presume to have knowledge in foreign fields, ended the discussion: "Well, I am not familiar with this kind of music."[98]

Another time, in a meeting with the young generation of Kibbutz Ein Gedi, he presented a long historical review of the early days of Zionism. When he finished, he sat on the grass like one of the guys, waiting for their questions. In response to the first questions—regarding his position about the Occupied Territories—he presented another analysis of the past, digressing into the stories of his first arrival to Palestine and giving Biblical examples. When he finished his lecture, convinced he made his position clear, he asked the young people to present further questions. After a long moment of silence, one of them said desperately: "But it took you an hour to answer the first one."[99] Ben-Gurion was undeterred, and ensured them he was willing to stay there the whole night. But his answer only convinced the audience to give up any further questions.

The soldiers in the platoon that was deployed in the kibbutz to protect him were another target for opinion exchange.[100] Due to their young age, the Old Man believed he could challenge them with questions about the ability of man to settle the moon, and other projections of this sort. But they were occupied by more mundane issues, and weren't carried away.[101]

The mental gap between him and the soldiers was also created by the fact that they considered him to be a historic hero, not someone you can make small talk with. His approach only highlighted his alienation from their life. He always asked the same questions: "Where are you from?" "What do your parents do?" "What is your position in the army?" The nervous soldier would usually give back some clipped answers, and embarrassed Ben-Gurion had no other choice but to keep on going.[102] His enthusiasm with soldiers of Eastern origins was not deemed. When he met paratroopers in Ein Yahav he remarked, disappointed: "Are there only blond soldiers in this unit?"[103] But the gathering of exiles venture had already been embedded in the reality of most soldiers. Some were embarrassed by his inquiries about their parents' countries of origin, and often, the commanders had to interfere and remind them to treat him with respect.[104]

10

Trying to keep him updated with the mindsets within the Israeli society, Teddy Kollek and his bodyguards were trying to convince him to install a television set in his cabin since he reached old age. It was not an easy task. He saw television broadcasts as one of the negative products of modern world. Since the 1950s, he was appalled by the power of TV and the hold it had over people's routine. In 1952, a retired US general offered to establish a television channel that would focus on Jewish issues "for the gathering of exiles," he wrote in his diary. But he refused nonetheless: "I doubt that Israel's balance allows it to spend unnecessary dollars."[105] As for the necessity of the television, he argued in the late 1950s with Charles de Gaulle as well: "I don't get you. With a head like yours and this face, you can easily win the elections,"[106] said the French president. But his arguments weren't tempting enough.

In face of the pressures put upon him, he ordered in 1961 an UNESCO report about the possible impact of the television over Israel. The conclusion was positive: A television channel will help instill the Hebrew language, encourage education, and bring the periphery closer to the center. As for noneducational programs, the commission recommended a governmental supervision.[107] Ben-Gurion remained skeptic. While he assessed that television can be used as an educational tool, he believed it will serve mainly for mass entertainment. Only in 1962, after meeting the staff of *Kol Israel* radio channel, who adamantly argued that progress demanded television broadcasts, he agreed reluctantly to establish an educational television channel. But he made an explicit condition. "I opposed the mixture of news, entertainment and things of no importance," he wrote in his diary. "For the entertainment part—one hour is enough. We shouldn't corrupt the listeners' good taste."[108] This statement revealed that despite his alienation from television, he could still predict the mixture that would later be presented on the collective radar screen in Israel and abroad.

He gave up his struggle against progress and agreed to install a set in his cabin only upon his retirement from the Knesset. He stressed in his diary: "Despite the fact I always objected it [television] when I served in the government, because I didn't perceive it as an intellectual or educational blessing. I know it may include positive aspects as well, and I hope to see there things that are of blessing."[109] After the television set was installed, though, he usually preferred to keep it turned off. "I don't like it, just like I haven't been to the cinema for 30 years,"[110] he concluded impatiently.

One time, he made an exception and watched a full television show: The show *Moked*, which featured his interview after retiring from the Knesset. "I saw it and got scared," he concluded, half smiling, the reflection of his image on the small screen.

He remained loyal only to the news broadcast from the big radio in his room. The radio sound, the kiss of pen on paper, the ruffling of the pages in his books—this was the soundtrack of his life. His clothes were of no interest to him as well. In summer, he wore a short-sleeved shirt, and in winter he liked to wear the turtleneck sweater and the long khaki coat, a reminder of his days as defense minister. Without Paula, his clothes were sent to the kibbutz's laundry on specific days and not according to need. Hence, he sometimes wore mismatched clothes: The socks didn't always match the shirt; the tie did not fit the pants. His bodyguards decided to check his attire before important meetings, and he would give in to their recommendation, although he never cared about it.[111] The only thing he did care about was his hair. Whenever he left his cabin, he would comb his hair with a small metal comb, pulling it forcefully backward.[112]

11

The "Ben-Gurion Youngsters," who surrounded him in his days of glory and were now mature and integrated into the political system, visited him rarely. When one of them, Yitzhak Navon—who had served his office's CEO between 1953 and 1962 and was now as a *Ma'arach* Knesset member—came to the cabin for old time sake, Ben-Gurion was revived, and inquired about various details. He concluded the meeting in his diary with satisfaction, mentioning that the IDF had bought four Phantoms and that a lot of very important weapons were on their way.[113]

Unlike the attitude of Israeli politicians, Richard Nixon's administration continued to believe he had crucial influence. Toward the end of July 1970, an American representative was sent to update him concerning the Rogers Plan. Ben-Gurion was asked to join the efforts to convince the prime minister, Golda Meir, that the program was crucial for Israel's survival.[114] The initiative, named after the US Secretary of State at the time, William Rogers, was a development of a 1969 suggested outline foe an Israeli-Egyptian peace treaty. According to the original plan, Israel was supposed to withdraw her troops from the Sinai Peninsula and deploy them along the international border in exchange for an Egyptian willingness to negotiate for peace agreement. The future of Gaza Strip and Sharm el-Sheikh was supposed to be discussed at a later stage. Additionally, the plan stated that after the negotiation over the future of the West Bank, Jerusalem will remain in Israeli sovereignty, but the Old City will be managed by a joint forum of representative from the three monotheist religions. Both the Egyptians and the Israelis rejected the proposal outright.

Now, in the summer of 1970, a new, more general plan was conceived. Israel and Egypt were to accept the mediation of the UN special envoy to the Middle East, Gunnar Jarring, and launch a negotiation based on the UN Security Council resolution 242, which dictated territorial concessions in exchange of a peace agreement. This time, the Egyptians accepted the offer, but Golda and the Israeli government remained skeptic.

Ben-Gurion supported the offer. Ever since 1967 War, he feared another cycle of violence and believed that Israel must strive for negotiation with its neighbors, even if it won't end with an agreement. The highest potential for peace with one of the Arab states was in the southern front, so he thought. Seven years before Prime Minister Menachem Begin met the Egyptian president Anwar Sadat, Ben-Gurion already stressed the fact that Egypt was the first state to sign the Rhodes Agreements, the armistice agreements at the end of the War of Independence, and argued that a peace agreement with Egypt will be signed within a decade.

Why a decade? It is an assessment of time, assessment of the Arabs' development. Even Nasser, toward the end of his reign, came to the conclusion that the
sole idea, the elimination of Israel, was absurd, and that the real big problem is
how to improve the Arab people's life. The whole world moves forward these
days. There's no longer states in Europe with a majority of poor, uneducated
peasants, whose situation deteriorate further every year [...] the chances of peace
are related to the development of Arabs, and this is a process I believe in.[115]

He even predicted a more profound revolution in Egypt, although at the
time, he couldn't have estimated the weight of the Islamic elements in the
transformation he projected:

The Egyptian intelligence will change the regime and strive to advance its
country. Indeed, animosity will not disappear any time soon. Peace will not be
here tomorrow, or the day after. But the biggest chance for a change among all
the Arab movements is in Egypt. The Egyptian regime will be change in about
10 or 12 years, I'm certain. There are three options for Egypt: The Muslim
Brothers, the Army officers and the intelligence. The Muslim Brothers will not
bring change. They are extremely oppressed, they are fanatics and they lack the
power to make changes. The officers are the same. They are afraid to talk freely,
even among themselves. The greatest opposition to Nasser is found among the
intelligence, and there lies the chance. There are over 100,000 students in Egypt
today. Some of them only study so they can get good positions and well-paying
jobs. But many of them, no doubt, are concerned about their country, and they
will reform the regime.[116]

Based on these views, he believed that Israel is obliged to negotiate with
Egypt over the Rogers Plan was, and blamed Golda Meir for misunderstanding the political situation. He wrote to a friend in the United States: "If the
plan is realized, there will be peace, but I am skeptic. Anyway, the current
situation cannot go on."[117] A few months after Ben-Gurion had received the
update about the program, Rogers called him personally and offered to meet
him during his visit to Israel. His basic assumption was that the Old Man
would have the power to change Golda's mind. Ben-Gurion waited for him
in his apartment in Tel Aviv. During the meeting, he clarified that his position was exactly the one he stated publicly: Israel mustn't reject any offer
for negotiation. He supported territorial withdrawal, except for the Golan
Heights and Jerusalem, as long as the peace is "not just empty words, but
also friendly neighboring and mutual help."[118] His last sentence suggested
that any peace agreement should include the development of financial, cultural, and social relations. As for Jerusalem, the Old Man stressed, he was
willing to grant the Christians and Muslims authority over their respective
holy sites in the Old City, as long as the city itself remains under Israeli
sovereignty.[119]

Rogers was satisfied with Ben-Gurion's position and proposed that he would try to influence the government in Israel. Indeed, upon returning to his cabin, Ben-Gurion requested to talk to the prime minister's office. As usual, he didn't linger much on small talk and explained impatiently that without negotiation, disaster was due to happen. Golda started detailing her concerns regarding a negotiation that was based on the formula of resolution 242 (land for peace), but Ben-Gurion's patience was short lived. He abandoned the receiver angrily while she was still talking, hearing Golda's desperate voice call him—"Ben-Gurion! Ben-Gurion!"—He returned angrily to his work station and didn't provide details about the conversation. A few seconds later, when his assistants put the receiver back in place and hanged out properly, he said quietly: "A war will break out soon."[120] Later he explained that Golda was capable of being prime minister, but she was "limited, somewhat limited in her perception, her understanding."[121]

12

With no power to influence any of the Israeli leaders, the Old Man dedicated himself to writing answers to the dozens of letters he received weekly from Israel and abroad. Outwardly, he complained about the numbers of letters and requests, and blamed them for the delay in writing his memoir. But they were definitely important to him. When the handwriting was unreadable, he even requested them to be printed out. Researchers of his life have learned a lot from following his correspondences. He used to send detailed responses, which included his opinions and feelings in a variety of issues, fascinating as well as mundane.

In fact, in the pre-Internet and social media era, the letters were a unique channel of direct communication between him and the citizens. Furthermore, as an old man, those citizens became his pen pals, in front of whom he could let out some steam.[122] He loved this way of communication, which was free of journalists' mediation and political sabotage. A free correspondence, which was honest, based on the extent of exposure he allowed himself.

But as Ben-Gurion was drifting further away from the center of action, he had to deal with a growing number of esoteric offers and requests. Some demanded him to write introductions to their books, now that he had time on his hands;[123] others tried to gain his support for revolutionary ideas like changing the direction of the Hebrew writing system; and yet others demanded explanations from "our leader" concerning the Biblical prohibition of sibling marriages.[124] One woman even invited him to a secret seminar, in which, using metaphysics, it will be discovered how many Jews were actually present during the Exodus.[125] Another woman urged him to take part in a confidential experiment aimed to expand the Suez Canal with the force of nuclear energy.

The Old Man sent serious responses to them all, although these kinds of letters further demonstrated the cruelty of his situation, as someone who used to exchange correspondence with the world's greatest leaders. A hushed tone of irony and self-sense of humor slipped into his letters only rarely. To a citizen who demanded his return to the premiership, he answered that he wasn't as young as he used to be forty years ago, nor was he young as he was sixty years ago. Another time, as some kind of a private joke, he noted in his diary that the next day would be dedicated to reinterpreting Samuel 1, Chapter 1, Verse 5, per the request of a pensioner from Haifa.[126]

And there were also some touching surprises. During the summer, he found the name of the woman who had yet to forget their youth between the envelops: Rachel Nelkin–Beit Halahmi. "David, writing is difficult for me, but holding back without writing is even more difficult [...] was our childhood nothing but a dream?"[127] She wrote, as if ignoring the decades that had passed since he was a boy full of dreams. Rachel was not young anymore either. She lost her husband, Yehezkel, many years before, and lived alone in Givatayim. Despite the many years that had gone by, her letter suggested that she was still convinced in her power to feel Ben-Gurion's heartbeat, the fibers of his being. She was one of the very few women who called him "David."

In her letter, she wrote she was aware of the burden of the passing years, and the different ways they were shaped by life; she recognized the fact that the boy she once knew grew up to be a wizard leader, who was now nearing the end of his life. And yet, she wanted to renew their youth, now that they were both widowers and had a few years left, and suggested he would come and visit her.[128] Her letter didn't reveal anything of importance. Nor did it include any new content. But pieces of life long gone from his life vibrated between the lines. Ben-Gurion was touched, but wasn't swept away by the romantic nostalgia. There were times when he regretted losing her. Three years after her wedding, he still tried to win her back: "How I yearn to see you. No need to tell you that. You should realize it yourself. And I believe you want to see me too."[129]

But now it was too late. She moved on, to the arms of another, and while he loved her innocently as a young boy, their hearts grew apart since then. The years have carved a place for another woman in his heart, the one who followed him, not just in her imagination, but in real life, in a no-man's land. Therefore, in his typical stubbornness, he urged her to give up her advances: "Dear Rachel (and I mean it!), your complaint is justified, and I won't ask for your forgiveness, because those would be just empty words. You are definitely right, and I feel your pain," he wrote, but kept on saying that while he wasn't sure how many years he had left, he had to dedicate them to another national mission—writing his memoir. "I tell you this not to seek forgiveness for my sin. The sin is what it is. Just so you'll know I'm not free to do whatever I would like to do."[130]

His refusal to renew his relationship with Rachel testified, once again, that Ben-Gurion lived throughout his life in two time dimensions—the past and the future. Almogi used to tell that he realized it when he was the general secretary of *Mapai*, and came to the Old Man one night, his face contorted due to the tensions within the party's leadership. "Almogi, what's wrong? Why are you upset?" Ben-Gurion wondered. Almogi replied that Ben-Gurion would understand if he read the newspapers' headlines. Ben-Gurion got up, looked at the state's map and said firmly: "Do you see the map? We should develop the Negev, the Galilee."

"This is the vision, but there's also the present," Almogi interrupted him.

"There's no such thing as the present," said Ben-Gurion. "Once you say 'present' it's already gone. There's only past and future."[131]

The latest victim of his approach to time dimensions was Rachel, whose proposition to renew their past in the present was rejected flat out.

Chapter 6

A Man of a Single Job

1

In 1970, while the newspaper headlines included occasional reports of another Israeli fatality in the southern front, the front pages' margins presented eulogies, which appeared almost monthly, of deceased past leaders and cultural heroes: The poet Leah Goldberg, the author Shmuel Yosef Agnon (although Agnon was a religious Jew, Ben-Gurion refused to wear a yarmulke in Agnon's funeral, "as a protest against the government's enforcement and hypocrisy regarding the Registration Law [Who is a Jew]"[1]), the artist Avigdor Hameiri, the ministers Haim Moshe Shapira, Zalman Aran, and Yitzhak Grinboim, and the poet Nathan Alterman.

Frequently, Ben-Gurion was asked to say a few words "in their memory." Whenever he wrote or said respectful things about the deceased, he always felt it like a wake-up punch to his stomach, because he was summarizing his life together with theirs. Or perhaps it wasn't just his life; he was summarizing his time, an era of long-lost cultural giants. Ben-Gurion was particularly mournful over Alterman, who authored the weekly "Seventh Column" in *Davar* newspaper, and whose poetry was Ben-Gurion's companion during his tenure as prime minister.

They maintained a close and mutually respectful relationship. In 1953, when Ben-Gurion retired and went to live in Sde Boker, Alterman wrote a poem celebrating his leadership.[2] More importantly, Alterman supported Ben-Gurion's position during the Lavon Affair—maybe the most significant political support granted to him by the poet, when Ben-Gurion's status had already been deteriorating. Alterman's critics claimed he was the establishment's poet laureate, though Alterman could also criticize Ben-Gurion, as he did in the cases of Ben-Gurion's attitude toward the *Palmah* and "the other Germany," and his tendency to cover-up immoral conduct of IDF soldiers.

Ben-Gurion, on his part, wrote an impassioned letter to Alterman for his fiftieth birthday:

> One expression of your literary and poetic greatness is your use of current events, which you artfully manage to present in a profound, poetic, enchanting and upgraded way, unlike any of our poets (as far as I know) [...] You won't be upset if I allow myself to express some of my feelings for you, feelings of appreciation, love, and wonderment.[3]

Alterman was also one of the few who were noted by Ben-Gurion that they had to Hebraizaited their name, only following an apology for this "cheeky remark."[4] Now, when the poet passed away at sixty, the Old Man dedicated a week for reading his works, in some kind of a private memorial.[5]

His recognition of the fact that he was one of the few survivors from his cohort, 1886, as well as the end of his political activity, raised existential questions about life and its meanings, death, and its essence.[6] One morning, when he returned from his daily walk, Ben-Gurion reviewed his archival materials, like he always did, and decided to skip the meticulous reading. Haim Yisraeli, who came to visit him, found him in bed, deep in thoughts. "I wonder what death is," said Ben-Gurion suddenly, as if talking to himself. "I know I'm getting closer to it." Yisraeli was embarrassed and kept silent, and then Ben-Gurion added, as if trying to rebel against the cycle of life once again: "But I still feel like a 40 year old."[7]

He analyzed his life in periods. Once in a while, he talked about his life being partitioned into periods of fifteen years each. He served as secretary of the Labor Union for fifteen years, was the head of the Jewish Agency for fifteen years, and then prime minister for fifteen years (including two years of hiatus in Sde Boker). "Do I still have any hope for the next fifteen years after my resignation from the government in June 1963?"[8] He wondered in his diary.

He was healthy, but worried about what was about to come—the body's betrayal and the mind's weakness. When the French ambassador's assistant expressed his surprise at Ben-Gurion's energetic and lively appearance, he mentioned it in his diary as the essence of their communication. Naive, as someone who forgot the etiquettes of French diplomacy, he wrote proudly that the ambassador's assistant was surprised to find him looking so young.[9] Meeting his doctor, he kept asking questions about the possibility of increased longevity. "Is it [getting old] a necessity? Can't you go on living for centuries, like in the days of Abraham and Methuselah?"[10] He felt that medicine was on the verge of a breakthrough, which would change life's quality and expectancy, but he wasn't convinced it would happen during his lifetime.

Thus, he tried to explore the medical possibilities with his own means.

In many ways, he was one of the first Israelis who adopted the New Age principles, as they were developed over the years. Ben-Gurion believed in a connection between the body and the soul, and dedicated time for reading about Buddhism[11] and practicing Yoga.[12] His attraction to Buddhism and meditation was also a testimony of the huge tension he felt. He learned the Buddhist preaching of recognizing four truths: the pain as a fact, the reason for it, the cessation of pain, and the way to cease it. These truths were meant to help humans to be released from the source of human suffering, which is a quality of human beings, derived from their temporal existence in the world—that is, to reach a nirvana. To Renana, his daughter, he wrote ecstatically that Yoga is important for him, since it leads to "reigning the mind, and eventually the urges and the spirit, so you can concentrate until you strip off your materialism."[13]

Due to his back and joint pains, he made a habit out of visiting the hot springs in Tiberias. He admired the healing power of the warm water, and enjoyed leaving his suffering body to the mercy of the currents.[14] Most of all, he enjoyed the saltiness of Ein Gedi hot springs, which allowed him to float.[15]

He looked for his own solutions to the miseries of the modern world. For example, after reading studies about the importance of vitamin D, he took off the sunglasses he used to wear during his daily walks, saying that he wanted the sunlight to touch his face.[16] He talked a lot about the need to reconnect to nature, and believed that the human brain had many undiscovered capabilities, which can overpower physical and mental pains.

Less than twenty years before, during the 1950s, he held a different position regarding man's needs and place in the modern era. Back then, he believed that human beings should improve their control over technological developments. He tried to master the art of typing in a typewriter, although he gave it up shortly, and considered the ability to drive a car to be one of the features of modern man. He resented the fact that he almost never drove himself. During one of his vacations as prime minister, he insisted on replacing the driver. He sat behind the wheel on his way to the Principality of Monaco with his staff. But as it turned out, it was a winding road between cliffs—not the ideal road for learning how to drive properly. This riding experience, led by the unskilled hands of the Old Man, was so terrifying, that one of his staff members almost forced him to stop, a minute before they went down the ravine.[17]

Now he concluded that machines had gained control over human beings in more than the other way around. He longingly remembered the days when he walked from Sejera to Jaffa for two and a half days. "What's the matter? Can't people walk? Not just me—all my friends. We walked. People don't do it anymore, and I'm not saying they have degenerated, but I liked walking. Things changed when I got back from America to Israel. Until then, people were embarrassed to drive. A man should walk. And I keep walking even today."[18]

He also had a solid position on the issue of smoking cigarettes, which was quite common in the 1970s. Until the age of fifty, he was a heavy smoker who sometimes smoked up to three packs a day, but in his later years he became an almost obsessive preacher against smoking. In many occasions, he mentioned that all he needed in order to stop smoking was to have a wager with his son saying he can do it, as if trying to demonstrate the power of will.[19] The individual will was almost a holy concept for him in many fields, because it—and not belief—was the main generator of changes; he believed that the will had the power to bring about self-realization and release from the burden of heteronomous morality. He was obviously inspired by the Nietzsche and Schopenhauer, who were known as great influences over Jewish intellectuals at the turn of the twentieth century.[20]

2

His working ability was still exceptional. Often, he would dedicate almost fifteen hours a day for reading and writing his memoir. While he did change his habits a bit, and retired for half-hour breaks a couple of times a day instead of taking a nap at lunchtime,[21] people much younger than him still watched him with envy. One of his greatest advantages as a man of action and realization was his ability to concentrate, the ability to put everything into one important issue and attack it from every angle, until it's done. One of his biographers, Shabtai Teveth, defined him as a person who had a complete control over opening and closing drawers in his mind according to need. Ben-Gurion described himself, based on Maimonides' words, as a "man of a single job"[22]—the job needed at the time.

This was his modus operandi throughout his life—immersing himself in what he identified as key issues. In late 1946, while the *Yishuv*'s leadership was still concerned by the British Mandate and the opposition of the local Arabs, Ben-Gurion requested the defense office in the JNC board, in order to focus on what he named "a security seminar." After delving into the military issue, he decided that the best model for the Hebrew future military was the British one. More importantly, he concluded that the *Hagannah* should be prepared to fight against the Arab states and not against the British or the Palestinian Arabs—a decision that contributed to the IDF's preparedness in the War of Independence. Similarly, he could focus all his efforts into one issue when it came to his struggle for the establishment of the nuclear venture in Dimona, and establishing the ties between the Jewish state and the Other Germany; another example was his concentrated intellectual effort on the need to answer the question about "Who is a Jew" in 1958.

But this same ability to focus on one thing was now an obstacle when he came to write his memoir. What he needed now was the ability to tell a story. He had to forgo some historical events in order to highlight the more attractive stories, and write the history against the background of the changing political and mental climate of his career.

Yet, he tended to dive deep into specific stories of unique events that popped up into his memory, and forget the main field he had to plow in his book. Reencountering past materials sometimes swept him toward a renewed contemplation of events and people, regardless of their significance in his biography. So much so, that some of the people who met him during these days and weren't aware of his current practice, felt he was living in another realm of reality. This was one of the reasons for the rumors spread by some of them, saying that the Old Man was not as lucid as he used to be.[23]

Another problem that made his task more difficult was his old-fashioned work methods. Although he could have used a copying machine, he preferred to copy the required documents by hand into his notebooks, even when it meant copying a complete protocol.[24] Hence, he spent days on copying documents from one source to another.[25] His obsessive insistence on double copies of many documents was derived, among other things, from the trauma of losing his diary as a young man—a diary he started writing at the age of fourteen, feeling that he had greatness in his future.[26] He took the diary with him when he went to study law in the University of Constantinople (Istanbul) in 1912. But when he came back to Palestine for a vacation, World War I broke out, and upon returning to Turkey, he discovered that his apartment was burned to the ground. His possessions, and most importantly, his documents and diaries, were lost.[27] Since then, he tended to keep a few copies of his documents in various places, a practice that turned his private archive into an overflowing mess. He had an enormous amount of materials in his archives: During his active years, he collected almost every paper clip concerning his activities that appeared in local and global newspapers. One of the main obstacles in writing his memoir was the need to filter the materials out of about half a million pages of hand and type writing, and organize chronologically in cardboard files.[28]

His archive was organized for years according to two main collections, accumulated in dozens of files. One collection included his speeches, notes he wrote, personal correspondence, and protocols of meetings and sessions he attended, including some he didn't attend, but were related to the matters of the state. The other collection included letters, articles, and essays, written about him or by him. And the main source was his diary, in which he wrote daily, or sometimes intermittently. The diary included his notes from many decades of events and various lists, starting with population censuses in kibbutzim and villages, through philosophical discussions and ending with confidential materials related to the state's security.

Sine he documented a huge amount of materials, he had a hard time creating a hierarchy of importance. In many chapters, he didn't summarize the most important or crucial things, but rather the ones that attracted his attention at the moment, without referring to any defined historical scale. Thus, for examples, crucial events during the War of Independence were marginalized in his diary in favor of his notes about the ground's quality in the north of Israel.[29]

One of the reasons for his pattern of documentation was the fact that he experienced different events according to the subjective emotional power triggered by them. The day in which he declared the establishment of the state, for example, occupied a similar space in his diary as the space dedicated to his speech in a youth convention during the 1950s, where he was thrilled to find a solid pioneering spirit. Looking from the wider perspective of his mission, both events reflected parts of a whole renaissance mosaic of the revival of the Jewish people in modern times. Another reason had to do with the fact that he preferred to marginalize specific events in the historical documentation left after him, while emphasizing others.

The amount and type of materials were not the only obstacles in writing his autobiography; the physical condition of the documents was another factor. The Old Man didn't always use the best-quality papers. Many letters and documents were outworn over the years, which made them more difficult to decipher. Furthermore, many documents from the pre-state era were coded, due to the fear that they would get into the wrong hands. The codes were constantly replaced, as were the different writing techniques, and he was the only one who knew them all, but at the age of 83, he sometimes struggled to remember the codes. An additional hardship was related to the fact that he used many abbreviations, and his handwriting was cramped and difficult to understand (often, he would write quickly during meetings).[30]

But there was something else that held back Ben-Gurion's progress. While writing came easily to him, most of the stuff he wrote was practical, businesslike. His detachment from the world of prose made it harder for him to act as an autobiographer and write a historic, compelling narrative. When writing his memoir, he had to deal with the intimate, the motivations of the soul, and he wasn't capable of such an exposure. All his life, he wanted to create, achieve, and lead. An eternal activist, he managed to avoid the mental dilemmas that weighted upon his good friend Berl Katznelson.[31] As a constructive leader, his practical side—the ability to stop pondering and make a decision—was a huge advantage. But now, his practical tendency became another weakness in his writing mission.

And so, despite his unique working abilities and his strong desire to complete his memoir, the gap between his intentions and actions became almost unbearable. Since retiring from premiership, he told almost anyone who would listen that he was occupied with writing his memoir. Indeed, he dedicated days and nights to the technical aspect of collecting the materials and writing factual descriptions. And yet, seven years had gone by, and the publishing of his cherished memoir was drifting further and further away.

3

His retirement from the Knesset didn't contribute to the acceleration of the process, and his affiliates decided to help him by finding a secretary. They devised a division of labor, deciding that Ben-Gurion will choose the materials required for the first chapters and move them on the secretary, who will then have to filter the overflowing files and extract the most important documents. After the filtering process, Ben-Gurion was supposed to process the materials into a flowing autobiographical text. The designated editor was Yehuda Erez.

The secretary chosen for the mission was the then-student Zeev Tzahor, who later became a professor. He was both excited and embarrassed to meet the founding father, whom he was supposed to meet on a daily basis now. Ben-Gurion was not comfortable either. For decades, he was used to working alone in his den, and the awkward glances he exchanged with Tzahor in the first few days reflected his distress. And yet, dedicated as ever to completing his mission, he never said a word.[32] There was another personality trait of Ben-Gurion, which remained relatively unknown: his shyness.[33] As long as he had an official position, he knew how to manage, direct, give orders, and express thoughts. But when he wasn't occupied by a specific issue, he felt uncomfortable in unofficial encounters.

One afternoon, after a day of work, the Old Man caught a moment of lingering before his secretary was leaving for the day, and asked him: "What do you do?" Tzahor was surprised and deliberated his answer for a moment, and Ben-Gurion repeated his question: "What do you do when you get off work?" He was definitely trying to start a more intimate conversation, unrelated to the mission at hand, to inquire about the schedule of a normal citizen. But like many who were embarrassed by the presence of the man who had already been a myth, Tzahor was lost for words, and Ben-Gurion didn't press the matter. The air was tinged with sadness. Despite his somewhat awkward attempt to start a small talk, it was too late for him to learn how to speak naturally with people of different generations and states of mind.[34]

As for work, although he needed Tzahor's assistance, in his first few day, Ben-Gurion mainly enjoyed competing with him. He wrote in his diary that the student had copied ten pages and worked until 4:00 p.m., while he finished fourteen pages by 8:00 p.m.[35]

Another problem that held back his progress was raised during writing: Ben-Gurion always had a fighting spirit, and he never avoided a conflict. This was one of the reasons for the huge anticipation created around his book—there were rumors that his autobiography will include embarrassing stories, defamations, and insults directed toward the state's greatest past and present leaders. This was definitely a viable possibility. Ben-Gurion was optimistic about the ability of people to change reality, but his views about the human soul were skeptic and unkind.[36] Because of that, many people were weary from the moment his opinion of them will be published, along with other things that were hidden in his diary for years.

At the same time, his memoir was also intended to create the opposite effect: To fixate the national consensus around his image as a founding father and marginalize his personal struggles against his opponents in favor of a more statist version.

The tension between his turbulent feelings toward the state's leading figures and his aspiration to be remembered as a national-consensus leader was a difficult one to master. His relationship with Golda was one example. Up until the 1960s, his appreciation and even affection toward her were unmistakable. His positive approach is evident in his diaries and letters from this period. But since his abandonment of *Mapai*, Golda became his political enemy. He said she was dangerous to the state as prime minister. How would he describe their close relationship in previous years? Was it a mere result of interests and hypocrisy on her part, as he wrote in his diary in his later years, or an honest relationship that had gone sour? On the other hand, the man who had become one of his friends in the state leadership in recent years, President Zalman Shazar, was described differently in his diary entries in 1934. Back when he was trying to convince his colleagues in the *Histadrut* to support his agreement with Zeev Jabotinsky, he met with Shazar (whose name was Rubashov at the time) in an attempt to gain his support. Shazar agreed, but Ben-Gurion wrote in his diary that Shazar will probably support those who opposed the agreement when he met them.[37] Zeev Tzahor pointed out the possible unpleasantness that might arise toward Shazar in the matter, specifically now, when he had the most important official position in the state. Ben-Gurion, as usual, didn't hesitate: "If I wrote it, it was true."[38]

His secretary was alarmed by the almost unbearable lightness in which the Old Man was willing to open new struggle fronts, even in his old age. Tzahor wasn't the only one who tried to calm him down. His assistant at the Defense Ministry, Haim Yisraeli, often had to moderate insulting phrases in angry letters he wrote: "When we meet, don't reach out to me, because I won't return the gesture."[39]

As a leader, Ben-Gurion could make pragmatic decisions, even when they contradicted his previous declarations. Some of the most prominent among those were his decision to accept the 1947 Partition Plan, despite the small portion of land allocated for the Jewish state (although in the 1920s he supported the Greater Israel approach); the status quo agreement, which enabled the Chief Rabbinate to monopolize family law, in return for the support of the Partition Plan by the Mizrahi movement (although he opposed the orthodox demands in principle, and personally was married by a civil ceremony[40]); the withdrawal from the Sinai Peninsula and Gaza strip under the pressure of the superpowers, having already declared the establishment of the "third Israelite kingdom"); and so forth.

But as for his personal character, he had what can be described as a Revisionist tendency: Die or conquer the hill. Those who adopted Jabotinsky's "One flag (*Had-Nes*)" motive—sticking to one sacred principle at all costs—were unwilling to divert even for a moment from their beliefs and principles concerning people and events. Now, in his final life mission—the writing of his memoir—which required the ability to tell a story with many different shades and provide insights into the souls of those around him, his persistence and uncompromising decisiveness became obstacles.

And if the ongoing struggle to keep writing was not enough, he was also the victim of a fishy affair: Among the many requests of foreign journalists who wished to speak with him, he got a request from a Swiss journalist, Mark Melville, who wanted to interview him for a film he planned to produce about him. Ben-Gurion, craving human contact, accepted the offer. He enjoyed sharing his insights and past experiences and describing them against the background of the various historical contexts more than he was anxious to see the final product on screen. In late 1970, a few months after their meetings, Ben-Gurion was surprised to receive many greetings, most of them enthusiastic, for finally completing his mission. A rumor was spread, apparently, saying that his autobiography was about to be published. As it turned out, Melville has published a book based on their interviews, and presented it as Ben-Gurion's own creation. While the book didn't shed a negative light on Ben-Gurion or on Zionism in general, it did include many inaccuracies. The damage was grave, because Melville's swift operation ridiculed the Old Man's repeating statements concerning his work on his memoir.

At first, he settled for a denial and personal explanation to each of his greeters that this was not his memoir. But the greetings kept coming, and made it clear that he had to take a more extreme step. The suggestion to stop the book's distribution through legal means seemed like a burden he wasn't interested in taking on. Eventually, he had no choice but to publish a statement about the deceit in the world's most important papers. "I did say some of the stuff in the book," he admitted desperately after reading the book, "but most of it is invented." When Melville was located in Paris, Ben-Gurion sent him a bitter letter. He regretted his acceptance of the interview, although admitting he was partly at fault. Anyway, he concluded: "My friends advised me to sue you, but I'll settle for never seeing you again."[41] Melville agreed to correct his initial evil and the book was reprinted and republished as a book about Ben-Gurion, and not his own work.

4

Summer became fall, and Ben-Gurion's eighty-fourth birthday was about to be celebrated on the following Sukkot holiday. His white mane of hair was growing again, and the echoes of his retirement from the Knesset were subdued. Ben-Gurion was starting to adjust to his final stage of life, trying to find his place in the mundane routine ahead of him. He refused to celebrate his birthday. There was no reason for celebration, and his biological age was always a sore spot for him. When he was eighty, he already wrote an ironic letter to Zalman Shazar:

> Why 80 is considered to be the age of heroism (*gvurot*), I do not know. Does it mean a man needs heroes at this age, or is it that this age requires heroism [...] when I lived in exile, I felt I was growing old each year. Since I came to the Land of Israel—60 years ago—I feel no age difference, although I know for sure that I am getting old.[42]

His struggle against his biological clock was evident in more sarcastic ways as well. One day, he was interviewed by Yaakov Ahimeir from the Israeli Television. At the end of their conversation, Ben-Gurion asked Yaakov what he remembered about his father, Aba Ahimeir, the leader of *Brit Ha-Birionim* (The Strongmen Alliance) and the radical revisionist right wing during the *Yishuv* period. Yaakov said he was too "young" to carry with him the trauma of the struggle between his father and Ben-Gurion. Ben-Gurion wondered about his age, and upon hearing Ahimeir's response he noted: "Thirty-three is not that young. Is thirty-three a young age?" and answered his own question: "It's not."[43] It was difficult to avoid the feeling that the Old Man was avenging the fear of his own old age with his sarcastic remark to Ahimeir. After all, he achieved so much more by the time he was thirty-three.

This anecdote is merely another proof of the huge amount of energy still stored inside Ben-Gurion despite his eighty-four years of age. It seemed that the chronological aspect was ahead of the biographic one, as if it was an intentional sabotage. He managed to avoid the birthday celebrations planned for him, but didn't have as much luck with the sarcasm of Rachel Beit-Halahmi, who refused to let go despite, or maybe because of his previous rejection. In a congratulatory letter for his birthday, she wrote that in his age, this day was not so much a happy event as it was an opportunity for nostalgia, and reminded him that his memories "are both yours and mine."[44] But he avoided her trap once again. Indeed, he opened his letter of response with the words: "My dear beloved Rachel," and continued with "I cannot tell you how happy I was to receive your letter," but then he drove their correspondence into less intimate realms, as he always did with her. His main subject was his hope for peace in Israel,[45] as if trying to console her with this hope. Later, he remarked in the ears of his bodyguard: "Rachel was very beautiful once, but now she's gotten old."[46]

5

At the beginning of 1971, after his birthday and following a long period of excruciating labor and soul-searching, a milestone was reached in the process of writing the memoir. Ben-Gurion managed to gather the required materials for wiring all that had happened to him since his birth and until 1933. There were close to thirty files filled with documents, papers, statistical data, and essays, which were supposed to be the basis for the first volume of his autobiography. This was the bare minimum that had to be included. His secretary moved on to filter the materials. After some hard work under the Old Man's scrutinizing gaze, they were left with eight files. The Old Man felt a surge of positivism, efficiency, and vitality, and started reading the materials in order to write them as a coherent narrative. A while later, Ben-Gurion gave all the files back with added remarks on the different documents. But that was not the original intention. Ben-Gurion was supposed to turn the materials into a coherent story line, both personal and national; to write his autobiography.

According to his own explanation, he reached the conclusion that the raw materials should be publicized as they were, since any correction would only harm them. Tzahor tried to convince him that many people, in Israel and abroad, were waiting for his book, and a book based on documents alone will be of interest to a mere few researchers. But Ben-Gurion kept insisting. He kept arguing that the materials were important, and urged his staff to prepare them for print, as if avoiding the rest of the writing task.

He was difficult to argue with, partly due to the awe they felt toward him,[47] in addition to the fact that he had honestly deliberated each paragraph for years. Only in 1969—six years after he began to work on his memoir—had he decided to start the second volume of his autobiography in the year 1930 rather than in 1933, arguing that his Zionist activity up until he was chosen as a member of the Zionist Board required additional background. Therefore, he decided the volume won't be titled "Memories from my years in the service of the Zionist movement" but rather "Zionist memories."[48] His precision was that far reaching. He gave no leeway to consideration of intriguing editing or an attempt to attract readers.

When the dispute ended with no result, Tzahor and the editor, Erez, offered an easier writing pattern: They would take the main entries from his diary and add some commentaries and hindsight explanations. The protocols and the rest of the documents can be added as annexes, they promised. As encouragement, they reminded him the interest raised by De Gaulle's memoir. The last volume was due to be published around that time. Ben-Gurion did not reject their offer right away, and requested some time to consider it. After a short while, he gave his response: I am not writing a novel. I am presenting my memories from the process of the state's establishment. Those who are not interested shouldn't read it. Eventually, the only result of their discussion was his agreement to remove statistical data, such as the population census conducted in Palestine in 1922, and move them to an annex at the end of the book.[49] Encouraged, Ben-Gurion continued to declare his work was progressing.[50] But his staff members were already starting to fear that the mission he took upon himself—his autobiography—would never be completed.

Chapter 7

Vision, Leadership, and Path

1

His self-induced retrospective while going through his archives flooded Ben-Gurion with feelings and tastes of his past. Unlike his continuing grudge toward his ex-colleagues in *Mapai*, the memories of his ideological struggles as prime minister brought on some nostalgic feelings to those days and their old disputes, which were often drought with personal circumstances as well, but seemed to him now more worthy and based on principle worldviews. One of his former rivals, who he now saw in a different light, was Moshe Sneh, a member of the Israeli Communist party (Maci) during the 1970s.

In the pre-state era, Ben-Gurion had appreciated Sneh's intellect, his integrity, and his operational skills, when he was a member of *Ha-Tzionim Ha-Klaliyim*. He saw him as a future leader. Sneh was appointed to be the head of the *Hagannah* national headquarters with the Ben-Gurion's unequivocal approve. They joined forces, for example, against Haim Weizman's leadership during the time of the Jewish Resistance Movement, which was too moderate for their taste.

To some extent, Sneh was the pre-state equivalent to Dayan with regard to his relationship with Ben-Gurion. Ben-Gurion considered him to be a young, brave, and promising leader, a security-oriented activist, and hoped he will continue to work under his wings. It seems that the seeds of their later personal conflict were planted back then. For Ben-Gurion, Sneh was one of his "boys,"[1] and while no one could say that Sneh considered himself to be Ben-Gurion's obedient follower, he certainly never denied his authority or importance until the state had been established. Yet, when Sneh rejected the Partition Plan and started getting closer to Ahdut Ha-Avoda members, Ben-Gurion's suspicions grew, and he deduced that Sneh was too independent.[2] In the early 1950s,

Sneh crossed the lines and moved to the Communist left, opening a personal and ideological unbridgeable gap between them.[3] Sneh's decision to join *Mapam*, and later the Communist Party, was a double insult for Ben-Gurion: Not only did Sneh abandon his own way, but he also joined the "other" camp while publishing an anti-Zionist booklet. Ben-Gurion could always lash out at his rivals, but he often avoided arguing with Sneh's sharpened tongue, saying that he had nothing to say to Sneh's camp anyway.

The change in the winding path of their relationship started with 1967 War. When the war broke out, Sneh supported an aggressive attack by Israel. After the war, while he continued to support the Palestinians' right for self-determination, he withdrew from his previous anti-Zionist positions, a step Ben-Gurion perceived as acknowledgment of his mistake, although Sneh never saw it as such. Sneh continued to be perceived as Ben-Gurion's rival, due to his demands to accelerate the efforts for peace with the Palestinians (obviously, Sneh never heard about Ben-Gurion's meetings with Mussa Alami), but it became an inter-Zionist dispute.[4] Anyway, they couldn't become close friends, but Ben-Gurion made a point of fixating Sneh's historical memory as a man who retracted and changed his mind. He was happy to tell that a short while before his retirement from the Knesset, he asked Sneh mockingly: "So, are you a Zionist now?" And Sneh didn't deny.[5] This was the Ben-Gurionist way of reaching out for peace: Draw his opponent closer to his own opinions.

At another time, he explained that Sneh never went through an ideological journey, because he was never a real communist in the first place. Sneh, Ben-Gurion analyzed, was a man who attempted to foresee the future. He believed that after the state's establishment, the Soviets will strengthen their hold in the Middle East, and therefore, tried to prepare for it. Sneh knew the Russians would need someone who "knew the land," that is, a local leader who is engaged with the society, "and actually, he does know the people and the land more than all of the communists combined."[6] Furthermore, Ben-Gurion assessed, it was no coincidence that 1967 War was the watershed that marked Sneh's change—the war made him understand that the Soviet's takeover option will not be realized. For Ben-Gurion, this was another proof that Sneh got closer to the communist idea for tactical reasons alone. He said with a smile that Hannah, Sneh's wife, was indeed "a very good communist," but Sneh always had been "a highly qualified Zionist."[7]

His softened approach toward Moshe Sneh—even if its justification would never have been accepted by Sneh himself—was not a rare exception in his later attitudes toward left-wing leaders. Specifically, this statement is relevant for Meir Yaari and Yaakov Hazan. Despite the verbal catapults thrown at them when they were sitting in the Knesset as an opposition to his government, now he stressed their contribution to Zionism:

Even when Russia was sacred to them, I believed they were Zionists. I believed in their Zionism. Hazan's statements at the time, about Russia being his second homeland, were empty words. Hazan never went to Russia. He was here, working in agriculture. I respect Yaari as well. He was always a Zionist. An honest man, a high-level intellectual.[8]

As a proof of Hazan's integrity, he presented his support of establishing kibbutzim by *Ha-Shomer Ha-Tzair* in the Golan Heights.[9] Yaari was portrayed as a role model of fair ideological rivalry: On the one hand, he opposed Ben-Gurion's path, and particularly his Western tendencies; on the other hand, he was one of the few members of *Ha-Shomer Ha-Tzair* who supported the decision of the *Palmah*'s desolation.[10]

Another reason for his positive opinion about the leaders of *Ha-Shomer Ha-Tzair* and *Mapam*, whom he cursed as prime minister and blamed them for blindly admiring the USSR,[11] was related to his deep frustration from *Mapai*, like many other of his positions at the time. He was pained knowing that unlike his fights against *Mapam*, his struggle against *Mapai* portrayed him as a bitter, stubborn man, while Golda and Eshkol were perceived as humane and warm hearted. Thus, when he praised his rivals from the communist left, he also highlighted the difference between an ideological rivalry and his struggles against *Mapai* leaders, which he saw as based on lust for power. Indeed, when Yaari and Hazan took the time to visit him in his cabin, they were surprised to see him smiling, moving impatiently, and demonstrating "an almost child-like excitement."[12]

Ideologically, his reconciliation gestures toward Sneh, Hazan, and Yaari didn't change his tendency of distancing himself further away from the socialist values. On the contrary, as he grew older, he developed a growing alienation toward the idea of the kibbutz. "Today, I would not call every young man and woman to go the Kibbutz, and I wouldn't dare saying the revival of Israel would not have been possible without the Kibbutzim, although the establishment of the Kibbutzim was a requirement as part of the effort to build the country. Those who want to—are welcome to go. But the Kibbutz is not the only way."[13] He also made a point of emphasizing the fact that his decision to settle in Sde Boker had nothing to do with the fact that it was a kibbutz. "There's nothing more important and cherished than bringing a barren place into life, and I went to the Negev because it was abandoned."[14] When angry, he was even blunter. He said that the only advantage of the kibbutz life was based on his hatred toward the big city: "Such a city is a disaster. I saw it in America and now in Israel. Robing, stealing, raping."[15]

His criticism against the city life was also derived from his disappointment: Against his ambition to create the New Jew, who will work in creative, labor-intensive jobs, by the 1970s it was clear that most of the Israelis were concentrating in the big cities and returning to professional, trade-based occupations. He resented the phenomenon that was developed after 1967 War, when agricultural and construction jobs were re-occupied by the Palestinians. This was the reason for his objection to the Defense Minister Dayan's "open bridges" policy—a policy designed to facilitate the transfer of goods between Jordan and the West Bank, as well as the movement of laborers from the West Bank and Gaza Strip into the Green Line territories.[16] Dayan believed that his policy was neutralizing the motivation for terror attacks, relieving the hostility toward the Israeli regime and strengthening the connections between Jordan and the Palestinians.[17] Ben-Gurion objected this policy based on educational and economical calculations. He feared that turning the Palestinians into a cheap workforce will jeopardize the basic Zionist principle he put forward in the early twentieth century: Hebrew labor, including manual labor.[18] He warned:

> If things continue this way, in 20 years there will be no more Hebrew laborers in Israel. The solution is a high-level technological education. We must reach the point where a Jewish laborer will remain a laborer, but will be able, through technology, to be productive like ten laborers of today.[19]

2

Ben-Gurion witnessed first-hand the intermediate period between the existence of Jews as separate groups around the world, and their gathering in Israel under one law and one government. One of his main fears was what he recognized one of the most prominent weaknesses of Jews throughout history: The lack of politicians who had the ability to unify, strengthen, and stir the people as one consolidated unit.

While he was a strong leader, who was sometimes even accused of totalitarianism by his rivals—his political path was paved with dozens of struggles, during which he repeatedly put himself and his positions to vote. Some of his struggles, he believed, were a consequence of the Jewish tendency toward sectarianism, a tendency he mentioned often, convinced that one unifying leader is a prerequisite for national revival. His disappointment from the current leadership in Israel was not a result of a specific situation, so he thought. Analyzing the people's history according to the quality of its leaders, he reached a gloomy conclusion:

> The Jewish people, which was the origin of some of the greatest figures in human history, has generated no great political leaders since the days of the old kings. The exceptions were two or three kings: David, Uzziah, and maybe

Jeroboam the second. Of course, two thousand years of exile, wandering, dependency on strangers, and persecutions didn't generate any statist qualities within this people.[20]

He found a role model of leadership in Jeremiah, the prophet of destruction who was active toward the end of the First Temple period. He praised Jeremiah, who was described as: "a man of strife and a man of contention to the whole earth" (Jeremiah, 16:10; this was the source of the Old Man's description of himself), mainly because he had the courage to present unpopular views, even when he had to pay a high personal cost. Ben-Gurion believed that Jeremiah's power was a result of his belief in his mission ("Say not: I am a child; for to whomsoever I shall send thee thou shalt go, and whatsoever I shall command thee thou shalt speak," Jeremiah, 1:7), and not his desire for power. He also praised Jeremiah because he appreciated his position, arguing that an honest answer doesn't involve sacrifices, but rather soul searching; and mainly due to his willingness to warn his people, who were gearing up for the battle, that they are about to be defeated by the Babylonians:

> The people of Israel had no statist perspective during the First Temple period, or the Second Temple period. Their war against the Romans during the Second Temple was an absurd, just like the war against the Babylonians during the First Temple. Jeremiah opposed the war. He knew that if we don't fight, the Babylonians will be fine. But the people of Jerusalem misunderstood Jeremiah. He was the greatest prophet of all. No prophet ever suffered like him. He was thrown into a deep hole in the ground. But he had a statist perspective. He knew we couldn't face the Babylonians, not because he liked them. But the people of Jerusalem wanted to fight, and that was the result.[21]

Ben-Gurion admired Jeremiah's independent character since his early political career. But now, at the end of his days, when he spoke about him again during his walks, his companions saw that he was identifying with the later chapters in the prophet's life, when he was persecuted by his people and thrown into jail after telling them the truth.[22] One day, Ben-Gurion added a surprising interpretation to the prophet's loneliness: "Jeremiah was a bachelor throughout his life, and never had a childhood love,"[23] he remarked without explaining any further.

3

He found some good qualities in other, less historical leaders as well. The first was Charles de Gaulle, the leader of Free France Army during World War

II and later the president of France in the years 1959–1969. The similarities between their personalities and behavior patterns are clearly visible. The French leader was also stubborn and brave, and knew how to navigate his country and gain achievements, while tramping over his political rivals from the left and from the right. He established the almost-totalitarian presidential regime of the Fifth Republic over on the ruins of the dilapidated infrastructure of the Fourth Republic; he developed France's nuclear capabilities; enhanced the control of the regime over the media; freed France from the burden of ruling Algeria in 1962; and pushed forward economic reforms that reduced unemployment rates, and were based on a free market, while giving some power to the government's guiding hand.[24]

But de Gaulle was also responsible for the decline of France–Israel alliance, which was formed during the 1950s, as part of what was named the "reassessment" of France's political interests in the Middle East after the withdrawal from Algeria.[25] He was the one who ordered the French military establishment to reduce the intensity of the relationship with Israel, and to stop their support in the development of the Dimona nuclear facility.[26] His policy was publicized in Israel during the 1960s, particularly after 1967 War, when he declared an embargo for weapon sales to Israel and expressed his unequivocal opinion against the occupation of the territories. In a press conference, which included some anti-Semitic undercurrents, he declared: "The Jews were always confident, elitist and controlling."[27]

But all of those things never stopped Ben-Gurion from appreciating him. Ben-Gurion admired de Gaulle's decision-making abilities, particularly because he managed to withdraw from Algeria despite the objection of the French officers and settlers. He did explain, however, that if he were French, he would do it differently.

> I was in France when de Gaulle opened his speech with the words: "Algeria for the Algerians." France was in shock. In our conversation, I told him: "If we were you, we would also grand Algeria its independence." But you have one million French people, who have lived there for decades. I would take them to the Tunisian border, from the Mediterranean Sea to the Sahara Desert, bring another million and a half French and Italians from Europe, settle them in the desert's outskirts, and secure the road along the Tunisian border. Algeria for the Algerians—but the Sahara could have remained French. He didn't do it. He took the French out, and that's it.[28]

Ben-Gurion praised the French leader in many occasions, but one thing he never said, but was evident in his approach to de Gaulle, was related to the similar life stories of both of them as old men. Like him, de Gaulle finished his tenure as a lonely man, robbed off the glory he once had, after being out-voted in the 1969 referendum, when he wanted to turn the French senate into a counseling body and empower the municipalities. Just like Ben-Gurion's struggle against *Mapai*'s leadership, de Gaulle also continued to rely on his belief in his the rightness of his way and the power of his charisma. He insisted on conducting the referendum despite the advices of his advisers, who realized that while the 1968 students' revolt in Paris was oppressed, the disappointment from the establishment felt by the young generation will be reflected in the polls.

De Gaulle retired about a year before Ben-Gurion left the Knesset, and dedicated himself to writing his memoir. The French leader was the only person Ben-Gurion requested to meet after retiring from politics, but he refused. In his diary, Ben-Gurion tried to repress his disappointment. He mentioned that the response was friendly, but that de Gaulle was now a civilian, and wasn't meeting anyone because he was busy with writing his memoir.[29]

Despite the personal and national disappointment caused by de Gaulle, Ben-Gurion rejected the hostility toward him in the Israeli public opinion. His statements about the need to understand de Gaulle regardless of his approach toward Israel were another chapter in his struggle against what he identified as an influence from the days of exile, judging foreign leaders according to one scale: "Are you with us or against us?" Just like he mentioned, during his final speech in the Knesset, that the USSR's policy toward Israel was not deterministic, he rejected hysterical expressions of hostility toward de Gaulle, and requested to judge him from realistic perspective:

> He shouldn't have declared the embargo, specifically after we've already paid the money. But after all, he is French, and he was concerned with the interests of France. He is not a small man—a great French men, honest in nature, and a man of truth. The Israeli press created a distorted image of him.[30]

He waited for a long time for the fourth volume of de Gaulle's autobiography, which included a reference to Israel–France relations. In September 1970, he got what he was longing for: The English edition of the memoir, with a personal dedication. The book did not present Israel or Ben-Gurion in a positive light. De Gaulle wrote that during one of his visits to France, the Old Man admitted that his strategic goal was to expand Israel's borders. We may assume he referred to the confidential preparatory meeting before the Sinai Operation, which was conducted at the end of 1956 in the Parisian suburb of Sevres with the French prime minister Guy Mollet and the British foreign minister Selwyn Lloyd.[31] Later reports argued that during this meeting, Ben-Gurion presented a political vision: Giving Iraq, which was under a British-oriented regime at the time, the East Bank of the Jordan River and settle the Palestinian refugees over there, at the same time, establishing autonomy in the West Bank under Israeli control. Ben-Gurion also suggested to expand

Israel's northern border to the Litani River and include the Strait of Tiran in its southern border.[32] Yet, he seemed to have suggested it when he was anxious, under the pressure of discussions before the operation, and it shouldn't be concluded that he actually meant to realize this vision.

Ben-Gurion, in any case, was enraged by the publication. Israel was portrayed in it as having almost imperialist territorial ambitions. Moreover, the text suggested that his political confession was the one that impacted de Gaulle's reassessment of France's relationship with Israel.

And so, he found a new front, another final battle with the leader he admired. He chose to send de Gaulle a long, detailed letter of response, designed to refute the argument in his book. In his letter, he defined de Gaulle again as a leader whose "historical acts for the salvation of France will be eternally remembered, not just in the history of France, but of entire Europe."[33] But he explained that as far as his relationship with Israel was concerned, de Gaulle was guilty of a basic misunderstanding. As a proof of the fact that he never wished to expand the state's borders, he mentioned his decision to accept the UN Partition Plan in 1947, and his speech at the Knesset after the War of Independence, in which he declared that he was satisfied with the 1949 borders as a status quo for the next century, if only the Arab states would accept Israel's existence. Finally, he stressed the fact that the occupations of 1967 War were a result of a defensive war enforced on Israel. He summarized:

> The Land of Israel belongs to the Arabs residing in it and to the members of the Jewish people, from every country, who want to return to the Land of Israel. This land can absorb all the Jews who feel the need and the desire to return to Israel without disowning even one Arab, while developing the empty territories and by helping to raise the local Arabs' financial and cultural level.[34]

Ben-Gurion waited for his letter to be translated into French, and he was planning on publicizing it in a press conference.[35] But when the translation was finally ready, on November 9, 1970, he was surprised by unexpected news: De Gaulle died of an asthma and heart attack. He was about eighty.

The lost letter was one thing. But for Ben-Gurion, de Gaulle's death was another line in the chain of loss stretching for over a year now, as warning signs, revealed in various places and moments, which were gathered to warn him against life's cruelty and transience. Normally, his diary included mainly brief reports, and lacked descriptions, but he made an exception with de Gaulle's death: He described how the French ex-president was sitting with his wife for a quite card game, when his heart suddenly gave out.[36]

A day after de Gaulle's death was announced, the telephone in the Old Man's cabin rang. The voice of a young, nervous soldier was heard—she wanted to connect him to the Prime Minister Golda Meir. The memory of their final angry talk was still vivid in his mind. But Golda, who knew how much de Gaulle had meant to the Old Man, surprised him. She asked him to represent the government in the public ceremony that was about to be held after the private funeral. It was a first step of goodwill, maybe an attempt to clear her conscience, which was further burdened by the reports she received about the Old Man's unglorified loneliness in his cabin.[37]

It is safe to assume that if it wasn't for de Gaulle, Ben-Gurion would have rejected her proposal. But while he tried to avoid trips abroad at this stage of his life, he was willing to take part in the public ceremony. Over there, he mingled with past world leader, tired heroes, who greeted each other and maybe realized that should have known their time would come, even when they were winning and overcoming their rivals.

Charles de Gaulle was buried in Colombey, where he grew up, and his tombstone carried only his name and dates of birth and death. Unlike the public funeral ceremony in his honor, de Gaulle ordered in his will that he should be buried in a simple funeral, with no politicians, acknowledging the fact he was a human being, only a human being. This order impressed Ben-Gurion immensely. He stressed in his diary: "[de Gaulle] ordered in his will that he should be buried in a garden, and no one outside of the village's population would be allowed to attend his funeral."[38] In 1970, Ben-Gurion had yet to draft his own will, but when he did so, a couple of years later, it was obvious he was inspired by de Gaulle.

4

The renewed encounter with current and past politicians inspired, so it seems, a new idea in Ben-Gurion's mind: To publish an annotated edition of his correspondence with the US president John Kennedy, who was murdered seven years earlier.[39] But he quickly deserted this plan. Kennedy's image, and the memory of their shaky relationship, didn't inspire him to write.

Generally, although he resided in the United States between the years 1915 and 1917, and directed the *Yishuv* toward the United States ever since the second St. James Conference in 1939,[40] his attitude toward the American nation was less than enthusiastic. In an article he wrote—but never sent—he described the United States as a superpower in a constant declining process. His estimation was that the United States will have problems in the future dealing with its characterizing social gaps and financial issues. "The intellectuals [in the United States] want peace at any cost, and those who support Nixon and Vietnam are the chauvinists, the anti-Semites, and anti-niggers," he wrote. "Add in a financial crisis, unemployment and inflation and you get a rather gloomy picture. Israel is dependent upon the mercy of this state, with Nixon as its leader. [...] Due to what is mentioned above, I lack the mental energy to further explain the situation over there."[41]

He resented the political system of the United States, because it allows the Congress to overpower the president,[42] and it seems that his approach was affected by the anti-Zionist and even anti-Semite tendencies, which were common in the State Secretary and the Pentagon during the 1920s and 1930s.[43] Even the "special relationship" developed between Israel and the United States since 1967 War was not enough to relieve his memories of the US attitude toward Israel in its early days. He often mentioned the State Secretary's hesitation concerning the establishment of Israel after the UN vote on November 29, 1947, and the administration's skepticism concerning the ability of the IDF to sustain itself during the War of Independence. Furthermore, he made a point of mentioning his disappointment from the American embargo on weapon sales to the Middle East during the war, which, while imposed on all the states involved in the battles, weakened only the Jews.[44] Since the War of Independence was the toughest security-related experience of his tenure, the embargo was a wound that didn't heal yet. We may assume that the pressures put by the Kennedy administration in demand to supervise the Dimona nuclear reactor didn't contribute to his positive attitude toward the United States.

Additionally, he criticized the Americans for their involvement in the Vietnam War.[45] He believed that the ambition to defeat the communist ideology by force was an oversimplification, and that the war was handled in a way that wouldn't grant the United States the desired political result. He had a disagreement with Dayan in this matter: Dayan was impressed with the military power demonstrated by the Americans, and during the 1960s he even covered the battles in Vietnam in a series of articles for an American magazine.

During his years as prime minister, Ben-Gurion refrained from revealing his opinions about the United States due to political considerations. But after he left the Knesset, his reservations were easily detectable. For example, he rejected the request of *LOOK* magazine to express his opinion about the American interests regarding Israel,[46] but highlighted the age-old friendship between the two nations. He mentioned a letter written by a Jewish officer in the American military during the days of President John Adams, where he expressed his hope that the Jews will establish a national home in Israel one day, and pointed out the fact that both houses of the Congress had approved the Balfour Declaration. While emphasizing the deeply rooted relationship between the nations, Ben-Gurion said over and over again that Israel must remember that political interests may change over time.

Unlike his lack of appreciation toward the United States, he was inspired by the qualities he attributed to the British people:

The English are a people who knew, despite the stormy times of war, to maintain their political freedom, their pillars of democracy, and while they did grant their government the unlimited power to confiscate property of any kind [...] they still retained their freedom of criticism, and every English person is entitled to criticize the government for every wrong-doing or injustice.[47]

When he advocated a change in the Israeli electoral system, he turned once again to the British model.[48] "The English people has invented the great wisdom of representatives, the world's most efficient system [...] it educates the opposition to be responsible, because every opposition can become a government."[49]

Winston Churchill, Britain's leader during World War II, was also considered by Ben-Gurion's to be a great leader, although, he explained, de Gaulle had better leadership skills, because he led "against the will of his people, who didn't want to fight Hitler and didn't want to leave Algeria, while Churchill had the support of all his people, except for a few English communists, during WWII."[50]

When discussing leadership, he mentioned: "He [Churchill] saved England, but right after the war, he was thrown off premiership and the Labour were elected. Everyone spoke highly of him, but they didn't want him as prime minister."[51] For a moment, a simple psychological interpretation seemed to suggest he was comparing himself to Churchill with regard to the ungratefulness of their respective peoples; but then he declared he understood the English people's choice to dismiss their leader, because Churchill was responsible for his own mistakes. What he meant was that leaders must comply to the same requirements as their people, and that a worthy leadership is rooted in the spirit of its people. "He wasn't elected for premiership, and rightly so. He didn't want to take apart the British Empire; he refused to grant India its independence and was willing to start a war. This only shows you what a healthy and wonderful political instincts the English have."[52]

5

As for the Israeli leaders, there's no doubt that Ben-Gurion preferred Moshe Dayan as his successor. He highly admired Dayan's analyses, perception, and composure. Although he never said it out loud, it seems that Dayan's refusal to ignore his advice during 1967 War was also considered by him to be a sign of independent thinker. "He is usually the only one who gets our situation,"[53] he concluded.

Aside from their shared love of Bible and archaeology, Ben-Gurion and Dayan shared a similar perspective on security issues: Both of them supported activism—harsh military reactions when needed, alongside a willingness to give up territories in return for an agreement, which would ensure security mechanisms and proper peaceful relationships. But even when they had disputes, as in the cases of the Lavon Affair, the establishment of *Rafi*, and 1967 War, Ben-Gurion still appreciated Dayan's position.

A typical example of their relationship can be found in early 1961, after Ben-Gurion had resigned from premiership in order to create a new coalition. The leaders of *Mapam, Ahdut Ha-Avoda,* and the Liberals wanted to take advantage of the circumstances and construct a government without Ben-Gurion, a suggestion that was out of the question for *Mapai*'s leaders. During a meeting of *Mapai*'s secretariat, Dayan was the only one, who declared that he wouldn't reject the idea of a government without Ben-Gurion, adding: "As long as the spirit of Ben-Gurionism prevails in it." Ben-Gurion's assistant, who knew that the Old Man was waiting in his house for the meeting's protocol, feared that a rift will be created between him and Dayan. But Ben-Gurion surprised him: "Dayan's words were true. He is a smart man. What is Ben-Gurion? Only flesh and blood. The important thing is the path, the policy, and not the person."[54]

Ben-Gurion insisted on defending Dayan in other contexts as well; once, when he happened to overhear a conversation between his children about Dayan's passion toward archaeological treasures, he went out of his den and stopped them.[55] A particularly interesting incident happened in the late 1950s, when an IDF officer, Colonel Dov Yirmiyah, discovered that Dayan was having an affair with his wife, Hadasah Mor. Yirmiyah was agitated, and sent a raging letter to Dayan: "You lowly, cursed adulterer [...] you took advantage of the weakness of a poor woman and dragged her into an abyss she can never get out of [...] and now, you fornicating man, you must help her [...] you are damned for eternity."[56] Dayan never bothered to respond, and Yirmiyah chose to approach Ben-Gurion in the matter. He demanded that Ben-Gurion will stay true to his words concerning the IDF moral aspect and dismiss Dayan from his military duties.

Ben-Gurion felt for Yirmiyah, and sent him a long and detailed letter, in which he explained that he wouldn't reprimand Dayan because he distinguished between two aspects of moral—the intimate and the public ones:

I sympathize with you, and I completely understand the sadness, pain and anger expressed in your words. It is the most natural thing [...] even if you were wrong, and your public conclusions are not the result of an objective reason—one should not blame you for not considering your words by the scale of reason [...] but I hope you won't be mad at me if I make a distinction between the personal and intimate aspect, and the public one, although I know very well how deep and sensitive is the personal aspect in matters like that, and I wouldn't tell you that you should be mad at the woman as well, and not just about the act (though there is a basis for reasonable anger in such experiences), and that you must realize that a woman is not a personal possession, she is a free human being. [...] Not just these days, but also in previous generations, and even in ancient times (during the days of the prophet Nathan, whom you quote), there was a distinction between two spheres—the private sphere between a man and a woman (not between one person and another, which is a social and statist matter), and the public sphere. A man can be a holy monk throughout his life, but he would be useless as a public figure, and vice versa. [...] The people of Israel have been singing "David, the king of Israel, is still alive" up until this day, although every Jew knows what King David had done to Uriah the Hittite, Bathsheba's husband.[57]

Beyond the Old Man's dedication to Dayan, which is clearly reflected in this letter, we can also find proofs for his feminist approach. He refused to view Yirmiyah's wife as a manipulated person, and saw her as an independent personality, thus deciding that both she and Dayan share the responsibility for their acts. Ben-Gurion always believed in gender equality. Despite his disappointment from *Davar* newspaper, which was used as a prominent platform for essays against him after his retirement from *Mapai*, he wrote to Hannah Zemer when she was appointed to be the newspaper's chief editor in the late 1970s, saying he was proud of the fact that a woman was appointed for this position for the first time. Despite his strained relationship with Golda Meir, he wrote to Hannah Zemer that in light of the fact that the prime minister was also a woman, he was hoping that gender equality in Israel would be promoted soon enough.[58] According to his daughter, Renana, his feminism was derived of the fact that "the mother figure was almost a holy concept for him."[59] Once, he surprised his grandson, Yariv, when he confessed that he was sorry for not being able to experience motherhood, because it was one of the most supreme feelings a human being can experience.[60]

Beyond the feminist aspect, in the last section of his letter, Ben-Gurion compared Dayan's actions to those of the revered British admiral, Horatio Nelson, who fornicated with the ambassador's wife, but was still considered to be a hero in his country. He wrote: "Dayan is no hypocrite either, because he never was, nor will he ever be, the preacher in intimate matters," and stressed that as far as the public sphere was concerned, Dayan "fought in the service of the people, with great skill as well as devotion [...] he led his soldiers to battle."[61]

Dov Yirmiyah was not persuaded by the moral system suggested by Ben-Gurion. He left the military and dedicated his life to political activity in peace-promoting NGOs. To this day, he believes that Ben-Gurion's back up for Dayan's actions contributed to the creation of the chauvinistic atmosphere in the defense and security establishment.[62] One of Ben-Gurion's rare criticisms against Dayan was, by the way, related to his divorce from his wife,

Ruth: "So strange, she is a great girl, such a good family, a noble woman." Later, he added quietly that he knew their marriage weren't a happy one, without adding any details.[63]

In any case, since Ben-Gurion's retirement from the Knesset, his interactions with Dayan were sporadic. Even when Dayan offered to update the Old Man on current events, he explained that due to his many occupations, he wouldn't be able to drive south all the way to Sde Boker. Ben-Gurion was understanding, and made the trip to Tel Aviv himself, although felt less comfortable in his apartment in the city.[64]

During one of these conversations, at the end of 1970, they exchanged their assessments concerning Egypt's goals. Ben-Gurion was optimistic. He insisted that due to the financial and cultural situation in Egypt, it would be willing to sign a peace agreement with Israel in the near future.[65] Furthermore, he believed that the rising of China and the threat it was imposing on the USSR might weaken the Russian influence over the Arab countries, thus further enhancing the chances of peace. Dayan was less optimistic. He assessed that a peace agreement with Egypt was improbable in the foreseeable future, and that China's dominant position in the international community will influence the Middle East power relations only in the longer run.[66]

6

Dayan's pessimist assessment regarding the chances for peace didn't convince Ben-Gurion to sit and wait. He was looking into the future, and feared the continuation of the Israeli-Arab conflict. One military defeat will be one too many, he used to explain, adding: "And no one could say it's impossible."[67]

Since he wasn't committed anymore to Israel's official policy, he nurtured a desire to better understand the Arabs' thinking patterns. In order to do so, he asked as many meeting as possible with representatives of the Israeli Arabs. One of these meetings was with the members of Jamal family from the village of 'Ar'ara in the center of Israel.[68] As usual, pleasantries and small talk were not his strong suit. Committed to his objective, he opened with a statement: "I would like to find out whether you see some way of talking and reaching mutual understanding with our neighbors, the Arab peoples."[69]

More than fifty years before his meeting with the Jamal family, Ben-Gurion had an original idea for the local Arabs: he wanted to integrate the peasants among them within the Jewish population. In an essay he published in 1917 in New York, titled "About the Origins of the *Falahiyun*,"[70] he distinguished between three types of Palestinians: Arabs who came from the Arab Peninsula; urban Arabs, who held strong national positions and were difficult to confer with; and the villagers, the *Falahiyun*, who were the majority among the peasants of Palestine. He was convinced that the later originated from the Jewish peasants left in the country, and particularly in the Galilee, after the failed revolt of Bar Kochba in 136 CE.

Together with Yitzhak Ben-Zvi, he tried to find out the historical origins of the Arabs in Israel—a research that relied on insufficiently supported historical assumptions—and concluded that the Jews who were left in Palestine after the revolt were the poor ones. Therefore, they weren't strict on keeping the religious laws and understanding their meaning. After the land was occupied by the Muslims in the seventh century, the Jewish peasants were impressed with the fact that the Muslims believed in a single god, unlike the Christians and their Holy Trinity. They felt religious proximity toward them.

Their motivation to become Muslims was based, so he thought, on two aspects: Their desire to stay in Palestine, and the financial consideration—by becoming Muslims, they exulted themselves from heavy taxes imposed upon non-Muslims. "The highest majority of the Muslim *Falahiyun* in Western Eretz Israel presents a different racial profile and a complete ethnic group, and there's no doubt that they have a lot of Jewish blood flowing in their veins—the blood of those Jewish peasants, the common people, who chose, under pressure, to deny their religion in order to stay in their country,"[71] he wrote.

His main objective in this essay was not to find out the origins of the *Falahiyun*, but rather to prove that the link between the Jews and their land was never cut off completely, even during exile. But an additional result was his belief that his historical theses could be translated into a practical move. He wanted to bring the *Falahiyun* back to their natural ethnic origin: the Jewish people.

His plan was received with bewilderment and resistance, which made him abandon it quickly. But he did make another attempt at implementing the basic idea—solving a part of the national conflict by integrating the local Arabs into the Jewish people—after the state was established. This time he referred to the Bedouins, particularly those who were friendlier toward the state and served in the military. He even explained that culturally, they were very similar to the Jews who came from the Atlas Mountains.[72]

In the spirit of this idea, he called Moshe Dayan and Haim Levakov in 1956 and instructed them to "Jewdify" the Bedouins—a term used in an attempt to overcome the resistance of religious circles to their conversion into Judaism. But the first religion minister, Rabbi Fishman of *Ha-Mizrahi* party, was not the only one who objected the plan. Military officials and Bedouin leaders were also confused. Finally, Dayan was the one who convinced him that the attempt to "Jewify" a few thousands of Bedouins will fail, and raise objection and anger in the Muslim world.

The echoes of that long-abandoned plan might have been the ones that caused Ben-Gurion to open his meeting with the Jamal family with another question: "Forgive me, this is another matter, but why do you pronounce 'b' instead of 'p'? Why 'bolitics' and not 'politics'?" Ben-Gurion had the most intriguing talent to throw unexpected questions, which seemed out of context. Usually, however, his question had a deep hidden meaning, even when the people he talked to could not understand it at first. It was an awkward moment, and the Jamal family members felt uncomfortable, but they responded that it was a habit. He urged them to overcome it, if it was really only a habit.[73]

After exhausting secondary issues, he asked for an advice that would help in promoting peace with the Palestinians and the Arab states. Mustafa Jamal's answer was similar to the one presented by Mussa Alami in their last conversation: "You must help the young generation in the West Bank, give them opportunities to improve their life, and talk to the Palestinians directly." Ben-Gurion, who refused to use the word "Palestinians," pretended he didn't understand: "You mean the Arabs in the West Bank?"[74]

The conversation moved on to the War of Independence, and Ben-Gurion asked why the Arabs "ran away." The Jamal family members—whether it was because they wanted to respect him, or because they truly believed it—didn't reject his basic assumption: The refugee problem was created because the Palestinians ran away on their own accord, fearing that the Jews would kill them, and believing that the Arab states will recover, win the war, conquer the land, and bring them back to their homes soon enough.

This time, Ben-Gurion was not interested merely in confirming his position. He wanted to find out whether, despite the national grudges created by wars, there is a possibility of shared existence. He wondered whether the Israeli Arabs could serve as a bridge between Jews and Arabs in the Middle East in general, and particularly in the Occupied Territories, and asked them about the education in Judea and Samaria and the number of university students. He was direct and to the point, although it was evident that he was no longer familiar with current events. The Old Man was surprised when Mustafa suggested that Israel should be encouraged to invest in various industries in the Occupied Territories, while he was under the impression that agriculture was still the main source of livelihood over there.

The main axis of the conversation was his attempt, probably inspired by his conversations with Alami, to find out whether Israel could find moderate Palestinian representatives for direct talks. He promised: "While I no longer belong to any party, I can connect the young leaders with leading figures in Israel."[75] His willingness to assist in finding a leadership among the Arabs in the Occupied Territories suggests, again, that while he refused to acknowledge the Palestinian nationality in public, he did realize that the West Bank Arabs were a distinguished political unit.

Ending the conversation, Ben-Gurion predicted: "In the next 50 years, if humanity is not destroyed by a nuclear war, there will be world peace." His argument was that the great wars of the nineteenth and twentieth centuries were influenced by Europe, and no European country was still eager to fight. Again, he expressed optimist concerning the peace with Egypt. Just like he told Dayan, he explained that unlike the Egyptian leadership, the Egyptian people are not interested in a war, but rather in changing their financial situation, and that the young intellectuals will lead to the change of regime. "I won't get to see it, but you might."[76]

7

After going to Charles de Gaulle's funeral, Ben-Gurion had already resolved that this would be his last trip abroad. But he changed his mind on February 1971. In a fit of stubbornness, he announced that he was going to speak at the World Jewish Congress in Brussels. It wasn't the most important convention of his life. But he believed in the historical significance of the main title: The right of the USSR Jews to immigrate to Israel. The Jewish immigration to Israel was the main pillar the state should be based on once its territorial goals are fulfilled, so he believed.

Like in so many other significant occasions in his life, his fever went up before the convention. The link between body and soul was evident in his case, and since he often developed high fever before significant occasions, this phenomenon was diagnosed as psychosomatic.[77] During the flight, he even developed symptoms of pneumonia. He flew without his doctor, and had to wait for the landing, breathing heavily, slumped heavily in his chair, with Lova Eliav and his bodyguard, who were worried about his health.[78]

Ben-Gurion was a strong man. Even at eighty-five, he was willing to take on the hard work that younger people rejected. But his health had been shaky since he was a young boy. When he came to Palestine and started working as an agricultural laborer in Sejera, he suffered from malaria and tended to faint. The physical effort and the mental stress related to his work as prime minister affected him in the 1950s, and he suffered severe back pains and recurrent dizziness. In an attempt to relieve his back pains—which attacked, among other occasions, before his meeting with President Truman in 1951—he used a primitive treatment method, which he nevertheless found efficient: Sticks tied to his back.

The dizziness, however, was harder to deal with. In the late 1950s, when he was bedridden for about a month due to dizziness, he was afraid he couldn't go on. He consulted senior doctors, but none of them could find a cure for his dizziness. After a long search, he was diagnosed with a rare condition, Ménière's Disease, which affects balance due to a problem in the inner ear.

Prof. Efrayim Katzir recommended that he see Dr. Moshe Feldenkrais, who developed an innovative system: physical exercises that strain the muscles, accelerate blood circulation, and improve balance.[79] One of the exercises was particularly tricky: standing on one's head.

Dr. Feldenkrais was controversial as a physician, but Ben-Gurion accepted the challenge and started mastering the exercises. Initially, he fell a lot, but he continued to practice until the mission was accomplished.[80] When he was in the right mood, after he gained confidence in his abilities, he would invite his assistants and some photojournalists to witness the charm, as if teasing them: The prime minister stands on his head at the beach. The photos taken by Paul Goldman became some of his most famous images.

The exercises did the job. His health was improved, and he also insisted on his daily walks, 2.5 miles in each direction, every morning and every evening. His enthusiasm of his ability to stand on his head—he used to tease his body-guards for not being able to do it—wasn't shared by Paula, who perceived it as a useless trick. She preferred the health advices she learned during her internship in the United States. Whenever Feldenkrais would come to train her husband, she would snap: "Here comes Mr. Hocus-Pocus."[81]

Ben-Gurion attributed significance to his health and physical strength almost like the political challenges he faced. Inspired by Max Nordau and his school of "muscle Jew," he believed that a healthy soul should reside in a healthy body. Personally, he was too old to portray the model of the "new Jew," the strong, toned native, but he never gave up his walks and standing on his head.

At the age of sixty-eight, when he was the defense minister, he even requested to try parachuting as a soldier. His assistants were anxious about the danger in parachuting and tried to persuade him to let it go. But he insisted on parachuting with the red berets. The crisis was averted only when the Dayan, the chief of staff at the time, intervened and told Ben-Gurion that if he wanted to be a soldier, he must obey orders, and Dayan ordered him to avoid it.[82]

Almost two decades had passed since those days of glory. Now, all he wanted to achieve during his flight to Brussels was to breathe evenly. Upon landing, he was exhausted, suffering from chills and a deep, dry cough. There was no doubt he wouldn't be able to speak in the opening ceremony as he planned. But during the couple of days in which he was lying, sick, in his hotel bed, he kept announcing that he will get through it and make the speech at the convention.[83]

Two days later, his entourage was surprised to find him better, and he offered to speak at the convention's final session. While he probably under-stood that the convention itself had no influence over the chance to open the gates of the USSR, he was willing to do anything as part of the effort of encouraging immigration. When an old Jew wrote to him she wanted to immigrate, but was afraid she couldn't afford the rent payments, he offered her to come and live in his cabin. He even prepared his family members for the roommate he was going to get at the age of eighty-five, but eventually it never happened.[84]

At the last day of the convention, he went up to the stand, pail and tired. The only compromise reached with his doctors was that he would give up the long speech he was going to give in English, and read a shortened Hebrew version instead. "Three great doctors suggested I should stay in bed," he opened his speech with a smile, talking in untypical quiet voice. He had no great news to portray; the significance of his speech was his ability to give it. He said that even after everything he's been through in his life, he was still excited to know that there were Jews out there who were willing to sit in jail because of their insistence to get to Israel, and that the era of exile gathering was not over yet.[85] The applause he got, so it seemed, suggested that beyond listening to his speech, people just wanted to witness his miraculous presence. For him, anyway, the mission was completed successfully, although when he got back, he did admit that he might have made an excessive effort. "An exhausting trip," he wrote.[86] The journey ended with a long healing vacation in Tiberias.[87] This was the last time he boarded a plane for a trip abroad.

Chapter 8

Memorandum

1

Generally speaking, Ben-Gurion's years after his retirement from the Knesset can be described as one long, uneventful stretching continuance; but this statement is based on a too-wide historical perspective. The year 1971, more than a year after his retirement from the Knesset, around his eighty-fifth birthday, marked the beginning of a new act in the final chapter of his life's play. A generous one, filled with a more reconciled atmosphere.

While his bitterness could not be completely dissolved, the pain and frustration he felt upon retiring were now blurred by a certain acceptance, recognition of the fact that his defiance could not make a change, and there was no point fighting his fate anymore. The facts of life had spoken. He no longer seemed to be the furious Old Man, who was judging reality and looking for a way to make it right; now he became a much softened version of himself. He stopped blaming *Mapai* for his inability to find a political home, and declared: "I'm only a member of the *Histadrut*. Beyond that, I am a member of the Jewish people and of human kind."[1] The depressing retrospective over his recent years was starting to be replaced by a wider perspective of the state's achievements. Bitter, raging Ben-Gurion, who declared upon retiring from the Knesset that "The State of Israel does not exist yet," started talking differently.

> I doubt if we could have a better state. We did the best we could, considering the circumstances. There is much to be done yet. The Negev has a space for millions of Jews. But I still remember Beer-Sheva as a Bedouin town without a single Jew in it. Today, it's a pure Jewish venture. The population is nearing 100 thousand people and growing. There were some mistakes, but the overall is

positive—extremely positive even. I only regret the things that were not done. I would like to see today in Israel not 3 million Jews, but 10. But I know this wouldn't be achievable in a year or two.[2]

While he still wasn't able to acknowledge his own mistakes, he did allow himself some self sense of humor when he said: "I don't know a single person in the world who never made mistakes, but if I did, I'm not aware of them."[3] His statements concerning the dissident organizations in the prestate era were also softened. The reason was his understanding of the expected development of ideological concepts, and mainly the weakening of the Zionist aspect. During the 1970s, when Israel was already a natural political phenomenon, the debate regarding disobedience during the *Yishuv* era was replaced by comparisons, both by outside elements and by the Israeli left, between the undergrounds and the terrorist organizations striving to free Palestine. In this context, he concluded that his ongoing dispute with the underground organizations, as part of the struggle over the intra-Jewish narrative, was becoming pointless. And so he found himself, in a historically ironic move, defending their actions:

> They did some grave things, and I'm sure they regret them today. I am talking about Altalena. But the *IZL* and the *Lehi* never meant to exterminate Arabs. Fatah and The Popular Front want to exterminate Jews. I opposed the Jewish terrorists, but they are different from the Arab terrorists. The Jewish terrorists fought against the British. Then, there were a few operations against Arabs. But I'm sure that any historian, who learns the issue carefully, won't be able to tie together the Arab terrorist organizations and the Jewish undergrounds. It would be impossible, even from a long perspective.[4]

On a similar note, one can also understand his more tolerant attitude toward Menachem Begin. Unlike his warnings against Begin before his retirement from premiership, in 1971, Begin no longer posed a threat to the Israeli establishment; he was already an integral part of it. Ideologically, Ben-Gurion continued to oppose his way, but now he no longer viewed the Altelana affair as a potential revolt, and defined it merely as "stupidity."[5] He added: "The man who did it back then, I am certain he wouldn't have done Altelana today."[6] This transformation of his view of the affair did not make him regret the attack on the *IZL*'s ship. As someone who tended to avoid psychological diagnoses, and against the Kantian concept, the Old Man believed that a person's acts, and not their intentions, dictate the attitude toward them (just like he couldn't understand the mental motivations of *Mapai* leaders when they became his rivals). So, he explained, even if, in hindsight, he learned that Begin had no intention of rebelling against the government's authority—as prime minister, he wasn't supposed to wonder about what Begin "intended to do or didn't intend to do."[7]

Additionally, one cannot ignore the personal aspect, which was another reason for his moderated approach toward Begin. Ben-Gurion was grateful for the fact that Begin suggested to make him prime minister just when he reached rock bottom, when he was watching Eshkol leading the state in the waiting period before 1967 War and his heart was bleeding. "I couldn't believe my ears," he recounted those days, excited. "The man I always said about: 'I will have an extended coalition, but not with his party,' comes to me and proposes that I'll be the leader."[8] Replying a citizen who expressed his wonderment about Ben-Gurion's moderate expressions toward Begin, he wrote:

> I resented the acts of *Herut* before the state was established, and a few years after. I'm not sorry about it and I don't regret my opposition [...] But actually, I must say that today's Begin is not pre-Six Day War Begin. Reality has also changed, and things the *IZL* did before and after the state's establishment are not to be done today. As a human being, Begin is an honest man. He was the man who came to me before 1967 War and demanded that I replace Eshkol as defense minister, and only after I turned him down (since my retirement from the government in 1963 was final, based on statist considerations) he demanded that Moshe Dayan will replace Eshkol.[9]

This chapter in Ben-Gurion-Begin relationship was not necessarily a romantic one; rather, it was another proof of life's power of influencing human beings. Time softens sharp edges and dulls the pain. After all, there were definitely days when the Old Man could ignore his feelings, just like he rejected Paula's request to leave Lavon alone when he was sick. But years have gone by, and now, when he needed some comfort and support, Ben-Gurion was no longer willing to discuss the principle question:

Is it possible that Begin had also a political interest when he offered a national union government, a move that paved *Herut*'s path into the coalition for the first time in the history of the state?[10]

2

Obviously, Ben-Gurion's diary was no longer what it used to be. During the decades of writing in his diary, it included reports, reflections, speeches, and stories; so much so, that the diary was seen at times to have a life of its own, as a soul mate. Now, the diary was no longer documenting any crucial storyline, but he still continued to write, although not daily, especially about his feelings, moments of satisfaction and disappointment, things that were less common during his heyday. Indeed, the Old Man always knew how to weave some lighter tones into his writing. When he met a foreign diplomat who made him angry, he concluded it was a meeting with "an ugly woman";[11]

when he got a visit from an American preacher, he noted that he met "a young woman, décolletage."[12] But those expressions were rare. Since he retired from the Knesset, his diary became more expressive, and he poeticized about a thirteen-year-old boy who played music "with a great talent" in Paula's memorial service, or about his happiness when he spent some quality time with his daughter, Renana, and his great-grandchild Uri.[13]

Now, he started allowing himself to enjoy a little the silence enforced on him, appreciate the freedom, and observe life from the outside. It was obvious he wanted to refute the image created for him, the one of the oh-so-vindictive bitter father of the nation. "Whatever happened—I forgot it,"[14] he concluded in a conversation with Mordechai Ben-Porat, who came to visit him, his current approach to past struggles. Yosef Almogi heard the same words.[15] He wasn't interested in rivalries anymore, and his only wish was to pass on the torch, to have a dignified farewell. A prime evidence for his abandoned struggles was his decision to send a copy of his memoir to the prime minister with a personal inscription: "To sassy and wise Golda, with appreciation and criticism."[16] While he didn't give up his "criticism," the mere fact he wrote an inscription signaled he no longer wished to denounce here, and that he realized he must adjust to life's halftones. And so, approaching his eighty-fifth birthday, the man who once defined himself as "a man of strife and struggle" now declared: "There is not one person in this country—dead or alive—who I still begrudge. I am interested only in the future now."[17]

His desire to discuss the future only was, probably, a reflection of his attempt to make peace with his past, but also a continuation of his life-long approach: History may be fascinating as an intellectual exercise, but one cannot deduce from it anything about the future. As prime minister, he had told IDF officers:

> Historical situations are almost always one-of-a-kind, and just like we must study previous periods and our history in the land, the history of the IDF and past wars, we must also see, if we want to be ready for future events, to learn the unique properties of our own time, and not make the mistake and be misled by historical examples that will never repeat themselves.[18]

Indeed, the Israeli society went through tremendous changes during the third decade of its existence. Financial transformations and cultural influences from Western countries were infiltrating Israel, slowly but steadily. The state's profile was different from the one familiar to the Old Man: By 1971, Shlomo Artzi won Singer of the Year; one of the most successful bestsellers, *Lapid's Guide to Europe* by Yosef Lapid, urged Israelis to explore new global experiences; more and more Israelis dressed according to the latest fashion trends—Ben-Gurion was oblivious to all of these development, and anyway, he was isolated in Sde Boker. He wasn't even skilled enough in telephonic small talk. Often, he would put down the receiver having finished his message, or ending with "goodbye" while the person on the other side was still talking.[19] He was also estranged from the first appearances of extravagance he encountered in early 1970s Israel. As someone who was used to ceremonies and celebrations in the spirit of *Mapai* tradition, he was surprised by the variety of private cars and houses he spotted during his road trips. During a reception at the wedding of Haim Yisraeli's daughter, he called his loyal assistant, looked at him closely and inquired: "How much did it cost you?" Yisraeli, who was surprised by the question, explained awkwardly that he will get the bill only after the celebration was over.[20] When Renana was excited to show him the house she bought on in Tzahala neighborhood in Tel Aviv, he wondered: "All that is yours? Why does a person need a carpet, a curtain, and a lamp shade? All one needs is a bed, a desk, and a book shelf."[21]

Official representatives were sometimes sent to update him on security matters—a representative from the Mossad reported about Israel's involvement with the Ethiopian Jews and the cholera epidemic over there.[22] But as far as culture and society were concerned, his distance from Israeliness was constantly growing. For example, he kept silent during the public debate that broke out in 1971 following Hanoch Levin's play, Queen of the Bathtub, which mocked the army and the Israeli arrogance after 1967 War.

Ben-Gurion had always defended the IDF, even when he had to lie. In October 1953, after Unit 101 with its commander, Ariel Sharon, conducted a reprisal operation in the village of Qibya, which resulted in the killing of sixty-nine people, half of them women and children, he insisted that the accusations against the IDF were a "fantastic lie," and explained that the incident might have ensued from a local operation by the residents, who suffered by the hands of the *Fidayun*.[23] Now, when asked about his position concerning the conflict that surrounded the play (which was played out only 19 times), he only confessed: "I'm not a theater or movie goer, and I know nothing about this play."[24]

Similarly, when he was asked about his opinion concerning *Michtav Ha-Shministim* (The Letter of High-School Seniors)—a letter sent to Golda Meir by some high-school graduates in protest against the occupation and the lack of peace efforts—he just said: "Generally, I don't appreciate Hebrew words which end with ist-nist." The new Israeli jargon didn't bother him as much as the fact that he was no longer familiar with the state of mind of these high-school graduates. Therefore, he avoided the subject. Only when asked again, he said: "Everyone has the right to criticize."[25]

It was only natural. At the age of eighty-five, the Old Man could no longer be involved in every cultural and social aspect in the state he had established.

And still, it was a somewhat sad realization, the fact that the man who was in on everything was no longer familiar with crucial issues.

Yet, he never stopped believing in the high quality of what he called "the youth."[26] Toward the end of the 1950s, he was already worried by the loss of the pioneering aspect among the younger generations, and arranged conventions where he preached Zionism to teenagers. Yet, he felt that the young people of the 1970s, who allegedly freed themselves of the burden of Zionism and were no longer speaking his language, represented a different kind of quality. He acknowledged the differences in culture and manners between the young people of his time and those of today, but recognized it as an advantage. "The young people of today lack the rhetoric of previous ages, and sometimes they even like to talk nonsense. But they are good young people. I doubt whether there are youth like them in the world. Maybe just in Japan."[27] The proof of their superiority was found in the book *Siah Lohamim* (Fighters' Conversations), in which the soldiers of the victorious army from 1967 War described their hesitations concerning the War's moral justification. He found in this book the combination he wished to instill in the IDF soldiers: The ability to hold both a gun and a moral standard.

> I doubt if you'll find such literature anywhere in the world—winning soldiers who talk like that [...] This is why the youth of our generation are better than those of the Hashmoneans [...] I doubt if there were ever such youth in the history of the Jewish People, and I know the old argument: "The youth of last year were better than today's, and those of the year before were even better." I said to myself: If they are right, we will sink deeper and deeper each year. Thank God they weren't right. Today's youth are dedicated pioneers, even if their words are laced with cynicism. I regret only one thing: Today's youth are unfamiliar with Jewish history, or the history of the state's establishment. I am writing my memoir so the youth will know about the good and bad things that had been done.[28]

3

While current culture was already alienated from him and his lifestyle, his perception of the deep currents of social processes in Israel was still precise, and he warned against problems that were not yet exposed in the fullest. Against the background of the Black Panthers' social protest—second generation Jews from Eastern countries who protested against their discrimination, he called the government to provide better housing and education options, and not to hide behind the argument that most of the budget was dedicated to security-related issues.[29]

At the same time, he continued to perceive the "melting pot" as a required practice, necessary for building the nation according to the "new Jew" model.

The effort required from the newcomers was necessary for the creation of a modern, engaged nation, based on Biblical values and scientific advancement. The "melting pot" was also meant to uproot what Ben-Gurion perceived as a patriarchal, unproductive culture, which was based on irrational beliefs, and was held by many new immigrants. As the product of nineteenth-century rationalism, Ben-Gurion didn't recognize the relativist, postmodern view, which respects different "truths" without trying to judge them. He believed in modern science, cultural hierarchy, and the right narrative versus the wrong one. Aristotle, Socrates, and Plato were the most important philosophers in ancient times, he thought, due to their tendency to look for the "truth" in life through rational inquiry.[30] Any attempt to understand and contain cultures which were wrong, in his eyes, would be against his truth. As a "transformational" leader—versus the "rewarding" leader like Begin or the "instructional" leader like Levi Eshkol and Yitzhak Shamir[31]—Ben-Gurion required constant effort and strive for improvement from the Israeli people.

That was also the reason he objected the method of affirmative action, which was presented in the 1970s as a way of fixing the melting pot's damages. "There is no discrimination in Israel, but there is deprivation," he distinguished between the idea he positioned as the society's foundation and its implementation:

> Not everything was done properly. The point is, we need a different education. I would very much like to see a Yemeni at a senior position. But I wouldn't like a Mizrahi president just because he came from there. We can't accept someone just because they come from a specific origin. This is discrimination as well. The problem is education. Many people, who were over 14 years old when they came to Israel, weren't raised properly. When people study, they understand. There is already a big change, but it is not enough. There is a problem. Those who came from Europe are still wealthier. There are still differences between origins, differences which shouldn't exist. But it's not what it used to be.[32]

The gap between Ashkenazi and Mizrahi Israelis was, in his eyes, a socioeconomic problem, or, alternatively, the result of a distorted phsyco-historic perception, which was developed in Jews during the years in exile and created hierarchies between different communities. "The gap problem must be perceived as a gap between Jews and Jews, not Ashkenazi and Sephardic Jews, because there are wealthy Sephardi Jews who ignore the poor, just like their Ashkenazi counterparts."[33]

He did, however, change his position concerning death penalties in Israel. As prime minister, he objected the idea: "Principally speaking, no man and no institution should have the right to kill a human being; practically, a verdict might be wrong, and we can't bring the dead back to life [...] I tend to support those who object death penalty."[34] But following the series of terrorist attacks in the early 1970s, he concluded that the state had no means to deter them except death penalty. This was the focus of his last public battle, trying to convince the political and judicial systems that death penalty should be used.

> The Arabs in Israel—both inside the Green Line and in the Occupied Territories—should be treated equally and be granted equal rights. But Israel must be defended against terrorism. We are making a mistake. Terrorists should be hanged, and not sent to jail. The threat of death will scare potential killers, and they will be deterred by the possibility of being hanged. What happens to them when we catch them? We put them in jail, take care of them, give them education. What do they have to lose? But if they know it might cost them their life, there won't be so many great heroes.[35]

In a conversation with the defense minister, he said there was no need for a special law, and proposed to make use of the law that enabled the execution of Adolf Eichmann. "The law that refers to death sentence for those who perform 'murder with the intention of genocide' can be applied on terrorists as well."[36]

4

In the midst of 1971, Ben-Gurion was waiting for a word from the printing house: The first volume of his memoir, which included mainly raw materials, was about to be published. Encouraged, he already planned another short literary project: An essay about the transformation in Israel-USSR relations. His motivation came from an entry in the Soviet Encyclopedia, which presented Israel as a colonialist venture. He was furious to read the "distorted and forged description; such lies and distortions can appear in a scientific publication only under the current Russian regime."[37] His fury was raised particularly by the presentation of Jews as ungrateful, after the Russians had supported the establishment of their state. "Those busters are not saying what really happened. They can only say that they demanded the establishment of a Jewish state."[38]

But before he started writing, he was faced with disappointment. The book defined as the first part of his memoir was presented to the public in two heavy, uninspiring volumes. His memoir was a kind of biographical hybrid: Only the first thirteen chapters out of a total of eighty-four were written as an autobiography. The rest were actually a collection of documents. Historians were quick to read it and publish their reviews, but when the press and the public discovered that the books included only a few new impressions about figures and events from the state's history, they lost interest pretty quickly.[39]

Years of anticipation for a book he worked so hard on died out in a whisper. While he never admitted it openly, he knew the result was disappointing and didn't generate any real interest. His vented his frustration, of all things, by complaining about his photo on the book cover—a photo that presented him as a somewhat unkempt old man, with a kind expression, which was meant to portray him as someone looking back with satisfaction. Before the book was published, he paid no notice to the photo. In light of the cool reactions, he insisted on replacing the photo with the one that appeared on the cover of his previous book, *Medinat Israel Ha-Mehudeshet* (The Renewed State of Israel), where his expression was firm and determined. His demand embarrassed his staff. Desperately, they tried to explain that the books were already printed, and it would look weird to change the photo now, but he insisted, holding on to the argument that the photo was doing the book injustice.[40]

After his photo-induced rage subsided, he said no more about the chilled reception of his book, which was supposed to be his final life project. The lack of enthusiasm seemed to ease some of the tension he felt, as if there was some relief in knowing that he won't be able to complete his literary mission.

He did continue to work on the next volume of his memoir, but the pace was slower. He blamed it on two elements that wouldn't allow him to complete his mission—letters from abroad and visitors[41]—but it seems that the responses to his first volume discouraged him a little. The order in his den, which was necessary for his writing, was gradually lost. The files he prepared were mounted on the desk, hiding the glass with the photos of his grandchildren and Paula underneath; the paper clips were spread around the wooden chairs. One day, Mazal, the housekeeper, found a photo of Berl Katznelson, which was usually positioned at the end of his desk, sitting on one of the archives' shelves.[42]

Beyond the aforementioned reasons for his failure to write his autobiography, we may ask why Ben-Gurion, who wasn't in the habit of making empty promises, insisted on writing more and fulfill his mission, despite the disappointment of the first volume. The explanation involves two key reasons: The first has to do with a letter he wrote in 1968 to the mother of his bodyguard, Aharon Eldan, in response to her question about one crucial and essential conclusion he got from his life. He responded: "The main thing I learned in life was that words without deeds are worthless. It is a simple but necessary truth, and not many acknowledge its significance."[43] Indeed, being active was his recipe for eternal redemption. It wasn't just a philosophical outlook on life; being active was necessary for him in order to continue feeling needed, existent, a human being.

But there may have been another reason. Ben-Gurion declared his intention to author further volumes, but it was no coincidence that he prioritized the collecting of historical documents over the actual writing of a narrative.

As a person who was a Biblical prophet in the modern era, his main inter-est—despite his declarations to the contrary—was not an autobiography that would attract attention of his and younger generations. He knew that his impact in Jewish history will be examined for centuries ahead. Just like Bibli-cal heroes, who never wrote an autobiography, but rather were immortalized by the books that were written about them in the Bible—his undeclared wish was to collect the archival materials that would direct future researchers in writing his story.

5

A short while after the publication of his book, he found a substitute of a kind for his autobiography by venting his grievances in conversations with *Ba-Mahane* journalists. As mentioned before, intimate revelation was not one of his strong suits. In many ways, he despised such acts of mental exposure. But this time, he talked in details about his feelings, family, childhood home, and upbringing.

As part of the interview, he mentioned the three books that shaped his worldview: Avraham Mapu's *Ahavat Zion* ("The Love of Zion," translated into English under the title *Amnon, Prince and Peasant*), which was consid-ered to be the first Hebrew novel, and described in a biblical fancy language the life of the Jews in the days of the kings Hezekiah and Isaiah (interestingly, the title of Mapu's second book, *'Ayit Tzavua*—"Hypocrite Eagle" was the nickname given to Pinhas Lavon by Ben-Gurion);[44] Harriet Beecher Stowe's *Uncle Tom's Cabin*, the famous nineteenth-century novel about the suffering of a black slave serving his master loyally; and Leo Tolstoy's *Resurrection*, which tells the story of the Russian peasants before the Bolshevik revolution.

The books he chose were fine testimonies of their reader. They could explain the ideological foundation for his social-Zionist worldview, as well as his hystoriosophic tendency to secularize the holy Bible and bring it into the national-ethical realm. He explained: "Mapu's stories revived the stories of the Bible, which I was studying at the time, and enhanced my longing for the Land of Israel"; "*Uncle Tom's Cabin* created a strong resentment against slavery, oppression and dependency"; while after reading *Resurrection*, he said, he became vegetarian.[45] But since he couldn't find vegetarian food in Israel, he started eating meat again, until his final years, when he stopped eat-ing beef, although chicken remained a part of his diet.[46]

His longing for those innocent times were joined by his nostalgic feelings toward his strict upbringing as a child, despite his suffering: The first time he felt the taste of a physical and mental slap was when his father hit him after he had stopped wearing *Tefillin*.[47] Now, he saw himself as a reflection of his father. "He was a famous lawyer and many of Plonsk's 5,000 Jews needed his advice. Yet, he was a rebel at heart, and made many enemies for himself. I guess I got from him,"[48] he said with a laugh.

Ben-Gurion wasn't completely honest when he described his relationship with his father, Avigdor Green, as ideal (nor was he accurate when describing his father as a proper lawyer, although he did represent people in front of the local court). Their relationship had known many ups and downs over the years. In late 1903, when Ben-Gurion was sick with malaria and couldn't support himself properly in Palestine, he partly blamed his father for his distress. In a letter to his father, he wrote angrily that the father shouldn't have misled him with false promises of financial support. "We both did a terrible mistake: You committed yourself to something that was too much for you, and I agreed to live under conditions that might destroy all my physical and moral strength."[49] During the 1930s, Avigdor Green decided to immigrate to Palestine, and asked his son to assist him in getting a certificate. Ben-Gurion, who was the *Histadrut* Secretary at the time, rejected him. He explained that due to his position, he didn't want to spread the rumor that he was using his power for a family interest[50] (yet, he gladly assisted his sister, Tzipora, in her immigration. Her husband, Moshe Kortini, was murdered in his clinic in Poland, probably by anti-Semitics, and Ben-Gurion got her a certificate, claiming she was his wife[51]).

Ben-Gurion's biographer, Shabtai Teveth, argued that his relationship with his father was tainted by his anger over the father's second marriage two years after his mother had died. Ben-Gurion himself never provided details, but interestingly, he never included his father's second marriage in his memoir and stories, and called his stepmother "aunty" in his letters to his father.[52]

Even when Avigdor Green did manage to get to Palestine, verging on seventy, their relationship was fragile. The father found a job as a clerk in an accounting office, and lived alternatively with his two daughters, Rivka and Tzipora. Despite their complicated relationship, Green made an effort to come to all his son's conventions, and was very proud of his leadership. One of those days, in the summer of 1934, when he was riding the bus to Haifa with his grandson, he heard one of the passengers curse Ben-Gurion. In response, he tried to hit the man with his walking stick, but luckily, hit only the bus's ceiling.[53]

Green passed away in 1942, while Ben-Gurion was encompassed with the Biltmore Conference, which was arranged in New York at the height of World War II and revolved around the future of Palestine.

Unlike his relative estrangement toward his father, Ben-Gurion used to tell that he never got over the death of his mother, who passed away when he was eleven years old. "The death of my mother, Sheindel, was the toughest blow I suffered as a child, and I felt the pain for many years after. I miss her to this day. A part of my world was gone with her."[54] Talking to his daughter, Geula, he remembered his mother's love fondly. He said that his mother used to take him to summer vacations in a village near Plonsk because of his fragile health, and stressed that it was only for him that she was willing to leave the house for a long period of time.[55] His version wasn't accurate: He failed to mention the fact that Tzipora, his sister, was also with included in those trips. There was, however, something touching in his insistence, at the age of almost 85, to fight for his position as his mother's preferred child.

David was the third out of five children. The relationships between the siblings were also complex. Avraham, the eldest, was the only religious member of the family, and a member of Ha-Mizrahi movement. He came to Palestine in 1943, and was known for his hot temper. In Palestine, he took part in confrontations with non-Zionist religious circles, and blamed the Gur Rabbis for not warning the Jews of Poland against the dangers of the Holocaust. His life ended in a tragedy: Less than two years after coming to Palestine, he was beaten with sticks by Gur Hassidim and was never the same again. He died on April 18, 1945.

Rivka, the sister who was born five years before David, didn't have a close relationship with Ben-Gurion as well. She came to Palestine in 1931 and settled in Borochov neighborhood in Tel Aviv. She was widowed at a young age, and remarried at fifty to Yehuda Har-Melah. His relationship with his younger sister, Tzipora, was closer, although she was also disappointed when he settled for a consolation letter when her second husband, Friedman Levov, passed away in 1953.[56]

His youngest brother, "Michel," was different: He had no interest in ideologies and was occupied with managing his snack shop. Although they were practically neighbors, the brothers David and Michel saw each other only rarely. Michel, who maintained his original surname, kept working until he was eighty-four, and according to the rumors among the shop's costumers in the 1950s, he was a supporter of *Herut* and Menachem Begin.[57]

Disappointment with Ben-Gurion's attitude was also created in more distant branches of the family. In 1964, when his cousin Hagay, the son of his uncle Arie, got married, Ben-Gurion and Paula were invited as the guests of honor. The Old Man, who was occupied at this stage of his life with his struggle against Levi Eshkol, was asked to talk about the bride's name—Shulamit. Without preparing ahead of time, he talked about the image of Ehud ben Gera, added a sarcastic political fable about *Mapai*, and held the guests' attention for almost an hour. Years later, Hagay and Shulamit still remembered how their famous relative almost destroyed their wedding.[58]

Ben-Gurion's relationships with his three uncles who immigrated to Chicago—David, Yehuda, and Nathan—were actually quite good. He met them and their children in Israel when they came to visit, but never mentioned them in his writings, mainly because they didn't implement the vision of settling the land and chose to live abroad.

6

At the end of 1971, David and Paula had three children, seven grandchildren, and two grand-grandchildren. His children visited him mainly during holidays and family occasions,[59] and were often reprimanded by Yehoshua Cohen for their scarce visits.[60] He didn't like talking about his relationships with his relatives, or about the relationships between his children.[61] As a father, he couldn't claim to be successful. In fact, he was present-absentee in his own house since his marriage in 1931. He left Paula a few minutes after their marriage for a meeting of *Poalei Tzion*'s committee. Just after she got pregnant, he announced that he was leaving in order to serve in the Jewish Legion. His family members knew that he was dedicated to the national project and didn't dare bothering him. During family gatherings, they would commit to silence every hour for the radio news broadcast. In family conversations, he would sometimes get lost in thoughts, writing political notes in his notebook.[62] Unlike Paula, who was committed to his lifestyle, his children were having a hard time accepting it.

His oldest daughter, Geula (1918–1998) was born in New York while he was away, serving in the Jewish Legion. Ben-Gurion, who hoped for a boy, planned to call him Yariv (derived from the Hebrew root of "struggle" or "fight"), named after the priest who came back to Zion with Ezra the Scribe and was supposed to "fight for our people."[63] When it turned out that Paula was going to have a daughter, he preferred the name Geula (redemption), his life's motto. Geula struggled to accept her father's attitude toward her. While she was a teenager, when she told her parents about one of her suitors, Ben-Gurion, serious and loving, said he was happy, and explained: "You are not a beautiful girl, but you have such beautiful suitors."[64] Her grievances about her relationship with her father caused her to leave her parents' home at a young age. "It's nice of you to finally remember you have a mother and a father and grace us with your letter,"[65] Ben-Gurion snapped at her once.

In 1937, Geula got married to Emanuel Ben-Eliezer, who worked at the Defense Ministry, and became a teacher. During World War II, when Emanuel considered joining the British Army, Ben-Gurion responded: "I can only tell you what I would do—I would enlist." Geula would prefer it if he had advised him to avoid it.[66] The Eliezers had two sons, Yariv and Moshe, and a daughter named Orit. Yariv became a communication professor, and Moshe specialized in psychology. Orit studied fashion and married Danny Etziony, an employee of the Israeli Military Industries who was known for his right-wing political views.

In his later years, Geula tried to take advantage of her father's detachment of politics in order to make him talk about the way he raised his children. He refused to talk about it: "There is no clear rule about the limit between familial and public commitment. The contradiction between family and public duties is uncomfortable, but you can't give up doing something else, something you must do, because of family commitments. It's not a question of importance; there are just things you must do."[67] Geula complained:

> There was no father in our house. Mom functioned as a father as well. There were no family holidays in our house. There were no family dinners on Saturday nights. Just once, when I was already married, we had a Passover dinner with both Mom and Dad. I remember these things clearly. There's no doubt they impacted me somehow. This is why I told myself: I will never marry a politician, or be a politician myself. When I saw the Sabbath dinner and the Kiddush at my in-law, the author Moshe Ben-Eliezer, I was jealous. I'm sure my brother, Amos, was also impacted by it. We were proud of our father, but we missed him very much. He never knew what grade we were on or how we did in our studies. He was dedicated to public affairs. This was his destiny. Somehow, he did remember he had three children, yes. He had a notebook with our birthdays. But Mom was the one who gave us our presents.[68]

Geula had complaints for Paula as well. She argued that Paula's attempt to defend her husband—"so we won't make noise, won't bother him"—prevented the creation of the natural, spontaneous connection between a father and his children.[69] When Ben-Gurion passed away, Geula refused to sit in the Shiva, arguing that her father did not appreciate religious rituals.

His son, Amos (1920–2008), grew up at the height of his father's activity as the *Yishuv* leader, and didn't get to spend much quality time with him. When he was nine, he once took his father's personal diary from his drawer and read it to his friends. Ben-Gurion slapped him. Amos never forgot the taste of this slap, and his father's many apologies after it.[70] Ben-Gurion acknowledged the fact that his son was missing a father figure. When Amos flunked in high-school, he said with regret: "When I'm old, I'll wonder if I gave enough to my children, and I'm sure that my unfortunate conclusion will be that I didn't give them enough attention. But I am busy, and not cut out for that. Make it easier for me."[71]

Amos volunteered to join the *Hagannah* and served as an officer in the British army during World War II. He was a Battalion Commander in the War of Independence, and later went on to develop a career in the Police. In 1955 he was accused by *Shurat Ha-Mitnadvim* (The volunteers' front)—a group that fought against corruption in Israel, and included Uri Avneri and Elyakim HaEtzni among others—that he illegally closed a criminal case of a friend,

Yeshaayahu Yarkoni (the husband of the singer Yaffa Yarkoni). Amos filed and won a libel suit (and was awarded damages). Ben-Gurion backed him up through his struggle to clear his reputation and assured him: "It's not you they are after. It's me. You are just the excuse."[72]

In 1958, Amos Ben-Gurion became a major general and was the active police vice-commander. Some hoped he would follow his father's footsteps, but he failed to comply. "Amos could have been the Chief Police Officer, but since it was up to me, I wouldn't let him, despite his leadership skills,"[73] Ben-Gurion regretted the turns in his son's life. After retiring from the police, Amos worked as the CEO of the textile company Ata. He married Merry and had two daughters, Galya and Ruthi, and a son named Alon.

Renana, Ben-Gurion's youngest daughter (1925–2008), a microbiology professor, was the closest to him out of his children. She maintained her distance from politics, and even asked her parents not to attend her wedding to engineer David Leshem, because she wanted to avoid the presence of politicians.[74] Ben-Gurion didn't complain, and when asked about the tailored suit he wore that day, he explained that this was his way of honoring "the celebration." Under Paula's pressure, Renana agreed to celebrate her marriage at a later occasion in her parents' home, which justified her fears: Hundreds of guests came to the occasion, and the groom had to wait in line in order to get into the house.[75] Renana and David had one son, Ori. In February 1970, a short while before his retirement from the Knesset, Ben-Gurion accepted Renana and David's request and presented an affidavit to the Ministry of Internal Affairs, asking to add the name Ben-Gurion to Ori's surname, Leshem.[76]

Now, seeing the loneliness of their father, his children tried to reach out to him, but he avoided their gestures, as if he was used to their loose connections. He hated being a burden. When Renana's husband offered they would come to live with him in his cabin, he retracted: "Don't you have your own apartment?"[77] Renana was so worried, she sometimes had to stalk him. One day, she was surprised to see his official car parked in front of his Tel Aviv house—they would usually meet when he left his cabin. She knocked on the door and found her father packing his things, getting ready to go back to Sde Boker. "Why didn't you tell me you were here, in Tel-Aviv?" She wondered. "I was here for two weeks, and now I'm going to the Kibbutz." He said. Renana was angry: "Two weeks and you haven't said a word?" And he replied: "I wanted to call you every day, but I didn't want to bother you."[78]

7

The man who couldn't nurture his relationships with his closest family members dedicated most of his time and effort to the past and future of the

Jewish people; or, to be more exact, to his attempt to revision of the Zionist historiography. He opposed the highlighted importance of his own generation, the Second Aliya, who were considered to be the founders of the local labor class[79] in the history of Zionism. The pioneering stories of this Aliya were a legend, he said:

> The Third *Aliyah* was much better than the Second *Aliyah*. I was a member of the Second *Aliyah*. While there were some good people in the Second *Aliyah*, they were very few. Less than ten percent of them stayed in Palestine. The Third *Aliyah* brought people who already learned Hebrew and were ready for agricultural work. They prepared themselves before they came, and learned agriculture. Most of the members of the Third *Aliyah* were much better than those of the Second. Except for the Fourth *Aliyah*—whose members were people who came to live in Palestine like they did in Poland and not to work—all the other *Aliyot* were better than the Second *Aliyah*.[80]

Now he made his disappointment known: "Most of the Second Aliya members used Arab laborers,"[81] and one can't ignore the fact that his criticism against his own generation had to do with his deep resentment against *Mapai*, which was originally based on the leaders of this Aliya.

He also resented the heroic aura given by historians and public figures to the suicide story of Yehuda extremists in Masada after their failed rebellion attempt against the Romans. While the story of Masada involved acts of heroism, which he usually preferred to nurture as founding myths of the revived nation, he rejected fatalist positions, and particularly those resulting in suicide. His criticism in this matter involved a hidden dispute with the Revisionist camp, with its historiographic tradition that emphasized the Second Temple period—between the Maccabean Revolt and Bar Kochba revolt—as a national role model.[82] "Masada is important as a historical story, and because they had to be brave to take their own lives. Yet, I cannot say they had to commit suicide."[83]

The greatest historical chapter in the Jewish history was the Bible times, so he believed. This was the statist and philosophical golden age of the nation, from which he wanted to draw inspiration for modern Israel. As part of his stubborn attempts to prove the ancient texts, he even said once, seriously, that during one of his visits to the Sinai Peninsula, he got to Kadesh Barne'a and saw water come out of a rock. He said that this might be the rock that Moshe hit in the Biblical story.[84]

His linkage to the Bible was reflected in two different aspects. First, he believed that the Bible was bringing man closer to a basic truth in his nature,[85] because it expresses an all-encompassing life philosophy. He found the "essence of Judaism and humanity" in a few selected Biblical verses:[86]

- "For thus saith the LORD that created the heavens, He is God; that formed the earth and made it, He established it (...) He formed it to be inhabited: I am the LORD, and there is none else" (Isaiah, 45:18)
- "[...] thou shalt love thy neighbor as thyself" (Leviticus, 19:18)
- "And if a stranger sojourn with thee in your land [...]" (Leviticus, 19:33), "and thou shalt love him as thyself; for ye were strangers in the land of Egypt [...]" (Leviticus, 19:34)
- I the LORD have called thee in righteousness (...) and set thee for a covenant of the people, for a light of the nations" (Isaiah, 42:6)
- [...] nation shall not lift up sword against nation, neither shall they learn war any more" (Isaiah, 2:4)
- "And I will turn the captivity of my people Israel, and they shall build the waste cities, and inhabit them; and they shall plant vineyards, and drink the wine thereof; they shall also make gardens, and eat the fruit of them. And I will plant them upon their land, and they shall no more be plucked up out of their land which I have given them, saith the LORD thy God" (Amos 9:14–15)

The second realm of his attitude toward the Bible was based on his famous declaration at the Peel Committee in 1937: "The Bible is our *Kushan* (ownership deed) for the Land of Israel." Thus, the holy book was also an educational and propaganda mean for establishing the people's linkage to the land. He stripped the Bible stories off their religious holiness so he could prove that the people of Israel was formed in Canaan as a nation with unique identity and characteristics, different from those of the peoples around them, even before the Exodus.[87] This conception was the basis for the first sentence of the Declaration of Independence—"The Land of Israel was the birthplace of the Jewish people," although anyone who reads the Bible will conclude that the people was formed in Egypt, based on their common religious faith, and wandered through the desert for forty years until they reached Canaan.

His aspiration to prove that the national aspect predated the religious one raised many disputes with Bible researchers,[88] but he stuck to his version and presented his own independent and original Biblical interpretations.[89] One of them was based on two chapters in the books Exodus and Numbers, where it was said that the population of Israel upon leaving Egypt was only "six hundred thousand" (*shishim ribo*). Ben-Gurion argued that since Jacob's family came to Egypt on its own, and came back to Canaan only two or three generations later, there was no way that this number was representing more than a few hundreds of people. Thus, he concluded that it was probably 600 people. But since 600 people cannot be called "a people," one must conclude that the Hebrew people, which Jacob's family was a part of, existed in Canaan even before the acceptance of the Tables of the Covenant, which proved that the national identity predated the religious faith.[90]

Another pillar for his theory was based on verses from Genesis (40:14–15), where Joseph says to Pharaoh's chief of the butlers: "For indeed I was stolen away out of the land of the Hebrews." This was another proof, he argued, that the land belonged to the Hebrew even before the Exodus.

The famous verse "Now the LORD said unto Abram: 'Get thee out of thy country, and from thy kindred, and from thy father's house, unto the land that I will show thee, and I will make of thee a great nation" (Genesis, 12:1–2) was also used by Ben-Gurion to prove that the basic idea of Judaism was based on nation and territory rather than commandments and faith.[91]

His interpretations were gathered into the book *Iyunim Batanach*, which he urged to be translated into English and German, so his arguments could be established abroad as well.[92]

Compared to the Bible period, the Second Temple represented a lower level of existence, since the Jews had no sovereignty, and since the model of center and diaspora was created in this period. Another reason for his lesser appreciation for this period was the political deadlock created after the revolt against the Romans.[93] This was the main reason for his avoidance of discussing rabbinical and Halachic texts that were developed in exile.

His effort to reject the model of the "exile Jew" was a recurring theme in his worldview. This was also the basis for his latest mission—to uproot exile mentality and its influence from among the Israelis and their leaders. The exile Jews were, in his mind, the "desert generation," those who were afraid of redemption and preferred the life of political slavery out of habits, wrong beliefs, and personal interests.[94] Like Plato's cave,[95] he compared the Jews in exile to those who lived in a cave, and weren't able to adjust themselves to the outside reality even after they left it.

His struggle against the exile mentality went hand in hand with his resistance to the Halachic Judaism, which characterized Jewish life in exile after the Second Temple period. He wanted to create a direct link between the Bible and the *Palmah*, in order to connect between the ancient and new culture in the Land of Israel. The exile Jewish culture, which focused on keeping the commandments, was an obsession with "mountains of explanations and interpretations of the Holy Scriptures, and our spiritual life, just like our material life, were reduced and shriveled [...] we lived in a political, economic, and spiritual ghetto [...] a giant eagle grew among us, Baruch Spinoza. [...] What did we do? We excommunicated him."[96] Against this background, in 1961, during the biggest population census in the history of Israel, he told the surveyor who interviewed him about his religion: "I am a Jew. Not by my religion. A Jew."[97]

In 1971, however, his attempts to dismiss the meaning of the Jewish religion and its meaning during exile was somewhat weakened. In his last important essay, "Al yihudo shel amenu u-Mikve Israel" (The uniqueness of our people and Mikve Israel), he wrote:

> Jewish faith and nationality are interlinked. The Jewish holidays are religious holidays, but also national ones. The Jewish people as a whole is one in faith and in nation [...] The sages of classic Greek wondered about the expressions of nature and wanted to understand them, which engaged them in the scientific and philosophical exploration. The sages of Israel in those days were not wondering about the origins of nature, because they already knew what it was, and Isaiah expressed it in one verse: "I am the LORD; and there is none else. I form the light, and create darkness; I make peace, and create evil; I am the LORD, that doeth all these things" (Isaiah 45:6–7). They didn't have to explore, because they already knew—everything was brought along by God, even evil [...] and while the Jewish people is different than any other people in its fate, history, nationality and faith, the faith of the Jewish people and the Bible is the most universal among all other faiths.[98]

He continued to advocate the Jews' obligation to take their fate into their own hands and not give up their sovereignty and depend on Heaven's mercy.[99] Still, the sting of his criticism against religious tradition in exile and its characteristics in the people's history was dulled. He was willing to emphasize the contribution of religion and keeping the commandments to preventing assimilation, and even attributed ideological significance to rabbinic religious works.

The second period in the history of Israel was the period of exile, spreading around the world and the ghetto—this was also the period of the Talmud and its interpreters, Maimonides and Joseph Caro, until the French Revolution, in the final decade of the eighteenth century. Jews in exile were hated by all the other nations. Their rights were denied and they were closed off in ghettos. "Only religion and the limitations of religion could save the people of Israel and maintain its faith and hope to return to its country [...] whether a different people could have prevailed for centuries under these conditions is doubtful [...] and there's no doubt that the number of commandments, which grew constantly since the destruction of the Second Temple until the French Revolution, allowed the Jews in the ghettos to maintain their existence and hope to return to their land."[100]

It seems that his positions regarding the role of religion during exile was moderated partly due to his growing confidence in the sovereign existence of Israel. By 1971, he had already realized that there was no need to ruin the past in order to build the future. Enough time had passed, and he realized that the real danger for Zionism lay with the weakening of the national ideals and not with returning to religious beliefs and traditions, which bore minor importance for most Jews in any case. And maybe, like many others,

Ben-Gurion the elder felt nostalgic toward his childhood, to Judaism as he knew it in his grandfather's house, before he embarked on the great journey of Zionist rebellion.

His interest in the concept of divinity was also increased at this stage of his life. In one of the final entries in his diary he wrote that he would like to read *Moreh Nevochim* by Maimonides, who tried to prove the existence of God through rational research tools.[101] Talking to prof. Ezra Spicehandler, one of the leaders of the Conservative Movement in the United States, he admitted: "I have two strict principles: Believing in God. I believe in the truth of God more than in any other truth; and I admire the prophet's morals."[102]

Since his childhood, Ben-Gurion's attitude toward God was inspired by the writings of Spinoza, whom he also admired because of his struggle against the religious establishment in Amsterdam, and considered him to be one of the ancestors of secular Zionism.[103] David Ben-Gurion adopted Spinoza's pantheistic stance, arguing that God is not an external being, but rather a being embedded in nature.[104] He often used the term "God." Impressed with the gathering of the Moshavim youth in Nahalal in 1954, he announced with excitement: "There is a God in this place!"[105] But his was not the traditional God of Israel, an external, holy power. On the contrary, based on his Spinoza-inspired assumption that God is immanent to nature, he thought that the natural order is the proof of God's appearance, while the belief in his excessive power and in miracles is a wrong concept of God.[106] Thus, Ben-Gurion's God was the result of distinct rationalism.[107]

Now, in his later days, he started reconsidering Spinoza's ideas as well. He sometimes wondered whether God was indeed the thing that was driving the world from within, as a part of it, or whether those who believed in his transcendental existence were right. "I'm a big believer in God—I believe in one God who creates everything,"[108] he said.

> What is God's nature and essence? I do not know. It is beyond me. I know what Spinoza thought. For him, God and nature were one and the same. I wouldn't say it wasn't true. I would say I don't know, and I doubt if Spinoza or Maimonides knew. Someday, in a hundred or ten thousand years, we will reach an understanding of God's essence (I do not doubt it). Today, I only know there is something beyond my understanding, which does it all.[109]

He added on the same topic:

> Without believing in God, there are things you can't understand. There are people, animals, birds, beasts, insects, and each has its own scale of brain. When I walk through Sde Boker, morning and evening, I meet a small insect which is also walking in the street, but when it notices me, it moves aside so I won't tramp him. Man has a brain, but there is more. There is a brain superior to the human brain, and that is God, because he decides everything.[110]

In any case, he distinguished between believing in God, whatever it may be, and the need to keep the commandments. He never went to the Synagogue except for Yom Kippur, and just like Baruch Spinoza, he believed that circumcision was the one significant commandment, because it establishes the people's uniqueness, in addition to medical considerations.[111]

I am certain of my faith in God—but not the God that an orthodox Jew believes in, a bearded Jew, with the angels around him. This is nonsense. This way of thinking is not consistent with Jewish faith as well. Maimonides didn't believe in it. There's no doubt there is God in the world, but not the one that the Satmar Rebbe believes in.[112]

To demonstrate the excessive weight attributed to the commandments and their interpretations by orthodox Judaism, he used a Talmudic legend from tractate Minhoth.[113] According to the legend, Moses asked God to send him through a time warp into the second century AD, to learn Torah with Rabbi Akiva. God accepted. While listening to the lecture, Moses was surprised to hear many rules he wasn't familiar with. He wasn't the only one who wondered. One of the students asked Rabbi Akiva how he knew that all these rules were true, and he said that they were all given on Mount Sinai and passed on from one generation to another. "This legend mocks the statement that the Halacha was dictated. Rules and religious laws were changed over time, according to the needs."[114]

Ben-Gurion even believed that Jesus and his teachings should be included in the Jewish canon. He argued that the Christian Messiah should be considered one of Israel's prophets, because he was born as a Jew and died as a Jew, but mainly because he didn't find in his opinions, as presented in the New Testament, any contradiction with the Jewish religion. He did explain, though, that the 2,000 years of hostility between Christianity and Judaism have made it impossible to implement this idea.[115]

To justify the uniqueness of the Jewish people without its faith, he had to use the elusive concept of "historical providence,"[116] but he never really explained its actual meaning. At times, the historical providence was the fruit of the rebellious character, which shaped the history of the Jews: "We can never understand the existence of the Jewish people and its ongoing struggle without noticing the phenomenon of pioneering throughout the history of Israel."[117] Other times, he just said that the "providence" was following the Jews because they were "different."[118] And so, even though he prioritized the national aspect over the religious one, he rejected the request of a citizen to define himself as a Jew with different religion.[119]

His perception concerning the "historical providence" held a linkage to the theological concept he dictated while drafting the Declaration of Independence: "The rock of Israel." Ben-Gurion chose this term as a compromise between

Rabbi Yehuda Fishman Maimon from *Ha-Mizrahi*, who requested to mention the God of Israel, and Aharon Zisling from *Mapam*, who objected it; but still, this concept was more than a political solution meant to create an agreement concerning the Declaration of Independence. "The rock of Israel" is an ambivalent term, which can be interpreted both as a belief in the people's historic uniqueness, and as a recognition of some transcendent element that accompanies it, included an intellectual solution to the question of his own faith.

8

As prime minister, he moved back and forth between the desired and the practical; and so, despite his known opinions about Jewish orthodoxy, he was willing to compromise with the religious circles. The outline of the relationship between state and religion in Israel was decided by him as early as June 1947, when he sent the "status quo" letter to the leaders of *Agudat Yisrael* as the head of the JNA. The status quo dictated that the *Shabath* will be the day of rest, state institutions will maintain Kashrut, the Chief Rabbinate will be the only authority in family affairs, and the ultra-orthodox community will have its own independent education system in the future state.[120] While the agreement was a political constraint—Ben-Gurion needed it in order to get the support of *Agudat Yisrael* for the Partition Plan—it was the origin of many other important arrangements that impacted the state's character, such as the exemption of Yeshiva students from military service and the adoption of the orthodox position on "who is a Jew" and the Law of Return.

He recognized the disadvantages of the linkage between state and religion, but even decades after the state was established, he rejected the separation from the rabbinic establishment, mainly due to practical reasons. He believed that the existing arrangement didn't enforce religion on the secular public, while at the same time maintaining the ties between religious and nonreligious Jews:

> This is not the time to provoke a severe dispute among the public regarding a hundred percent separation between state and religion. Even today, religious doesn't rule: In Haifa, everyone is driving on Saturday and no one bothers the cars [...] Rabbis put obstacles before marriage in a few and far between cases, but the time is not right, considering the people's unity, to abolish this law [...] We must consider the damage of the current law in comparison to the possible damage of a constitution.[121]

The philosopher Prof. Yeshayahu Leibowitz attributed another argument to Ben-Gurion, one he confessed in their private conversations, although it was never pronounced in public. Ben-Gurion created the linkage between religion and state so the state can "keep an eye on religion" and won't allow the religious circles too much independence.[122] If, indeed, Ben-Gurion wanted to limit the power of the rabbinic establishment by tying it to the state, there's no doubt his assessment was wrong. Later, he admitted that he didn't estimate correctly the rabbinic approach to conversion and family laws after being given sole authority in these matters. One lesson was learned after a bitter family experience.

The story begins with true love: After being injured while serving in the British army, Amos Ben-Gurion fell in love with Merry, the Christian nurse who took care of him. When he told his parents he was going to marry her, Paula was horrified by the possibility that he would marry a gentile girl. She asked Ben-Gurion to use his influence. The Old Man, on his part, took notice of other things: Merry's beauty and her love to his son. He wouldn't dare saying it in front of Paula, but he did tell Amos that not only did he approve of his marriage, it was also "good for genetic improvements."[123] Paula's objection was put to rest when Merry agreed to convert to Judaism.

After going through a reformist conversion, Amos and Merry started a family in Israel. But when their oldest daughter, Ruthi, wanted to get married, she was faced with an unexpected obstacle: The Rabbinate announced that since her mother went through a reformist conversion process, she was not considered to be a Jew. Ben-Gurion was appalled. Furious, he said that the religious education given by Amos and Merry to their children was more meaningful than his education to his own children. In their son's Bar-Mitzva, he said, "They [even] forced me to go to a Synagogue, although I usually enjoy going to Synagogues only when I'm abroad."[124] When no Rabi was willing to ratify Merry's conversion, he had to intervene. Ben-Gurion approached the IDF Chief Rabi, Rabi Shlomo Goren—"a great Rabi like any of them"—and he was willing to marry the couple. But the bitter taste of rejecting his granddaughter's Judaism stayed with him.[125]

In a letter he sent to Shulamit Aloni, who was *Mapai* member in those days, and handled many issues of state religion and women's status, he admitted that in hindsight, his willingness to give away family matters to the rabbinic establishment was a mistake.[126] Although, he explained apologetically, there was no better alternative at the time. As usual, he wasn't practiced in remorse, and justified his position by his desire to unify the Israeli society.

During the first Knesset, I supported the Law of Marriage according to the Halacha. I had my reasons at the time. As you know, after the Second World War, people came from Asia and Africa, not just from Europe as before. And I knew that these Jews, although they were believers, weren't strict on following the Halacha, and they had only one holy idea: Family purity. I saw no harm in marriage by a Rabi. I knew that if we wouldn't enact a law that marriage should be according to the Jewish religion, many Jews will have to start checking who this boy is and who this girl is when they marry them. And what will we have then? [Furthermore], Rabbi Maimon was the Religion Minister at the time, and he didn't allow Rabbis to use their rights in marriage [that is, to use their power and disqualify marriages between partners whose Jewish identity was questionable to them]. Now I think it's unnecessary. We must be like in America: Religious marriage for those who want it, and civil marriage for those who want that.[127]

He had reservation concerning conversion as well. He proposed to integrate gentiles into the Jewish people in a process based on the concept he suggested concerning the Bedouins in the 1950s—"Jewification." The practical implementation of Jewification was integrating into the Israeli society.[128]

> If a family of mixed marriage comes to Israel, they merely reinforce Judaism. When I came to work in Sejera, 62 years ago, I found a school teacher and master whose wife was Russian, but she spoke Hebrew and their children, of course, were Jews. She never went through a formal conversion, but she became a Jew in practice. Why should they make it harder for mixed families to be part of the Jewish people in its own land?[129]

To anchor his position in the Jewish tradition, he used the famous verse from Deuteronomy (10:19) "for ye were foreigner in the land of Egypt." The Hebrew term used in this verse, "Ger," appears here as a "foreigner" which means that the whole concept of conversion, "Giyur," is based on an error. Another support of his argument concerning the distortion of the concept of "conversion" was found in the *Book of Esther*, where it was written that gentiles who became Jews were "Jewified" (*Nityahadu*) rather than "converted" (Nitgayru). Hence, he argued, joining the Jewish people after the state was established should not be performed according to the Halachaic conversion rules as in the days of exile—but according to the biblical concept, in which the Jewish people was a national phenomenon and not religious one.[130]

In the late 1950s, he sent a letter to dozens of Rabbi and Jewish intellectuals, whom he considered to be the "sages of Israel," in an attempt to answer the question "who is a Jew." Now he had a decisive answer: To be a Jew is to know the Bible in Hebrew, be versed in Jewish history and literature, and settle in the Land of Israel.[131]

Chapter 9

Eternal Redemption

1

In October 1971, Ben-Gurion was about to celebrate his eighty-fifth birthday. He had already taken back his public statements against the state's leadership, and the government wanted to compensate him for his final years, to express some of the gratitude and the appreciation felt by his supporters and rivals alike. A special committee appointed by the government was charged with organizing his birthday events, which were supposed to take place throughout the whole year.

Making an exceptional decision, and against his habit of dismissing honorary ceremonies, he didn't reject the proposals to declare that this would be "The Year of Ben-Gurion." Since retiring from the Knesset, he never stopped reminding everyone around him that his father passed away at eighty-seven, and time, he knew, could not hold still. Who could say how many more birthdays he had left?

A few months before his birthday, at the end of June 1971, he stopped writing in his diary. The last entry in the diary was a technical one: A reminder that he had to locate some essays he wrote at the end of the 1930s.[1] He could still fill his diary with reflections, feelings, and retrospectives, but he was no longer interested. His diary was his constant companion, a core in which he processed the heart of his activities. It seems that after accepting the fact that his final life project—his memoir—was not going to be completed, the last active chapter in his life was closed, and his diary was no longer needed. He wrote no special announcement, nor did he add an intimate reference to the end of a chapter. He simply put his pen down without adding another word.

Alongside parting with his diary and putting an end to the verbal bashing with the state's leaders, his willingness to take part in the ceremonies for his birthday was the most significant reflection of the mellowing process he was going through over the last year. The first convention celebrating his birthday was scheduled for early October 1971. Of all things, it was a convention of Ha-Avoda party in Beit Berl, and he promised to attend it, after boycotting the party's events for years.

2

In Beit Berl's dining room, together with past and present *Mapai*'s members, the plates were filled with traditional comfort food: "Gefilte fish," white Roze wine, roasted chicken, and some fruits. Most of the members wore their typical white dress-shirts. Ben-Gurion, strangled in a black suit, sat at the head table next to Prime Minister Golda Meir, the ministers, and the Knesset Chairman, Reuven Bareket. The Old Man seemed to be excited than ever. He sampled only a little of the food in front of him. His musical taste wasn't particularly diverse, and it was easy to choose his favorite song: "*Yerushalayim shel zahav*" (Jerusalem of gold) by Neomi Shemer.[2] He even did his best to hum along with the singer.

The greatest excitement was felt by Prime Minister Golda Meir, who was seated again next to the Old Man after years of complicated relationship. Opening her speech, she declared: "Anyone who has to say something to Ben-Gurion over the next few weeks will probably be embarrassed just like me." She defined Ben-Gurion as "a man of action," and added:

> He taught me not to make decisions just by taking the easy, non-risk road. He taught us all, and specifically me, to live without illusions, and not to make decisions based on illusions. The necessary courage requires us to see the difficulties, and if something is necessary—to do it despite the difficulties. If something is grave and dangerous, but it is still the only way—this is the way we must follow.[3]

For a long moment, it seemed that the barriers between them were collapsing. She even ended her speech by calling Ben-Gurion to return to Ha-Avoda. "Come with us, together. We deserve it. And if you will, you deserve it too. You are sitting among us. We don't need a formal act. Come back to your party, our party."[4]

Silence spread around the hall when David Ben-Gurion got up on his way to the stand. His speech was prepared ahead of time, but he opened with a cold rejection of her proposal. He wasn't interested in fighting anymore, but he also didn't absolve completely. "I won't say everything I feel," he insinuated that his bitterness was not yet dissolved, "but I won't be a member of any party. My being or not being a member of a party is worthless anyway. There is only one thing I wish to do—dedicate the years I have left for talking to our youth—in order to help them fulfill their roles in the state's leadership in the future—about what happened in my days, so they can fix and improve the negative and learn from the positive."[5]

After avoiding the attempt to use his birthday for political support of *Ha-Avoda* party, he went on to his speech, which was optimistic, although tinged with sarcasm toward the current generation of leaders. He focused his speech on the six landmarks that, according to him, ensured the revival of the people of Israel: Adolphe Crémieux, "who recognized the fact that Jews must be brought back to working in the fields"; Charles Netter, "who was sent by Crémieux to convince the Jews to go back to working in the fields"; Edmond de Rothschild, "who did more than any other Jew in order to implement this goal"; and Joel Salomon, Yehoshua Stampfer, and Samuel Gutman, "the young men who set out to establish the first Hebrew village with their own two hands."[6] Politically, it seemed that he also wanted to remind the audience that the roots of the Jews' revival in their own country was not *Mapai*, but rather the foundations, the pillars built by the first Zionist. Historically, the six figures he mentioned were all chosen due to their capability of implementing the vision. Life, to him, was a jigsaw puzzle of actions. What people do defines their consciousness.[7] The greatness of the state's visionary, Benjamin Ze'ev Herzl, was also dictated by his ability to realize his vision, and not by the mere presentation of this vision. "There were even some gentiles who thought about a Jewish state before him. But he was the first one who gathered the Jewish people and made them into a political unit. He was the only one who managed to mobilize most of the people and fight for the idea of a Jewish state."[8] Based on the same realization scale, he also concluded that the value of Haim Weizman, with whom he fought during the 1940s over the *Yishuv*'s policy versus the Mandate,[9] was greater than Herzl's: "Weizman was the greatest Zionist I've ever known. He was greater than Herzl in many ways. He, for example, was linked to the Land of Israel, while Herzl was not. Weizman had his faults as well. Particularly since the immigration of Jews was not the main thing for him most of the time. But his greatness overpowered his weaknesses."[10]

3

Ben-Gurion's speech in front of the members of his ex-party was just an exposition to the chain of birthday events. The main event was the Knesset session that was scheduled especially in his honor. When he came to the parliament, it seemed in many ways as if he was able to move through a time warp. For one festive day, he became the center of attention for the Knesset members, the state's leaders and its citizens, as if ignoring the twenty-three years that passed since he declared its establishment. Fancy looking in his black suit and dark diamond tie, he went up to the stand, slowly but decisively. His cheeks still had a pink, vital tone about them. His eyes were still clear, and his forehead wrinkled with worry, insights, and anger of the kind that stick to revolutionaries even when they are old.

Before he started talking, he rejected the usher's offered glass of water, just like he rejected any other gesture that could have been interpreted as related to his age. No. He wouldn't drink any water before he made some effort. He started his words with a promise: "I will address mainly the future," but still presented his analysis of the Jewish history from beginning to end in details. "The people of Israel," he emphasized, "is not one of the oldest peoples in the world: Egypt, Assyria, Babylonia, China, and others have predated it. But the Jewish people has a unique feature: The Jewish nationalism and faith were tied to each other since the beginning of our history and up until today."[11]

As if predicting the post-Zionist era, which broke out after his death, he talked for a long time about the justification for the establishment of Israel. It was important for him to embed the information about its modern independence as an inseparable part of the people's historical continuous existence. His arguments were presented against the claims that Israel's establishment was part of a worldwide trend of granting independence to various nationalities, *and only* as response to the Jew's cruel fate during the Holocaust, or even as a Western colonial venture.[12] He noted that Israel was indeed established alongside other states—India, Burma, and Ceylon (Sri Lanka), but stressed the fact that the Jewish phenomenon was different:

> Other peoples were left in their lands even when they lived under foreign regimes, and when they got rid of these foreign regimes, they became independent. But not Israel. The revival of Israel is also different from those of the United States, Canada, Australia, and South America. Those were lands that were rediscovered by travelers–conquerors: Spanish, Portuguese, British and others, and the European cities sent immigrants to settle them. The redemption of Israel was renewed in a land that was populated by Arabs for 1,400 years, and is surrounded by Arab countries from the south, east and north. The land was poor and the living standards were lower than that of the original countries of the Jewish settlers who came back to Israel, to revive its Jewish existence.[13]

The core of the modern Jewish phenomenon, he said, was the revival of the Hebrew language, which was formerly considered to be a dying language, used for scriptures alone, until Zionism; as well as the agricultural and manual labor, after years of trade and religious sophistry in exile.

The ability to renew the people's youth was derived, so he argued, from the Jews' age-old linkage to the homeland and the Bible›s original language. The Jewish consciousness had dictated their national existence. He elaborated about the Messianic aspect of his perception, arguing that the existence of Jews is based on the "Jewish and human redemption" and their ambition to be "the chosen people"—otherwise, their fate would be similar to that of other nations in history.

In contrast to his bitter statements after retiring from the Knesset—"The state of Israel doesn't exist yet," he said now: "The revival of Israel in 1948 opened a new chapter, not just in the history of the land, but also in the history of Judaism. We cannot boast the fact that the people of Israel is already the chosen people, although during our short period of independence we made significant advancement, probably more than any other nation in a similar period of time."[14]

Interestingly, he avoided mentioning the Holocaust, except as one of a series of a national tragedies suffered by the people. This avoidance was another proof of his desire to marginalize the Holocaust chapter, which he perceived as the height of the Jewish helplessness in exile. He wanted to guide the nation in the spirit of the heroic myths needed to create the "new Jew."[15] His almost outrageous avoidance of the Holocaust may have included some admission that the *Yishuv* under his leadership didn't do enough to try and save European Jewry from extinction, but if it did—he kept it to himself, loyal as ever to his perception that a nation must look to its future and not on its past weaknesses.

As for the future, he again pointed out two main targets: Increasing the efforts to encourage Jews' immigration to Israel and implementing the Law of Return, and implementing the values of Jewish culture, which is rooted in the Bible's moral and social aspects. All of these can be done through education, and specifically, the State Education Law:

> This law traces the main lines of our ambition to be the chosen people and a role-model state, and maintain our eternal linkage to the Jewish people around the world; our historic destination is a new society based on freedom, equality, tolerance, mutual aid, and love of man, that is, a society with no exploitation, discrimination, slavery, the rule of one man over the other, moral imposing, totalitarianism. This rule fixates our ambition to develop in Israel a culture that is built on the eternal values of Judaism together with scientific achievements.[16]

Only toward the end of his speech did he touch the topic of relationship with the Arab countries. He pointed out the paradox in the fact that the peoples closest to the Jews geographically, racially, and linguistically, "are sadly our worst enemies,"[17] as if assuming that the opposite—a Jewish-Arab alliance in the Middle East—was also possible. This is the utopian and most desired future solution, even if only in the very long run.

He finished with a somewhat pessimistic message to future leaders: They must make political alliances based on the national interests, but remember: "Israel has only one loyal ally in the world: the Jewish people." This time, he didn't call on the world Jewry to come to Israel, and focused on the need to avoid their assimilation into foreign nations. He suggested that they should maintain their linkage to Israel by strengthening Hebrew education, visiting Israel, and investing in it. Additionally, he asked diaspora Jews: "to deepen the linkage to the vision of the Jewish and human redemption according to the prophets of Israel, and thus unite the religious, conservative, modern and free Judaism, and enhance the relationship between diaspora and the people in Israel."[18]

He continued his series of lectures in front of the crowd of the Zionist Congress, which convened a few months later in Jerusalem. It was in this forum that he chose to declare that the concept of "Zionist" is no longer relevant since the Jews have realized their ambition to establish a national home in the Land of Israel. "What is the Zionist movement these days, I do not know. And what is a Zionist? I do not know either. I only know that the Jewish people is interested in the Land of Israel and the Jews reside in the Land of Israel."[19] The perception at the background of what sounded like a typical Ben-Gurionist defiance was cultivated by Ben-Gurion since the state was established, arguing that a Zionist can only be a person who realized the Zionist idea and came to live in Israel. In December 1953 he already wondered, in a letter to the Zionist General Council: "Can there be, after the state has already been established, a Zionist movement without the personal obligation to immigrate, and if it can be, what is the difference—if there is indeed such a difference, as some Jewish lobbyists abroad believe—between Zionism with no obligation to immigrate and the affection toward the State of Israel, which is felt by almost any Jew?"[20]

He reminded the Congress members that since the state was already established, and offered opportunities for individuals as well as the entire nation, there was no longer a reason for those who identified with Zionism not to implement it by living in Israel. He did recognize the fact that global Jewry was not going to settle in Israel in the near future, but clarified that in principle, maintaining a linkage to Israel while staying in diaspora is not a Zionist act, but merely one that characterizes "Jews who support Israel."[21]

The series of speeches he made between October 1971 and early 1972 was a physically exhausting task. His doctor ordered his staff: "The man is like a pump, and you shouldn't pump it too hard. You must make sure that the Old Man won't make long speeches."[22] But mentally, those days brought him happiness at his old age. His persona was graced with a thin aura of authority.

If people's life stories would have been narrated by kind-hearted storytellers, this period might have been the most suitable one to say farewell to the founding father.[23] But he still had a long way ahead of him.

4

By 1972, he was no longer the "man of anger and strife." His reconciliation process with Golda Meir continued over the summer. He took a helicopter ride to Kibbutz Revivim to celebrate her seventy-fourth birthday and the fiftieth anniversary to her immigration to Israel. During the celebration, Ben-Gurion gave Golda a booklet of letters he sent her during their days as colleagues.[24] He also added a new, somewhat emotional letter:

> Today I send my honest congratulations, because you are almost 12 years my younger, and your life work is not done yet, and you still have things to do, and a few decades and creative projects still await you, some of them only you can produce. Go and be successful, go back to continue your blessed work for the decades to come (I wouldn't dare to say "centuries"). Your admirer and friend, David Ben-Gurion.[25]

Their relationship could never go back to what it used to be, especially since they were based on Ben-Gurion's seniority, which was no longer relevant. But his willingness to moderate his attitude toward her proved that unlike his conflicts with Levi Eshkol, Pinhas Lavon, and others, his disputes with Golda seemed more like a love-hate relationship.

He had very few intimate friends in his life, and his introverted character was one of the main culprits. He mentioned only three true friends: Berl Katznelson, Yitzhak Ben-Zvi, and Shlomo Lavi,[26] another Plonsk native and one of the founders of Kibbutz Ein-Harod. By that time, they had all passed away. When he heard about Berl's death in 1944, before the age of sixty, he panicked and told his son: "I lost the only true friend I ever had."[27] After Ben-Tzvi's death in April 1963 he wrote: "When he died, I felt lonely and orphaned."[28]

Now he developed longing for friends, people he could talk to, especially people of his own generation, who spoke his language and shared his world. By 1972, he had only one childhood friend left, Shlomo Tzemah. But they too had a long-lasting quarrel. Tzemah was his partner in crime when they decided to immigrate to Palestine while swimming together in the river near Plonsk. He found the courage and immigrated before Ben-Gurion, and sent him a weekly detailed letter, reporting about what was going on in Palestine. Ben-Gurion had said that Tzemah's poetic description introduced him intimately to the landscapes before he ever set foot on them.[29] But a short while after he came to Palestine, their paths were separated. Ben-Gurion chose *Poalei Tzion* party, which highlighted the socialist aspect of the Zionist revolution, while Tzemah chose *Ha-Poel Ha-Tzair*, which advocated the uniqueness of the local culture and tried to dismiss the influences of foreign class ideologies.[30]

But their split wasn't just the result of ideological dispute; they also derived from the limitations of human nature. Tzemah grew up in a more privileged family than that of Ben-Gurion, and felt superior to his friend throughout their childhood. His father even used to warn him against visiting the Green family house, and sometimes mentioned condescendingly that people played cards over there. Tzemah was also more physically capable than Ben-Gurion. He was disappointed by the fact that Ben-Gurion betrayed their original dream, couldn't keep up with the hardship of manual labor, and became a politician. "He was a very poor laborer," Tzemah wrote in his book.[31]

Ben-Gurion didn't deny the fact that he wasn't the best laborer in the country. He often told the story about the times he couldn't budge the donkey he was supposed to lead, and preferred reading instead.[32] But the fact that he had given up manual labor was not considered by him to be an ideological weakness. He always said that he wanted to excel as a laborer, but he was often sick and even got malaria.[33] Tzemah, who continued to work in agriculture and eventually became a teacher, believed Ben-Gurion was too quick to give up the manual labor vision of Zionism.

But since they came to Palestine, Ben-Gurion ascended the steps of leadership in a quick pace, while Tzemah was left behind. His bitterness became a grudge against Ben-Gurion after he experienced a financial crisis in the 1930s. He asked for his friend's help, but felt that Ben-Gurion looked at him condescendingly, as if saying: "You are the son of Aba Tzemah. Look how things have changed, here I am now, and you come to ask for my help."[34] After their meeting, Tzemah was offered a job as an emissary of the Zionist Movement in South Africa, but the bitter taste of his friend's patronizing look stayed with him ever since.

Over the years, Ben-Gurion's relationship with Tzemah was pushed away when he was a busy prime minister. Toward the end of his tenure, when he was asked about it, he argued that their split was based on an ideological gap from the days of rivalry between *Ha-Poel Ha-Tzair* and *Poali Tzion*. He even explained that their rivalry was greater because Tzemah also supported "Magnes' approach [the *Brit Shalom* movement, which supported a binational autonomy during the *Yishuv* period] and didn't look kindly at my political struggle."[35] It seemed, however, that by emphasizing the ideological dispute, he also meant to disguise the personal uncomfortable circumstances.

We can never know what actually went down between them. It is possible that Ben-Gurion took pleasure of avenging his father's lower position; it is also possible that Tzemah, who felt bad because of his financial distress, overinterpreted Ben-Gurion's expression. Knowing human nature, we may assume that they both overreacted a little. Now, when the years had gone by, Ben-Gurion was no longer interested in past rivalries. He searched for healing, comfort, attentive ear, and his assistant, Yisraeli, wanted to reconcile the two of them. He presented an old letter from Tzemah to the Old Man, and told him that the letter didn't get to him at the time by mistake. Ben-Gurion believed that this was the reason for the deterioration of their relationship, and said he must apologize. He requested to visit Tzemah in his house in Jerusalem as a sign of his respect.[36]

But the reunion in the ninth decades of their life was not a successful one. They were quickly engulfed by ideological conflicts: Tzemah blamed Ben-Gurion for stalling his immigration to Palestine. He explained that the Old Man should have established a strong working class among the Israeli society. Instead, he did two mistakes. First, when he was charmed as a young man by Marxism, and then, when he completely abandoned the class struggle in favor of the national idea. Ben-Gurion replied that Tzemah was wrong in his interpretation of the Zionist project, because he was still captivated by exile class perceptions. Their conversation, which was meant to renew their friendship, was stopped only when the Old Man's bodyguards thought he was getting too tired.[37] On his way back to Sde Boker, he told his bodyguard innocently: "He [Tzemah] has gotten so old. He doesn't look good,"[38] as if trying to emphasize the human aspect of their encounter and put aside the ideological arguments.

5

Following his attempts to repair his relationships with Golda Meir and Shlomo Tzemah, he felt a new desire to reexplore topics and people he fought against in the past. One of them was Aba Ahimeir, a leader of the Revisionist camp and the founder of The Strongman Alliance. Ben-Gurion resented Ahimeir and his worldview.[39] He saw him as one of the most radical members of the Revisionist movement, and said that while Ahimeir advocated the rights of Jews, he was inspired by European Fascism at the turn of the nineteenth century.[40] Ben-Gurion's hostility toward Ahimeir was born in the *Yishuv* period and survived the state's establishment. A short while before his retirement from premiership, Ben-Gurion used Ahimeir's essays, in which he presented his radical nationalist worldview, as a proof of the fascist concepts that guided *Herut* as well.[41]

Now, he demonstrated a surprising attitude toward Aba Ahimeir. "Enough, it's over. If I thought his actions were damaging—I fought against him. But that's in the past now. He wasn't the worst one among the Revisionist movement."[42] The years that had gone by were not the only reason for his weakened hatred. When he preached against Ahimeir and *Herut* in 1963, he feared that Begin's power will increase and that the nuclear venture will be jeopardized: He was concerned that *Herut*'s induced dispute over the relationship with Germany will improve its public position and hurt the military aid he requested of Adenauer, including some "deterrent weapons" he hoped to get.

Ideological matters were not the only consideration that impacted Ben-Gurion's attitude toward Ahimeir; another one was his alleged involvement in the murder of Haim Arlosoroff, head of the Political Department of the Jewish Agency, in 1934, which was widely discussed above. Ahimeir, the editor of *Hazit HaZa'am* newspaper, blamed Arlosoroff for "trading in Jewish blood" based on his attempts to reach a deal with the Nazi regime in which Germany would get goods in exchange of Jews' lives. After the murder, Ahimeir was charged with incitement for murder and was put in jail.

The identity of the murderers was never proved. In a trial that took place in 1934, two Revisionist activists, Abraham Stavsky and Tzvi Rosenblatt, were charged with the murder. Rosenblatt was equated, while Stavsky was sentenced to death based on the testimony of Sima Arlosoroff, who escorted her husband in their walk on the beach at the time of the murder. Stavsky appealed and won, because according to the British criminal law, one cannot be convicted based on eyewitness testimony.[43]

The story remained an open wound even after the state was established, but its echoes were silenced over the years. Now, Ben-Gurion regained his interest in it. In one of his conversations with the president, Zalman Shazar told him that according to the rumor, Sima Arlosoroff had admitted in a private conversation that she was no longer convinced in her testimony. Ben-Gurion felt scruples for blaming the Revisionists for murder incitement. Was it possible that he overreacted? Were Stavsky and Rosenblatt charged in vain?[44]

As always, he wanted to find out the truth for himself. In March 1972, he invited Sima Arlosoroff to a meeting in his cabin. During their conversation, he wondered about the rumor of her doubts. Arlosoroff didn't hesitate, and told him she was still certain she knew who the murderers were. Ben-Gurion was relieved, and later said he was impressed by her personality and mental strength.[45] Instead of keeping the information to himself, he sent a letter to Yosi, Ahimeir's youngest son, in which he recreated the chain of events and insisted that he was right during the affair.

> I hear you when you say that no Revisionist had anything to do with the murder of Arlosoroff. You respect your father's dignity, and like you, I don't believe your father had anything to do with this murder. But I do know who murdered

Arlosoroff—one of my Revisionist friends—and how I know it. Because Arlosoroff's wife was walking alongside him that night (I was abroad at the time) and saw the man who shot Arlosoroff. And I have no reason not to believe her, because I know her and she was there, she saw the shooter. And I have no reason to doubt her [...] about a year ago, a few people came and told me that Arlosoroff's wife told them she didn't see Arlosoroff's murderer. I met her and she said it was a false rumor, and I have no reason to doubt her.[46]

Arlosoroff's murder kept haunting him until his final days, and he continued to rely on Sima Arlosoroff's testimony as a proof for the Revisionists' involvement in the murder.[47]

6

There was another affair that consumed his attention in 1972: The murder attempt he himself was saved from in the 1920s, a story that was marginalized in the *Yishuv*'s historiography. One night, Ben-Gurion told his secretary that he clearly remembered that in 1926 a group of *Ha-Kibbutz Ha-Hashai* members wanted to murder him. This mysterious affair started with the *Bar-Giora Society*, which was established at the early twentieth century by Israel Shohat. The members of *Bar-Giora* were active mainly in the field of advocating Hebrew guards for the Jewish settlements and replacing the Arab and Circassian guards with Jewish ones. *Ha-Shomer* organization was established in 1909 by the principal members of *Bar-Giora*, and its members maintain a confidential, elitist organizational pattern. In 1920, the leaders of the *Histadrut* demanded that the organization will be subordinated to the *Histadrut* as a popular militia. *Ha-Shomer* was dissolved, and the *Hagannah* was established instead.

Israel Shohat refused to accept this move, and established the organization *Ha-Kibbutz Ha-Hashai*, a group of about eighty people, most of them members of *Gdud Ha-Avoda*, including Alexander Zaid and Yitzhak Sade. The group members were inspired by socialist revolutionary ideas: They aspired to establish a courageous society, which would live in village communes, and their enemies were the Arabs, the British, and probably some of the ultra-orthodox leaders. Violence was a viable option for implementing their goals. The Labor camp leadership, with its different variations, was not revolutionary enough for them.[48]

Ben-Gurion, who was the head of the Labor Union at the time, believed that their intentions and independence were dangerous. He wanted to dismantle them or subordinate them to the *Yishuv*'s leadership. But since most of their operations were confidential, he found it difficult to find a viable reason to do so. The justification was found only when Alexander Zaid,[49] one of the founders of *Ha-Shomer* and *Bar-Giora*, left *Ha-Kibbutz Ha-Hashai* and revealed evidence of robberies and murders committed by its members.[50] The members of *Ha-Kibbutz Ha-Hashai* blamed Zaid for spreading around false accusations, and Zaid, on his part, claimed they were planning to kill him.

In 1926, an inquiry committee was established by the *Histadrut* leadership in order to explore the issue. During the sessions, Ben-Gurion argued that the members of *Ha-Kibbutz Ha-Hashai*, headed by Hanoch Rochel, were threatening to murder him because of his attempts to stop them. The written evidence for this plan was never found, but he avoided visiting Kfar Giladi ever since.

Why did he want to re-discuss this long-forgotten affair at this stage of his life? He never explained. Did he want to investigate the story and make it part of the history of the Zionist Movement? Did he suddenly panic as an old man? Either way, he abandoned the issue shortly after raising it, and never discussed it again.

7

Dealing with past affairs did nothing to relieve the Old Man's loneliness, going into his eighty-sixth year. Sometimes, his bodyguards would call old friends before the end of their shift and urge them to come and visit him. Even his loyal followers during his heyday, those who were nicknamed "Ben-Gurion's youth," drifted farther and farther away. He met Dayan only a couple of times a year; Yitzhak Navon was occupied with his own affairs; Kollek tried to do more for the Old Man, as well as Shimon Peres, but the frequency of their visits was reduced.

Ben-Gurion's attitude toward Peres was complex. He never admired his personality like that of Dayan's, nor did he feel "fatherly love" toward him, like he did for Kollek.[51] He did, however, greatly appreciate Peres's operational and practical skills. Peres said they met for the first time in the early 1940s, when Peres, one of the secretaries of *Ha-Noar Ha-Oved Veha-Lomed*, got to ride with Ben-Gurion in his car when he toured the country. During the trip, the Old Man talked to Peres about politics, worthy leadership, and specifically the need to make a decision and be willing to pay the price. During the War of Independence, Ben-Gurion appointed Peres to be his assistant, and in December 1953, one day before his retirement from the government, he appointed him to be the Defense Ministry's CEO. He was impressed by Peres's ability to get weapon deliveries from France, including jet planes,[52] which the IDF needed to reinforce its power. He gave him a long line of credit to advance the establishment of the military industries and create the "peripheral alliance" with Iran, Turkey, Ethiopia, and Sudan. In 1957, upon signing the French-Israeli agreement concerning the nuclear reactor in Dimona, Ben-Gurion put Peres in charge, and in 1959 he made him deputy defense minister. According to Peres's testimony, Ben-Gurion intended to make him defense minister, but his retirement in 1963 prevented it.

Shimon Peres, on his part, remained completely loyal to Ben-Gurion, and it seemed that this loyalty allowed him to act more independently in his contacts with other official entities. While the Old Man was aware of the resentment against the overactive Peres among many of *Mapai*'s senior leaders in the 1950s,[53] he believed Peres was a valuable asset: A man with original ideas and rare execution capabilities. Ben-Gurion's main scale, according to which he judged his people, was their usefulness. This was the reason he supported Peres even when the foreign minister, Golda Meir, complained time and again that the deputy defense minister gave inaccurate reports and was undermining her. Ben-Gurion defended Peres against Paula's grievances as well: She doubted his loyalty to Ben-Gurion, just like she doubted the loyalty of many others. (When *Rafi* was established, Paula forbade Peres from using her husband's designated car, so he wouldn't get the feeling he was Ben-Gurion's political heir.[54])

Did Ben-Gurion mean for Peres to be his heir? During a conversation about the generational change in *Ha-Avoda* party, Ben-Gurion pointed out Peres's impressive work as his assistant: "When I was the Chairman of the Zionist Leadership, I already had six or seven assistants. None of them was any good, except for Peres. He was my personal assistant. The only one who was very successful. He was young, very young, but he is still young."[55] But Ben-Gurion never mentioned Peres as a candidate for premiership. This fact should not be seen as an indication of Ben-Gurion's negligence of this question. During the 1950s, Dayan was his candidate for the job. As mentioned, he often described Dayan as a potential leader, and at times he also pointed out Haim Tzadok, the development minister in Eshkol's government and a member of the Jewish Police during the *Yishuv* period. As an old man, he even lamented that Enzo Sereni "could have been a leader" if he wasn't caught by the Nazis during his mission in Hungary.[56]

Shimon Peres was never explicitly mentioned by Ben-Gurion as a potential leader. He may have believed that the lack of military combat experience was a weakness.[57] This assessment is supported by his famous essay from the 1950s, where he discussed the need for generational change in *Mapai*'s leadership. Ben-Gurion's argument was that the young generation leaders were better than the Third *Aliyah* generation, because they "fought in the War of Independence and the Sinai Operation and proved their skills."[58] Peres's unrestricted loyalty toward him may have been another factor, which caused the Old Man to prefer some more independent leadership candidates (Yigael Yadin, like Moshe Dayan, confronted him often). And maybe he really meant what he said: In 1972, Peres was still too young for the job, and the Old Man believed he should get some more experience.

Another interesting aspect of Ben-Gurion-Peres's relationship was Peres's wife, Sonia, who shared Peres's admiration toward the Old Man. Zalman Shoval, one of the founders of Ha-Reshima Ha-Mamlachtit, said she remained loyal to Ben-Gurion even after her husband had left *Rafi*, and admitted that she even voted for his last party.[59] But now everyone was drifting away, busy with their jobs and their own lives.

Chapter 10

Confessions

1

In 1972, feeling his approaching demise, Ben-Gurion wanted to tour the country once more in order to impress himself with its development, its landscapes, and its people. His mind was still precise and curious, although more associative than in the past, shifting in circles from the mundane to world-important issues, from the concrete to remembrance of his youth in Sejera and beyond. When answering questions it seemed that he tended to wander, but he knew how to return to the starting point and to rearrange his thoughts, having taken the listeners on a years' journey on the way. His tendency to repeat things over and over was attributed to his old age—but in that regard, precisely, he had not changed. He was never afraid of repeating himself over and over until his words sunk in. "There is only one truth, anyway," he used to joke about this tendency of his.[1]

In July he visited one of the Military Industries' factories. Nineteen years had passed since his former visit there. He surprised his listeners by noting that the *Yishuv* had not been in danger of annihilation in the War of Independence, as Zionist historiography usually has it:

The danger of being wiped out was theoretically expected. Not in this war. They did not know how to fight. The only ones who knew how to fight were the Jordanians—the Bedouin. All the rest didn't know how to fight. Lebanon didn't want to fight at all. All the rest didn't know how, including the Syrians and the Egyptians. I feared we would lose 60,000 and we lost 6,000. They tried to fight, some of them fought, but the majority ran away or gave themselves up, officers and soldiers alike. Very few fought.[2]

This was a rare Ben-Gurionist confession. For decades he described the War of Independence as the most heroic chapter in the state's history. He even inculcated the founding myth, according to which the Israelis won as the "Few against Many." He often recalled how American Secretary of State George Marshall warned his colleague Moshe Sharett that the Jews were going to be defeated due to their military inferiority:

> He (Marshall) feared that the state would be swiftly destroyed by the Arab states' resoundingly superior forces. He feared that the Arab states would attack us if we declared our independence and that our poor and inadequate army would be vanquished [...] Marshall was right to note that we could field only the partisan force we had [...] and indeed they had decisive numerical superiority in manpower and arms.[3]

The sudden change in Ben-Gurion's version of history cannot be explained only as a passing remark.[4] It is no coincidence that precisely when he visited the Military Industries and was impressed by the weapons developed there he warned that Israel should not be so sure of its might. For years he feared that, in contrast to the Arab countries, for Israel one defeat will mark the end of the state.

Israel's complacency, the certainty that the Arabs could be routed in any situation, frightened him. In spite of Israel's military achievements he worried that it would not withstand a decades-long conflict, if only for the Arab states' huge advantage due to the size of their populations:

> I do not think that we are ready for a decades-long war, and they are ready for it. The Arabs have not only over 100 million, but allies of their faith, more than 300 million Muslims who will always say "we are all Muslims" and stand by them. Therefore, if there is a chance of peace, it would be better to return all the territories.[5]

In his surprising confession that in the War of Independence the IDF's power was superior, he meant to say that the balance of power might also change for the worse. He feared a fixation with the power of military innovations, as if they were the Golden Calf. When examining the arms race in the Middle East he did not dismiss the possibility that the IDF would be hard-pressed to widen the quality gap forever. He warned: "there is a danger that they will yet learn how to fight. One cannot say that they will never do."[6] Therefore, he wanted to achieve security by striving for a peace accord. Those days, in a talk with an unnamed French historian he surprisingly, for the first time, told of his willingness to accept the development of the Palestinian autonomy to real statehood. "If the Arabs want to establish a state on the west bank of the Jordan, it is their business. Why not?"[7]

In August 1972 he went on a tour of Sharm el-Sheikh and the military bases in the Sinai Peninsula. During his life he went on dozens of trips to various IDF units. He loved to feel close to the troops, to see in them the embodiment of the ingathering of the exiles. On these trips he frequently wore his khaki suit as if he were "one of the guys." For him, there was no more impressive and material example of the War of Independence, the forging of the New Jew, than the IDF soldiers. This time he dispensed with the khaki suit, but was immersed in a special feeling. He asked his son Amos to accompany him and during the flight he held his doctor's hand excitedly as if knowing that this was his last visit with the troops. After they landed in Sinai he strode in awe after Defense Minister Moshe Dayan, who spoke of the progress of the settlement project and the defense situation, and agreed to be photographed with every soldier until he had to be reminded of the delay in the schedule.[8]

One year before this visit he disapproved of Dayan's famous announcement—"Sharm-el-Sheikh without peace is better than peace without Sharm-el-Sheikh." He firmly responded: "Although I understand why he said this, control of Sharm guarantees freedom for Israeli vessels, for true peace I will return Sinai."[9] Now, in the course of the tour, he was somewhat carried away in his excitement about the civilian outposts set up in Sinai. He did not retract his assertion that if peace was to be attained, the peninsula would have to be returned, but chose to emphasize over and over again that the settlements did not constitute an obstacle to peace because they could remain in place under a foreign flag. Now, seemingly under Dayan's influence, he expressed his grave doubt whether they were ready for peace, and said: "[In that case] at the present we go in and settle."[10]

On the way back from Sharm-el-Sheikh he stopped at a military installation near the Suez Canal, where he met Arik Sharon, then the chief commander of the Southern Command. Sharon seemed excited and slightly bashful and kept casting his gaze downward.[11] Ben-Gurion did not say much. Clearly the trip had exhausted him, but his fondness of Sharon was unmistakable.

Like the way he viewed Dayan, Ben-Gurion saw Sharon, from his days as a young officer in Unit 101, as the figure of the New Jew he wished to uphold—one who knew how to grasp both the plow and the sword. His overriding criterion for judging people was the quality of their deeds, and so he esteemed Sharon as a fighter, and as with his attitude toward Dayan, he tended to forgive him for his flaws of character, even though he recognized them. In 1960 he wrote in his diary: "[Sharon] is an original thinking fellow of—if only he weaned himself of his faults of not saying the truth nor refraining from gossip he would have been a model military leader,"[12] but in fact was his patron in the army. Despite Sharon's many clashes with his commanders, Ben-Gurion defended him and saw to his promotions. "Pay attention to Arik,"[13] he said to Yitzhak Rabin after he was nominated as chief of staff. Sharon was also one of the last to receive a personal letter from him. He wrote to him in the summer of 1973 and expressed his sorrow over his retirement from the IDF.[14]

In their meeting in Sinai Ben-Gurion was asked for his opinion of Sharon. He repeated the question, "What do I think of Sharon?" as a kind of intellectual joke, smirked and mumbled "Nice boy, good soldier." In Ben-Gurion's shortened code, "Nice boy, good soldier" was a sort of letter of forgiveness and encouragement. He meant to say that he had not forgotten that he was troubled by problematic aspects of Sharon's character, but on the bottom line, he was worthy.[15]

Something else in the meeting seemed anecdotal at the time, but in context of the war that broke out the following year, received further meaning. At the end of the briefing he was given, Ben-Gurion wondered about the distance between the Suez Canal and Cairo. An officer answered that it was some 100 kilometers. Sharon was quick to point out "If we burst onwards from here we'll be in Cairo within six hours." The Old Man looked westwards as if trying to judge the distance, nodded his head as if in doubt and said nothing further.[16]

2

It was not only in matters concerning the country and the region that Ben-Gurion was interested; his gaze stretched to more distant regions. He dreamt of a federative framework in which the countries of the world would be joined together as part of the messianic vision of Israel's place in history. He hoped the purpose of the state would manifest itself into becoming the advance guard in service of mankind which will lead history toward an era of redemption.[17] Like the visionary of the state Theodore Herzl, Ben-Gurion believed in an inevitable historical progress.[18] Scientific achievements attested in his eyes to the positive possibilities inherent in the future, and he thought that mankind was marching toward prosperity with the advancement of time.

He saw the proliferation of knowledge among Earth's inhabitants as the principal difference between the wisdom of the ancient world and that of the modern one. Humankind had astounding achievements in olden times but then knowledge was the part of few. The scientific achievements of the modern world do not merely stand for themselves but also benefit most of humankind, and this was "the most comprehensive spiritual success of our times."[19] The era of redemption, therefore, would not be achieved by political agreements between leaders of states but only after citizens of all nations develop all-human awareness that they have an obligation to care for a measure of equal opportunity between the nations. The modern world needs a correction that would bring about "peace and equality among peoples, eradicate the gap between the rich developed peoples and the poor undeveloped peoples of Asia, Africa and Latin America."[20] In this context of realizing the Jewish vision of the "correction of the world," he wished to promote a union between the states of South America, in a similar pattern as that of the United States. He reasoned that the South American states had an unrealized potential for prosperity and that there were no significant differences of religion or language between them.[21]

In his opinion only one dangerous obstacle stood in the way to the era of redemption: the flaring up of a nuclear war. But contrary to conventional though in the 1970s, he did not fear a nuclear war between East and West but a conflict between the Soviet Union and China. He repeatedly stated that if the atom bomb were not used in the next fifty years, we would indeed enter an era of world peace.[22]

China fascinated him more than many other countries. Of all places in the world, he regretted that he never managed to see the Great Wall of China.[23] His interest in the Chinese nation was no quirk of his later years. His esteem for Chinese culture stemmed also from the similarities he found between it and the Jewish notion of the "Chosen People"—the Jews and the Chinese were unique, in his opinion, in that ever since becoming nations they regarded foreign cultures as inferior; they only wanted to entrench themselves in their positions, not to conquer them. Beyond the identical philosophical-cultural dimension, he considered that China held the key to reformatting the world and that it had the power to break the hegemony of the United State and the Soviet Union.

As a prime minister he held conflicting attitudes toward the Chinese. With the establishment of the state, before the communist revolution wrought by Mao Zedong, he tried to explore the possibility of diplomatic relations.[24] The Chinese rejected the offer. When the Korean War broke out in 1950, Ben-Gurion was forced to take sides in the conflict between the Western and Eastern blocs: he chose the West, led by the United States, and was even ready to send in support by the IDF. Israeli interests at the time were the justification of his choice, but he opposed American enmity to communist China, regarding its policy as a mistake owing to political shortsightedness. During Kennedy's presidency he tried to convince the administration that the United States was hurting its own interests and the Chinese should be regarded favorably, despite the inter-bloc struggle between capitalism and communism:[25]

Unlike the powerful European states in the last 150 years, until the end of the Second World War America maintained friendly relations with China and later changed its course. But Mao will not be China's leader forever. And although I can understand why the Chinese masses revere him, he made China independent, the Chinese people is not communist in its views. It is important for America to maintain good relations with China, which in 10–15 years will become a rising power, the second power in the world after the United States [...] I am no communist either, but I doubt if a huge nation like China can be ignored [...] I offered this prediction to Kennedy and I was convinced he would change his policy if elected to a second term, but as is well known he was assassinated.[26]

His words show that his major concern was that the years of enmity between the Chinese regime and the American administration would imbue a hatred of the West in the citizens of China even after the dissolution of the communist rule. He also assessed that if the West would not find a peaceful way to it, it would be unable to deter an armed nation having a strong economy and such a huge population. "The Chinese will strengthen both in arms and economy. If they acquire the same arms as the Russians, they will have no fear [...] the Chinese don't care if even 250 million of them are killed."[27]

He was not content with assessments for the distant future and promoted the expansion of the Hebrew University's Department of Eastern Asia Studies.[28] In February 1972, on the eve of President Richard Nixon's famous visit to China, he asked him by means of a common friend not to content himself with empty gestures.[29] He advised the United States to support China's claim over territory the Soviet Union had conquered on their northeastern border.[30]

Following the success of the visit, Ben-Gurion sent Nixon his last political message. He encouraged him to persevere in his policy and promised that his steps were hastening the vision of the End of Days and will contribute to the possibility of "uniting the world according to the vision of the prophets."[31]

Chapter 11

Farewell

1

He was called The Old Man even before he reached fifty. Sitting in a coffee house, while he was the Head of the JNA, a young girl pointed at him and asked her parents out loud: "Who is this old man?" The legend, which is more powerful than any fact, tells that the nickname had spread between his friends until it became his trademark.

Ben-Gurion felt comfortable with this description: He was the Old Man in the Biblical sense of the term, the wise one, the sage, the authority. But now, the famous nickname was not only a sign of respect, but also a biological crisis. His old age bothered him, but his passion for life was not vanished. "I would go back to being 20 and start all over again,"[1] he told Renana. This wasn't just an abstract ambition, but a natural expression of his vitality. He had a vision in this area as well. In recent years, he had read many researches, which proved that the damages of old age can be battled by replacing damaged tissues or old cells. His imagination was ignited by this issue, and he often shared his thoughts with his doctor. He explained, apologetically, that the quality of life was more important to him than longevity. Sometimes he would even mention that Churchill and Adenauer were interested in the subject, as if quoting them to legitimize his hope.[2]

His ambition to overcome what most people accepted as a necessary deterioration process was only typical. At the height of his career, at the end of the 1950s, he visited the Ramon Crater. Admiring the landscape, he wondered why the crater wasn't filled with water and made into a fertile land. When his entourage explained it was impossible, he asked who said it wasn't. "Experts," was the answer. And then he wondered, half-jokingly: "Why won't you replace the experts?"[3]

He never suggested replacing his doctor, but he often talked to Dr. Bolek Goldman about an antiaging clinic in Switzerland, which presumably delayed the aging process, until Dr. Goldman took the hint. Skeptic, yet excited by his Ben-Gurionist task, the good doctor sailed to his mission. His visit to Switzerland was kept as a secret. He found a fancy clinic and many promises, but couldn't find the secret for longevity.[4] A while after the disappointing report, Ben-Gurion admitted: "I am more than 85 years old. This is not a very young age. How much do I have left? Five, ten, fifteen years? They wish me 'May you live to be 120,' and think their wish will make a difference."[5]

Before his eighty-sixth birthday, when it finally looked like he reached some level of tranquility, he was having health problems that were threatening to affect his ability to function.[6] Muscle and back pains and breathing difficulty were felt often. His bodyguards even found him semiconscious in his den a couple of times. When they asked him why he hadn't called for help, he didn't respond. His doctor knew it was difficult to talk to Ben-Gurion about his weakness, because he hated feeling needy and preferred to ignore any signs of distress.[7] A medical report about his condition said: "He can't define what's bothering him, like you see with kids and sometimes adults, who are totally uninterested in physical pains."[8]

In contrast to the state-wide celebrations of the year before, his eighty-sixth birthday was celebrated modestly in his kibbutz. Ben-Gurion was not feeling too well. Dressed in a worn out suit, without the fancy tie he wore the year before, Shimon Peres at his side, the Old Man settled for a few limp congratulatory words. He gazed tiredly at the chocolate cake with the number 86 written in cream and tasted just a small bite. His doctor limited his diet to porridge, vegetables, fruits, and sometimes some low-fat chicken dish. He didn't complain about that either. Only once in a while, when he craved for something tasty, he wondered out loud whether there were any rolls in the kibbutz's dining room. His bodyguards were used to his insinuations, and would go find a roll in the kitchen; when they couldn't find one, some volunteer would drive all the way to Yeruham to satisfy the Old Man's craving, but he never knew about all the trouble for his sake.[9]

During this period, he was already rejecting offers to be involved in current events and in historical issues that used to fascinate him not so long ago.[10] He was still busy with writing his memoir, copying archival materials and notes to his notebook, but he was now burdened by another problem: His right hand, his main working tool, was weak and painful.[11] Some advised him to let go, to give up the writing of his memoir and write only when he had to. Some advised the opposite: They were concerned that inactivity will accelerate his aging process and wanted to treat his hand in any way possible.[12] His doctor knew what writing had meant to him, but wanted to avoid shots. His bodyguards suggested he use a recording device and hire a typist to put his words into writing, but Ben-Gurion refused. His independence was sacred to him. "I must write everything myself. I never even signed a letter that I didn't write myself."[13] When he could no longer hold the pen, he demanded his doctor to treat him, so that he could write again.[14]

The shot had a positive impact, and not just on his hand. His ability to write affected his mood as well.[15] His doctor saw it clearly: When Ben-Gurion kept bothering him with the need to Hebraicize his name, and even presented a document with possible alternatives—Barak or Baruch instead of Bolek—he knew that his patient was feeling better.

But his palm was only one of his health problems. One morning, his bodyguard was horrified to find him lying on the floor, covered in cold sweat, his gaze unfocused. An ambulance was rushed to his cabin and took him to Tel Ha-Shomer Hospital. A few long moments of anxiety passed before the tests showed he was suffering from exhaustion. He went out on a recovery vacation to Tiberias, but the same symptoms appeared again over there: fainting and cold sweat. This time he was sent to Poriya Hospital, where the doctors diagnosed a hernia in his diaphragm, which caused symptoms similar to those of a heart attack. When he was released from the hospital, he went to the Defense Ministry to meet Haim Yisraeli. He told him bravely about his health problems and explained that he was feeling better now. But something was off: He kept repeating the same sentences again and again. Yisraeli believed those were insignificant symptoms of old age. But Ben-Gurion, who was clear minded enough to realize he wasn't well, was anxious and frustrated.

In his good years, he was famous for his excellent memory: Talking on the phone, he could quote the specific page of the book from which he was trying to find a citation, out of the thousands of books in his library.[16] At eighty-six, there were still things he said or wrote that were a fascinating proof of his ability to remember and analyze events clearly and accurately, but sometimes he wasn't up for it anymore.[17]

His memory was deteriorating, in fact, in a slow process that lasted over a decade, and affected, among other things, his decision to resign from premiership. Just before his retirement, he ordered, according to Renana's advice, an Irish book for memory improvement on a DIY basis.[18]

One day, he read in the newspaper some esoteric news about the development of a memory-improving drug. He tried to get more information about the pill. When he failed, he turned to Dr. Haim Shiba, former director of the Health Ministry:

The newspapers over here published a piece about a pill that is marketed through Europe, Ribaminol. Tests performed on old people and students have shown that it improves memory. Do you know of such a thing? Could you find out if there is indeed such a pill, and if so, if it really improves memory skills?

In recent years, I have been feeling that my memory is weakened, especially concerning names, and I would seriously consider a memory-improving pill.[19]

Shiba's response was less enthusiastic. He explained that the medicine should be treated like "Mephisto's promise to Faust," a false promise.

But Ben-Gurion continued his effort to find cure for his distress, and even read some biology and medicine books. "During my years in Israel, I've read a lot in the Bible, I took interest in philosophy, in Buddhism. But if I were young and starting again, I would study biology. Biology of the human mind. Because what is a thought? How do we think? How do we remember? I read a lot of books, but I never found an answer,"[20] he sadly admitted. "I used to have good memory. If I talked to someone, I could write down our conversation, word by word, up until 3 or 4 hours later. Now it is a bit broken."[21] But not everyone realized his distress.

Teddy Kollek, Jerusalem's mayor, approached him one day and asked to renew his lectures and expand the discussion about Jerusalem's significance. Ben-Gurion agreed. His new public appearance attracted interest, and dozens of participants gathered to listen. He even asked his daughter Geula to come with him. But during the lecture, he forgot some details of the story for a moment. He closed his eyes, trying to focus his mind, but the bitter feeling of not being able to say what he wanted was clearly visible on his face.[22] The gap between firm, decisive, energetic Ben-Gurion and the old man who stood embarrassed in front of everyone was touching, tragic, and very human.

He admitted honestly: "My memory fails me," and asked for a short break before continuing, but his weakness generated a laugh among a young couple in the audience, like young people naturally do. Geula, who chose, unfortunately, to sit next to this couple, couldn't stand it: "I felt like I might die. He was embarrassed, pitiable. I felt that if I wasn't going to run out of the stadium, I would go hysteric. I ran out."[23] Kollek was concerned and went out to calm her down. Geula had just one request: "If you love him, make it stop." Since this incident in late 1972, Ben-Gurion tried to avoid talking in front of large audiences.

2

His decisive expression, his raging hair, his sparkling eyes—all started to fade away, until it seemed, in early 1973, that an external force undermining his power had revealed a less familiar person. His gaze was hesitant, tending to avoid contact, and his steps became fragile and indecisive. His connections with the kibbutz members were severed almost completely. He didn't like to be seen in his weakness, and even when he did leave his cabin, he didn't wave the passers-by anymore. The gazes turned toward him were easy to interpret: They were whispering behind his back, noticing the weakness of the nation's father. Even his daily walk, which he continued to practice, was getting shorter.[24]

Once, when walking with his bodyguard, Yehoshua Cohen, he stopped after a few hundred feet and presented an unusual request: "Yehoshua, let's go back."[25] Yehoshua was concerned. Ben-Gurion was already in his eighty-seventh year, but even his close companion and bodyguard, who had seen him through thick and thin, couldn't detach himself from the aura of the Ben-Gurioninst myth. He didn't dare asking for the reason, and Ben-Gurion didn't explain. They turned together toward the cabin, where the Old Man got settled in his room and went back to reading his documents.

His decision to give up walking seemed justified. His legs were sore and his back was aching, and his health condition required him to rest and avoid unnecessary effort. But giving up his walks, which were one of his trademarks, signified his acceptance of the nearing end. His will power had always been his most prominent feature. Walking daily, in all types of whether; writing in his diaries almost in any type of mood; self-educating, even at an old age (at 56, he started learning ancient Greek and Spanish so that he could read Plato and *Don Quijote de la Mancha* in their original language); his insistent repentance of his principles and the myths he wanted to instill—Ben-Gurion could achieve all of those by producing his best effort through his relentless will power. Now he was giving up. He never walked any more, mornings or evenings, holidays or weekdays.

3

His weakening caused him to reflect on his will, realizing that he will reappear after his death—this time as a historic founding myth.

The first surprise was the man entrusted with the will: The Justice Minister, Yaakov Shimshon Shapira, who wasn't one of his greatest advocates. Shapira had objected to quite a few of Ben-Gurion moves, and even headed the internal tribunal that dismissed Ben-Gurion of the party—after the latter announced the establishment of *Rafi*—and described his followers as "neo-Fascists." Shapira himself wondered about the decision. But Ben-Gurion had his reasons to choose him as responsible for his will, even if these reasons seamed contradicting. The first was a proof of his burning desire to leave the world in peace, and the extent to which his soul was tortured by his political struggles as an old man.

The second reason takes us back to the Lavon Affair. In 1968, after the affair was finally put to rest, Shapira was the one to initiate the "Commissions of Inquiry Law." The law defined the practices of investigations initiated by the government. In fact, these inquiries were taken away from the government's authority and moved to the judicial system. Basically, the law was a stamp of approval over Ben-Gurion's struggle. After all, he protested against the procedure of a government that investigates and judges itself. And so, the Old Man's decision to entrust Shapira with his will was a conciliatory gesture, but also a further proof that his way has won.[26]

The location he chose for his grave was also significant. His decision to be buried in the Negev, and not in *Helkat Gedolei Ha'Uma* (The Nation's Greatest Burial Plot) on Mount Herzl, Jerusalem, was, first and foremost, a testimony of his perception concerning his position in the history of Israel. By avoiding the burial ground of the rest of the founding fathers, he not only professed modesty, but also immortalized his own uniqueness and central position. From a national point of view, his decision to be buried in the Negev was also a heritage: The revival project is not completed, and there are many regions still waiting to be redeemed and conquered.

But the exact position of his grave, close to Sde Boker College, overlooking the Wadi of Tzin, seemed to contradict his call to bring life to the desert: The canyon below his grave is out of reach. It is a wild, powerful natural landscape that can't be settled. Yehoshua Cohen, as well as his son Amos, noticed the paradox and tried to convince him to pick out another plot, within the boundaries of the kibbutz.[27] Ben-Gurion's refusal projected his deliberate intention to emphasize the gap between wild nature, which people can only be impressed by its greatness, and the general location—the Negev spaces, which can be settled. His decision was also a symbol of his political practice of "utopian realism." But the paradox is actually a symbol of the tension felt by Ben-Gurion between the pioneering element and the statist one. By choosing the Negev over Mount Herzl, he prioritized the pioneering aspect—the need to act as an individual and revive the desert with pure will power. But since the reviving of the desert was not just an adventure, but a move designed to advance the state—the statist aspect was still included in his act.[28]

And maybe there was also another justification, simple but typical one, for his decision to be buried on the edge of Wadi Tzin, where the people of Israel went through during their Exodus from Egypt. This was an expression of the bitterness he felt in his final years, and a reminder of the way he ended his life. Just like Moses, he too never got to come into the promised land, and his work was not done.

Concerning his funeral, Ben-Gurion gave few instructions and left many parts open for interpretation. He requested that no eulogies will be read, as if refusing to believe the power of the current state's leaders to interpret him properly, and preferred to be buried in a deafening silence. He did not ask for a religious ceremony, but didn't prohibit the reading of a *Kadish*.

His possessions—his houses in Sde Boker and in Tel Aviv, his archives, and some art pieces he accumulated—were left to the state, with the intention of establishing a museum and spreading his teachings. Before doing so, he requested his children's permission. He promised that if they demand the rights to themselves, he will accept their position.[29] They gave their consent, and he left them his savings. In order to maintain the value of his money, he chose to invest it in a yielding bank deposit for the first time in his life, at the age of 86.[30]

4

In early 1973, David Ben-Gurion had to move to Tel Aviv to be closer to his doctor and to Tel Ha-Shomer Hospital. The aura around him still affected anyone who met him. But what was left of the man, who seemed superhuman even in his later years, was no longer as familiar as before. He spent most of his time alone in his home, walking around in his pajamas and slippers, reading in the den or in his bed.[31] A lion at the winter of his life. His tone was quite, dull, and the familiar decisiveness came up only rarely. His eyes were sunk deep under his tall forehead, and when he was angry, they still looked like balls of fire. But usually he was reflective. Once in a while, he browsed through his writings in order to write his memoir, but he was no longer committed to complete his task. For the first time in his life, he had no defined daily routine. He didn't write too much, and most of the letters he wrote were congratulatory letters for happy occasions and condolences letters in cases of mourning.[32]

His terrifying loneliness was enhanced in the big house in *Ha-Keren Ha-Kayemet* Boulevard in Tel Aviv, amidst the urban roar. Renana, who recognized his distress, suggested that Mira Avrech, *Yedioth Aharonoth*'s gossip columnist, would come to visit him. The two women had a close relationship for years, since Avrech wrote a best seller about Paula.[33] Avrech was embarrassed. In her mind, Ben-Gurion was a giant from a different world than her own. Renana assured her that she had no reason to be afraid.

Ben-Gurion welcomed her sitting on his couch, with a cup of tea in his hand—he had all the time in the world. Later, he went up to his room and came back with a bunch of letters. He read for her things written to him by world leaders. Avrech wondered why the Old Man wanted to talk to her—a gossip columnists—of all people. But when the meeting ended and he encouraged her to come again, she realized: He needed her to listen to him more than she needed his stories. Once, she found him in the small room that was adjacent to his study, lying on the couch, wrapped up in a blanket, and his gaze was alert, as if he could be called back to a job at any moment.[34]

In March 1973, he experienced his last political disappointment when Ephrayim Katzir was elected as *Ha-Avoda*'s presidency candidate. Ben-Gurion supported Yitzhak Navon, and his rejection brought back memories from his struggle against *Mapai*, since his followers blamed Navon's affiliation with *Rafi* for his failure. In a letter to Navon, Ben-Gurion admitted:

> I am one of many who currently feel sorry for the fact that the only man who should have been president was not elected. I have nothing against the one who was chosen. I deeply cherish Ephrayim Katzir and his important activity. But he is not the one that should have been elected. I am deeply sorry that he chose this position for himself, and even more sorry that you were not elected. I believe that the Hebrew nation will recognize your right to this position in the future, and that we shall see you as the nations' president.[35]

Katzir's election was the final political issue he was passionate about, and he was deeply engaged in it. When the state was established, Ben-Gurion believed that the president's position is mainly ceremonial and limited to its symbolic value. He supported Haim Weizman's appointment as president because he wanted to give him an honorary position with no power or execution capabilities. His position didn't change. Beyond his disappointment from Katzir's election, he wondered why Katzir, a biophysics professor, was willing to leave his more important position in the Weizman Institute for presidency.[36]

Around Passover, his health condition was improved. This was evident in the long letters he wrote. He sent Golda another greeting letter for her 75th birthday, ending it with words that left no doubt about his feelings: "With love."[37] He insisted on spending the Passover feast in his kibbutz, where he read the sentence of the *Hagadah* he loved the most: "with a strong hand and with an outstretched arm."[38] During the spring of 1973, Israel was getting ready to celebrate its twenty-fifth anniversary, and Ben-Gurion was preparing for a comprehensive interview for *TIME* Magazine.[39]

He sounded firm and proud of the state's achievements. He promised that the gates of the USSR will be open for Jews who will come to Israel and predicted an immigration wave from the United States sometime in the future. He estimated that by the time Israel will celebrate its fortieth anniversary, the Jewish population will include five or six million people. The reasons for immigration remained practically the same since the early days of Zionism: They are all based on the Jews' linkage to the Land of Israel, but the circumstances change. He made a point by emphasizing that the Arab citizens of Israel were not discriminated against, and invited the interviewers to take a tour of the Arab communities and see their financial situation. He refused to say when the Occupied Territories would be returned, and clarified that the state had to focus on populating the Negev and the Galilee and on encouraging Jewish immigration.

Personally, he admitted he would have preferred to stay in Sde Boker, and that he didn't like the big city, but he had to remain in the center of Israel due to his medical condition. Optimistic as ever, he promised that he will go back to his cabin and even renew his efforts to write his memoir. He defied the skeptic reporter: "I may not be as young as you are, but I've written books. And yes, if I live—I will have time to write my memoir."[40]

He even agreed to talk, after years of boycotting it, with a reporter from *Kol Ha-Am*, the Communist Party's newspaper, a party that Ben-Gurion declared unworthy of being part of the political arena in Israel (his motto was "no *Herut* and no Maki"). *Kol Ha-Am* became famous in 1953, when it blamed Ben-Gurion for "starting a war" when the foreign affairs minister, Aba Even, declared that Israel was willing to send her troops to fight in the Korea War.[41] The internal affairs minister, Israel Rokah, ordered to shut down the newspaper, arguing that the article was jeopardizing "public safety." The newspaper's editors appealed to the Supreme Court, which overruled the decision and ordered to republish it. This ruling of Judge Shimon Agranat has since become a milestone in the struggle for freedom of speech in Israel.

During his short interview, Ben-Gurion couldn't hide the grudge he still bore for the newspaper. When he was asked if Israel was also responsible for the failure to achieve peace in the Middle East, he said: "I don't know." And when he was asked what he would do differently after all, he replied with sarcasm: "If I would still be serving the state, I wouldn't do anything differently. My expectations from 25 years ago were fulfilled almost to the full during my tenure as Prime Minister."[42]

During the summer, some of the members of his last party, Ha-Reshima Ha-Mamlachtit, negotiated with *Gahal*'s people, led by Menachem Begin, in an attempt to join the Likud party—a union of *Herut* and the Liberals. Zalman Shoval, the Knesset member who replaced Ben-Gurion after his resignation, updated the Old Man about the negotiations. He gingerly added that the negotiations will be stopped if Ben-Gurion objected them. Ben-Gurion said sarcastically that they should do what they think is best for them.[43] He continued to observe the political life, but did it through a transparent screen. He had no energy or desire to be directly involved. Yet, for a long time he resented the attempts of his last party members to join Begin's party. When Yoel Lavi, one of the members of *Ha-Reshima Ha-Mamlachtit*, asked his opinion, he wrote that while he was no longer interested in the past, he would join *Ha-Avoda* if he was younger.[44] This was the only time he mentioned *Mapai* in a positive context throughout his final years.

During the spring of 1973, he focused all his energy on the state's twenty-fifth Independence Day. He even engaged in the dispute regarding the relevance of the military parade, and said that the arguments about the parade being a wasteful militarist gesture were "nonsense."[45] But just before Independence Day, his fever went up again, and he had to miss most of the ceremonies. In the haze of his fever, he told Avraham Tzivion, who came to celebrate with him at home, about his visit to South America in 1969. It was the most exciting trip of his life, he remembered, because the ancient Hebrew of the Jewish school's students was very similar to the language he and his friends spoke in Plonsk before their immigration. His conclusion was that the power of Jewish existence was still very much alive.[46]

His condition improved at the end of the summer. He wanted to tour the country again, particularly to places he's never been before, like Caesarea.[47] When he was in a good mood, he even promised he will complete his memoir in ten years,[48] and explained that the state needed between eight and ten million Jews in order to ensure its existence, and therefore, immigration and settlement were the most important missions.[49]

Against his habit of avoiding awards, he accepted the title "City Notable of Givatayim." The reason was simple, he explained: Rachel Beit-Halahmi was one of the names signed on the proposal. "If there is one person alive that I can't say no to, it is my childhood friend and my hometown comrade Rachel."[50]

5

On September 1973, a month before his birthday, his condition deteriorated. When the Yom Kippur War broke out, he was no longer aware of what was going on.[51] During the war, he had a stroke that immobilized the right side of his body. He didn't know that his grandson, Alon, Amos' son, was severely injured. The sadness in his eyes was evident when the president, Zalman Shazar, came to visit him at the hospital, and asked him if he was reading the war reports in the newspapers.[52] Reading was difficult for him, but he asked Shazar to send his best wishes to Prime Minister Golda Meir and to Defense Minister Dayan.

He recovered a little, and was even sent to rest at home. Blurred, his eyes dim, and his tongue heavy, he responded dryly to the developments and the despair atmosphere that was spread through the state during the war. He was particularly interested in the numbers of casualties.[53] When he heard that Elhanan Yishai, his personal assistant during the 1950s, lost his son in the war, he made an effort and wrote a short condolences letter: "I was sorry to hear about the loss of your son in Sinai. We have faced many challenges, but this war is the worst and most brutal of all. I am certain we will prevail, and it is unfortunate that many of our best youth are dying to protect our existence. Be strong."[54] Those were the last sentences he ever wrote.

His nephew, Arie Ben-Gurion, Tzipora's son, came to visit him at home and asked him to sign some book. He was horrified when his famous uncle, who spoke eight languages, could hardly move his hand and settled for the letter B as his signature.[55] In late November, after the war's turning point, when the IDF troops crossed the Suez Canal and the cease-fire agreement was signed, he had another severe stroke. This time, he lost his ability to speak.[56]

In the hospital, on a gray iron bed, under a white sheet, hooked up to tubes and his head sinking into his pillow, he seemed to Dayan, who came to visit him, like Gulliver in the land of tiny people. "A powerful expression," Dayan felt, was still covering his face.[57] The bitten defense minister wrote in his diary that the eulogies will probably distinguish between his golden age, his period of greatness, and his final, unimportant final years. Those were two completely different periods of time. There were times when Dayan himself tried to distinguish between the man and his path, but now he concluded it was a mistake.[58] Ben-Gurion in his days of glory was the same person he was at the end of his days. Ben-Gurion was also Ben-Gurionism. And when his heart gave out, on the early morning of December 1, 1973, it was also the end of an era.

Epilogue

Avi Shilon

Movements' thoughts, like people's thoughts, lag behind events. The thought hangs on to inertia, routine, habit [...] The thought is always lazy, and assumes that whatever has been will always be. But events are not so. Indeed, events are driven by inertia, but also by dynamics. Life and nature are always filled with powers' clashes and struggles. The world never stagnates, neither does history, or nature or human beings. But the thought usually lags behind, and when, at a specific time, a specific system is shaken, the thought still refuses to see it, because it would require it to make big efforts, to find new paths. And it is difficult, because a man has a limited amount of energy, and he can't turn his thought on observing transformations in history.[1]

NOTE

1. Ben-Gurion, in his speech in front of the council *HaIhud HaOlami Poalei Zion Hitahadut*, April 26, 1939, in: David Ben-Gurion, *Zichronot min ha-izavon* [Memoirs from the archives], ed. Meir AviZohar (Tel-Aviv: Am Oved, 1987), 270.

Notes

CHAPTER 1

1. An interview I conducted with his doctor, Dr. Bolek Goldman, on July 16, 2011 [all the interviews listed hereafter were conducted by me].

2. Diary of Yehuda Erez, October 22, 1973, Testimonies Collection, BGA.

3. Diary of Shimon Peres, October 14, 1973.

4. An Interview with Mordechai Ben Porat, August 23, 2011.

5. Matilda Guez, August 1, 1979, Testimonies Collection, BGA.

6. An Interview with Bolek Goldman, July 16, 2011.

7. Diary of Shimon Peres, October 14, 1973. After the gathering Peres told a *Davar* journalist that Ben-Gurion expressed his confidence in victory, but according to all other testimonies, this was not so. Meshulam Ad, "Ma amar BG al ha-milhama [What Ben-Gurion said about the war]," *Davar*, December 15, 1973.

8. Bar-Zohar, *Ben-Gurion*, Vol. 3, p. 1522.

9. Bar-Zohar, *Ben-Gurion*, p. 528.

10. Bar-Zohar, *Ben-Gurion*, Vol. 3, p. 1556.

11. Ibid.

12. Ibid.

13. Bar-Zohar, *Ben-Gurion*, p. 541.

14. Yosef Almogi, *Ha-Maavak al Ben-Gurion* [The struggle over Ben-Gurion] (Tel Aviv: Idanim), 1988.

15. Yechiam Weitz, "Ha-Preda meha-av ha-meyased: Prishato shel David Ben-Gurion me-rashut ha-memshala be-1963 [Beeding goodbye to the founding father: Ben-Gurion's retirement as prime minister in 1963]," in *Medina ba-derech* [State in construction] (edited by Anita Shapira) (Jerusalem: The Zalman Shazat Center), 2001, p. 93.

16. Many books and articles were written on Ben-Gurion's attitude to the Holocaust, for example, Friling's book (mentioned in the introduction); Shabtai Tevet, "Ha-Hor ha-shahor: Ben-Gurion bein sho'a li-tekuma [The black hole: Ben-Gurion

between the Holocaust and revival]," *Alpayim* 10 (1994): 111–95; Eliezer Don Yihye, "Mamlachtiyut ve-yahadut ba-haguto uve-mediniyuto shel Ben-Gurion [Judaism and statism in Ben-Gurion's thought and politics]," *Ha-Tziyonut* 14 (1989): 51–88; Dina Porat, "Ben-Gurion ve-sho'at yehudey eropa [Ben-Gurion and the Holocoast]," *ha-Tziyonut* 12 (1987): 293–314; Dina Porat, "Be'aya be-historiografiya: Yahaso shel David Ben-Gurion le-yehudey eropa bi-tkufat ha-sho'a [A Problem in Historiography: Ben-Gurion's attitude towards the Jews of Europe in times of the Holocaust]," *Massua* 19 (1991): 154–65.

17. Ben-Gurion with newspaper editors, March 31, 1961, Protocols Collection, BGA.

18. Bareli, *Lehavin et Ben-Gurion*, p. 70.

19. Ben-Gurion to Yitzhak Ben Aharon, July 14, 1963, Correspondence Collection, BGA.

20. In fact, Harel also headed the *Shin Bet*, the Internal Security Service.

21. "It should be mentioned that Hitler's treats to eliminate the Jews were treated lightly [...] and the 'liberation of Palestine' cannot be attained without destroying the people in Israel [...] Despite my belief that we will prevail over the tree of them [Iraq, Egypt and Syria] in a power-struggle, if it is indeed unavoidable [...] I suggest that the US President and the USSR Prime Minister will publicize a shared statement, saying that the two states guarantee the territorial integrity and safety of every state in the Middle East." A letter from the prime minister to the president of the United States, April 25, 1963, Correspondence Collection, BGA.

22. Kennedy's response was skeptic, and even a bit condescending: "Knowing the full range of dangers related to the situation in Jordan, it seems like danger has decreased, and we share your assessment that Israel is capable of protecting itself against any early Arab attack." US president response to the prime minister, May 26, 1963, Correspondence Collection, BGA.

23. Meron Medzini, *Golda* [Golda] (Tel-Aviv: Yedioth Aharonoth), 2008.

24. Diary of Ben-Gurion, August 19, 1958, ABG.

25. Avner Cohen, "Kennedy, Ben-Gurion veha-krav al Dimona: April-yuni 1963 [Kennedy, Ben-Gurion and the battle over Dimona: Aprile-June 1963]," *Iyunim bi-Tekumat Yisra'el* 6 (1996): 110–46.

26. Conversation protocol between Shimon Peres and President Kennedy, April 2, 1963, Protocol Collection, ABG.

27. Ibid.

28. According to Gidon Tadmur, the second secretary in the Israeli embassy in Washington at the time. "Ben-Gurion ve-Kennedy [Ben-Gurion and Kennedy]," *Ha'aretz*, May 12, 2009, Letters to the Editor.

29. Diary of Ben-Gurion, March 19, 1960.

30. Michael B. Oren, *Power, Faith and Fantasy* (New York: W. W. Norton & Company), 2007: 521–22.

31. An Interview with Shimon Peres, September 20, 2012.

32. Bar-Zohar, *Ben-Gurion*, p. 492.

33. Moshe Pearlman, *David Ben Gurion* (Tel Aviv: Am Oved), 1987, p. 159. According to UNRWA data, about 700,000 Palestinians left or were deported during the War of Independence.

34. Bar-Zohar, *Ben-Gurion*, Vol. 3, p. 1526.

35. Diary of Ben-Gurion, June 7, 1962.

36. Yuval Ne'eman, "Yisrael be-idan haneshek hagarini: Iyum ve-hartaa meever le-1955 [Israel in the nuclear era: Threat and deterrence beyond 1955]," *Nativ* 5 (September 1955), p. 38. It should be noted that Shimon Peres, the deputy defense minister at the time, did not share this assessment. An interview with Shimon Peres, September 20, 2012.

37. Ben-Gurion even suspected that Golda was objecting to the relationship with Germany in an attempt to flatter public opinion, even if it would hurt his position within the party. Diary of Ben-Gurion, June 16, 1963.

38. Ibid.

39. "He was very concerned by forgetting a person's or a place's name at this time, although it was completely natural in light of his age and workload. But compared to his extraordinary memory and his perfectionism, this phenomenon was bothering him tremendously. He used to tell me that human body cells can be renewed, unless they are memory cells. He also consulted his daughter, Renana, who was close to him and beloved by him, and specialized in chemistry and biology, and asked her about it. I think this concern had to do with his decision to resign." An interview with Shimon Peres, September 20, 2012.

40. Diary of Ben-Gurion, September 23, 1953.

41. "*Mapai*'s secretariat has unanimously decided that Levi Eshkol will construct the next government," Maariv, June 18, 1963.

42. Shalom, *Ka-Esh be-atzmotav*, p. 34.

43. Haim Yisraeli, *Megilat Hayim* [A life's story] (Tel-Aviv: Yedioth Aharonoth), 2005, pp. 132–33.

44. Diary of Yehuda Erez, May 13, 1954, Testimonial Collection, October 20, 1978, BGA.

45. Ben-Gurion to Benjamin Akzin, September 19, 1959, Correspondence Collection, BGA.

46. Pearlman, *David Ben Gurion*, p. 136.

47. For further reading see: Jean-Jacques Rousseau, *The Social Contract* (Translated by G. D. H. Cole), online source: http://www.marxists.org/reference/subject/economics/rousseau/social-contract/.

48. Yechiam Weitz, "Ha-Peh she-hitir: Ben-Gurion, hakamat *Rafi* veha-herem al tnu'at ha-*Herut* be-1956 [The Change in Ben-Gurion's Attitude toward the *Herut* Movement during the 1960s]," *ISRAEL* 17 (2010): 134.

49. Diary if Ben-Gurion, July 28, 1963; July 29, 1963.

50. Shalom, *Ka-Esh be-atzmotav*, pp. 32–35.

51. An interview with Amos Degani, a member of *Rafi*, June 21, 2011.

52. Shalom, *Ka-Esh be-atzmotav*, p. 38.

53. *Protocols: Divrei Ha-Knesset* [The Knesset Minutes], August 16, 1949, 2, pp. 1359–60.

54. Ibid.

55. Ben-Gurion to Haim Guri, Correspondence Collection, May 15, 1963, BGA.

56. Diary of Ben-Gurion, January 16, 1964.

57. Official relationship between Israel and the Vatican were established only in December 1993, after the Oslo Accords.

58. For more details about the visit and its significance see: "The Pilgrimage of Pop Poal the Sixth," *LIFE*, January 7, 1964, pp. 18–30.

59. Diary of Ben-Gurion, May 2, 1967.

60. Shalom, *Ka-Esh be-atzmotav*, pp. 15–16.

61. For more details see: Bareli, *Lehavin et Ben-Gurion*, p. 174.

62. For more details see: Hagai Eshed, *Mi natan et ha-hora'a? "ha-esek ha-bish," parashat Lavon ve-hitpatrut Ben-Gurion* [Who gave the order? Lavon affair and Ben-Gurion's resignation] (Jerusaelm: Idanim), 1979; Eyal Kafkafi, *Lavon—anti-masiah* [Lavon—anti-messiah] (Tel-Aviv: Am Oved), 1998; David Ben-Gurion, *Dvarim ke-havayatam* [Thing as they are] (Tel Aviv: Am ha-Sefer), 1965.

63. Weitz, "ha-Preda meha-av ha-meyased," pp. 98–99.

64. Gibli refused to speak to the press for years, but in a testimony for the Ben-Gurion Heritage Archive in 1978, he said that Dayan was informed about the network's activity and Egypt, but chose to deny his responsibility once they were caught: "Moshe never knew how to be loyal to people [...] he knew about the letter, about the operation, he was informed." Binyamin Gibli, July 4, 1978, Video Testimonial Collection, BGA. Gibli's testimony was hidden in BGA and publicized only five decades after the Affair, declaring that Dayan authorized the operation and supporting Lavon's claims. See: Boaz Gaon, "Binyamin Gibli: Dayan natan et hahoraa [Binyamin Gibli: Dayan gave the order]," NRG Website, October 6, 2008, http://www.nrg.co.il/online/1/ART1/796/168.html.

65. In his book, *Dvarim ke-havayatam*, Ben-Gurion offered a rather peculiar justification for his decision to get involved in the Affair only in 1960: "I heard nothing about the 1954 Affair until 1960 [...] on May 5, 1960 I was approached by Lavon, who said that some lieutenant colonel told him there were documents counterfeited by the IDF [...] I immediately told my military secretary [...] to look at it," p. 26.

66. Ben-Gurion's speech in the Knesset about security issues, June 20, 1950. In: David Ben-Gurion, *Yihud ve-yeud: Dvarim al bithon Israel* [Uniqueness and destiny: about Israel's security] (Tel-Aviv: Ma'arachot), 2008, pp. 136–37.

67. David Ben-Guion, "Cariyera o shlihut [career or a mission]," *Hazon va-derech*, 1974, p. 211.

68. Almogi, *Ha-Maavak al Ben-Gurion*, p. 119.

69. Diary of Ben-Gurion, June 16, 1963.

70. David Ben-Gurion, "Sherut halutzi Le-yisrael," a national convention of the party's activists in the rural periphery, Kiryat Haim, May 26, 1950, *Mapai* Collection, special meetings and conventions, pp. 3–4, BGA.

71. Ben-Gurion, "Cariyera o shlihut," p. 212.

72. For more details see: Bareli, *Lehavin et Ben-Gurion*, pp. 144–86.

73. For further reading about Buber's position regarding Ben-Gurion's statehood see: Keren, *Ben Gurion veha-intelektualim*, pp. 85–86.

74. "The IDF—everything would have been gone without it," he highlighted in one of his letters. David Ben-Gurion to Yehezkel Schuster, February 17, 1970, Correspondence Collection, BGA.

75. Diary of Ben-Gurion, June 16, 1963. Ben-Gurion saw the IDF as the key mean for combining the pioneering spirit with that of statehood—a far more important mission than its function as a military organization. Hence, he wanted to require each

soldier to work in agriculture in his/her first year of service (the idea was partially realized in the Nahal Brigade). Aharonson, *Ben-Gurion: Manhig ha-renesans she-shaka*, p. 32.

76. "Neum Ben-Gurion bifney noar ha-moshavim, 1.11.1974 [Ben-Gurion's speech before the Moshavim youth, November 1, 1974], in: Ben-Gurion, *Zichronot min ha-izavon*, Vol. 4, pp. 454–55.

77. Ben-Gurion in a conversation with one of *Mapam*'s leaders (unidentified), 1969, The IDF Archive, file no. 240791.

78. Aharonson, *Ben-Gurion: Manhig ha-renesans she-shaka*, pp. 358–62.

79. Yosef Goldstein, *Eshkol, biografiyah* [Eshkol: A biography] (Jerusalem: Keter Publishers), 2003, p. 518.

80. "You shouldn't prove to me by the history of 'the official' [Isser Harel] that a citizen has no right to keep official documents without permission [...] as for my authority regarding top-secret material—you must have forgotten that I used to be prime minister and defense minister, and I could look at any document." Ben-Gurion to the Labor Minister, Yigal Alon, December 2, 1964, Correspondence Collection, BGA. For further details about Ben-Gurion's deep insult following Alon's demand to investigate him, see: Yisraeli, *Megilat Hayim*, pp. 148–71.

81. Nili Friedlander, "Eich efshar lichtov kach? Shaal aba u-vacha ka-yeled [How can you write like that? Dad asked and wept like a child]," *Maariv*, November 20, 1974, p. 19.

82. "He didn't appreciate him as a great or a good leader. Not at all. He said: 'Alon was a good soldier, he was in the *Palmah*, he was Okay.' But when it came to positions with wider, deeper perspective [...] to some extent, he is Arab. He grew up with the Arabs, he learnt with the Arabs, rode horses with them—he has an Arab mentality, and to some extent, he retained this narrow perspective [...] he is underdeveloped [...] not qualified enough." Aharon Tamir, July 30, 1978, Testimonial Collection, BGA.

83. "Sharett's policy does not correspond with our essential needs [...] I told a few friends—not in the government—that I cannot sit with him, and they went and told him he should resign, and he accepted. I knew that our security policy was our key problem, and Moshe didn't get it." David Ben-Gurion, to M. Ben Elul, June 12, 1970, Correspondence Collection, BGA.

84. Anita Shapira (ed.), *Anu machrizim ba-zot: 60 ne'umim nivharim be-toldot ha-medina* [We hereby declare: Sixty selected speeches from the State's history] (Tel-Aviv: Kinneret–Zmora–Bitan–Dvir), 2008, pp. 98–100.

85. Bareli, *Lehavin et Ben-Gurion*, pp. 148–50.

86. Medzini, *Golda*, p. 400.

87. Ben-Gurion to Dr. Y. Goldstein, July 25, 1957, Correspondence Collection, BGA.

88. An Interview with Amos Degani, June 21, 2011.

89. Yeshaayahu Porat, "24 hashaot she-kadmu le-hitpatruto shel Ben-Gurion [The 24 hours before Ben-Gurion's resignation]," *Yedioth Aharonoth*, May 29, 1964.

90. Medzini, *Golda*, p. 400.

91. "These were the people he nominated. He trusted them and gave them responsibilities—people who worked knowingly to fulfill his mission. And these people were him. It was the system he created. And if they did it—he was the one. I, in any

case, cannot find another explanation. Since the struggle seemed unnecessary. He wasn't involved in the affair, he had no responsibility over the affair." Yitzhak Ben-Aharon, January 27, 1978, Testimonial Collection, BGA.

92. Yehoshua Arieli, *Historiya u-folitika* [History and politics] (Tel-Aviv: Am Oved), 1992, pp. 124–25.

93. Shalom, *Ka-Esh be-atzmotav*, pp. 85–103.

94. Isser Harel, *Bitahon u-demokratya* [Security and democracy] (Jerusalem: Yedioth Aharonoth-Idanim), 1989, pp. 452–53. Harel resigned from his position he got after resigning from the Mossad, Eshkol security advisor, claiming that Eshkol's function as a leader was lacking with regard to the affair. He argued that Eshkol gave the Mossad an ambiguous order regarding Ben-Barka, thus deeply affecting Israel-France relationship. According to Zaky Shalom's research, it is possible that Ben-Gurion's main concern was France would relinquish its support of the nuclear project—which was, in his mind, a key element in the security of the state—and thus, his accusations toward Eshkol were louder because of that. See also: Shlomo Aharonson, "Derech ha-yisurim shel ha-optziya ha-gar'init [The Via Dolorosa of the nuclear option]," *Kivunim Hadashim* 26 (2012): 41–67.

95. Ibid., p. 45.

96. Shalom, *Ka-Esh be-atzmotav*, pp. 85–103.

97. Ibid., p. 107.

CHAPTER 2

1. "I wasn't invited, but I decided to come." Diary of Ben-Gurion, June 27, 1965.

2. Michael Bar-Zohar, *Ke-Of ha-hol—Shimon Peres* [Shimon Peres: The biography] (Tel Aviv: Yedioth Aharonoth), 2006, p. 386.

3. Ibid., pp. 387–89.

4. Shabtai Teveth, *Moshe Dayan* [Moshe Dayan: A biography] (Jerusalem: Schoken), 1971, pp. 526–27.

5. "Be-Hazara labayit ba-sdera [Beck to the house in the boulevard]," *Maariv*, January 30, 1987, p. 2.

6. "[He had] a motivation and a rebellion against the society that was developed under his own leadership and rule. I do not know if he saw everything that was created in this society. I believe he only saw one thing: the monstrous face of the mechanism he built. When he saw the faces of the mechanisms, which were slowly slipping away from his control, he wanted to create a cultural revolution like in China." Yitzhak Ben-Aharon, January 27, 1978, Testimonial Collection, BGA.

7. Menachem Michelson, *Murik—sipur hayav shel Meir Bar'eli* [Murik: the life story of Meir Bareli] (Tel-Aviv: Elilev), 2007, p. 399.

8. Refael Bashan, "Ha-Regaim hagdolim behayay—reayon hashavua im David Ben-Gurion [The greatest moments of my life—the weekly interview with David Ben-Gurion," *Maariv*, May 22, 1970, p. 16.

9. Eli Eyal, "Bi-Shnat 1952 hitzaaty leshahrere et yerushalayim umahoz hevron ach harov bamemshala hitnaged—siha im David Ben-gurion [In 1952, I

suggested we free Jerusalem and Hebron municipality, but the majority of ministers objected—a conversation with David Ben-Gurion]," *Maariv*, April 28, 1971, p. 20.

10. Shimon Peres, *Lech im ha'anashim: Shivah dyokanot* [From these men: Seven founders of the State of Israel] (Tel Aviv, Yedioth Ahronoth), 1979, p. 139.

11. An interview with Shimon Peres, September 20, 2012.

12. Cf. *"Rafi"* in Ynet Encyclopedia, available at: http://www.ynet.co.il/home/ 0,7340,L-1361,00.html.

13. Avraham Wolfenzon, *David Ben-Gurion: Asor le-moto, 1886–1973* [David Ben-Gurion: A decade to his death, 1886–1973] (Tel-Aviv: *Ha-Histadrut Ha-Klalit Shel Ha-Ovdim Be-Eretz Yisra'el*), 1983, p. 30.

14. Diary of Ben-Gurion, June 11, 1965.

15. Ibid., October 8, 1965.

16. Yisraeli, *Megilat Hayim*, p. 175.

17. An interview with Amos Degani, June 21, 2011.

18. The prime minister's speech before senior officers, April 6, 1950, Speeches and Articles Collection, BGA.

19. The melting pot concept was the subject of many books and articles. See, for example, one of the latest most comprehensive among them: Eli'ezer Don-Yihya, *Mashber u-temurah bi-medinah hadashah* [Crisis and Change in a New state] (Jerusalem: Yad Yitzhak Ben-Zvi), 2008.

20. "I was the general secretary of the Histadrut during its first 13 years, and I'm responsible, to a large extent, for its structure and distribution [...] but conditions have changed since then: It is a small crowd, and almost all of them are pioneers from Eastern Europe." Diary of Ben-Gurion, September 17, 1965.

21. Avi Shilon, *Begin 1913–1992* (Tel Aviv: Am Oved), 2008, pp. 243–44.

22. Diary of Ben-Gurion, November 1, 1965.

23. Yosef Almogi, May 30, 1978. Testimonial Collection, BGA.

24. Bar-Zohar, *Ben-Gurion*, Vol. 3, p. 1403.

25. Ben-Gurion to A. Neeman, December 23, 1959, Correspondence Collection, BGA.

26 Diary of Yehuda Ererz, May 27, 1967, November 20, 1978. Testimonial Collection, BGA.

27. Yosef Almogi, May 30, 1978, Testimonial Collection, BGA. For further details about the meeting, see: Medzini, *Golda*, p. 407.

CHAPTER 3

1. Tom Segev, *1967* (Jerusalem: Keter), 2005, pp. 111–12.

2. Nevo, Joseph. *Ha-Mizrah ha-tichon be-yameinu: Yarden: ha-hipus ahar zehut* [The contemporary Middle East: Jordan—In Search of an Identity] (Ra'anana: The Open University), 2005, p. 123. According to them, the operation shifted King Hussein's attitude toward Israel. Following the operation, he feared that Israel planned on destroying his regime, which pushed him to join 1967 War.

3. "Ben-Gurion loved Yitzhak, and was grateful to him for the rest of his life for remaining in the army after the *Palmah* was desolated, although he did participate in the desolation ceremony." An interview with Yariv Ben-Eliezer, June 9, 2011.

4. Diary of Ben-Gurion, July 23, 1970.

5. Shalom, *Ka-Esh be-atzmotav*, pp. 36–37.

6. Yitzhak Rabin (with Dov Goldstein), *Pinkas sherut* [Service book] (Tel-Aviv: Ma'ariv), 1979, p. 55.

7. Shaul Webber, *Yitzhak Rabin—Tzmichato shel manhig* [Yitzhak Rabin—A Growth of a Leader] (Tel Aviv: Maariv), 2009, pp. 230–34.

8. Rabin and Goldstein, *Pinkas sHerut*, p. 86.

9. Yigal Eilam, *Ma hitrachesh kan* [What happened here] (Tel-Aviv: Am Oved), 2012.

10. Diary of Ben-Gurion, May 22, 1967.

11. Ibid.

12. The prime minister with newspapers' editors, March 13, 1964, Protocole Collection, BGA.

13. Rabin and Goldstein, *Pinkas sHerut*, p. 150.

14. Yohanan Bader, Oral Documentation Collection, The State Archive.

15. Segev, *1967*, pp. 268–91.

16. Aviezer Golan and Shlomo Nakdimon, *Begin* (Tel Aviv: Yedioth Aharonoth), 1978, p. 223.

17. Segev, *1967*, p. 335.

18. An interview with Shimon Peres, September 20, 2012. "These were the hardest 24 hours in my life," he said later.

19. Ibid.

20. Ibid. See also a similar description in: Bar-Zohar, *Ke-Of ha-hol*, pp. 398–400.

21. After completing the mission, Ben-Gurion said to the members of *Rafi*: "I knew many people in my life, but none was as unselfish as Shimon." An interview with Shimon Peres, September 9, 2012.

22. Bar-Zohar, *Ke-Of ha-hol*, p. 400.

23. An interview with Prof. Bolek Goldman, July 16, 2011.

24. Ben-Gurion to Yigal Yadin, March 9, 1964, Correspondence Collection, BGA.

25. Moshe Dayan, *Avnei derech* [Milestones] (Jerusalem: Yedioth Aharonoth-Idanim), 1976, p. 691.

26. Moshe Dayan, *Lihyot im ha-tanach* [Living with the Bible] (Jerusalem: Yedioth Aharonoth-Idanim), 1978, pp. 177–78.

27. Diary of Ben-Gurion, June 1, 1967.

28. Bar-Zohar, *Ben-Gurion*, p. 553.

29. Dayan, *Avney Derech*, p. 432.

30. Shalom, *Ka-Esh be-atzmotav*, p. 260.

31. Dayan, *Avney derech*, p. 410.

32. Shalom, *Ka-Esh be-atzmotav*, p. 274.

33. Diary of Ben-Gurion, June 9, 1967.

34. Oren, *Power, Faith and Fantasy*, pp. 523–25.

35. Ben-Gurion to Yoseph Weitz, June 12, 1967, Correspondence Collection, BGA.

36. Bar-Zohar, *Ben-Gurion*, p. 556.

37. Diary of Ben-Gurion, January 31, 1969.

38. An interview with Michael Bar-Zohar, November 21, 2011.

39. Ben-Gurion repeated his objection to returning the Golan Heights in many occasions, in both oral and written statements. In a television program, he explains his objection by describing a personal experience: "I worked in the region of the Golan Heights for three years, as a laborer. I came to the Golan Heights in the seventh day of the war, and when I saw it, I said: 'Dear God, how did they survive?' [The soldiers and communities at the foot of the Golan Heights]. Those on top can do whatever they want with those at the bottom. And those at the bottom can do nothing. I saw it, and I knew they wanted to destroy the communities in the Galilee. How could they not do it? It just shows you that they [the Arabs] are incompetent, how incompetent do you need to be in order to lose that." Ben-Gurion in a conversation with an unidentified French interviewer, March 1, 1972, Correspondence Collection, BGA. See also: Moked, The Israeli Television, May 1, 1970, Correspondence Collection, BGA.

40. Diary of Ben-Gurion, June 8, 1967.

41. Aharon Tamir, July 30, 1978, Correspondence Collection, BGA.

42. Ben-Gurion to Shoshana Zehavi, July 17, 1967, Correspondence Collection, BGA.

43. Aharon Tamir, July 30, 1978, Correspondence Collection, BGA.

44. David Ben-Gurion, "Jerusalem's sister," January 25, 1970, Chronologic Documentation Collection, BGA. The article was later published in: Oded Avishar (ed.), *Sefer Hevron* [The Hebron book] (Jerusalem: Keter), 1970, pp. 14–15.

45. Ben-Gurion to David Snir, April 10, 1970, Correspondence Collection, BGA.

46. Ben-Gurion to Ezer Weizman, August 13, 1972, Correspondence Collection, BGA.

47. Bar-Zohar, *Ben-Gurion*, p. 443.

48. Ben-Gurion in a government meeting, September 26, 1948, Protocol Collection, BGA.

49. Diary of Ben-Gurion, June 7, 1967.

50. Dayan, *Avney derech*, p. 552.

51. Moked, The Israeli Television, May 1, 1970, Protocol Collection, BGA.

52. Ben-Gurion to Meir Baruch, July 19, 1967, Correspondence Collection, BGA.

53. Moked, The Israeli Television, May 1, 1970, Protocol Collection, BGA.

54. Ben-Gurion to Binyamin Nahary, September 18, 1979, Correspondence Collection, BGA.

55. Ben-Gurion to Shmuel Peer, July 17, 1967, Correspondence Collection, BGA.

56. Regarding his unison aspiration see: *Mapai* meeting, November 23, 1961, LPA, 61/23.

57. Diary of Ben-Gurion, November 25, 1950. After the electoral achievement of HaZionim HaKlaliyim in November 1950 election, he wrote in his diary: "This

is obviously not a mere conjectural rise, but the beginning of the formation of the Bourgeoisie."

58. Bareli, *Lehavin et Ben-Gurion*, p. 181.

59. An interview with Mordechai Ben-Porat, August 23, 2011.

60. Ben-Gurion to Shimon Peres and Yoseph Almogi, January 24, 1968, Correspondence Collection, BGA.

61. An interview with Aharon Eldan, September 8, 2011.

62. Mira Avrech, *Paula* [Paula] (Tel Aviv: Am ha-Sefer), 1965, p. 16.

63. An interview with Avraham Tzivion, August 31, 1968.

64. "At 2:00pm, she will be buried in the grave reserved for me (I was always certain I'll die first)." Diary of Ben-Gurion, January 30, 1968.

65. Ben-Gurion to Lea Edelman, June 13, 1968, Correspondence Collection, BGA.

66. Shabtai Keshev, "Paula Ben-Gurion (shloshim li-ftirata) [Paula Ben-Gurion (thirty days after her death)], *Davar*, February 28, 1968, p. 6.

67. Ben-Gurion to Moshe Glokin, March 13, 1968, Correspondence Collection, BGA.

68. Ben-Gurion to Moshe Soroka, January 12, 1968, Correspondence Collection, BGA.

69. Ben-gurion to S. L. Shragai, September 18, 1968, Correspondence Collection, BGA. The letter is based on an interview he gave in 1962 to *LOOK* magazine, which is quoted here with some abbreviations.

70. "Zionist Conspiracy for World Government from Jerusalem," in http://mail-star.net/tmf.html.

71. "The accusation of dispossession was first heard in Shaw Commission, after the 1929 Palestinian wave of violence. It was later inspected by English investigators and was found to be false. At the time, the JNA representatives argued in front of the royal commission that the Jews came to Palestine not in order to improve the Arabs' position, but in order to build themselves a national home. The settlement of the Jews has no external motive. It is a goal within itself: To solve the problem of the Jewish people and to re-root it in its old homeland. But the nature of the Jewish immigration and settlement, the essence of the Jewish creative process, is such that all the residents of the land enjoy the results of these immigration and settlement process. The royal commission examined this argument and reached the conclusion that the Jewish settlement was a blessing to the entire residents of the land and improved the Arabs' standard of living." David Ben-Gurion, *Ba-Ma'aracha* [In Battle], Vol. 2 (Tel Aviv: Am-Oved), 1957, p. 150.

72. For further details, see: Yosef Gorny, *Ha-Sheela haarvit ve-habaya ha-yehudit, 1948–1882* [Zionism and the Arabs, 1882–1948: A study of ideology] (Tel Aviv: Am-Oved), 1985.

73. Mordechai Barkai, "David Ben-Gurion be-reayon meyuhad le-*Davar*" [David Ben-Gurion in a special interview to *Davar*], *Davar*, July 24, 1970, pp. 14, 17.

74. Shabtai Teveth, *Ben-Gurion ve-arviey Israel: Me-hashlam le-haslama* [Ben-Gurion and the Palestinian Arabs: From peace to war] (Jerusalem: Schoken), 1985, p. 225. Concerning his approach to Israeli Arabs, see: Shabtai Teveth, "Ben-Gurion veha-sheela ha-arvit [Ben-Gurion and the Arab question]," *Kathedra*, 43 (March

1978): 52–68; Gabriel Shefer, "Pitron kolel mul mitun ha-sichsuch ha-yisra'eli-aravi: bhina mehudeshet shel ha-hitnagshut bein Moshe Shart ve-David Ben-Gurion [Comperhansive solution versus conflict moderation: reexamining the collision between Moshe Sharet and David Ben-Gurion]," in *Ha-Tziyonut veha-she'ela ha-aravit* [Zionism and the Arab Question] (edited by Menachem Stern), 119–163 (Jerusalem: The Zalman Shazar Center), 1979.

75. Zeev Jabotinski, "Al kir ha-barzel," November 11, 1923. Retrieved from Jabotinski Institution's website: http://www.jabotinsky.org/multimedia/upl_doc/doc_241007_29453.pdf.

76. Concerning Ben-Gurion's adoption of the Iron Wall concept see: Avi Shlaim, *Kir ha'barzel* [The Iron Wall: Israel and the Arab World] (Tel Aviv: Yedioth Ahronoth), 2005.

77. "A constant, energetic and dynamic striving to ensure friendly and mutual-assistance relationship without neighboring countries—first and foremost, the Arab states—is the highest priority of Israel's foreign policy. The current animosity of the Arab states towards Israel is exaggerated and artificial, and won't necessarily hold on after the state is established. As much as the Arab citizen in our state will feel at home, and his status will be no different than that of the Jew, and maybe better than that of Arabs in Arab states, and the state will constantly and honestly help him to achieve the Jewish *Yishuv*'s financial, social and cultural standard of living, the Arab suspicion will be reduced and a bridge of Semitic, Arab-Jewish alliance will be built in the Near East." David Ben-Gurion at *Mapai*'s meeting, December 13, 1947, Protocol Collection, BGA.

78. Bar-Zohar, *Ben-Gurion*, Vol. 3, p. 1411.

79. Divrey HaKnesset, February 20, 21, 1962. Retrieved from Daat website: http://www.daat.ac.il/daat/ezrachut/begin/neum11-2.htm.

80. Pearlman, *David Ben Gurion*, p. 155.

81. Ibid., pp 152–62.

82. The Ambassador in London to Shlomo Hilel, Foreign Ministry Deputy Director, November 6, 1969, Chronologic Documentation Collection, BGA.

83. Ibid.

84. Ibid.

85. The first meeting with Alami, which was reported in the embassy's telegram, was not mentioned in Diary of Ben-Gurion. But after two weeks, he used the code name Musa to mention in his diary the second meeting. I found no documentation of the meeting's details. His enthusiasm is evident in the fact that he mentioned it immediately when he was told that Alami was willing to meet again: "Just now, at qarter past five, Aharon Remez phoned me from London and said that Musa wants to meet." Diary of Ben-Gurion, August 25, 1969. It is possible that the details of this meeting appear in the part of his diary which is still confidential.

86. The last political meeting of his career did not result in any practical breakthrough, but the similarities between the outlines designed in the meeting and the beginning of the negotiation between Israel and the Palestinians, as drafted in Madrid Conference in 1991, are visible: More than twenty years after Ben-Gurion–Alami meeting, the Likud government, headed by Yitzhak Shamir, agreed to meet Palestinian

representatives, as part of a joint Jordanian-Palestinian delegation. Following this negotiation, the Oslo Accords were signed two years later by the *Ma'arach* government under Yitzhak Rabin and the PLO under Yasser Arafat.

87. Refael Bashan, "ha-Regaim ha-gdolim be-hayay—Reayon ha-shavua im David Ben-Gurion [The greatest moments of my life—The weekly interview with David Ben-gurion]," *Maariv*, May 22, 1970, p. 16.

88. Ibid.

89. Ha-Kibbutz ha-meuhad Archive, 141–43, Danni Operation headquarters to Yiftah and Hativa 8 headquarters, July 12, 1948, in: Webber, *Yitzhak Rabin – Tzmichato shel manhig*, p. 223.

90. Even if Rabin's testimony was true, it can be interpreted in different ways. According to Yoav Gelber, Ben-Gurion always paid attention to documentation and clear instructions, and such an order cannot be attributed to him based on a hand gesture alone. Thus, it seems that Alon and Rabin chose the interpretation to what they saw. See: Yoav Gelber, *Komemiyut ve-nakba* [Independence and nakba] (Or Yehuda: Kinneret, Zmora-Bitan, and Dvir), 2004.

91. Diary of Ben-Gurion, January 29, 1969.

92. Ben-Gurion to Golda Meir, January 29, 1969, Correspondence Collection, BGA.

93. Ben-Gurion to Menachem Begin, February 6, 1969, Correspondence Collection, BGA. At the end of his letter, Ben-Gurion mentioned: "Reading my letter to Golda, you will understand why I perceive a disaster and a danger if Levi Eshkol's government will continue to exist. Of course, you are free to judge things according to your discretion."

94. According to his grandson, Yariv Ben-Eliezer, Ben-Gurion continued to despise Begin in personal conversations, despite his reconciliation letter. An interview with Ben-Eliezer, July 9, 2011. His son, Amos, also said: "He never change his mind nor his appreciation of Begin, and if it seemed like his position was softened in his later years—it was all due to my mother." Dov Goldstein, "David Ben-Gurion—Avi [David Ben-Gurion – My father]," *Maariv*, October 17, 1986, pp. 29–30.

95. Diary of Ben-Gurion, February 26, 1969.

96. Ben-Gurion to Zakai, March 4, 1969, Correspondence Collection, BGA.

97. An interview with Mordechai Ben-Porat, August 23, 2011.

98. Moshe Dayan, *Avney Derech*, p. 551.

99. "Ben-Gurion believed that his marriage to Miryam was one of the reasons to the change [...] during our conversations, he specifically said that she wasn't a positive influence. She was deeply involved [...] 'he has changed,' this wasn't Eshkol as he knew him, he said." Aharon Tamir, August 18, 1978, Testimonial Collection, BGA.

100. Anita Shapira, *Yigal Allon, aviv heldo, [Igal Alon: Spring of his Life]* (Tel Aviv: ha-Kibbutz ha-Meuhad), 2004, pp. 420–25.

101. Shlomo Nakdimon, "Medinat Israel od eina kayemet [The state of Israel still doesn't exist]," *Yedioth Aharonoth*, May 22, 1970, pp. 5, 15.

102. Yigal Alon, "Le-Ahar kenes talmidim [after a meeting with students]," *La-Merhav*, Vol. 2, June 16, 1954, p. 1.

103. Tzahor, "Ben-Gurion kotev biyografiya," pp. 144–56.

104. "*Mapam* is a Communist semi-cult, which can see the big picture concerning the state's problems." Diary of Ben-Gurion, June 27, 1965.

105. Ibid., June 29, 1965.

106. Ben-Gurion in a conversation with one of *Mapam*'s leaders (unidentified), 1969, Protocol Collection, BGA.

107. Tzahor, *Ha-Hazon veha-heshbon*, p. 197.

108. David Ben-Gurion, "Parashat Drachim [Crossroads]," in *Mi-Maamad le-am* [From class to people], p. 21 (Tel-Aviv: Am Oved), 1974. The article was first published in *Der Yiddisher Kemper*, New York, January 4, 1918.

109. *Divrei Ha-Knesset*, January 16, 1950, p. 536.

110. Meir Avizohar, May 12, 1976, Correspondence Collection, BGA.

111. Ben-Gurion to S. Tzukerman, Kibbutz Hulda, December 12, 1953, Correspondence Collection, BGA.

112. "David Ben-Gurion be-reayon meyuhad le-yovel ha-*Histadrut* [David Ben-Gurion in a special interview for the *Histadrut*'s 50 anniversary]," *Davar*, December 28, 1970, p. 15.

113. Ben-Gurion in a conversation with one of *Mapam*'s leaders (unidentified), 1969, IDFA, file no. 240791.

114. Tzahor, Ze'ev. "Ya'akov Hazan: Naftuley ha-derech shel ha-hanhaga ha-historit [Yaakov Hazan: The vicissitudes of the historical leadership]," *ISRAEL* 3(2003): 97–110.

115. Shlomo Nakdimon and Nissim Taito, "BG be-pgisha im studentim shel ha-Avoda bi-Sde-Boker [BG in a meeting with ha-Avoda students in Sde-Boker," *Yedioth Aharonoth*, December 13, 1970.

116. Ben-Gurion in a conversation with one of *Mapam*'s leaders (unidentified), 1969, Protocol Collection, BGA.

117. An interview with Amos Degani, June 21, 2011.

118. "Ben-Gurion was the Messiah to me. I followed him without even thinking about myself. And when I believed him, I believed in myself. I wasn't the only one who saw him as a Messiah. I heard it for the first time on Berl's funeral." Zeev sherf, the government secretary in the years 1948–1957, Testimonial Collection, August 5, 1975, BGA.

119. Diary of Ben-Gurion, August 14, 1969.

120. Bareli, *Lehavin et Ben-Gurion*, pp. 190–91.

121. Bar-Zohar, *Ben-Gurion*, Vol. 3, p. 1413.

122. Ben-Gurion commented that in 1933 he got "louder and louder standing ovations," compared to the applause to the rest of the Zionist board members. David Ben-Gurion, *Zichronot* [Memoirs], Vol. 1 (Tel-Aviv: Am Oved), 1964, p. 663. Zeev Tzahor referred me to this source.

123. Diary of Ben-Gurion, February 16, 1969.

124. "Stern came to me in the morning. He wants me to organize a list for the next Knesset, and he will join it. I told him I might use the press sometime soon to approach *Rafi*'s voters and supporters, to ask them to notify me whether they are interested in another *Rafi* party, in which case I will join as the last candidate on the list. Because I will not go back to official activity anymore." Diary of Ben-Gurion, February 10, 1969.

125. An interview with Amos Degani, June 21, 2011.

126. Diary of Ben-Gurion, February 10, 1969.

127. Ibid., March 4, 1969.
128. Ibid., August 21, 1969.
129. *Ha-Reshima Ha-Mamlachtit* to its supporters, December 24, 1969, Protocol Collection, BGA.
130. An interview with Yariv Ben-Eliezer, July 8, 2011.
131. Diary of Ben-Gurion, April 13, 1969.
132. After resigning from his job as the chief commander of the Mossad, Isser was appointed to be Eshkol's security adviser, but later resigned, following disputes with Eshkol about Ben-Barka's assassination and other issues. Shalom, *Ka-Esh be-atzmotav*, p. 105.
133. Yehoshua Cohen, May 21, 1979, Testimonial Collection, BGA.
134. An interview with Zalman Shoval, September 8, 2011.
135. Ben-Gurion in a conversation with one of *Mapam*'s leaders (unidentified), 1969, IDFA, file no. 240791.
136. Ben-Gurion, "Lama *Rafi* [Why vote for *Rafi*]," January 1, 1970, Speeches and Articles Collection, BGA.
137. An interview with Zalman Shoval, member of *Ha-Reshima Ha-Mamlachtit*, September 8, 2011.
138. Diary of Ben-Gurion, November 6, 1969; November 9, 1969.
139. Ibid., October 30, 1969.
140. Ibid., November 6, 1969.
141. An interview with Amos Degani, June 21, 2011.
142. Ben-Gurion's speech at a convention of *Ha-Reshima Ha-Mamlachtit*, Sde-Boker, April 18, 1970, Protocol Collection, BGA.
143. Ibid.
144. Ibid.
145. Ibid.
146. Yosef Gorny, "Ha-Re'alizem ha-utopi ba-tziyonut [Utopian realism in Zionism]," in *Reshafim: Hebetim historiyim, filosofiyim ve-hevratiyim shel ha-hinukh: Asupah le-zikhro shel Prof. Shim'on Reshef, zal* [Reshafim: Historical, philosophical, and social aspects of education: a collection in memory of Prof. Shim'on Reshef], edited by Rina Shapira, 37–49 (Tel-Aviv: Tel-Aviv University Press), 1991.
147. According to an interview with Prof. Tuvia Friling conducted in August 2012.
148. Ben-Gurion's speech at a convention of Ha-Reshima Ha-Mamlachtit, Sde-Boker, April 18, 1970, Protocol Collection, BGA.
149. Ibid.
150 "Sikum shel divrey Ben-Gurion be-moetzet *Mapai*, 16.4.1939 [A summary of Ben-Gurion's speech in *Mapai*'s secretariat, April 16, 1939," in Aharonson, *David Ben-Gurion: Manhig ha-renesans she-shaka*, p. 63.

CHAPTER 4

1. Yehoshua Cohen, May 21, 1979, Testimonial Collection, BGA.
2. Refael Bashan, "Ha-Regaim hagdolim behayay," *Maariv*, May 22, 1970, p. 16.
3. Aharon Tamir, July 30, 1978, Testimonial Collection, BGA.

4. Ben-Gurion to Yaakov Tzur, June 12, 1970, Correspondence Collection, BGA.

5. Yona Cohen, *Ha-Keneset kemot she-hi: Diyunim ve-hiyukhim* [The Knesset as it is: Discussions and conflicts] (Tel Aviv: Am ha-Sefer), 1972, p. 119.

6. Concerning the myth and its significance, see: David Ohana and Robert S. Wistrich, "Mavo: Nochehut ha-mitosim ba-yahadut, ba-tziyonut uva-yisra'eliyut [Introduction: The presence of myths in Judaism, Zionism and Israelism]," in *Mitos ve-zikaron*, pp. 11–37.

7. David Ben-Gurion to Esther Herlitz, December 19, 1971, Correspondence Collection, BGA.

8. "He threatened the hairstylist. 'This time you'll cut it, no matter what. Cut it short.' Off course, I had warned the hairstylist beforehand. I stood behind him and signed him 'that's it.'" Aharon Tamir, April 3, 1979, Testimonial Collection, BGA.

9. Another person who mentioned in his memoirs the funny feeling created by Ben-Gurion's short haircut was Elimelech Ram, from the Israeli Television, who met him that day. "The first thing I noticed was his new haircut. His white mane, which was signature look, disappeared completely. Instead, the hairdresser gave him a short haircut, which exposed his robbed-looking face, if one may say so." Elimelech Ram, *Be-Kol ram* [Out loud] (Tel-Aviv: Yedioth Aharonoth), 2011, p. 80.

10. Shlomo Nakdimon, "Medinat Israel od eina kayemet [The state of Israel still doesn't exist]," *Yedioth Aharonoth*, May 22, 1970, pp. 5, 15.

CHAPTER 5

1. Diary of Ben-Gurion, January 1, 1970.

2. An interview with Dr. Avraham Tzivion, the founder and first CEO of Sde-Boker College, August 31, 2011.

3. Yehoshua Cohen, May 21, 1979, Testimonial Collection, BGA. During the 1950s, according to Yehoshua's calculation, Ben-Gurion was walking one kilometer in twelve minutes.

4. Refael Bashan, "Ha-Regaim hagdolim behayay: Reayon ha-shavua im David Ben-Gurion [The greatest moments of my life: The weekly interview with David Ben-Gurion]," *Maariv*, p. 16. October 22, 1970.

5. An interview with Aharon Eldan, Commander of the *Shin Bet*'s VIP Protection Unit in the 1970s and Ben-Gurion's security detail when he was prime minister, September 8, 2011.

6. Aharon Tamir, July 30, 1978, Testimonial Collection, BGA.

7. An interview with Avraham Tzivion, August 31, 2011.

8. Refael Bashan, "Yom im BG [A day with BG]," *Ba-Mahane*, September 14, 1971, p. 27.

9. Y Rabi, "Dvarim she-amar BG li [Things I heard from BG]," *Al Ha-Mishmar*, March 9, 1971, pp. 4–5, 26.

10. Ezer Weizman, May 4, 1992, Testimonial Collection, BGA. According to Weizman, after Ben-Gurion had passed away, he regretted the fact he rejected the proposal for a lunch with him.

11. Yehoshua Cohen (1922–1986) was a *Lehi* member who commanded the attempted assassination of the High Commissioner of the British Mandate in Palestine, Harold MacMichael, and was the one who shot and killed the UN mediator, Count Folke Bernadotte, in 1948. In 1952, after his request to join the standing army forces was rejected due to his past as a *Lehi* member, Cohen joined Sde-Boker. When Ben-Gurion decided to settle there in 1953, Cohen was made responsible for his safety. They became close friends over the years.

12. An interview with Michael Bar-Zohar, November 21, 2011.

13. Yehoshua Cohen, May 21, 1979, Testimonial Collection, BGA.

14. Ibid.

15. Pearlman, *David Ben-Gurion*, p. 75.

16. His assessment that the dissidents' activities will have negative effect over public opinion in the world and unite it against Zionism, as well as his desire to establish the authority of the Labor camp in the *Yishuv*, was among the reasons for his struggle against them. See: Ben-Gurion to the Zionist Board in Jerusalem, October 3, 1938, Correspondence Collection, BGA.

17. Aharonson, *David Ben-Gurion: Manhig ha-renesdsans she-shaka*, p. 307.

18. "I remember some harsh expressions about Begin, not dismissing him as a person, but rejecting his whole method, his entire ideology, even a year or two before he died. Even after Altelana was forgotten by most of the public. He never believed the weapon on Altelana posed a threat to the state's security, but it bothered him that there was a government, and there was a group of people who may have been dedicated to the Zionist idea in their own way, but it was their own." Aharon Tamir, April 3, 1979, Testimonial Collection, BGA.

19. David Ben-Gurion, "Ha-Medina veha-Etzel [The state and the *IZL*]," *Maariv*, August 27, 1971, pp. 21–22.

20. Yehoshua Cohen, May 21, 1979, Testimonial Collection, BGA.

21. For further details see: Shlomo Nakdimon, *Altalena* [Altalena] (Tel-Aviv: Yedioth Aharonoth), 1978, pp. 109–33; Uri Benner, *Altalena: Mehkar medini u-tzva'i* [Altalena: Political and military research] (Tel Aviv: ha-Kibbutz ha-Meuchad), 1978, pp. 70–86.

22. David Ben-Gurion, "Ha-Medina veha-Etzel [The state and the *IZL*]," *Maariv*, August 27, 1971, pp. 21–22.

23. Ibid.

24. Ben-Gurion in a meeting with Jewish students, July 13, 1971, Protocol Collection, BGA.

25. Yehoshua Cohen, May 21, 1979, Testimonial Collection, BGA.

26. The omission was revealed by the journalist Tom Segev, who examined the original diary. Tom Segev, "Ulay ze mikre, aval kol anshei ha-mishmar, yesh laem partzuf shel ha-olam ha-tahton [It might be a coincidence, but all of the Mishmar people look like criminals]," *Haaretz*, July 10, 1983.

27. During the Saisons, when Ben-Gurion was asked why the *IZL* members are being persecuted rather than the *Lehi* members, he answered: "*Lehi* is an organization that honestly believes they could bring about salvation through murder, while actually striving to control the *Yishuv*." Yaacov Shavit, *Onat ha-tzayid: ha-Seison* [The hunting season: The saison] (Tel-Aviv: Hadar), 1976, p. 92.

28. Ben-Gurion to Geula Cohen, January 20, 1962, Correspondence Collection, BGA.

29. The story about Ben-Gurion's statement saying the cannon that shot at Altelana was a "holy cannon" was a myth, based on his statement that this cannon "should be positioned next to the Holy Temple, if it is ever constructed," cited in: Brenner, *Altalena*, p. 275. According to Bar-Zohar, who interviewed Yehoshua Cohen, the *Lehi* member considered Ben-Gurion's letter to Geula Cohen as an apology for their past animosity and a willingness to reconcile.

30. According to Christoph Schmidt, political theology means using religious terms in order to describe the release of the human being from the ropes of religion in favor of national and civil ideals. Similarly, Ben-Gurion used theological terms to highlight the importance of the state, its institutions, and values.

For further details see: David Ohana, "Meshihiyut hilonit ke-teologia politit: Ha-Mikre shel Ben-Gurion [Secular messianism as political theology: Ben-Gurion's case study]," in Christoph Schmidt (ed.), *Ha-Elohim lo ye'alem dom: ha-Moderna ha-yehudit veha-te'ologiya ha-politit* [God will not stand still: Jewish modernity and political theology], pp. 204–20 (Jerusalem: The Van Leer Institute), 2009.

31. For further reading about Ben-Gurion's statism concept see: Nir Kedar, *Mamlachtiyut: ha-tfisa ha-ezrahit shel David Ben-Gurion* [Statism: David Ben-Gurion's civic thought] (Jerusalem: Ben-Gurion University Press and Yad Yitzhak Ben-Zvi), 2009.

32. Yehoshua Cohen, May 21, 1979, Testimonial Collection, BGA.

33. Shlomo Nakdimon, "Medinat Israel od eina kayemet [The state of Israel still doesn't exist]," *Yedioth Aharonoth*, May 22, 1970, pp. 5, 15.

34. Aharonson, *David Ben-Gurion: Manhig ha-renesdsans she-shaka*, p. 287.

35. Shlomo Nakdimon and Nissim Taito, "BG be-pgisha im studentim shel Ha-Avoda be-Sde-Boker [BG in a meeting with Ha-Avoda students in Sde-Boker]," *Yedioth Aharonoth*, December 13, 1970, p. 7.

36. Ibid.

37. Ben-Gurion to S. Shhariya, February 17, 1970, Correspondence Collection, BGA.

38. Ben-Gurion to William Smith, NY, May 14, 1970, Correspondence Collection, BGA.

39. Ben-Gurion to Y. Winstok, February 16, 1970, Correspondence Collection, BGA.

40. Ben-Gurion to the members of Kibbutz Ein-Gedi, December 17, 1970, Protocol Collection, BGA.

41. Yisraeli, *Megilat Hayim*, p. 225.

42. An interview with Aharon Eldan, September 8, 2011.

43. Ben-Gurion to Haim Shiba, December 21, 1970, Correspondence Collection, BGA.

44. "He was invested fully in his goal, his activity, a man with no tricks or pretending. Even if you were close to him, you couldn't ask him about insults and stuff like that." An interview with Shimon Peres, September 19, 2012.

45. Ben-Gurion to Zeev Sherf, April 13, 1970, Correspondence Collection, BGA.

46. Diary of Ben-Gurion, February 6, 1959.

47. Ben-Gurion's meeting schedule, May–June 1970, Chronological Documentation Collection, BGA.

48. Tzahor, *Ha-Hazon veha-heshbon*, p. 237.

49. An interview with Aharon Eldan, September 8, 2011.

50. Ben-Gurion to Sara Rozenfeld, January 13, 1954, in: Zehava Ostfeld (Ed.). *Ha-Zaken veha-am: Mivhar igrot ishiyot shel David Ben-Gurion* [The old man and the people—Selected Letters of David Ben-Gurion] (Tel-Aviv: The Ministry of Defense), 1988, p. 217.

51. Ben-Gurion to David G., January 17, 1954, Correspondence Collection, BGA.

52. Ben-Gurion to Menachem Begin, February 6, 1969, Correspondence Collection, BGA.

53. Diary of Ben-Gurion, September 26, 1963.

54. Elhanan Shai, Ben-Gurion's assistant when he first retired to Sde-Boker, September 12, 1977, Testimonial Collection, BGA.

55. "At some point, he called me to the kitchen and asked: 'Yariv, what book would you like me to give you as a wedding present?' I had to say something, so I said: 'You know what? This is too important. I'll have to consult Dalia.' We left the kitchen, I approached Grandma and said: 'Is he kidding me? A book as a wedding present?' Of course, Grandma made him sign a check. The point is that for him, a book was something sublime, and everyday needs were insignificant to him." Yariv Ben-Eliezer, Ben-Gurion's grandson, August 8, 1976, Testimonial Collection, BGA.

56. Ben-Gurion in a conversation with Levi Yitzhak Hayerushalmi, February 28, 1972, Protocol Collection, BGA.

57. Ben-Gurion in the documentary dedicated to him in 1972, "Ben-Gurion zocher [Ben-Gurion remembers]." The producer Tzi Speilman allowed me to see the whole film on November 18, 2011.

58. Daniela Shemi, "Kmo yeled katan she-ibed et olamo [Like a young child who lost everything]," *Anashim*, December 28, 1981, pp. 25, 50.

59. Diary of Ben-Gurion, August 9, 1970.

60. Ibid., September 25, 1970.

61. Ibid.

62. Geula Ben-Eliezer, July 30, 1976, Testimonial Collection, BGA.

63. Diary of Ben-Gurion, August 15, 1970.

64. An interview with Yariv Ben-Eliezer, July 9, 2011.

65. Ben-Gurion's speech before the Journalists Association, November 29, 1951, in: Zaki Shalom, "Ben-Gurion veha-itonut—halacha le-maase [Ben-Gurion and the press—theory and practice]," *Kesher* 20 (November 1996), pp. 57–60.

66. Ben-Gurion's speech in *Noar Ha-moshavim* convention, Nahalal, June 11, 1954, Articles and Speeches Collection, BGA.

67. Diary of Ben-Gurion, May 6, 1971.

68. Ben-Gurion to Benjamin Akzin, October 17, 1959, Correspondence Collection, BGA.

69. Diary of Ben-Gurion, May 9, 1970.

70. Ibid.

71. For further details about Nehemiah Argov's story and his significance in Ben-Gurion's life see: Yisraeli, *Megilat Hayim*, pp. 36–50.

72. Bar-Zohar, *Ben-Gurion*, pp. 505–6.

73. "He claimed that Nehemiah was loyal and dedicated to him for many years, day and night, and he never knew and never asked what he was going through in his personal life." Yehuda Erez, November 14, 1978, Testimonial Collection, BGA.

74. Diary of Ben-Gurion, October 23, 1970.

75. David Ben-Guion, *Michtavim el Poula ve-el ha-yeladim* [Letters to Paula and the kids] (Tel-Aviv: Am Oved), 1969.

76. Ben-Gurion to Haim Hazaz, May 24, 1968, in: Ostfeld (Ed.), *Ha-Zaken veha-am*, p. 24.

77. Diary of Ben-Gurion, May 25, 1970.

78. Shlomo Nakdimon and Nissim Taito, "BG be-pgisha im studentim shel Ha-Avoda be-Sde-Boker [BG in a meeting with *Ha-Avoda* students in Sde-Boker]," *Yedioth Aharonoth*, December 13, 1970, p. 7.

79. Geula Ben-Eliezer, July 30, 1976, Testimonial Collection, BGA.

80. Ibid.

81. From Yehuda Erez's diary, Mat 11, 1954, Testimonial Collection, BGA.

82. Yehoshua Cohen, May 21, 1979, Testimonial Collection, BGA.

83. Ben-Gurion to Malka Cahana, September 18, 1968, in: Ostfeld (Ed.), *Ha-Zaken veha-am*, p. 31.

84. Bar-Zohar, *Ben-Gurion*, Vol. 1, pp. 491–94.

85. Ben-Gurion to Geula, December 20, 1953, Correspondence Collection, BGA.

86. Yisraeli, *Megilat Hayim*, p. 192.

87. Aharon Meidan, April 3, 1979, Testimonial Collection, BGA.

88. Geula Ben-Eliezer, July 30, 1976, Testimonial Collection, BGA.

89. Ibid.

90. An interview with Aharon Eldan, September 8, 2011.

91. Ben-Gurion to Paula, March 31, 1954, Correspondence Collection, BGA.

92. Ben-Gurion to Geula, December 30, 1953, Correspondence Collection, BGA.

93. An interview with Yariv Ben-Eliezer, June 9, 2011.

94. David Ben-Gurion, *Beit-avi* [My father's house] (Tel Aviv: ha-Kibbutz ha-Meuchad), 1975, p. 57.

95. Mordechai Naor, Yoram Teharlev and Amos Nevo, "'Im Ben-Gurion – Ktaim mitoch shtei sihot she-kiyma maarecht 'Ba-Mahane Gadna' in David Ben-Gurion [With Ben-Gurion—parts of two conversations between the editorial board of Ba-Mahane Gadna and David Ben-Gurion]," *Ba-Mahane*, December 16, 1973, pp. 3–5.

96. Tzahor, "Ben-Gurion kotev otobiyografiya," pp. 144–56.

97. "Reayon im David Ben-Gurion [An interview with David Ben-Gurion]," *Haaretz*, January 7, 1971.

98. "'What is pop?' Ben-Gurion asked the minister Yoseph Almogi," *Yedioth Aharonoth*, September 8, 1971, p 32.

99. Ben-Gurion to the members of Kibbutz Ein-Gedi, December 17, 1970, Protocol Collection, BGA.

100. An interview with Dr. Tzvi Shiloni, the commander of his bodyguards unit in 1970, November 24, 2011.

101. Ibid.

102. Tzahor, *Ha-Hazon veha-heshbon*, p. 242.

103. An interview with Dr. Tzvi Shiloni, November 24, 2011.

104. Ibid.

105. Diary of Ben-Gurion, July 26, 1952.

106. Bar-zohar, *Ben-Gurion*, Vol. 3, p. 1397.

107. Diary of Ben-Gurion, January 1, 1961.

108. Ibid., December 9, 1962.

109. Ibid., March 27, 1969.

110. Refael Bashan, "Yom 'im BG [A day with BG]," *Ba-Mahane*, September 14, 1971, p. 27.

111. Tzahor, *Ha-Hazon veha-heshbon*, p. 243.

112. Aharon Tamir, July 30, 1978, Testimonial Collection, BGA.

113. Diary of Ben-Gurion, July 30, 1970.

114. "A day before, I secretly got Rogers Plan." Ibid.

115. Refael Bashan, "Yom 'im BG [A day with BG]," *Ba-Mahane*, September 14, 1971, p. 27.

116. Mordechai Barkai, "David Ben-Gurion be-reayon meyuhad le-*Davar* [David Ben-Gurion in a special interview for *Davar*]," *Davar*, July 24, 1970, pp. 14, 17.

117. Ben-Gurion to Mrs. Archibald Silverman, September 18, 1970, Correspondence Collection, BGA.

118. Diary of Ben-Gurion, May 6, 1971.

119. "Jerusalem will remain one city, but each religion will control its own holy places." Ibid., May 2, 1969.

120. Zeev Tzahor, "Hanhagat Israel shuv omedet le-mivhan ha-historia [The Israeli leadership faces yet another historical test]," *Yedioth Aharonoth*, April 1, 2007, p. 21.

121. Aharon Tamir, July 30, 1978, Testimonial Collection, BGA.

122. Zeev Tzahor, "Hanhagat Israel shuv omedet le-mivhan ha-historia [The Israeli leadership faces yet another historical test]," *Yedioth Aharonoth*, April 1, 2007, p. 21.

123. Diary of Ben-Gurion, July 5, 1970.

124. Shmuel Peer to Ben-Gurion, December 6, 1970, Correspondence Collection, BGA.

125. Ben-Gurion to Efrayim Risfeld, May 12, 1970, Correspondence Collection, BGA.

126. Diary of Ben-Gurion, December 14, 1970.

127. Rachel Beit-Halahmi to Ben-Gurion, June 12, 1970, Correspondence Collection, BGA.

128. Ibid.

129. Avner Falk, *David melech yisrael: BiogRafiya psichoanalitit shel David Ben-Gurion* [David king of Israel: Psychoanalytic biography of David Ben-Gurion] (Tel Aviv: Tammuz Publishing), 1987, p. 60.

130. Ben-Gurion to Rachel Beit-Halahmi, June 12, 1970, Correspondence Collection, BGA.

131. Almogi, *Ha-Maavak al Ben-Gurion*, p. 114.

CHAPTER 6

1. "Golda was already there, the room was full. I didn't cover my head this time, as a protest against the government's enforcement and hypocrisy regarding the Registration Law." Diary of Ben-Gurion, February 18, 1970.

2. See: Nathan Alterman, *The Seventh Column*, Vol. 3 (Tel-Aviv: ha-Kibutz ha-Meuhad), 1972, pp. 313–16.

3. Ben-Gurion to Nathan Alterman, August 12, 1960, Correspondence Collection, BGA.

4. Ibid.

5. Diary of Ben-Gurion, April 3, 1970.

6. An interview with Avraham Tzivion, August 31, 2011.

7. Yisraeli, *Megilat Haim*, p. 225.

8. Diary of Ben-Gurion, December 8, 1969.

9. Ibid., October 11, 1969.

10. Prof. M. Rachmilewitz to Batya Even-Shohsan, February 7, 1970, Chronological Documentation Collection, BGA.

11. Diary of Ben-Gurion, March 10, 1969.

12. Ibid., March 15, 1969.

13. Ben-Gurion to Renana Ben-Gurion-Leshem, September 28, 1957, Correspondence Collection, BGA.

14. Diary of Ben-Gurion, March 2, 1969.

15. Ibid., December 12, 1970.

16. Yehoshua Cohen, May 21, 1979, Testimonial Collection, BGA.

17. Bar-Zohar, *Ben-Gurion*, p. 358.

18. Ben-Gurion in a meeting with the residents of the Arab village Ar'ara, Sde-Boker, June 8, 1970, Protocol Collection, BGA.

19. Ben-Gurion used to tell about his surprise, in the early 1940s, when he saw his son, Amos, enjoying a cigarette in their home. "Why are you smoking?" He asked, and was asked back in response. The Old Man refused to give up: "If I quit, will you quit?" Amos said yes, but argued that he couldn't make sure that his father will maintain his promises during his trips abroad. Ben-Gurion promised to write him if he felt he couldn't do it. "When I got to London," he said, "It was difficult not to smoke. I was used to smoking for years. But when I remembered I had to send a telegram to my son, I made an effort and stopped. It is very dangerous for many people, and can cause serious illnesses. It isn't always damaging, but it can be." Ibid.

20. For further reading about the concept of free will according to Nietzsche and Schopenhauer see: Friedrich Nietzsche, *The will to power* (translated by Walter Kaufmann and R. J. Hollingdale, edited by Walter Kaufmann) New York: Random House, 1967; Arthur Schopenhauer, *The world as will and idea* (translated by R. B. Haldane and J. Kemp) (London: Kegan Paul, Trench, Trübner & Co), 1909. A short summary of Arthur Schopenhauer can be found in: Michael Tanner, *Schopenhauer* (New York: Routledge), 1999. For further reading about Nietzsche and pioneering, see, for example: David Ohana, "Zarathustra in Jerusalem: Nietzsche and the 'New Hebrews,'" in *Mitos ve-zikaron*, pp. 269–89. We have no way of knowing whether

Ben-Gurion actually read Nietzsche and Schopenhauer thoroughly, but Nietzsche's renowned book, *Human, All Too Human*, published in 1878, was known to have influenced Jewish intellectuals in Europe, particularly its call to acknowledge the activist approach, which is based on the free spirit. Ben-Gurion's belief in the power of will went hand in hand with his resentment against the Jewish belief in miracles.

21. Tzahor, "Ben-Gurion kotev otobiyografiya," pp. 144–56.

22. Meir Avizohar, *Ha-Zionut ha-lohemet: Mavo le-yoman Ben-Gurion ule-zichronotav (1939)* [Fighting Zionism—an introduction to Ben-Gurion's dairy and his memoirs (1939)] (Sde Boker: The Bialik Institute & Ben-Gurion University), 1985, p. 61.

23. Tzahor, "Ben-Gurion kotev otobiyografiya," pp. 144–56.

24. An interview with Zeev Tzahor, April 2011.

25. Diary of Ben-Gurion, February 12, 1970.

26. Ibid., September 16, 1966.

27. David Ben-Gurion, *Igrot David Ben-Gurion* [The Letters of David Ben-Gurion], Vol. 1 (Tel Aviv: Am Oved), 1971, p. 13, note 2.

28. Tzahor, "Ben-Gurion kotev otobiyografiya," pp. 144–156.

29. Zaky Shalom, "Yomanei Ben-Gurion ke-makor histori [Ben-Gurion's diaries as a historical source]," *Kathedra 56* (June 1990): 136-149.

30. Tzahor, "Ben-Gurion kotev otobiyografiya," pp. 144–156.

31. Aharonson, *David Ben-Gurion: Manhig ha-renesans she-shaka*, pp. 1–2, 8–9.

32. An interview with Zeev Tzahor, April 2011.

33. Erez, "Ben-Gurion eino kotev otobiyografiya," p. 155.

34. An interview with Zeev Tzahor, April 2011.

35. Diary of Ben-Gurion, July 28, 1970.

36. Shlomo Avineri, *David Ben-Gurion: Dmuto shel manhig tnuat poalim* [David Ben-Gurion as a Labor Leader] (Tel-Aviv: Am Oved), 1988, pp. 110–17. Diary of Ben-Gurion, November 12, 1934, in: Tzahor, "Ben-Gurion kotev otobiyografiya," pp. 144–56.

37. Diary of Ben-Gurion, November 12, 1934, in: Tzahor, "Ben-Gurion kotev otobiyografiya," pp. 144–56.

38. Tzahor, "Ben-Gurion kotev otobiyografiya," pp. 144–56. It should be noted, that Yehuda Erez's response article presents a different version, claiming that Ben-Gurion was willing to moderate his expressions in order to avoid insults to well-known figures, and that the work process was smoother and easier. Furthermore, Erez argues that Ben-Gurion never meant to write an autobiographic narrative, but rather to leave a documentary summary of his life. See: Erez, "Ben-Gurion eino kotev otobiyografiya," p. 157. I chose to adopt Tzahor's version, since it is supported by the rest of the testimonies about Ben-Gurion in his later years.

39. Yisraeli, *Megilat haim*, p. 145.

40. For further reading see: Asher Cohen and Baruch Susser, *Me-Hashlama le-haslama* [From Accommodation to Escalation] (Jerusalem: Shocken), 2003.

41. Ben-Gurion to Mark Mellvile, December 30, 1970, Correspondence Collection, BGA.

42. Ben-Gurion to Zalman Shazar, November 11, 1969, Correspondence Collection, BGA.

43. Ben-Gurion to Yaakov Ahimeir, October 4, 1971, Protocol Collection, BGA.

44. Rachel Beit-Halahmi to Ben-Gurion, November 28, 1970, Correspondence Collection, BGA.

45. Ben-Gurion to Rachel Beit-Halahmi, November 28, 1970, Correspondence Collection, BGA.

46. Aharon Tamir, August 18, 1978, Testimonial Collection, BGA.

47. Erez, "Ben-Gurion eino kotev otobiyografiya," p. 152.

48. Diary of Ben-Gurion, February 1, 1969.

49. Tzahor, "Ben-Gurion kotev otobiyografiya," pp. 144–156.

50. An interview with Avraham Tzivion, August 31, 2011.

CHAPTER 7

1. Teveth, *Kin'at David,* Vol. 4, pp. 540–43.

2. Eli She'altiel, *Tamid be-meri: Moshe Sneh, biographiya, 1909–1948* [Moshe Sneh: A Life, Vol. 1, 1909–1948] (Tel-Aviv: Am Oved), 2000, pp. 409–13.

3. Ibid., pp. 432–33.

4. Moshe Sneh, "Dvarim be-imut im Moshe Dayan al ha-derech le-shalom [A dispute with Moshe Dayan about the road to peace]," in: Shapira, *Anu machrizim ba-zot,* pp. 132–38.

5. Refael Bashan, "Reayon ha-shavua im David Ben-Gurion [The weekly interview with David Ben-Gurion]," Maariv, May 22, 1970, p. 16.

6. Shlomo Nakdimon and Nissim Taito, "BG be-pgisha im studentim shel *Ha-Avoda* be-Sde-Boker [BG in a meeting with Ha-Avoda students in Sde-Boker]," *Yedioth Aharonoth*, December 13, 1970, p. 7.

7. Ibid.

8. Z. Yoeli, "Ha-Memshala shagta be-hash'ayat sihot Jaring: Reayon meyuhad le-*Davar* [The government was wrong in suspending the Jaring talks: A special interview for *Davar*]," *Davar*, September 18, 1970, p. 9.

9. Before his death, in the 1990s, Hazan even compared the settlers in the Occupied Territories to the pioneers of *Ha-Shomer Ha-Tzair*. Tzahor, "Ya'akov Hazan: Naftuley ha-derech shel ha-hanhaga ha-historit," pp. 97–110.

10. Yisraeli, *Megilat haim*, p. 85.

11. Tzahor, *Ha-Hazon veha-heshbon*, p. 200.

12. "When we visited him, Hazan and me, he was happy to see us, and he had some openness to him, even emotionality, almost child-like. Around this time, he may have pronounced a more balanced opinion [about us]. Basically, we were friends." Meir Yaari, July 15, 1975, Testimonial Collection, BGA.

13. Arie Palgi, "Tzarich leehov et binyan *Haaretz* [You must love the development of the land]," *Al Ha-Mishmar*, April 4, 1972, p. 3.

14. Ben-Gurion to Rastam, February 5, 1954, Correspondence Collection, BGA.

15. Arie Palgi, "Tzarich leehov et binyan *Haaretz* [You must love the development of the land]," *Al Ha-Mishmar*, April 4, 1972, p. 3.

16. For further reading see: Shlomo Gazit, *Ptaim be-malkodet* [Cuptured snakes] (Tel-Aviv: Zmora-Bitan), 1999, pp. 75–61.

17. Eilam, *Ma hitrachesh kan*, p. 37.

18. Meir Avizohar, May 12, 1976, Testimonial Collection, BGA.

19. "David Ben-Gurion be-reayon meyuhad le-yovel ha-*Histadrut* [David Ben-Gurion in a special interview celebrating 50 years for the *Histadrut*]," *Davar*, December 28, 1970, p. 15.

20. Ben-Gurion to Lova Eliav, October 3, 1970, Correspondence Collection, BGA.

21. Eli Eyal, "Siha in Ben-Gurion [A conversation with Ben-Gurion]," *Maariv*, April 28, 1971, p. 20.

22. An interview with Avraham Tzivion, August 31, 2011.

23. From Yehuda Erez's diary, November 14, 1972, Testimonial Collection (audio-visual), November 20, 1978, BGA.

24. For further details see: Avner Ben-Amos, "Ha-Shilton nimtza ba-rehov: Mered ha-studentim be-May 1968 veha-merhav ha-parisai [The street rules: May 1968 students revolt and the Parisian sphere]," *Zmanim* 109 (Winter 2010): 40–57.

25. For further details about Israel-France relationship see: Benjamin Pinkus, *Me-ambivalentiyut li-vrit bilti Ktuva: Israel, Tzarfat ve-yehudei Tzarfat 1947–1957* [From ambivalence to a tacit alliance: Israel, France and French Jewry 1947–1957] (Sde-Boker: Ben-Gurion University), 2005.

26. For further details see: Shlomo Aharonson, *Neshek garini ba-mizrah ha-tichon [Nuclear weapon in the Middle East]*, Vol. 2 (Jerusalem: Academon), 1996, p. 45 and thereafter.

27. "De Gaulle be-mesibat itonaim [de Gaulle in a press conference]," The Israeli Television Archives, November 27, 1967.

28. Mordechai Barkai, "David Ben-Gurion be-reayon meyuhad le-*Davar* [David Ben-Gurion in a special interview for *Davar*]," *Davar*, July 24, 1970, pp. 14, 17.

29. Diary of Ben-Gurion, October 16, 1969.

30. Mordechai Barkai, "David Ben-Gurion be-reayon meyuhad le-*Davar* [David Ben-Gurion in a special interview for *Davar*]," *Davar*, July 24, 1970, pp. 14, 17.

31. Yitzhak Bar-On, "Leidata u-nefilata shel yedidut: Yahasei tzarfat-yisra'el 1965–1967 [The rise and fall of a friendship: France-Israel relations 1965–1967]," *Medina, Mimshal ve-Yahasim Bein-Le'umiyim 35* (1992): 69–98.

32. Shlaim, *Kir ha'barzel*, pp. 177–78. It must be mentioned that the fear expressed by Ben-Gurion in 1958 of the possibility that Israel will have to conquer the West Bank if King Hussein's regime will be overthrown contradicts the suggestions he allegedly made during this meeting before the Sinai Operation.

33. Ben-Gurion to de Gaulle, 1970 (no specific date), Correspondence Collection, BGA.

34. Ibid.

35. The letter was read in a press conference held by him. "BG metaken tauyot de-Gaulle [BG fixed de Gaulle's errors]," *Davar*, p. 3.

36. Diary of Ben-Gurion, November 10, 1970.

37. According to her biographer, Meron Medzini, Golda acknowledged her partial responsibility for pushing Ben-Gurion away, but she explained he had to resign in 1963, for his own good and the government's proper management, and she was sorry he chose, since then, a conflicting, dangerous, and teasing path. Medzini, *Golda*, p. 405.

38. Diary of Ben-Gurion, November 10, 1970.

39. Ibid., November 22, 1970.

40. The Second Saint James Conference was arranged by the British government, in a final mediation attempt between the Jews, the Palestinians, and the Arab states. The conclusion at its end was that there was no solution and that the preferred situation is a binational state. For further details see: Friling, *Hetz ba-arafel*, pp. 401–3.

41. Ben-Gurion, unaddressed letter, January 1, 1970, Correspondence Collection, BGA.

42. Aharonson, *David Ben-Gurion: Manhig ha-renesdsans she-shaka*, p. 263.

43. Oren, *Power, Faith and Fantasy*, pp. 379–445.

44. Ben-Gurion to *LOOK* magazine, 1971, Protocol Collection, BGA.

45. Ibid. The famous meeting of Ben-Gurion and Moshe Sneh with Ho Chi Minh in the summer of 1946 may have affected his assessment concerning the power of Vietnam.

46. Ben-Gurion to *LOOK* magazine, 1971, Protocol Collection, BGA.

47. Aharonson, *David Ben-Gurion: Manhig ha-renesdsans she-shaka*, pp. 133–34.

48. Refael Bashan, "Reayon ha-shavua im David Ben-Gurion [The weekly interview with David Ben-Gurion]," *Maariv*, May 22, 1970, p. 16.

49. Aharonson, *David Ben-Gurion: Manhig ha-renesdsans she-shaka*, p. 28.

50. Ben-Gurion to *LOOK* magazine, 1971, Protocol Collection, BGA.

51. Mordechai Barkai, "David Ben-Gurion be-reayon meyuhad le-*Davar* [David Ben-Gurion in a special interview for *Davar*]," *Davar*, July 24, 1970, pp. 14, 17.

52. Ibid.

53. Shlomo Nakdimon, "Medinat Israel od eina kayemet [The state of Israel still doesn't exist]," *Yedioth Aharonoth*, May 22, 1970, pp. 5, 15.

54. Yisraeli, *Megilat haim*, p. 124.

55. Dov Goldstein, "David Ben-Gurion, Avi [David Ben-Gurion, my father]," *Maariv*, October 17, 1986, pp. 29-30. The story is also mentioned by Yariv Ben Eliezer, August 8, 1976, Testimonial Collection, BGA.

56. The letter, dated August 17, 1959, was preserved by Dov Yirmiyah and quoted in: Shalom Cohen, *Ha-Olam ha-zeh* [This world] (Tel-Aviv: Tfahot), 1972, p. 103.

57. Ibid., pp. 103–7.

58. Ben-Gurion to Hannah Zemer, September 13, 1970, Correspondence Collection, BGA.

59. Avigdor Ben-Dov, "Lama ala li-Sde-Boker [Why did he come to Sde-Boker]," *Ba-Mahane*, November 24, 1976, pp. 8–9.

60. Yariv Ben-Eliezer, August 8, 1976, Testimonial Collection, BGA.

61. Cohen, *Ha-Olam ha-zeh*, pp. 103–7.

62. Even in 2011, at the age of ninety-eight, Yirmiyah was still affected by the ordeal. He argued that Ben-Gurion's letter included the foundations for the perception that unofficially guided generations of IDF officers, about their right to be unfaithful to their wives, as long as they perform their national duty. An interview with Dov Yirmiyah, October 10, 2011.

63. "He thought of Dayan as a very original, exceptional, unusual man, with independent opinions and the ability to analyze and see things clearly. And mainly, he

appreciated Dayan's ability to maintain contacts with our surroundings, that is, Arabs, Arab leaders. I remember he mentioned Yael's talents as well, and said she was like her father—writing skills, originality [...] he referred to Dayan's personal life only once. After reading one morning about his divorce, although the Old Man really liked her [Dayan's wife]. He was surprised and said: 'So strange. She is a great girl, such a good family, a noble woman.' He said he heard, he knew, that their life together weren't good, something like that. He added no details." Aharon Tamir, July 30, 1978, Testimonial Collection, BGA.

64. An interview with Avraham Tzivion, August 31, 2011.

65. Diary of Ben-Gurion, September 9, 1970.

66. Ibid.

67. Ibid., April 16, 1969.

68. Ben-Gurion in a meeting with the residents of the Arab village Ar'ara, Sde-Boker, June 8, 1970, Protocol Collection, BGA.

69. Ibid.

70. David Ben-Gurion, "Le-Verur motza ha-falahim [About the origins of the *Falahiyun*]," in: David Ben-Gurion and Yitzhak Ben-Zvi, *Eretz Israel be-avar uva-hove* [The Land of Israel in the past and in the present] (Jerusalem: Yad Yitzhak Ben-Zvi), 1980, pp. 118–27.

71. Ibid. Ben-Gurion and Ben-Tzvi presented no concrete evidence for the Fala-hiyun's Jewish origins, but relied on historical facts which might support their argument. For example, the revolt of the Galilee Jews against Constantius Gallus broke out in 361. The story of the revolt was a proof that many Jews remained in Palestine even after the Bar Kohba revolt, and Ben-Gurion argued that they disappeared over time when they became Muslims.

72. "In the 1950s, he wanted to convert the Bedouins into Judaism. He told me: 'Elhanan, tell me, what's the difference between them and the Jews who came from the Atlas Mountains? Why can't the Bedouins be Jews? Let's make them Jews. We'll have more Jews, and Jews of this kind will settle the land.' A long argument ensued about the need to convert the Bedouins into Judaism, particularly those who were not Muslims but pagans. He saw their level and said they were like the Jewish newcomers. You need a revolution here and there." Elhanan Yishai, September 12, 1977, Testimonial Collection, BGA.

73. Ben-Gurion in a meeting with the residents of the Arab village Ar'ara, Sde-Boker, June 8, 1970, Protocol Collection, BGA.

74. Ibid.

75. Ibid.

76. Ibid.

77. Haim Yisraeli, February 23, 1990, Testimonial Collection, BGA.

78. Arie (Lova) Eliav, *Olam male* [The Entire World] (Tel-Aviv: Am Oved), 1980, pp. 71–78.

79. Bar-Zohar, *Ben-Gurion*, p. 405.

80. Moshe Feldenkrais, November 3, 1976, Testimonial Collection, BGA.

81. Aviva Lori, "Ha-Ish she-limed et Ben-Gurion laamod al ha-rosh [The man who taught Ben-Gurion how to stand on his head]," *Haaretz*, June 9, 2004. In: http://www.*Haaretz*.co.il/misc/1.973254.

82. Bar-zohar, *Ben-Gurion*, Vol. 3, p. 1408.

83. Eliav, *Olam male*, pp. 71–78.

84. Emanuel Ben-Eliezer (Geula Ben-Gurion's husband), July 30, 1976, Testimonial Collection, BGA.

85. Maurice Jacques, "10 ha-dakot shel Ben-Gurion [Ben-Gurion's 10 minutes]," *Davar*, February 26, 1971, p. 1.

86. Diary of Ben-Gurion, March 3, 1971.

87. Ibid.

CHAPTER 8

1. "David Ben-Gurion be-reayon meyuhad le-yovel ha-*Histadrut* [David Ben-Gurion in a special interview celebrating *Histadrut*'s 50th anniversory]," *Davar*, December 28, 1970, p. 15.

2. Mordechai Naor, Yoram Teharlev and Amos Nevo, "Im Ben-Gurion – Ktaim mitoch shtei sihot she-kiyma maarecht 'Ba-Mahane Gadna' in David Ben-Gurion [With Ben-Gurion—parts of two conversations between the editorial board of Ba-Mahane Gadna and David Ben-Gurion]," *Ba-Mahane*, December 16, 1973, pp. 3–5.

3. Shlomo Nakdimon and Nissim Taito, "BG be-pgisha im studentim shel *Ha-Avoda* be-Sde-Boker [BG in a meeting with Ha-Avoda students in Sde-Boker]," *Yedioth Aharonoth*, December 13, 1970, p. 7.

4. Shlomo Givon, "Talmidim shoalim Ben-Gurion megiv [Students ask, Ben-Gurion responds]," *Maariv*, October 22, 1970.

5. Shlomo Nakdimon and Nissim Taito, "BG be-pgisha im studentim shel *Ha-Avoda* be-Sde-Boker [BG in a meeting with Ha-Avoda students in Sde-Boker]," *Yedioth Aharonoth*, December 13, 1970, p. 7.

6. Ibid.

7. Ibid.

8. Ibid.

9. Ben-Gurion to Yitzhak M. Giladi, March 2, 1969, Correspondence Collection, BGA.

10. Shilon, *Begin 1992–1913*, pp. 209–6.

11. Diary of Ben-Gurion, July 15, 1958.

12. Ibid., July 23, 1957.

13. Ibid., January 31, 1971.

14. An interview with Mordechai Ben-Porath, August 23, 2011.

15. Yoseph Almogi, May 30, 1978, Testimonial Collection, BGA.

16. Diary of Ben-Gurion, March 2, 1971.

17. Shlomo Nakdimon and Nissim Taito, "BG be-pgisha im studentim shel *Ha-Avoda* be-Sde-Boker [BG in a meeting with Ha-Avoda students in Sde-Boker]," *Yedioth Aharonoth*, December 13, 1970, p. 7.

18. Ben-Gurion, "Ha-Beayot hamediniyot hakovot et torat mediniyut habitahon [The political issues that dictated our security paradigm]," a lecture before the IDF's senior commanders, January 14, 1951, Speeches and Articles Collection, BGA.

19. Aharon Tamir, September 13, 1978, Testimonial Collection, BGA.

20. Yisraeli, *Megilat haim*, p. 105.

21. Geula Ben-Eliezer, July 30, 1976, Testimonial Collection, BGA.

22. Diary of Ben-Gurion, December 12, 1970.

23. Ben-Gurion declared that the accusations against the IDF soldiers for conducting the operation were a "fantastic lie," although he approved it himself. See: Yemima Rosenthal (ed.), *Documents on the foreign policy of Israel*, Vol. 8: 1953 (Jerusalem: The State Archive), 1996, p. 844. Even more than a decade after the operation, he expressed no regret, and even believed it was an example of a "real" military activity: "Until Qibiya, the IDF did almost nothing in the reprisals [...] Arik and Har-Tzion, who were parachutists, started conducting real operations." Diary of Ben-Gurion, August 22, 1965.

24. Ben-Gurion in an interview to *Haaretz*, January 7, 1971, Protocol Collection, BGA.

25. Ibid.

26. "Youth" in Ben-Gurion's terms was anyone between teenagers and forty-year-olds. David Ben-Gurion, *Ba-Ma'aracha*, Vol. 4 (Tel-Aviv: Am Oved), p. 75.

27. Shlomo Nakdimon and Nissim Taito, "BG be-pgisha im studentim shel *Ha-Avoda* be-Sde-Boker [BG in a meeting with *Ha-Avoda* students in Sde-Boker]," *Yedioth Aharonoth*, December 13, 1970, p. 7. Ben-Gurion admired the Japanese's wisdom and hard-working nature, and expressed it often. His bodyguard also said: "He often said that the Japanese were an example of a people that had to find solutions and found them in quality development." Aharon Tamir, September 13, 1978, Testimonial Collection, BGA.

28. Mordechai Naor, Yoram Teharlev and Amos Nevo, "Im Ben-Gurion – Ktaim mitoch shtei sihot she-kiyma maarecht 'Ba-Mahane Gadna' in David Ben-Gurion [With Ben-Gurion—parts of two conversations between the editorial board of Ba-Mahane Gadna and David Ben-Gurion]," *Ba-Mahane*, December 16, 1973, pp. 3–5.

29. "If there are families who live five people together in one room, it creates awful things. The kid doesn't go to school, roams around the streets, and the corruption grows bigger. There are security expenses, but the state must do more." Eli Eyal, "Siha im Ben-Gurion [A conversation with Ben-Gurion]," *Maariv*, April 28, 1971, p. 20.

30. Aharonson, *David Ben-Gurion: Manhig ha-renesdsans she-shaka*, p. 27.

31. Nadir Tsur, *Retorika politit: Manhigim Yisraeliyim be-matzavei lahatz* [The rhetorics of Israeli leaders in stress situations] (Tel-Aviv: Ha-Kibbutz Ha-Meuhad), 2004, pp. 24–29.

32. Ben-Gurion in a conversation with Levi Yitzhak Hayerushalmi, February 28, 1972, Protocol Collection, BGA.

33. Bareli, *Lehavin et Ben-Gurion*, p. 85.

34. Ben-Gurion to the students of Kiryat Shmuel high-school, Tiberias, April 30, 1962, Correspondence Collection, BGA.

35. Juaque Mourice, "Yesh litlot mehablim aravim [Arab terrorists must be hanged]," *Davar*, May 4, 1970, p. 8.

36. Refael Bashan, "Reayon ha-shavua im David Ben-Gurion [The weekly interview with David Ben-Gurion]," *Maariv*, May 22, 1970, p. 16. According to his bodyguard, he expressed rage against terrorists in private conversations, and said they

were "bastards." His justification for death sentence was: "When they kill women, children, old people—this is no war, it's murder." Aharon Tamir, August 18, 1978, Testimonial Collection, BGA.

37. Diary of Ben-Gurion, February 16, 1971.

38. Ben-Gurion with A. Disinchek and Shalom Rosenfeld, March 13, 1971, Protocol Collection, BGA.

39. Tzahor, *Ha-Hazon veha-heshbon*, p. 252.

40. Tzahor, "Ben-Gurion kotev otobiyografiya," pp. 144–56.

41. Ben-Gurion to the Israeli Television, October 4, 1971, Protocol Collection, BGA. He explained in the interview that he needed 15 hours per day to complete his mission, but he couldn't find the time between all the letters he had to write and the meetings he had to attend. See also: Ben-Gurion in a conversation with Levi Yitzhak Hayerushalmi, February 28, 1972, Protocol Collection, BGA.

42. Tzahor, "Ben-Gurion kotev otobiyografiya," pp. 144–56.

43. Ben-Gurion to Lea Adelman, June 13, 1968, Correspondence Collection, BGA.

44. Diary of Ben-Gurion, June 16, 1963.

45. Mordechai Naor, Yoram Teharlev and Amos Nevo, "Im Ben-Gurion – Ktaim mitoch shtei sihot she-kiyma maarecht 'Ba-Mahane Gadna' in David Ben-Gurion [With Ben-Gurion—parts of two conversations between the editorial board of Ba-Mahane Gadna and David Ben-Gurion]," *Ba-Mahane*, December 16, 1973, pp. 3–5.

46. Ben-Gurion to Shimon Reem, February 16, 1970, Correspondence Collection, BGA.

47. Teveth, *Kinat David*, Vol. 1, p. 28.

48. Mordechai Naor, Yoram Teharlev and Amos Nevo, "Im Ben-Gurion – Ktaim mitoch shtei sihot she-kiyma maarecht 'Ba-Mahane Gadna' in David Ben-Gurion [With Ben-Gurion—parts of two conversations between the editorial board of Ba-Mahane Gadna and David Ben-Gurion]," *Ba-Mahane*, December 16, 1973, pp. 3–5.

49. Teveth, *Kinat David*, Vol. 1, p. 217.

50. Shimon Peres and David Landau, *Ben Gurion a political life* (New York: Nextbook-Schocken), 2011, p. 37

51. Ibid.

52. Shabtai Teveth, "Ha-Shanim haneelamot behayey Ben-Gurion [The absent years in Ben-Gurion's life]," *Siman Kria*, 9 (May 1979), pp. 350–57.

53. Amira Hagani, *Be-Guf rishon rabim: Arie Ben-Gurion, hayav u-fo'alo* [A biography: Aryeh Ben Gurion] (Tel-Aviv: Ha-Kibbutz Ha-Meuhad), 2010, p. 162.

54. Ben-Gurion, *Beit Avi*, p. 15.

55. Geula Ben-Eliezer, July 30, 1976, Testimonial Collection, BGA.

56. Hagani, *be-Guf rishon rabim*, p. 21.

57. An interview with Haya Arkis, Michel's daughter, January 28, 2006.

58. Hagani, *Be-Guf rishon rabim*, p. 164.

59. Tzahor, *Ha-Hazon veha-heshbon*, p. 242–35.

60. Yair Sheleg, *Ruah ha-midbar: Sipuro shel Yehoshu'a Cohen* [Desert's wind: The story of Yehoshua Cohen] (Tel-Aviv: The ministry of Defence), 1998, p. 221.

61. From Yehuda Erez's diary, October 26, 1972, Testimonial Collection, BGA.

62. Hagani, *Be-Guf rishon rabim*, p. 166.

63. An interview with Yariv Ben-Eliezer, June 9, 2011.

64. Sarit Levi-Yishai, "Kuch-much lezecher Paula [Kuch-much in Paula's memory]," *Ha-Olam Ha-Ze*, October 4, 1983, pp. 55–57, 60.

65. Ben-Gurion to Geula, December 30, 1953, Correspondence Collection, BGA.

66. Geula Ben-Eliezer, July 30, 1976, Testimonial Collection, BGA.

67. Ben-Gurion and Geula, February 28, 1972, Protocol Collection, BGA.

68. Ben-Gurion and Geula, March 10, 1972, Protocol Collection, BGA.

69. Geula Ben-Eliezer, July 30, 1976, Testimonial Collection, BGA.

70. Dov Goldstein, "David Ben-Gurion, Avi [David Ben-Gurion, my father]," *Maariv*, October 17, 1986, pp. 29–30.

71. Ibid.

72. Ibid.

73. Ben-Gurion and Geula, February 28, 1972, Protocol Collection, BGA.

74. "Dr. Renana Ben-Gurion nis'aa [Dr. Renana Ben-Gurion got married]," *Maariv*, March 25, 1956.

75. Aliza Volach, "Aba, lo mitos [A father, not a myth]," *Davar HaShavua*, October 17, 1986, pp. 10–12.

76. Yigal Lev "Nechdo shel BG yisa et shem mishpahat savo [BG's grandson will get his grandfather's surname]," *Maariv*, February 5, 1970.

77. Aliza Volach, "Aba, lo mitos [A father, not a myth]," *Davar HaShavua*, October 17, 1986, pp. 10–12.

78. Ibid.

79. The second *Aliyah* was discussed in many books and researches. See, for example: Mordechai Naor (Ed.), *Ha-Aliyah ha-shniyah 1903–1914* [The second *Aliyah* 1903–1914] (Jerusalem: Yad Yitzhak Ben-Zvi). 1988; Boaz Neumann, *Tshukat Ha'halutizm* [The pioneers' passion] (Tel Aviv: Am Oved), 2009.

80. Ben-Gurion in a conversation with Nathan Volach and Uri Gordon about the integration of generations within the family, January 28, 1971, Protocol Collection, BGA.

81. Ben-Gurion with Mark Segal, March 19, 1972, Protocol Collection, BGA.

82. Yaacov Shavit, "Bein Pilsudsky ve-Mickiewicz: Mediniyut u-meshihiyut ba-reviziyonizem ha-tziyoni be-heksher shel ha-tarbut ha-politit ha-polanit ve-zikato le-polin [Between Pilsudsky and Mickiewicz: Policy and messianism in Zionist Revisionism]," *Ha-Tziyonut* 10 (1985): 7–31.

83. Ben-Gurion in a meeting with American students, July 13, 1971, Protocol Collection, BGA.

84. Refael Bashan, "Ha-Regaim hagdolim behayay," *Maariv*, May 22, 1970, p. 16.

85. For further reading about the equivalent perception in American culture see: Allan Bloom, *The Closing of the American Mind* (New York: Simon & Shuster Inc), 1987.

86. Ben-Gurion to Meir Shaham, The Israeli Ambassador to Uruguay, January 9, 1972, Correspondence Collection BGA.

87. Many researches have been written about Ben-Gurion's national perception. For further reading, see: Yigal Donyets, "ha-Ideologiya ha-le'umit shel Ben-Gurion,

1930–1942 [The national ideology of David Ben-Gurion, 1930–1942]," PhD diss., The Hebrew University of Jerusalem, 2008.

88. Benjamin Oppenheimer, "Ben-Gurion veha-tanach [Ben-Gurion and the Bible]," in *Ben-Gurion veha-tanach – am ve-artzo* [Ben-Gurion and the Bible—a people and its land], edited by Mordechai Cogen, 59–61 (Sde-Boker: The Ben-Gurion Institution), 1989.

89. An interview with Avraham Tzivion, August 31, 2011.

90. David Ben-Gurion, *Iyunim ba-tanach* [Bible review] (Tel-Aviv: Am Oved), 1969.

91. Ben-Gurion to Yaakov Rabbi, March 28, 1971, Protocol Collection, BGA.

92. Diary of Ben-Gurion, December 15, 1970.

93. Don-Yehiya, *"Mamlachtiyut* ve-yahadut," p. 58.

94. See: Yosef Gorny, "Shlilat ha-galut veha-shiva el ha-historiya [Rejecting the exile and returning to history]," in *Ha-Tziyonut veha-hazara la-historiya: Ha'araha me-hadash* [Zionism and returning to history: a reevaluation], edited by Shmuel Eisenstadt and Moshe Lisk, 349–60. Jerusalem: Yad Yitzhak Ben-Zvi. 1999.

95. The Allegory of the Cave, which is presented in Plato's *The Republic*, tells, in a nutshell, about a group of prisoners, who were caged in a group since childhood, and due to their chains, their heads were turned to one side. A wall stood behind the prisoners, with an eternal fire, which lit the wall seen by the prisoners. The shadows of people moving between the fire and the wall were seen on the wall seen by the prisoners, and they were convinced that these shadows represent reality. One of the prisoners managed to free himself, and after a while, he came back to the cave to convince his fellow prisoners that the actual reality is found outside of the cave, and they can only see its shadows. But they wouldn't believe him.

96. Pearlman, *David Ben-Gurion*, p. 199.

97. http://www.youtube.com/watch?v=NhM4GnSK8QI&feature=related.

98. David Ben-Gurion, "Yihudo shel amenu u-Mikve Israel [The singularity of our people and Mikve Israel]," 1971, Articles and Speeches Collection, BGA.

99. "Prayer alone didn't help the Jews during the centuries. Only after the French Revolution, when the Jews of France got equal rights, a new era started in the history of the Jewish people." Ibid.

100. Ibid.

101. Diary of Ben-Gurion, June 3, 1971.

102. Ben-Gurion to prof. Ezra Spicehandler, March 1, 1970, Correspondence Collection, BGA.

103. "If the foundations of their religion have not emasculated their mind they may even, if occasion offers, so changeable are human affairs, raise up their empire afresh, and that God may a second time elect them." Benedict de Spinoza, *A Theologico-Political Treatise, and a Political Treatise* (Translated by R.H.M. Elwes) (New York: Cosimo Books), 2007, p. 56.

104. For further reading see: Yosef Ben-Shlomo, *Prakim be-torato shel Baruch Spinoza* [Lectures on the Philosophy of Spinoza] (Tel-Aviv: The Ministry of Defense), 1983.

105. Zeev Zivan, "Tguva al shnei maamarim [A response for two articles]," *Iyunim bi-Tekumat Yisra'el* 9 (1999): 4.

106. Gideon Katz, *Le-etzem ha-chiloniyot—nituach filosofy shel ha-chiloniyut be-heksher yisraeli* [To the core of Secularism—a philosophical analysis of secularism in the Israeli context] (Jerusalem: Yad Yitzhak Ben Zvi), 2010, pp. 28–29.

107. "I believe we stop living randomly if there is a mission for our life here, on Earth, in the territories we know and understand. 'The big mystery' (and there is one) is indeed a mystery, and it drives us to know more without eliminating the big mystery, but I don't know what is the meaning of getting closer to it, since it is mysterious, infinite, and will forever be that way." Ben-Gurion to Yosef Shechter, September 2, 1952, Correspondence Collection, BGA.

108. Y. Rabi, "Dvarim she-amar BG li [Things I heard from BG]," *Al Ha-Mishmar*, March 9, 1971, pp. 4–5, 26.

109. Ben-Gurion to Ezra Ben-shalom, March 16, 1971, Correspondence Collection, BGA.

110. David Ben-Gurion, *Hagut ba-mikra* [Bible studies] (Tel-Aviv: Am Oved), 1973, p. 86.

111. "Circumcision is a different commandment, because we share it with Abraham, and it is also a creation." Ben-Gurion to Avraham Stern, New York, May 12, 1971, Correspondence Collection, BGA. Another time, Ben-Gurion mentioned Spinoza's remark that the Jews were promised eternal existence due to circumcision, and that even Ha-Shomer Ha-Tzair's members did it. See: Ben-Gurion to Dr. Moshe Zilberberg, December 7, 1970, Correspondence Collection, BGA.

112. David Ben-Gurion, *Hagut ba-mikra*, p. 86.

113. Babylonian Talmud, Tractate Minhoth, 22: 9.

114. Ben-Gurion to the residents of Kibbutz Ein-Gedi, December 17, 1970, Protocol Collection, BGA.

115. "They said there was born a man who had the will of God—Jesus—and from history I know that he was a Jew and he died as a Jew but there are many others who say, no: He was born a Jew but he died as a Christian. But he continued to believe what Jews have always believed, and no other people believed, that you must have one God only [...] But I don't think that a Christian will ever accept my view." Ben-Gurion with Paul Simon, March 17, 1973, Protocol Collection, BGA.

116. Tzahor, *Ha-Hazon veha-heshbon*, p. 212.

117. Ben-Gurion, "Al hatmadat ha-halutziyut [About the continuation of pioneering]," *Hazon va-derech*, Vol. 2, pp. 263–69.

118. Ben-Gurion to Walter Fellon, November 28, 1971, Correspondence Collection, BGA.

119. Ben-Gurion to Reuven Adivi, March 1, 1970, Correspondence Collection, BGA.

120. For further reading see: Asher Cohen and Baruch Susser, *me-Hashlama le-haslama*.

121. Ben-Gurion to Dr. S. Feldman, February 8, 1967, Correspondence Collection, BGA.

122. Yeshayahu Leibowitz, *Emunah, historiah va-arakhim* [Faith, history, and values] (Jerusalem: Academon), 1982, pp. 185–86.

123. Dov Goldstein, "David Ben-Gurion, Avi [David Ben-Gurion, my father]," *Maariv*, October 17, 1986, pp. 29–30.

124. Mordechai Barkai, "David Ben-Gurion be-reayon meyuhad le-*Davar* [David Ben-Gurion in a special interview for *Davar*]," *Davar*, July 24, 1970, pp. 14, 17.

125. Shlomo Nakdimon and Nissim Taito, "BG be-pgisha im studentim shel *Ha-Avoda* be-Sde-Boker [BG in a meeting with Ha-Avoda students in Sde-Boker]," *Yedioth Aharonoth*, December 13, 1970, p. 7.

126. Ben-Gurion to Shulamit Aloni, July 26, 1970, Correspondence Collection, BGA.

127. Shlomo Nakdimon and Nissim Taito, "BG be-pgisha im studentim shel *Ha-Avoda* be-Sde-Boker [BG in a meeting with *Ha-Avoda* students in Sde-Boker]," *Yedioth Aharonoth*, December 13, 1970, p. 7.

128. Ben-Gurion to Prof. Ezra Spicehandler, March 1, 1970, Correspondence Collection, BGA.

129. Ben-Gurion to Haim Atzur, February 17, 1970, Correspondence Collection, BGA.

130. Ben-Gurion to the residents of Kibbutz Ein-Gedi, December 17, 1970, Protocol Collection, BGA.

131. Ben-Gurion to *LOOK* magazine, 1971, Protocol Collection, BGA.

CHAPTER 9

1. Diary of Ben-Gurion, June 20, 1971.

2. Ben-Gurion to Iris Karlinsky, May 12, 1970, Correspondence Collection, BGA.

3. Dan Patir, "Yom huledet le-Ben-Gurion [Ben-Gurion's birthday]," *Davar*, October 1, 1971, p. 1; "BG mesarev lahzor la-avoda [BG refuses to go back to work]," *Ha-Tzofe,* October 1, 1971.

4. Ibid.

5. Ibid.

6. Ibid.

7. Ben-Gurion was constant in measuring the historical importance of Zionist leaders according to their level of implementation. For example, when asked about Ahad Ha'Am's position in the Zionist pantheon, he replied: "When compared to Arthur Rupin, who wasn't so much a politician but was active in the field of settlements, and none of that would have happened without him; Cremieux, who was one of the first to identify the need of a Jewish state; Charles Netter, who build the first pillar of the state, Mikve Israel, and Rothschild's famous contribution to developing the land—I believe that Ahad Ha'Am is a little over rated. He did affect Jewish intellectuals in Europe. But he had a minor influence on the Israeli project, and there were a few things he couldn't understand or grasp (like Hebrew work, and the Hebrew language as well, for a long time)." Ben-Gurion to prof. Benjamin Shwadran, May 10, 1970, Correspondence Collection, BGA.

8. Ben-Gurion in a conversation with Levi Yitzhak Hayerushalmi, February 28, 1972, Protocol Collection, BGA.

9. After retiring from premiership, he explained that between the White Paper in 1939 and the Partition Plan in November 29, 1947, "Weizman was overcome with

embarrassment, confusion and frustration, which ate him from the inside and prevented him from finding his way." Pearlman, *David Ben-Gurion*, p. 62.

10. Ben-Gurion in a conversation with Levi Yitzhak Hayerushalmi, February 28, 1972, Protocol Collection, BGA.

11. Protocols: *Divrei Ha-Knesset*, October 25, 1971, 62, pp. 3–6.

12. "Seeing modern Israel as a continuation of the Jewish past is crucially important. Under no other circumstances can we understand how the State of Israel was created in 1948 and why, or what we are trying to achieve here." Pearlman, *David Ben-Gurion*, p. 226.

13. *Protocols: Divrei Ha-Knesset*, October 25, 1971, 62, pp. 3–6.

14. Ibid.

15. Eliezer Don-Yehiya, "Galut in Zionist Ideology and in Israeli Society," *Israel and Diaspora Jewry: Ideological and Political Perspectives* (edited by Eliezer Don-Yihya), pp. 219–259 (Tel-Aviv: Bar-Ilan University), 1993.

16. *Protocols: Divrei Ha-Knesset*, October 25, 1971, 62, pp. 3–6.

17. Ibid.

18. Ibid.

19. Ben-Gurion to Gil Sahar, December 31, 1971, Correspondence Collection, BGA.

20. David Ben-Gurion, "Michtav lavaad hapoel hatziyoni [A letter to the Zionist General Council]," *Hazon va-derech*, Vol. 5, p. 33.

21. Ben-Gurion in the twenty-eighth Zionist Congress, January 1972, Protocol Collection, BGA.

22. Yisraeli, *Megilat haim*, p. 233.

23. His relative, Prof. David Green, said that his family used to say: "He lived two years too long." A conversation with Green, June 2010.

24. Yisraeli, *Megilat haim*, p. 233.

25. Ben-Gurion to Golda, May 1, 1972, Correspondence Collection, BGA.

26. Bareli, *Lehavin et Ben-Gurion*, p. 89.

27. Anita Shapira, *Berl: Biographia* [Berl: A biography] (Tel Aviv: Am Oved), 1980, p. 708.

28. Ben-Gurion to Shlomo Tzemah, June 17, 1963, Correspondence Collection, BGA.

29. Pearlman, *David Ben-Gurion*, pp. 19–20.

30. Ze'ev Tzahor, "Hitgabshut manhiguta shel ha-aliyah ha-shniyah [The formation of the Second *Aliyah*'s leadership]," in *Ha-Aliyah ha-shniyah 1903–1914* [The second *Aliyah* 1903–1914], edited by Mordechai Naor, 26–36 (Jerusalem: Yad Yitzhak Ben-Zvi), 1988.

31. Shlomo Tzemach, *Sipurim me-hayey ha-aretz* [Stories from the Life of the Land] (Jerusalem: Rubin Mass Press), 1939.

32. Ben-Gurion in a conversation with Yosef Evron, August 17, 1971, Protocol Collection, BGA.

33. Pearlman, *David Ben-Gurion*, pp. 23.

34. Shlomo Tzemach, *Sipur hayay* [Story of my life] (Tel-Aviv: Dvir), 1983, p. 171.

35. Ben-Gurion to Shlomo Tzemah, September 16, 1961, Correspondence Collection, BGA.

36. Yisraeli, *Megilat haim*, pp. 218–19.

37. Ibid.

38. "He was shocked when he left the meeting, and said: 'He has gotten very old, very old, he doesn't look good.' He never said: 'We are supposed to be at the same age, look at him and look at me'—although maybe he thought about it." Aharon Tamir, August 18, 1978, Testimonial Collection, BGA.

39. Bareli, *Lehavin et Ben-Gurion*, p. 62.

40. "Aba Ahimeir was not the only one [in the Revisionist Movement] who preferred Hitler and Mussolini." Diary of Ben-Gurion, September 15, 1963.

41. Weitz, "ha-Preda meha-av ha-meyased," pp. 84–89.

42. Ben-Gurion to Yaakov Ahimeir, October 4, 1971, Protocol Collection, BGA.

43. For further reading see: Shlomo Avineri, *Arlozoroff* [Arlozoroff] (Tel-Aviv: Idanim), 1991; Shabtai Teveth, *Retzah Arlosoroff* [The Arlosoroff murder] (Jerusalem: Shocken), 1982.

44. On March 1982, Menachem Begin as prime minister ordered to establish an inquiry committee for this issue. The committee, headed by Justice David Bechor, concluded that Stavistky and Rosenblatt were most probably not the ones to pull the trigger, by they couldn't say who did. Many speculations, some less founded than others, were raised over the years. Some argue today that the shooters were Palestinians from the Communist party.

45. Yisraeli, *Megilat haim*, p. 222.

46. Ben-Gurion to Yosef Ahimeir, March 16, 1972, Correspondence Collection, BGA.

47. From Yehuda Erez's diary, June 17, 1973, Testimonial Collection, BGA.

48. For further reading see: Ze'ev Tzahor, "Va'adat ha-berur li-vdikat 'ha-kibbutz ha-hasha'i' bi-gdud ha-avoda [The committee to investigate the 'clandestine commune' in *Gedud ha-Avoda*]," *Katedra* 58 (1990): 128–54.

49. Alexander Zaid (1886–1938) immigrated to Israel in 1904, inspired to support the Zionist idea after witnessing the Jews' hopelessness during the Kishinev Pogrom. He was an exceptionally courageous guard, and was one of the founders of the first Hebrew guards organizations—*Bar-Giora*, *Ha-Shomer*, *Ha-Kibbutz* and *Agudat Ha-Shomrim*. He was murdered by a Bedouin during the Great Arab Revolt in 1938.

50. One unproven assessment was that the members of *Ha-Kibbutz Ha-Hashai* murdered in 1924 Israel de Haan—a Netherlands-born Jew, who was raised in a religious family, became secular and was a Zionist activist as a young boy, but later became religious again and led a struggle against the Zionist *Yishuv* as a representative of extreme ultra-orthodox circles. For further reading about his life story see: Shlomo Nakdimon and Shaul Mayzlish. *De-Haan: Ha-retzah ha-politi ha-rishon be-yisrael* [De-Haan: The first political murder in Israel] (Tel-Aviv: Modan), 1985.

51. An interview with Michael Bar-Zohar, November 21, 2011.

52. Bar-Zohar, *Ka-Of ha-hol*, p. 163.

53. Yoseph Almogi, May 30, 1978, Testimonial Collection, BGA.

54. Ibid.

55. Ben-Gurion in a conversation with Nathan Volach and Uri Gordon about the integration of generations within the family, January 28, 1971, Protocol Collection, BGA.

56. Enzo Sireni (1905–1944) was raised in a Jewish-Italian family, came to Palestine in 1972, and was one of the founders of Kibbutz Givat Brenner. He was known for his literary talent and his combative personality. In 1944, despite the objection of the *Yishuv*'s leaders and Ben-Gurion among them, he went to Europe with a group of paratroopers, in an attempt to assist the partisan operations against the Nazis. He was captured by the Nazis and executed in Dachau. Quoted in: Tzahor, *ha-Hazon vehaheshbon*, p. 253.

57. An interview with Yariv Ben-Eliezer, June 9, 2011.

58. Diary of Ben-Gurion, May 2, 1958.

59. An interview with Zalman Shoval, September 8, 2011.

CHAPTER 10

1. Bareli, *Lehavin et Ben-Gurion*, p. 31.

2. Ben-Gurion in a talk with Yosef Evron, 17.7.1972, Protocols Collection, BGA.

3. Perlman, *David Ben-Gurion*, p. 10. He also said a year before that General Marshall gave a characteristic alarming forecast that in view of the imbalance of power after the fighting not a single Jew would remain alive. See: Eli Eyal, "A Talk with David Ben-Gurion," *Maariv*, April 28, 1971, p. 20.

4. Ben-Gurion to Dr Tzitron, 11.8.1972, Correspondence Collection, BGA.

5. Ben-Gurion, discussion with members of Kibbutz Ein-Gedi, 17.12.1970, Protocols Collection, BGA.

6. Ben-Gurion in a talk with Yosef Evron, July 17, 1972, Protocols Collection, BGA.

7. Ben-Gurion in a talk with unidentified French historian, March 1, 1972, Protocols Collection, BGA.

8. Interview with Bolek Goldman, 16.7.2011.

9. Ben-Gurion to *LOOK* magazine, 1971, Protocols Collection, BGA.

10. Ben-Gurion in a talk with Yosef Evron, July 17, 1972, Protocols Collection, BGA. He also reiterated a similar statement two months later in a talk with Roman Frister, September 8, 1972, Protocols Collection, BGA: "Immediately after 1967 War I said that if peace arises we will have to return all the territories except for Jerusalem and the Golan Heights. But if there is no willingness for peace on the Arab side, we are not obligated either."

11. The meeting was filmed for the film "Ben-Gurion Remembers." It was made in 1972 and was mainly marketed abroad. It was intended to be screened in Israel also, but on the opening night, Saturday October 6, 1973, the theater was empty because of the war, and after it the film was archived.

12. Ben-Gurion's diary, 29.1.1960.

13. Ibid., 11.10.1963.

14. "Dear Arik, it is with deep sorrow that I heard you are leaving the army. I do not understand why, but I am sorry with all my heart. I well remember your blessed and important work in the IDF and hope and am sure that you will continue to

contribute of your talent and your experience for the state and for the people as you have done so far." Ben-Gurion to Arik Sharon, Correspondence Collection, BGA.

15. "He used the expression 'good guy' often when he wanted to say 'talented for Zionist activity.'" Aharon Tamir, 30.7.1978, Testimonies Collection, BGA.

16. Dov Goldstein, "David Ben-Gurion, Avi [David Ben-Gurion, My Father]," *Maariv*, October 17, 1986, pp. 29–30.

17. Ohana, *Meshihiyut u-mamlachtiyut*, pp. 1–2.

18. Shlomo Avineri, *Ha-Raayon ha-zioni li-gvanav* [Varieties of Zionist Thought] (Tel Aviv: Am Oved), 1980, pp. 105–18.

19. Perlman, *David Ben-Gurion*, p. 196.

20. Ibid.

21. "This morning many guests came to me. A prof. from Argentina: Dr Oswaldo and his wife [...] [I asked him] why Latin America, which has one language and one religion, does not unite. [He] replied: [Because] only three countries similar to one another: Argentina, Uruguay, and Chile. [The] Other countries a mix of colors and races." Ben-Gurion Diary, May 2, 1969.

22. Ben-Gurion to Moshe Z. Frank, September 14, 1970, Correspondence Collection, BGA.

23. Ben-Gurion in conversation with Paul Simon, Tiberias, Protocols Collection, BGA.

24. Nationalist China abstained from the vote on the establishment of the state of Israel on November 29, but in February 1949 announced that it would recognize it once it was accepted to the UN. But in October 1949 a revolution broke out: Mao Zedong rose to power, declared the establishment of the People's Republic, and the move stalled. Contrary to the United States' position, Ben-Gurion announced that Israel recognized China, and Israel was one of the first Middle Eastern states to officially do so.

25. Ben-Gurion to Kenneth Triem, July 17, 1970, Correspondence Collection, BGA.

26. Ibid.

27. Mordechai Barkai, "David Ben-Gurion in a special interview to *Davar*," *Davar*, July 24, 1970, pp. 14, 17.

28. Ben-Gurion to Prof. Paul Friedland, March 1, 1970, Correspondence Collection, BGA.

29. "My health has not been good for a while'" noted Ben-Gurion in the opening of his letter to Ogden R. Reid, but clarified that he took the trouble of writing because the approachment of the West toward China was a major step on the way to imposing future world peace. Ben-Gurion to Ogden R. Reid, January 4, 1972, Correspondence Collection, BGA.

30. After the dissolution of the Soviet Union a series of agreements were signed between Russia and China that resolved their territorial dispute. In 2008, following forty years of strife, Russia and China signed the final arrangement, as a part of which the Russians agreed to transfer to China another strip of land of 174 sq. km.

31. Ben-Gurion to Nixon, November 12, 1972, Correspondence Collection, BGA.

CHAPTER 11

1. Aliza Volach, "Aba, lo mitos [A father, not a myth]," *Davar* HaShavua, October 17, 1986, pp. 10–12.
2. An interview with Prof. Bolek Goldman, July 16, 2011.
3. Yehoshua Cohen, May 21, 1979, Testimonial Collection, BGA.
4. An interview with prof. Bolek Goldman, July 16, 2011.
5. Ben-Gurion in a conversation with Levi Yitzhak Hayerushalmi, February 28, 1972, Protocol Collection, BGA.
6. An interview with Avraham Tzivion, August 31, 2011.
7. An interview with Prof. Bolek Goldman, July 16, 2011.
8. Prof. M. Rahmilewitz to Batya Even-Shoshan, February 7, 1970, Chronological Documentation Collection, BGA.
9. Tzahor, "Ben-Gurion kotev otobiyografiya," pp. 144–56.
10. Ben-Gurion to David Snir, December 19, 1972, Correspondence Collection, BGA. Snir wanted him to help in a research about the village of Midia, which he recognized as ancient Modi'in, but Ben-Gurion refused.
11. Meir Avizohar, May 12, 1976, Testimonial Collection, BGA.
12. An interview with Yariv Ben-Eliezer, July 9, 2011.
13. Ben-Gurion with A. Disinchek and Shalom Rosenfeld, March 13, 1971, Protocol Collection, BGA.
14. An interview with Prof. Bolek Goldman, July 16, 2011.
15. Yisraeli, *Megilat haim*, pp. 233-234.
16. An interview with Michael Bar-Zohar, November 21, 2011.
17. Bar-Zohar, *Ben-Gurion*, Vol. 3, p. 1421.
18. Diary of Ben-Gurion, March 1, 1963.
19. Ben-Gurion to Haim Shiba, November 11, 1969, Correspondence Collection, BGA.
20. Mordechai Barkai, "David Ben-Gurion be-reayon meyuhad le-*Davar* [David Ben-Gurion in a special interview for *Davar*]," *Davar*, July 24, 1970, pp. 14, 17.
21. Ben-Gurion with Mark Segal, March 19, 1972, Protocol Collection, BGA.
22. Geula Ben-Eliezer, July 30, 1976, Testimonial Collection, BGA.
23. Ibid.
24. An interview with Avraham Tzivion, August 31, 2011.
25. Bar-Zohar, *Ben-Gurion*, p. 559.
26. An interview with Mordechai Ben-Porath, August 23, 2011.
27. Sheleg, *Ruah ha-midbar*, p. 164.
28. David Ohana and Michael Feige, "Halvaya al saf ha-tzuk: Israel nifredet mi-Ben-Gurion [Funeral at the edge of a cliff: Israel Parts from David Ben-Gurion]," *Israel 17*, 2010: 25.
29. Geula Ben-Eliezer, July 30, 1976, Testimonial Collection, BGA. In any case, after many struggles and arguments between public figures who were interested in being part of commemorating his heritage, as well as different notes made on his decision, his will was officially singed only in May 1973.
30. Ben-Gurion to Bank Ha-Poalim, November 5, 1972, Correspondence Collection, BGA.

31. An interview with Prof. Bolek Goldman, July 8, 2011.

32. In January, he sent a condolences letter to the widow of the thirty-sixth US president, Lyndon Johnson, who passed away after an unexpected heart attack. Ben-Gurion to Lady Bird Johnson, January 24, 1973, Correspondence Collection, BGA.

33. Mira Avrech, *Paula* [Paula] (Tel Aviv: Am ha-Sefer), 1965.

34. Mira Avrech, *Dvarim she-lo katavti* [Things I never wrote] (Tel-Aviv: Yedioth Aharonoth), 2011, pp. 42–46.

35. Mati Golan, "BG: Navon – Haadam harauy lihiyot nesi hauma [BG: Navon—The best candidate for presidency]," *Haaretz*, March 26, 1973, p. 1.

36. From Yehuda Erez's diary, April 2, 1973, Testimonial Collection, BGA.

37. "Dear Golda—I read that you just celebrated your 75th birthday. So you are still young—you still have decades ahead of you. Whether or not you are prime minister, it is not important. The important thing is your dedication to the State of Israel and the people of Israel, and I have no doubt you still have many years before you. With love and appreciation, Ben-Gurion." Ben-Gurion to Golda, April 30, 1973, Correspondence Collection, BGA.

38. Aharon Tamir, September 13, 1978, Testimonial Collection, BGA.

39. Ben-Gurion in an interview to *TIME* magazine, April 19, 1973, Protocol Collection, Ben-Gurion Archive.

40. Ibid.

41. "Yelech Aba Even Lehilahem levad [Aba Even can go to war by himself]," *Kol ha-am*, March 18, 1953.

42. "Ben-Gurion le-Kol ha-am [Ben-Gurion to Kol ha-am]," *Davar*, May 17, 1973, p. 9.

43. An interview with Zalman Shoval, September 8, 2011.

44. Ben-Gurion to Yoel Lavi, July 10, 1971, Correspondence Collection, BGA. Ben-Gurion even added at the end of his letter: "If I wanted to continue living in the present I would join *Ha-Avoda* party, despite the faults I see in it."

45. Dani Tzidkoni, "Ha-shalom yusag be-vinyan ha-aretz [Peace will be achieved by building the country]," *Davar*, April 25, 1973, p. 3.

46. An interview with Avraham Tzivion, August 31, 2011.

47. Yehuda Erez's Diary, April 7, 1973, Testimonial Collection, BGA.

48. Ibid., July 13, 1973.

49. Ben-Gurion to Ziv Av, president of the Peasants Union, September 2, 1973, Correspondence Collection, BGA.

50. Ben-Gurion to Mayor Kuba Keizman, September 5, 1973, Correspondence Collection, BGA.

51. Yehuda Erez's diary, November 4, 1973, Testimonial Collection, BGA.

52. Geula Ben-Eliezer, July 30, 1976, Testimonial Collection, BGA.

53. Haim Yisraeli, February 12, 1981, Testimonial Collection, BGA.

54. David Ben-Gurion to Hannah and Elhanan Yishai, October 30, 1973.

55. Hagani, *Be-Guf rishon rabim*, p. 165.

56. Michelson, *Murik*, p. 379.

57. Dayan, *Avney derech*, pp. 688–91.

58. Ibid.

Bibliography

ARCHIVES

Ben-Gurion Archive (BGA)
The Jabotinsky Institute
The Moshe Sharet Israel Labor Party Archives (LPA)
The IDF Archives (IDFA)
The Israeli Television Archives
The Central Zionist Archives (CZA)
Israel State Archives (ISA)
YouTube—Israel State Archives channel
Protocols: Divrei Ha-Knesset [The Knesset Minutes]

NEWSPAPERS AND MAGAZINES

Ba-Mahane
Davar
Haaretz
Yedioth Aharonoth
Maariv
Al Ha-Mishmar
LIFE
LOOK
TIME

WORKS BY DAVID BEN-GURION

Ba-Ma'aracha [In Battle]. Two Vols. Tel Aviv: Am-Oved. 1957.

Yihud ve-yeud: Dvarim al bithon Israel [Uniqueness and destiny: about Israel's security]. Tel-Aviv: *Ma'arach*ot. 2008.

Medinat Israel ha-mehudeshet [The renewed State of Israel], vols. 1–2. Tel-Aviv: Am Oved. 1969.

Igrot David Ben-Gurion [The Letters of David Ben-Gurion]. Tel Aviv: Am Oved. 1971, 1973, 1975.

Eretz Israel be-avar u-va-hove [The Land of Israel in the past and in the present] (co-written with Yitzhak Ben-Zvi). Jerusalem: Yad Yitzhak Ben-Zvi. 1980.

Beit-avi [My father's house]. Tel Aviv: ha-Kibbutz ha-Meuchad. 1975.

Dvarim ke-havayatam [Thing as they are]. Tel Aviv: Am ha-Sefer. 1965. Hagut ba-mikra [Bible studies]. Tel-Aviv: Am Oved. 1973.

Michtavim el Poula ve-el ha-yeladim [Letters to Paula and the kids] . Tel-Aviv: Am Oved. 1969.

Mi-Maamad le-am [From class to people]. Tel-Aviv: Am Oved. 1974.

Pgishot im manhigim aravim [Meetings with Arab leaders]. Tel-Aviv: Am Oved. 1967.

Iyunim ba-tanach [Bible review]. Tel-Aviv: Am Oved. 1969.

Zichronot min ha-izavon [Memoirs from the archives]. Tel-Aviv: Am Oved. 1982, 1987, 1993, 1997; Sde Boker: Ben-Gurion Institution. 2008.

Yoman ha-milhamah [War dairy], vols. 1–2. Tel-Aviv: The Security Ministry. 1982.

Zichronot [Memoirs], Vol. 1–4. Tel-Aviv: Am Oved. 1964–1971.

Hazon va-derech [vision and path], Vol. 1–5. Tel-Aviv: Am Oved. 1951–1964.

BOOKS

Aharonson, Shlomo. *David Ben-Gurion: Manhig ha-renesans she-shaka* [David Ben-Gurion: renaissance leader and the waning of an age] Jerusalem: The Ben-Gurion Institution and Ben-Gurion University. 1999.

Aharonson, Shlomo. *Neshek garini ba-mizrah ha-tichon* [Nuclear weapon in the Middle East]. Vol. 2. Jerusalem: Academon. 1996.

Almogi, Yosef. *Ha-Maavak al Ben-Gurion* [The struggle over Ben-Gurion]. Tel Aviv: Idanim. 1988.

Alteras, Isaac. *Eisenhower and Israel: U.S.-Israeli Relations, 1953–1960*. University Press of Florida. 1993.

Alterman, Nathan. *Ha-Tur ha-shvi'i* [The seventh column]. Vol. 3. Edited by Dvora Gilula. Tel-Aviv: Ha-Kibbutz Ha-Meuhad. 1972.

Arieli, Yehoshua. *Historiya u-folitika* [History and politics]. Tel-Aviv: Am Oved. 1992.

Avineri, Shlomo. *David Ben-Gurion: Dmuto shel manhig tnuat poalim* [David Ben-Gurion as a Labor Leader]. Tel-Aviv: Am Oved. 1988.

Avineri, Shlomo. *Ha-Raayon ha-zioni li-gvanav* [Varieties of Zionist Thought]. Tel-Aviv: Am Oved. 1980.

Avrech, Mira. *Dvarim she-lo katavti* [Things I never wrote]. Tel-Aviv: Yedioth Aharonoth. 2011.

Avrech, Mira. *Paula [Paula]*. Tel Aviv: Am ha-Sefer. 1965.

Avizohar, Meir. *Bi-Rei saduk: Idialim hevratiyim u-leumiyim ve-hishtakfutam be-olama shel Mapai* [In a Cracked Mirror: Social and National ideals and their reflection in the world of *Mapai*]. Tel-Aviv: Am Oved. 1990.

Avizohar, Meir. *Ha-Tziyonut ha-lohemet: Mavo le-yoman Ben-Gurion ule-zichronotav* (1939) [Fighting Zionism—an introduction to Ben-Gurion's dairy and his memoirs (1939)]. Sede Boker: The Bialik Institute & Ben-Gurion University. 1985.

Avineri, Shlomo. *Arlozoroff* [Arlozoroff]. Tel-Aviv: Idanim. 1991.

Bareli, Avi. *Mapai be-reshit ha-atzma'ut 1948–1954* [*Mapai* in the first years of Israel: 1948–1953]. Jerusalem: Yad Ben Zvi Press. 2007.

Bareli, Meir. *Lehavin et Ben-Gurion* [Understanding Ben-Gurion]. Tel-Aviv: Yedioth Aharonoth. 1986.

Bar-Nir, Dov. *Ha-'Imut: Ben-Gurion ve-harevizionism* [The confrontation: Ben-Gurion and Revisionism]. Tel-Aviv: Am Oved. 1987.

Bar-Zohar, Michael. *Ben-Gurion* [Ben Gurion: a biography]. Tel Aviv: Magal. 1980 (updated 1992, 2003).

Bar-Zohar, Michael. *Ben-Gurion*. Vols. 1–3. Tel Aviv: Am Oved. 1978.

Bar-Zohar, Michael. *Ke-of ha-hol—Shimon Peres* [Shimon Peres: The biography]. Tel Aviv: Yedioth Aharonoth. 2006.

Ben-Aharon, Yitzhak. *Be-'Ein ha-se'ara* [In the eye of the storm]. Tel-Aviv: Ha-Kibbutz Ha-Meuhad. 1978.

Ben-Refa'el, Eliezer, Yosef Gorny, and Shalom Ratzabi (Eds.). *Zehuyot yehudiyot: Tshuvot hachmei yisrael le-Ben-Gurion* [Jewish identities: The sages of Israel's responses to Ben-Gurion]. Sde-Boker: The Ben-Gurion Institution. 2001.

Ben-Shlomo, Yosef. *Prakim be-torato shel Baruch Spinoza* [Lectures on the Philosophy of Spinoza]. Tel-Aviv: The Defense Ministry. 1983.

Bloom, Allan. *The Closing of the American Mind*. New York: Simon & Shuster Inc. 1987.

Brenner, Uri. *Altalena: Mehkar medini u-tzva'i* [Altelana: Political and military research]. Tel Aviv: Ha-Kibbutz Ha-Meuhad. 1978.

Cogen, Mordechai (Ed.). *Ben-Gurion veha-tanach—Am ve-artzo* [Ben-Gurion and the Bible—a people and its land]. Sde-Boker: The Ben-Gurion Institution. 1989.

Cohen, Asher, and Baruch Susser. *Me-Hashlama le-haslama* [From Accommodation to Escalation]. Jerusalem: Shocken. 2003.

Cohen, Avner. *The Worst Kept Secret: Israel's Bargain with the Bomb*. Columbia University Press. 2010.

Cohen, Shalom. *Ha-Olam ha-zeh* [This world]. Tel-Aviv: Tfahot. 1972.

Cohen, Yona. *Ha-Keneset kemot she-hi: Diyunim ve-hiyukhim* [The Knesset as it is: Discussions and conflicts]. Tel Aviv: Am Ha-Sefer. 1972.

Dayan, Moshe. *Avnei derech* [Milestones]. Jerusalem: Yedioth Aharonoth-Idanim. 1976.

Dayan, Moshe. *Ha-Lanetzah tochal herev* [Shall the sword devour forever?]. Jerusalem: Yedioth Aharonoth-Idanim. 1981.

Dayan, Moshe. *Lihyot im ha-tanach* [Living with the Bible]. Jerusalem: Yedioth Aharonoth-Idanim. 1978.

De Spinoza, Benedict. *A Theologico-Political Treatise, and a Political Treatise.* Translated by R.H.M. Elwes. New York: Cosimo Books. 2007.

Don-Yihya, Eli'ezer. *Mashber u-temurah bi-medinah hadashah* [Crisis and Change in a New state]. Jerusalem: Yad Yitzhak Ben-Zvi. 2008.

Eilam, Yigal. *Ha-Hagannah: ha-Derech ha-ziyonit el ha-ko'ach* [The *Hagannah*: The Zionist path to power]. Tel-Aviv: Zmora-Bitan and Modan. 1979.

Eilam, Yigal. *Ma hitrachesh kan* [What happened here]. Tel-Aviv: Am Oved. 2012.

Eilon, Eli. *Yetsira atsmit: Haim, adam ve-yetsira al pi Nietzsche* [Self Creation: Life, man, and creation according to Nietzsche]. Jerusalem: Magnes. 2005.

Eliav, Arie (Lova). *Olam male* [The Entire World]. Tel-Aviv: Am Oved. 1980.

Eshed, Hagai. *Mi natan et ha-hora'a? "ha-esek ha-bish," parashat Lavon ve-hitpatrut Ben-Gurion* [Who gave the order? Lavon affair and Ben-Gurion's resignation]. Jerusalem: Idanim. 1979.

Falk, Avner. *David melech yisrael: BiogRafiya psichoanalitit shel David Ben-Gurion* [David king of Israel: Psychoanalytic biography of David Ben-Gurion]. Tel Aviv: Tammuz Publishing. 1987.

Friling, Tuvia. *Hetz ba-arafel: David Ben Gurion, hanhagat ha-Yishuv ve'nisyunot hatzala ba-shoha* [Arrows in the Dark: David Ben-Gurion, the Yishuv Leadership and Rescue Attempts during the Holocaust] (2 Volumes). Jerusalem, Sde Boker: Ben Gurion Institute and The Hebrew University, 2001.

Gazit, Shlomo. *Ptaim be-malkodet* [Cuptured snakes]. Tel-Aviv: Zmora-Bitan. 1999.

Gelber, Yoav. *Komemiyut ve-nakba* [Independence and nakba]. Or Yehuda: Kinneret, Zmora-Bitan, and Dvir. 2004.

Golan, Aviezer and Shlomo Nakdimon. *Begin.* Tel Aviv: Yedioth Aharonoth. 1978.

Goldberg, Giora. *Ben-Gurion against the Knesset.* Frank Cass, 2003.

Goldstein, Yosef. *Eshkol, biogRafiyah* [Eshkol: A biography]. Jerusalem: Keter Publishers. 2003.

Gorny, Yosef. *Ha-Sheela Ha-arvit veha-be'aya ha-yeodit, 1948–1882* [Zionism and the Arabs, 1882–1948: A study of ideology]. Tel-Aviv: Am-Oved. 1985.

Hagani, Amira. *Be-Guf rishon rabim: Arie Ben-Gurion, hayav u-fo'alo* [A biography: Aryeh Ben Gurion]. Tel-Aviv: ha-Kibbutz ha-Meuhad. 2010.

Harel, Isser. *Bitahon u-demokratya* [Security and democracy]. Jerusalem: Yedioth Aharonoth-Idanim. 1989.

Harel, Isser. *Kam ish al ahiv: Ha-nituah ha-musmach veha-mematze shel parashat Lavon* [When man rose Against Man]. Jerusalem: Keter Publishers. 1982.

Hazony, Yoram. *The Jewish state: The struggle for Israel's soul.* Basic Books. 2000.

Kafkafi, Eyal. *Lavon—anti-masiah* [Lavon—anti-messiah]. Tel-Aviv: Am Oved. 1998.

Katz, Gideon. *Le-etzem ha-chiloniyot—nituach filosofy shel ha-chiloniyut be-Heksher yisraeli* [To the core of Secularism—a philosophical analysis of secularism in the Israeli context]. Jerusalem: Yad Yitzhak Ben Zvi. 2010.

Kedar, Nir. *Mamlachtiyut: ha-tfisa ha-ezrahit shel David Ben-Gurion* [*Mamlachtiyut*: David Ben-Gurion's civic thought]. Jerusalem: Ben-Gurion University Press and Yad Yitzhak Ben-Zvi. 2009.

Keren, Michael. *Ben-Gurion veha-intelektualim, otzma, da'at ve-carisma* [Ben Gurion and the intellectuals: Power, knowledge and charisma]. Sde Boker: Ben Gurion Institute, 1984.

Kurzmam, Dan. *Prophet of fire: Ben-Gurion, a political biography*. Maurice Edelman. 1983.

Leibowitz, Yeshayahu. *Emunah, historiah, va-arakhim* [Faith, history, and values]. Jerusalem: Academon. 1982.

Levey, Zach. *Israel and the western powers, 1952–1960*. University of North Carolina Press. 1997.

Mann, Rafi. *Ha-Manhig veha-tikshoret: David Ben-Gurion veha-ma'avak al ha-merhav ha-tziburi 1948–1963* [The Leader and the Media: David Ben-Gurion and the Struggle over Israel's Public Sphere, 1948–1963]. Tel-Aviv: Am Oved. 2012.

Medzini, Meron. *Golda* [Golda]. Tel-Aviv: Yedioth Aharonoth. 2008.

Michelson, Menachem. *Murik – sipur hayav shel Meir Bar'eli* [Murik: The life story of Meir Bareli]. Tel-Aviv: Elilev, 2007.

Nakdimon, Shlomo and Shaul Mayzlish. *De-Haan: Ha-retzah ha-politi ha-rishon be-yisrael* [De-Haan: The first political murder in Israel]. Tel-Aviv: Modan. 1985.

Nakdimon, Shlomo. *Altelena* [Altelena]. Tel-Aviv: Yedioth Aharonoth. 1978.

Naor, Mordechai (Ed.). *Ha-Aliyah ha-shniyah 1903–1914* [The second *Aliyah* 1903–1914]. Jerusalem: Yad Yitzhak Ben-Zvi. 1988.

Neumann, Boaz. *Tshukat ha-halutizm* [The pioneers' passion]. Tel Aviv: Am Oved, 2009.

Nevo, Joseph. *Ha-Mizrah ha-tichon be-yameinu: Yarden: ha-hipus ahar zehut* [The contemporary Middle East: Jordan—In Search of an Identity]. Ra'anana: The Open University. 2005.

Nietzsche, Friedrich. *The will to power*. Translated by Walter Kaufmann and R. J. Hollingdale, edited by Walter Kaufmann. New York: Random House. 1967.

Ohana, David. *Meshihiyut u-mamlachtiyut: Ben-Gurion ve-haintelektualim, bein hazon medini le-teologya politit* [Messianism and statism: Ben-Gurion and the intellectuals, between political vision and political theology]. Sde Boker: The Ben-Gurion Institution. 2003.

Oren, Michel. *Power, faith and fantasy*. W.W Norton & company. 2007.

Ostfeld, Zehava (Ed.). *Ha-Zaken veha-am: Mivhar igrot ishiyot shel David Ben-Gurion* [The old man and the people—Selected Letters of David Ben-Gurion]. Tel-Aviv: The Ministry of Security. 1988.

Pa'il, Meir and Pinchas Jurman. *Mivhan ha-tnu'a ha-ziyonit 1931–1948: Marut ha-hanhaga ha-medinit mul ha-porshim* [The test of the Zionist movement 1931–1948: The authority of the political leadership vs. the dissidents]. Tel-Aviv: Cherikover Publishing. 2002.

Pearlman, Moshe. *David Ben-Gurion*. Tel Aviv: Am Oved. 1987.

Peres, Shimon and David Landau. *Ben Gurion, a political life*. Nextbook- Schocken. 2011.

Peres, Shimon. *Lech im ha-anashim: Shivah dyokanut* [From these men: Seven founders of the State of Israel]. Tel Aviv: Yedioth Ahronoth. 1979.

Pinkus, Benjamin. *Me-ambivalentiyut li-vrit bilti Ktuva: Israel, Tzarfat ve-yehudei Tzarfat 1947–1957* [From ambivalence to a tacit alliance: Israel, France and French Jewry 1947–1957]. Sde-Boker: Ben-Gurion University. 2005.

Rabin, Yitzhak (with Dov Goldstein). *Pinkas sHerut* [Service book]. Tel-Aviv: Ma'ariv. 1979.

Ram, Elimelech. *Be-Kol ram* [Out loud]. Tel-Aviv: Yedioth Aharonoth. 2011.

Robert, William. *Builder of Israel: The story of Ben-Gurion.* Doubleday. 1961.

Rosenthal, Yemima, (Ed.). *Documents on the foreign policy of Israel.* Vol. 8: 1953. Jerusalem: The State Archive. 1996.

Rousseau, Jean-Jacques. *The Social Contract.* Translated by G. D. H. Cole. online source: http://www.marxists.org/reference/subject/economics/rousseau/social-contract/.

Schmidt, Christoph (ed.). *Ha-Elohim lo ye'alem dom: Ha-Moderna ha-yehudit vehate'ologiya ha-politit* [God will not stand still: Jewish modernity and political theology]. Jerusalem: The Van Leer Institute. 2009.

Schopenhauer, Arthur. *The world as will and idea.* Translated by R. B. Haldane and J. Kemp. London: Kegan Paul, Trench, Trübner & Co. 1909. http://www.gutenberg.org/files/38427/38427-pdf.pdf.

Segev, Tom. *1967.* Jerusalem: Keter, 2005.

Shalom, Zaki. *David Ben-Gurion, Medinat Yisrael ve-haolam ha-arvi, 1949–1956.* Sde Boker: Ben Gurion Institute. 1995.

Shalom, Zaki. *Ka-Esh be-atzmotav: David Ben-Gurion u-ma'avakav al dmut ha-medina ve-hanhagata 1963–1967* [With heart aflame: David Ben-Gurion and the struggle for the image of Israel and its leadership, 1963–1967]. Sde-Boker: The Ben-Gurion Institution. 2004.

Shapira, Anita, ed. *Anu machrizim ba-zot: 60 ne'umim nivharim be-toldot ha-medina* [We hereby declare: Sixty selected speeches from the State's history]. Tel-Aviv: Kinneret–Zmora–Bitan–Dvir. 2008.

Shapira, Anita. *Berl.* (2 Vol). Tel Aviv: Am Oved. 1980.

Shapira, Anita. *Me-Piturey ha-ramatkal ad peruk ha-Palmah: Sugiyot ba-ma'avak al ha-hanhaga ha-bithonit, 1948* [The army controversy: Ben-Gurion's struggle for control, 1948]. Tel-Aviv: Ha-Kibbutz Ha-Meuhad. 1985.

Shapira, Anita. *Yigal Allon, Aviv Heldo* [Igal Alon: Spring of his Life]. Tel Aviv: Ha-Kibbutz Ha-Meuhad. 2004.

Shavit, Yaacov and Yaacov Goldstein. *Lelo psharot: Heskem Ben-Gurion-Jabotinsky ve-kishlono* [No compromises: The Ben-Gurion-Jabotinsky agreement and its failure]. Tel-Aviv: Hadar. 1979.

Shavit, Yaacov. *Onat ha-tzayid: Ha-Seison* [The hunting season: The Saison]. Tel-Aviv: Hadar. 1976.

She'altiel, Eli. *Tamid be-meri: Moshe Sneh, biography, 1909–1948* [Moshe Sneh: Life, Vol. 1, 1909–1948]. Tel-Aviv: Am Oved. 2000.

Shealtiel, Eli (ed.). *David Ben-Gurion rosh ha-memshala ha-rishon: Mivhar te'udot 1947–1963* [David Ben-Gurion, the first prime minister: A selection of documents 1947–1963]. Jerusalem: The state archive. 1997.

Sheleg, Yair. *Ruah ha-midbar: Sipuro shel Yehoshu'a Cohen* [Desert's wind: The story of Yehoshua Cohen]. Tel-Aviv: The Defence Ministry. 1998.

Shilon, Avi. *Menachem Begin: A life*. Translated by Danielle Zilberberg and Yoram Sharett. New Haven, Connecticut: Yale University Press. 2012.

Shlaim, Avi. *Kir ha-barzel* [The Iron Wall: Israel and the Arab World]. Tel Aviv: Yedioth Aharonoth. 2005.

Sneh, Moshe. *Ktavim* [Writings]. Vol. 5, 1966–1972. Edited by Matityahu Mintz. Tel Aviv: Am Oved and The Chaim Weizmann Institute for the Study of Zionism and Israel in Tel-Aviv University. 2002.

Tanner, Michael. *Schopenhauer*. New York: Rutledge. 1999.

Teveth, Shabtai. *Ben-Gurion ve-arviyey Israel: Me'-Hashlam le-haslama*. Jerusalem: Schoken. 1985.

Teveth, Shabtai. *Kalban: Al ma nafal David Ben-Gurion* [Ben-Gurion's spy: the story of the political scandal that shaped modern Israel]. Tel Aviv: Ish Dor, 1992.

Teveth, Shabtai. *Kin'at David: Hayey Ben-Gurion* [David's Jealousy: Ben-Gurion's life]. 1st Vol.: *Ben-Gurion Hatza'ir* [The Young Ben-Gurion]. 1977; 2nd Vol.: *Ben-Gurion: Ish-marut* [Ben-Gurion—Man of Authority]. 1981; 3rd Vol.: *Ha-Karka bo'er* [The Ground is Burning]. 1987; Vol. 4: *Ish riv* [A Man of Strife]. 2004. Jerusalem: Schoken.

Teveth, Shabtai. *Moshe Dayan: BiyogRafiya* [Moshe Dayan: A Biography]. Jerusalem: Schoken. 1971.

Teveth, Shabtai. *Onat ha-gez: Kitat yorim be-Beit Jiz, Kalaba"n* [Shearing Time: Firing Squad At Beth-Jiz]. Tel Aviv: Ish Dor. 1992.

Teveth, Shabtai. *Retzah Arlosoroff* [The Arlosoroff murder]. Jerusalem: Shocken. 1982.

Tsur, Nadir. *Retorika politit: Manhigim yisraeliyim be-matzavei lahatz* [The rhetorics of Israeli leaders in stress situations]. Tel-Aviv: ha-Kibbutz ha-Meuhad. 2004.

Tzahor, Ze'ev. *Ha-Hazon veha-heshbon: Ben-Gurion bein idiologya u-politika* [Vision and Reckoning—Ben Gurion: Ideology and politics]. Tel-Aviv: Yedioth Aharonoth and Sifriyat Po'alim. 1994.

Webber, Shaul. *Yitzhak Rabin – Tzmichato shel manhig* [Yitzhak Rabin—A Growth of a Leader]. Tel Aviv: Maariv, 2009.

Wolfenzon, Avraham. *David Ben-Gurion u-medinat Yisrael* [David Ben-Gurion and the State of Israel]. Tel-Aviv: Am Oved. 1974.

Wolfenzon, Avraham. *David Ben-Gurion: Asor le-moto, 1886–1973* [David Ben-Gurion: A decade to his death, 1886–1973]. Tel-Aviv: Ha-*Histadrut* Ha-Klalit Shel Ha-Ovdim Be-Eretz Yisra'el. 1983.

Yisraeli, Haim. *Megilat Hayim* [A life's story]. Tel-Aviv: Yedioth Aharonoth. 2005.

Zemach, Shlomo. *Sipur hayay* [Story of my life]. Tel-Aviv: Dvir. 1983.

Zemach, Shlomo. *Sipurim me-hayey ha-aretz* [Stories from the Life of the Land]. Jerusalem: Rubin Mass Press, 1939.

RESEARCH DISSERTATIONS

Donyets, Yigal. "Ha-Ideologiya ha-le'umit shel Ben-Gurion, 1930–1942 [The national ideology of David Ben-Gurion, 1930–1942]." PhD diss., The Hebrew University of Jerusalem, 2008.

Kabalo, Paula. "Ben-Gurion: Ra'ayon ha-halutziyut ve-nosav [Ben-Gurion: The idea of halutzyut]." PhD diss. Tel-Aviv University, 2000.

INTERVIEWS

Ya'ari, Me'ir. July 15, 1975. BGA.
Ya'ari, Me'ir. July 15, 1975. BGA.
Sherf, Ze'ev. August 5, 1975. BGA.
Avizohar, Me'ir. May 12, 1976. BGA.
Ben-Eli'ezer, Ge'ula. July 30, 1976. BGA.
Feldenkrais, Moshe. November 3, 1976. BGA.
Elchanan, Ishai. September 12, 1977. BGA.
Ben-Aharon, Yitzhak. January 27, 1978. BGA.
Almogi, Yosef. May 30, 1978. BGA.
Gibli, Binyamin. July 4, 1978. BGA.
Tamir, Aharon. July 30, 1978. BGA.
Erez, Yehuda. October 22, 1973, November 20, 1978. BGA.
Meidan, Aharon. April 3, 1979. BGA.
Cohen, Yehoshua. May 21, 1979. BGA.
Guez, Mathilda. August 1, 1979. BGA.
Bader, Yochanan. February 17, 1999. The State Archives.
Tzahor, Ze'ev. April 2011.
Ben-Eli'ezer, Yariv. June 9, 2011.
Degani, Amos. June 21, 2011.
Goldman, Bolek. July 16, 2011.
Ben-Porat, Mordechai. August 23, 2011.
Tzivion, Avraham. August 31, 2011.
Eldan, Aharon. September 8, 2011.
Shoval, Zalman. September 8, 2011.
Yirmiyah, Dov. October 10, 2011.
Spielmann, Zvi. November 18, 2011.
Bar-Zohar, Michael. November 21, 2011.
Shiloni, Tzvi. November 24, 2011.
Bareli, Avi. July 2012.
Friling, Tuvia. August, 2012.
Peres, Shimon. September 20, 2012.

MOVIES

Spielmann, Zvi. *Ben-Gurion Zocher* [Ben-Gurion remembers]. Tel-Aviv, 1973.

ARTICLES

Aharonson, Shlomo. "Derech ha-yisurim shel ha-optziya ha-gar'init [The Via Dolorosa of the nuclear option]." *Kivunim Hadashim* 26 (2012): 41–67.

Aharonson, Shlomo. "Huka le-yisra'el – ha-degem ha-briti shel David Ben-Gurion [A constitution for Israel—David Ben-Gurion's British model]." *Politica* 2 (1998): 9–30.

Avineri, Shlomo. "Mekomo shel manhig ba-historiya: Al manhiguto shel Ben-Gurion [A leader's place in history: About Ben-Gurion's leadership]," in *Manhig ve-hanhaga [Leader and leadership]*, edited by Irad Malkin and Ze'ev Tzahor, 327–38. Jerusalem: The Zalman Shazar Center, 1992.

Bar-On, Yitzhak. "Leidata u-nefilata shel yedidut: Yahasei tzarfat-yisra'el 1965–1967 [The rise and fall of a friendship: France-Israel relations 1965–1967]." *Medina, Mimshal ve-Yahasim Bein-Le'umiyim* 35 (1992): 69–98.

Bar-Or, Amir. "'Min ha-yesod': Naftuleha shel tnu'a politit-ra'ayonit ['*Min Hayesod*': The story of a political movement]." *Iyunim bi-Tekumat Yisra'el* 4 (1994): 478–93.

Ben-Amos, Avner. "Ha-Shilton nimtza ba-rehov: Mered ha-studentim be-May 1968 veha-merhav ha-parisai [The street rules: May 1968 students revolt and the Parisian sphere]." *Zmanim* 109 (Winter 2010): 40–57.

Bialer, Uri. "Ben-Gurion u-she'elat ha-oriyentatziya habien-le'umit shel yisra'el, 1948–1956 [Ben-Gurion and Israel's poreign policy orientation, 1948–1956]." *Katedra* 43 (1987): 145–72.

Cohen, Avner. "Kennedy, Ben-Gurion veha-krav al Dimona: April-yuni 1963 [Kennedy, Ben-Gurion and the battle over Dimona: Aprile-June 1963]." *Iyunim bi-Tekumat Yisra'el* 6 (1996): 110–46.

Don-Yehiya, Eliezer. "*Mamlachtiyut* ve-yahadut ba-haguto uve-mediniyuto shel Ben-Gurion [Judaism and statism in Ben-Gurion's thought and politics]." *Ha-Tziyonut* 14 (1989): 51–88.

Eliezer Don-Yehiya, "Galut in Zionist Ideology and in Israeli Society," in *Israel and Diaspora Jewry: Ideological and Political Perspectives*, edited by Eliezer Don-Yehiya, pp. 219–59. Bar-Ilan University. 1993.

Erez, Yehuda. "Ben-Gurion eino kotev otobiyografiya [Ben-Gurion is not writing an autobiography]." *Keshet* 65 (1975): 151–65.

Friling, Tuvia. "Bein otzmah le-da'at: Be-Ikvot Shlomo Aharonson, 'David Ben-Gurion, mangig ha-renesans she-shaka' [Between power and knowledge: On Shlomo Aharonson's book, David Ben-Gurion: The renaissance leader and the waning of an age]." *Israel* 3 (2003): 21–56.

Friling, Tuvia. "David Ben-Gurion veha-sho'a, shorashav ve-gilgulav shel stere'otip shlily [David Ben-gurion and the Holocaust, the roots and transformations of a negative stereotype]," in *Tshuvah le-amit post tziyoni [Answer to a post-Zionist colleague]*, edited by Tuvia Friling, 418–56. Tel-Aviv: Yedioth Aharonoth-Sifrey Hemed. 2003.

Friling, Tuvia. "Li-Vhinat ha-stere'otip: Ben-Gurion ve-sho'at yehudei eropa [Examining the stereotype: Ben-Gurion and the Holocoast, 1939–1945]," in Yad va-Shem: *Kovetz Mehkarim* [Yad va-Shem: Anthology], 329–51. Vol. 17–18 (1987).

Gal, Allon. "Hesped u-mediniyut: divrei David Ben-Gurion ba-azkara le-Louis D. Brandeis, London, 21 be-October 1941 [Eulogy and policy: David Ben-Gurion's address at a memorial meeting honoring Louis D. Brandeis, London, October 21, 1941]." *Katedra* 44 (1987): 108–15.

Gorny, Yosef. "Ha-Re'alizem ha-utopi ba-tziyonut [Utopian realism in Zionism]," in *Reshafim: Hebetim historiyim, filosofiyim ve-hevratiyim shel ha-hinuch: Asupah le-zikhro shel Prof. Shim'on Reshef, zal* [Reshafim: Historical, philosophical, and social aspects of education: a collection in memory of Prof. Shim'on Reshef], edited by Rina Shapira, 37–49. Tel-Aviv: Tel-Aviv University Press. 1991.

Gorny, Yosef. "Shlilat ha-galut veha-shiva el ha-historiya [Rejecting the exile and returning to history]," in *Ha-Tziyonut veha-hazara la-historiya: Ha'araha mehadash* [Zionism and returning to history: a reevaluation], edited by Shmuel Eisenstadt and Moshe Lisk, 349–60. Jerusalem: Yad Yitzhak Ben-Zvi. 1999.

Greenberg, Yitzhak. "David Ben-Gurion ve-Pinhas Lavon: Shtei gishot be-mahshevet hevrat ha-ovdim [David Ben-Gurion and Pinhas Lavon: Two approaches in labour economy thought]." *Iyunim bi-Tekumat Yisra'el* 3 (1993): 154–67.

Keren, Michael, "Biography and Historiography: The Case of David Ben-Gurion." *Biography* 23, No. 2 (Spring 2000): 332–51.

Mann, Rafi. "Olam ha-sfarim shel David Ben-Gurion: Hazon actu'ali bi-kricha kasha [Ben-Gurion's book world: a hardcover topical dream]." *Zmanim* 114 (2011): 100–11.

Ohana, David and Michael Feige. "Funeral at the edge of a cliff: Israel Parts from David Ben-Gurion." *Israel* 17, 2010, 25–57.

Ohana, David and Robert S. Wistrich. "Mavo: Nochehut ha-mitosim ba-yahadut, ba-tziyonut uva-yisra'eliyut [Introduction: The presence of myths in Judaism, Zionism and Israelism]," in *Mitos ve-zikaron: Gilguleha shel ha-toda'a ha-yisra'elit* [Myth and memory: Transfigurations of Israeli consciousness], edited by David Ohana and Robert S. Wistrich, 11–40. Jerusalem: The Van Leer Institute.

Ohana, David. "Zarathustra in Jerusalem: Nietzsche and the 'New Hebrews,'" in *Mitos ve-zikaron: Gilguleha shel ha-toda'a ha-yisra'elit* [Myth and memory: Transfigurations of Israeli consciousness], edited by David Ohana and Robert S. Wistrich, 269–89. Jerusalem: The Van Leer Institute.

Orren, Elhannan. "Yoman ha-milhama shel Ben-Gurion ke-makor histori le-milhemet ha-atzma'ut [Ben-Gurion's war diary as a historical source]." *Katedra* 43 (1987): 173–92.

Porat, Dina. "Ben-Gurion ve-sho'at yehudey eropa [Ben-Gurion and the Holocoast]." *ha-Tziyonut* 12 (1987): 293–314.

Porat, Dina. "Be'aya be-historiografiya: Yahaso shel David Ben-Gurion le-yehudey eropa bi-tkufat ha-sho'a [A Problem in Historiography: Ben-Gurion's attitude towards the Jews of Europe in times of the Holocaust]." *Massua* 19 (1991): 154–65.

Rojanski, Rachel. "Ha-omnam safa zara ve-tzoremet? Li-She'elat yahaso shel Ben-Gurion la-Yiddish le-ahar ha-sho'a [Ben-Gurion's attitude to Yiddish in the 1950s]." *Iyunim bi-Tekumat Yisra'el* 15 (2005): 463–83.

Shalom, Zakai, "Ben Gurion and Tewfik Toubi Finally Meet (October 28, 1956)." *Israel Studies* 8, No.2 (Summer 2003): 45–69.

Shalom, Zaki. "Ben-Gurion veha-itonut: halachah le-ma'ase [Ben-Gurion and the press: in practice]." *Kesher* 20 (1996): 57–60.

Shalom, Zaki. "Yomanei Ben-Gurion ke-makor histori [Ben-Gurion's diary as a historical source]." *Katedra* 56 (1990): 136–49.

Shapira, Anita. "Ben-Gurion ve-hatanach: Yetzirato shel nerativ history? [Ben Gurion and the Bible: The forging of an historical narrative?]." *Alpayim* 14 (1997): 207–31.

Shavit, Yaacov. "Bein Pilsudsky ve-Mickiewicz: Mediniyut u-meshihiyut ba-reviziyonizem ha-tziyoni be-heksher shel ha-tarbut ha-politit ha-polanit ve-zikato le-polin [Between Pilsudsky and Mickiewicz: Policy and messianism in Zionist Revisionism]." *Ha-Tziyonut* 10 (1985): 7–31.

Shefer, Gabriel. "Pitron kolel mul mitun ha-sichsuch ha-yisra'eli-aravi: bhina mehudeshet shel ha-hitnagshut bein Moshe Shart ve-David Ben-Gurion [Comperhansive solution versus conflict moderation: reexamining the collision between Moshe Sharet and David Ben-Gurion]," in *Ha-Tziyonut veha-she'ela ha-aravit* [Zionism and the Arab Question], edited by Menachem Stern, 119–63. Jerusalem: The Zalman Shazar Center. 1979.

Tal, David. "Milhemet tashah: Milhamto shel David Ben-Gurion [Israel's War of Independence—David Ben-Gurion's war]." *Iyunim bi-Tekumat Yisra'el* 13 (2003): 115–38.

Teveth, Shabtai. "Ben-Gurion veha-she'ela ha-aravit [Ben-Gurion and Palestinian Arabs]." *Katedra* 43 (1987): 52–65.

Teveth, Shabtai. "Ha-Hor ha-shahor: Ben-Gurion bein sho'a li-tekuma [The black hole: Ben-Gurion between the Holocaust and revival]." *Alpayim* 10 (1994): 111–95.

Tzahor, Ze'ev. "Ben-Gurion kotev otobiyografiya [Ben-Gurion is writing an autobiography]." *Keshet* 65 (1974): 144–56.

Tzahor, Ze'ev. "Nitzahon atzuv: Ben-Gurion ve-gdud ha-avoda [Sad victory: Ben-Gurion and *Gedud ha-Avoda*]." *Katedra* 43 (1987): 33–51.

Tzahor, Ze'ev. "Va'adat ha-berur li-vdikat 'ha-kibbutz ha-hasha'i' bi-gdud ha-avoda [The committee to investigate the 'clandestine commune' in Gedud ha-Avoda]." *Katedra* 58 (1990): 128–54.

Tzahor, Ze'ev. "Ya'akov Hazan: Naftuley ha-derech shel ha-hanhaga ha-historit [Yaakov Hazan: The vicissitudes of the historical leadership]." *ISRAEL* 3(2003): 97–110.

Weitz, Yechiam. "El ha-fantaziya uva-hazara: Madu'a hehlit Ben-Gurion laredet li-Sde Boker? [David Ben-Gurion's first resignation, 1953]." *Iyunim bi-Tekumat Yisra'el* 8 (1998): 298–319.

Weitz, Yechiam. "Ha-Peh she-hitir: Ben-Gurion, hakamat *Rafi* veha-herem al tnu'at ha-*Herut* be-1956 [The Change in Ben-Gurion's Attitude toward the *Herut* Movement during the 1960s]." *ISRAEL* 17 (2010): 131–67.

Weitz, Yechiam. "Ha-Preda meha-av ha-meyased: Prishato shel David Ben-Gurion me-rashut ha-memshala be-1963 [Beeding goodbye to the founding father: Ben-Gurion's retirement as prime minister in 1963]," in *Medina ba-derech* [State in construction], edited by Anita Shapira, 73–108. Jerusalem: The Zalman Shazat Center. 2001.

Weitz, Yechiam. "Yahaso shel Ben-Gurion la-reviziyonizm uli-zramav [Ben-Gurion's attitude towards the Revisionist movement and its offshoots]." *Iyunim bi-Tekumat Yisra'el* 19 (2009): 306–44.

Yizhar, S. "Hoo haya savur sheha-sofrim ya'aniku la-am et ha-mabat ha-histori... [He demanded of the writers to convey a historical outlook to the people...]." *Iyunim bi-Tekumat Yisra'el* 3 (1993): 1–9.

Ynet Encyclopedia, available online at: http://www.ynet.co.il/home/0,7340,L-1361,00. html.

Zak, Moshe. "Ha-Tmura be-yahaso shel David Ben-Gurion le-mamlechet yarden [The shift in Ben-Gurion's attitude toward the Kingdom of Jordan]." *Iyunim bi-Tekumat Yisra'el* 6 (1996): 109–85.

Zameret, Zvi. "Eich mitztayer Ben-Gurion be-sifrei limud [The Portrayal of Ben Gurion in Israeli textbooks]." *Kivunim Hadashim* 19 (2009): 34–52.

Zivan, Ze'ev. "Mi-Toch yomano shel Ben-Gurion [From the Ben-Gurion's Archives]." *Iyunim bi-Tekumat Yisra'el* 3 (1993): 565–71.

Index

About the Author

Avi Shilon, PhD, is a historian and a political science expert. His PhD dissertation focuses on "The Revisionist Movement Leaders' Attitudes toward Jewish religion, 1925–2005," and deals with the prominent leaders of the right-wing stream of Zionism—Ze'ev Jabotinsky, Menachem Begin, Yitzhak Shamir, Ariel Sharon, and the current prime minister, Benjamin Netanyahu.

His first book, *Menachem Begin: A Life*, was published by Yale University Press in 2012 and won as the finalist of the Jewish book council award on 2013.

Shilon is also a journalist who contributes a bi-weekly column for the *Ha'aretz* op-ed section. He was born in Israel and lives in Tel Aviv; currently, he is an Israel Institute-Taub Center for Israel Studies postdoctoral fellow at New York University.